SPSS

SPSS® 6.1 Base System User's Guide
Part 2

Marija J. Norušis / SPSS Inc.

SPSS Inc.
444 N. Michigan Avenue
Chicago, Illinois 60611
Tel: (312) 329-2400
Fax: (312) 329-3668

SPSS Federal Systems (U.S.)
SPSS Latin America
SPSS Benelux BV
SPSS GmbH Software
SPSS UK Ltd.
SPSS France SARL
SPSS Hispanoportuguesa S. L.
SPSS Scandinavia AB
SPSS India Private Ltd.
SPSS Asia Pacific Pte. Ltd.
SPSS Japan Inc.
SPSS Australasia Pty. Ltd.

For more information about SPSS® software products, please write or call

Marketing Department
SPSS Inc.
444 North Michigan Avenue
Chicago, IL 60611
Tel: (312) 329-2400
Fax: (312) 329-3668

SPSS is a registered trademark and the other product names are the trademarks of SPSS Inc. for its proprietary computer software. No material describing such software may be produced or distributed without the written permission of the owners of the trademark and license rights in the software and the copyrights in the published materials.

The SOFTWARE and documentation are provided with RESTRICTED RIGHTS. Use, duplication, or disclosure by the Government is subject to restrictions as set forth in subdivision (c)(1)(ii) of The Rights in Technical Data and Computer Software clause at 52.227-7013. Contractor/manufacturer is SPSS Inc., 444 N. Michigan Avenue, Chicago, IL 60611.

General notice: Other product names mentioned herein are used for identification purposes only and may be trademarks of their respective companies.

SPSS® 6.1 Base System User's Guide, Part 2
Copyright © 1994 by SPSS Inc.
All rights reserved.
Printed in the United States of America.

No part of this publication may be reproduced, stored in a retrieval system, or transmitted, in any form or by any means, electronic, mechanical, photocopying, recording, or otherwise, without the prior written permission of the publisher.

1 2 3 4 5 6 7 8 9 0   96 95 94

ISBN 0-13-438870-4

Preface

SPSS is a comprehensive and flexible statistical analysis and data management system. SPSS can take data from almost any type of file and use them to generate tabulated reports, charts, and plots of distributions and trends, descriptive statistics, and complex statistical analyses.

The SPSS Base system includes procedures for:
- Frequencies
- Descriptive statistics
- Exploratory statistics
- Crosstabulation
- Multiple response or multiple dichotomy sets
- Comparing means: means, one-sample t test, independent-samples t test, paired-samples t test, and one-way analysis of variance
- Simple factorial analysis of variance (ANOVA)
- Bivariate and partial correlation
- Linear regression
- Curve estimation
- Nonparametric tests
- Lists of cases and reports that include tables of summary statistics
- The following high-resolution charts:

bar charts	histograms
line charts	Pareto charts
area charts	control charts
high-low-close charts	error bar charts
difference charts	normal probability plots
boxplots	sequence charts
scatterplots	time series charts

This manual provides examples and descriptions of how to use all of these procedures. For information on how to use SPSS on a specific computer system, consult the *SPSS Base System User's Guide, Part 1*, which came with the system. Other statistical procedures are available in SPSS add-on options.

Compatibility

The SPSS Base system is designed to operate on many computer systems. See the installation instructions that came with your system for specific information on minimum and recommended requirements.

Serial Numbers

Your serial number is your identification number with SPSS Inc. You will need this serial number when you call SPSS Inc. for information regarding support, payment, a defective diskette, or an upgraded system.

The serial number can be found on the diskette labeled Installation that came with your Base system. Before using the system, please copy this number to the registration card.

Registration Card

STOP! Before continuing on, *fill out and send us your registration card*. Until we receive your registration card, you have an unregistered system. Even if you have previously sent a card to us, please fill out and return the card enclosed in your Base system package. Registering your system entitles you to:

- Technical support services
- Favored customer status
- New product announcements

Don't put it off—send your registration card now!

Customer Service

Contact Customer Service at 1-800-521-1337 if you have any questions concerning your shipment or account. Please have your serial number ready for identification when calling.

Training Seminars

SPSS Inc. provides both public and onsite training seminars for SPSS. All seminars feature hands-on workshops. SPSS seminars will be offered in major U.S. and European cities on a regular basis. For more information on these seminars, call the SPSS Inc. Training Department toll-free at 1-800-543-6607.

Technical Support

The services of SPSS Technical Support are available to registered customers of SPSS. Customers may call Technical Support for assistance in using SPSS products or for installation help for one of the supported hardware environments.

To reach Technical Support, call 1-312-329-3410. Be prepared to identify yourself, your organization, and the serial number of your system.

If you are a Value Plus or Customer EXPress customer, use the priority 800 number you received with your materials. For information on subscribing to the Value Plus or Customer EXPress plan, call SPSS Software Sales at 1-800-543-2185.

Additional Publications

Additional copies of SPSS product manuals may be purchased from Prentice Hall, the exclusive distributor of SPSS publications. To order, fill out and mail the Publications order form included with your system, or call toll-free. If you represent a bookstore or have an account with Prentice Hall, call 1-800-223-1360. If you are not an account customer, call 1-800-374-1200. In Canada, call 1-800-567-3800. Outside of North America, contact your local Prentice Hall office.

Lend Us Your Thoughts

Your comments are important. So send us a letter and let us know about your experiences with SPSS products. We especially like to hear about new and interesting applications using the SPSS system. Write to SPSS Inc. Marketing Department, Attn: Micro Software Products Manager, 444 N. Michigan Avenue, Chicago, IL 60611.

Contacting SPSS Inc.

If you would like to be on our mailing list, write to us at one of the addresses below. We will send you a copy of our newsletter and let you know about SPSS Inc. activities in your area.

SPSS Inc.
444 North Michigan Ave.
Chicago, IL 60611
Tel: (312) 329-2400
Fax: (312) 329-3668

SPSS Federal Systems
Courthouse Place
2000 North 14th St.
Suite 320
Arlington, VA 22201
Tel: (703) 527-6777
Fax: (703) 527-6866

SPSS Latin America
444 North Michigan Ave.
Chicago, IL 60611
Tel: (312) 494-3226
Fax: (312) 494-3227

SPSS Benelux BV
P.O. Box 115
4200 AC Gorinchem
The Netherlands
Tel: +31.1830.36711
Fax: +31.1830.35839

SPSS GmbH Software
Rosenheimer Strasse 30
D-81669 Munich
Germany
Tel: +49.89.4890740
Fax: +49.89.4483115

SPSS UK Ltd.
SPSS House
5 London Street
Chertsey
Surrey KT16 8AP
United Kingdom
Tel: +44.1932.566262
Fax: +44.1932.567020

SPSS France SARL
72-74 Avenue Edouard Vaillant
92100 Boulogne
France
Tel: +33.1.4684.0072
Fax: +33.1.4684.0180

SPSS Hispanoportuguesa S. L.
Paseo Pintor Rosales, 26-4
28008 Madrid
Spain
Tel: +34.1.547.3703
Fax: +34.1.548.1346

SPSS Scandinavia AB
Gamla Brogatan 36-38
4th Floor
111 20 Stockholm
Sweden
Tel: +46.8.102610
Fax: +46.8.102550

SPSS India Private Ltd.
Ashok Hotel, Suite 223
50B Chanakyapuri
New Delhi 110 021
India
Tel: +91.11.600121 x1029
Fax: +91.11.688.8851

SPSS Asia Pacific Pte. Ltd.
10 Anson Road, #34-07
International Plaza
Singapore 0207
Singapore
Tel: +65.221.2577
Fax: +65.221.9920

SPSS Japan Inc.
2-2-22 Jingu-mae
Shibuya-ku, Tokyo
150 Japan
Tel: +81.3.5474.0341
Fax: +81.3.5474.2678

SPSS Australasia Pty. Ltd.
121 Walker Street
North Sydney, NSW 2060
Australia
Tel: +61.2.954.5660
Fax: +61.2.954.5616

Contents

1 Data Transformations 1

Computing Values 1
   Calculator Pad 2
   Functions 3
   Conditional Expressions 7
   Variable Type and Label 8
   Syntax Rules for Expressions 9

Random Number Seed 10

Counting Occurrences 10
   Defining Values to Count 11
   Selecting Subsets of Cases 12

Recoding Values 12
   Recode into Same Variables 13
   Recode into Different Variables 15

Ranking Data 18
   Ranking Method 19
   Rank Ties 21

Creating Consecutive Integers from Numeric and String Values 22

Time Series Data Transformations 23
   Generating Date Variables 24
   Creating Time Series Variables 26
   Replacing Missing Values 28

Pending Transformations 30

2 File Handling and File Transformations 31

Sorting Data 31

Transposing Cases and Variables 32
   Missing Values in Transposed Data Files 33

Combining Data Files 33
   Merging Files That Contain Different Cases 33
   Merging Files That Contain Different Variables 37

Applying a Data Dictionary 42
   Weighted Files 43

Aggregating Data 43
   Aggregate Functions 45
   New Variable Names and Labels 47
   Aggregate Filename and Location 47

Split-File Processing 47
   Turning Split-File Processing On and Off 48
   Sorting Cases for Split-File Processing 49

Selecting Subsets of Cases 49
   Selecting Cases Based on Conditional Expressions 51
   Selecting a Random Sample 52
   Selecting a Range of Dates or Times 52

Case Selection Status 54

Weighting Cases 54
   Turning Weights On and Off 55
   Weights in Scatterplots and Histograms 55

3 Data Tabulation 57

A Frequency Table 57
   Visual Displays 58
   What Day? 60
   Histograms 60
   Percentiles 61
   Screening Data 62

How to Obtain Frequency Tables 62
  Frequencies Statistics 63
  Frequencies Charts 65
  Frequencies Format 66
  Additional Features Available with Command Syntax 67

4 Descriptive Statistics 69

Examining the Data 69

Summarizing the Data 71
  Levels of Measurement 71
  Summary Statistics 73
  The Normal Distribution 76
  Who Lies? 79

How to Obtain Descriptive Statistics 79
  Descriptives Options 81
  Additional Features Available with Command Syntax 82

5 Exploring Data 83

Reasons for Exploring Data 83
  Identifying Mistakes 83
  Exploring the Data 84
  Preparing for Hypothesis Testing 84

Ways of Displaying Data 84
  The Histogram 84
  The Stem-and-Leaf Plot 85
  The Boxplot 87

Evaluating Assumptions 89
  The Levene Test 89
  Spread-versus-Level Plots 90
  Tests of Normality 91

Estimating Location with Robust Estimators 93
  The Trimmed Mean 94
  M-Estimators 94

How to Explore Your Data 97
  Explore Statistics 98
  Explore Plots 99
  Explore Options 101
  Additional Features Available with Command Syntax 101

6 Crosstabulation and Measures of Association 103

Crosstabulation 103
  Cell Contents and Marginals 104
  Choosing Percentages 105
  Adding a Control Variable 105

Graphical Representation of Crosstabulations 107

Using Crosstabulation for Data Screening 107

Crosstabulation Statistics 108
  The Chi-Square Test of Independence 108
  Measures of Association 111
  Nominal Measures 112
  Ordinal Measures 118
  Measures Involving Interval Data 121
  Estimating Risk in Cohort Studies 121
  Estimating Risk in Case-Control Studies 122

How to Obtain Crosstabulations 123
  Crosstabs Statistics 124
  Crosstabs Cell Display 126
  Crosstabs Table Format 127
  Additional Features Available with Command Syntax 128

7 Describing Subpopulation Differences 129

Searching for Discrimination 129
  Who Does What? 129
  Level of Education 131

Beginning Salaries 132
Introducing More Variables 134

How to Obtain Subgroup Means 134
Means Options Dialog Box 135
Additional Features Available with Command Syntax 136

8 Multiple Response Analysis 137

Introduction to Multiple Response Data 137
Set Definition 138
Crosstabulations 140

Analyzing Multiple Response Data 143

How to Define Multiple Response Sets 143

How to Obtain Multiple Response Frequencies 144
Additional Features Available with Command Syntax 146

How to Crosstabulate Multiple Response Sets 146
Define Value Ranges 147
Options 148
Additional Features Available with Command Syntax 149

9 One-Sample T Test 151

Summary Statistics 151

Results from Samples 152
Are the Sample Results Unlikely? 154

The One-Sample T Test 155

Confidence Intervals 156

Hypothesis Testing 157

How to Obtain a One-Sample T Test 158
One-Sample T Test Options 158

10 Testing Hypotheses about Differences in Means 161

Testing Hypotheses 161
Samples and Populations 162
Sampling Distributions 162
Sampling Distribution of the Mean 164

The Two-Sample T Test 166
Significance Levels 167
One-Tailed versus Two-Tailed Tests 168
What's the Difference? 168

Using Crosstabulation to Test Hypotheses 169

Independent versus Paired Samples 170
Analysis of Paired Data 170

Hypothesis Testing: A Review 171
The Importance of Assumptions 172

How to Obtain an Independent-Samples T Test 172
Define Groups for Numeric Variables 173
Define Groups for String Variables 174
Independent-Samples T Test Options 174

How to Obtain a Paired-Samples T Test 175
Paired-Samples T Test Options 176
Additional Features Available with Command Syntax 177

11 One-Way Analysis of Variance 179

Examining the Data 179
Sample Means and Confidence Intervals 180

Testing the Null Hypothesis 181

Assumptions Needed for Analysis of Variance 182
The Levene Test 182

Analyzing the Variability 182
Between-Groups Variability 183
Within-Groups Variability 183
Calculating the F Ratio 184

Multiple Comparison Procedures 185

How to Obtain a One-Way Analysis of Variance 187
   One-Way ANOVA Define Range 188
   One-Way ANOVA Contrasts 188
   One-Way ANOVA Post Hoc Multiple Comparisons 190
   One-Way ANOVA Options 191
   Additional Features Available with Command Syntax 192

12 Analysis of Variance 193

Descriptive Statistics 193

Analysis of Variance 194
   Testing for Interaction 196
   Tests for Sex and Attractiveness 197

Explanations 197

Extensions 197

How to Obtain a Simple Factorial Analysis of Variance 198
   Simple Factorial ANOVA Define Range 199
   Simple Factorial ANOVA Options 199
   Additional Features Available with Command Syntax 202

13 Measuring Linear Association 203

Examining Relationships 203

The Correlation Coefficient 204
   Some Properties of the Correlation Coefficient 206
   Calculating Correlation Coefficients 206
   Hypothesis Tests about the Correlation Coefficient 207
   Correlation Matrices and Missing Data 208
   Choosing Pairwise Missing-Value Treatment 209
   The Rank Correlation Coefficient 209

How to Obtain Bivariate Correlations 210
   Bivariate Correlations Options 211
   Additional Features Available with Command Syntax 213

14 Partial Correlation Analysis 215

Computing a Partial Correlation Coefficient 215
   The Order of the Coefficient 216
   Tests of Statistical Significance 216

Detecting Spurious Relationships 216

Detecting Hidden Relationships 218

Interpreting the Results of Partial Correlation Analysis 219

How to Obtain Partial Correlations 219
   Partial Correlations Options 220
   Additional Features Available with Command Syntax 221

15 Multiple Linear Regression Analysis 223

Linear Regression 223
   Outliers 224
   Choosing a Regression Line 224
   From Samples to Populations 226
   Goodness of Fit 229
   Predicted Values and Their Standard Errors 232
   Searching for Violations of Assumptions 236
   Locating Outliers 242
   When Assumptions Appear to Be Violated 246

Multiple Regression Models 250
   Predictors of Beginning Salary 250
   Determining Important Variables 253
   Building a Model 255
   Procedures for Selecting Variables 258

Checking for Violations of Assumptions 263
Looking for Influential Points 265
Measures of Collinearity 267
Interpreting the Equation 269

How to Obtain a Linear Regression Analysis 270
Linear Regression Statistics 272
Linear Regression Plots 273
Linear Regression Save New Variables 275
Linear Regression Options 277
Additional Features Available with Command Syntax 278

16 Curve Estimation 279

Selecting a Model 279
The Health Care Composite Index 279

Predicted Values and Residuals 281

Testing for Normality 283

How to Obtain Curve Estimation 284
Saving Predicted Values and Residuals 287

17 Distribution-Free or Nonparametric Tests 289

The Mann-Whitney Test 289
Ranking the Data 290
Calculating the Test 290
Which Diet? 291
Assumptions 292

Nonparametric Tests 292
One-Sample Tests 292
Tests for Two or More Independent Samples 298

How to Obtain the Chi-Square Test 301
Chi-Square Test Options 303
Additional Features Available with Command Syntax 303

How to Obtain the Binomial Test 304
Binomial Test Options 305
Additional Features Available with Command Syntax 306

How to Obtain the Runs Test 306
Runs Test Options 307
Additional Features Available with Command Syntax 308

How to Obtain the One-Sample Kolmogorov-Smirnov Test 308
One-Sample Kolmogorov-Smirnov Options 310
Additional Features Available with Command Syntax 310

How to Obtain Two-Independent-Samples Tests 311
Two-Independent-Samples Define Groups 312
Two-Independent-Samples Options 313
Additional Features Available with Command Syntax 313

How to Obtain Tests for Several Independent Samples 314
Several Independent Samples Define Range 315
Several Independent Samples Options 315
Additional Features Available with Command Syntax 316

How to Obtain Two-Related-Samples Tests 316
Two-Related-Samples Options 318
Additional Features Available with Command Syntax 318

How to Obtain Tests for Several Related Samples 319
Several Related Samples Statistics 320

18 Listing Cases 321

How to Obtain Case Listings 321
Additional Features Available with Command Syntax 323

19 Reporting Results   325

Basic Report Concepts 325
  Summary Reports 325
  Listing Reports 327
  Combined Reports 328
  Multiple Break Variables 329
  Summary Columns 330
  Grand Total Summary Statistics 331
Formatting Reports 332
  Titles and Footnotes 333
  Column Headings 333
  Displaying Value Labels 334
How to Obtain Listing Reports and Reports with Summaries in Rows 334
  Data Column Format 336
  Break Category Summary Statistics 338
  Break Spacing and Page Options for Summaries in Rows 340
  Break Column Format 340
  Report Total Summary Statistics 341
  Report Options for Summaries in Rows 341
  Report Layout for Summaries in Rows 342
  Titles and Footers 344
How to Obtain a Report with Summaries in Columns 345
  Data Column Summary Statistic for a Variable 347
  Composite Summary (Total) Columns 348
  Data Column Format 350
  Break Options for Summaries in Columns 350
  Break Column Format 351
  Report Options for Summaries in Columns 351
  Report Layout for Summaries in Columns 352
  Titles and Footers 353
  Additional Features Available with Command Syntax 353

20 Bar, Line, Area, and Pie Charts   355

Chicago Uniform Crime Reports Data 355
Simple Charts 356
Clustered Bar and Multiple Line Charts 358
Drop-Line Charts 359
Stacked Bar and Area Charts 360
Variations in Bar, Line, and Area Charts 361
  100% Stacked Bar and Area Charts 361
  Hanging Bar Charts 362
  Mixed Charts 362
How to Obtain Bar, Line, Area, and Pie Charts 363
  Bar Charts 364
  Line Charts 374
  Area Charts 384
  Pie Charts 392
Transposed Charts 397
  Summary Functions 399

21 High-Low Charts   405

Simple High-Low Charts 405
Clustered High-Low Charts 406
Difference Line Charts 407
How to Obtain High-Low Charts 408

22 Boxplots and Error Bar Charts   429

Boxplots 429
Error Bar Charts 431
How to Obtain a Boxplot 433
  Defining Boxplots 436
How to Obtain an Error Bar Chart 439
  Defining Error Bar Charts 441

23 Scatterplots and Histograms   445

A Simple Scatterplot   445
  Profits, Growth, and Compensation   447

Scatterplot Matrices   449
  Smoothing the Data   450

Plotting in Three Dimensions   450

How to Obtain a Scatterplot   452
  Defining Simple Scatterplots   453
  Defining Scatterplot Matrices   454
  Defining Overlay Scatterplots   456
  Defining 3-D Scatterplots   457
  Displaying Case Labels in Scatterplots   458

How to Obtain a Histogram   458

24 Pareto and Control Charts   461

Pareto Charts   461

Control Charts   462

Using the Same Data in Pareto and Control Charts   464

How to Obtain a Pareto Chart   465

How to Obtain a Control Chart   474
  Control Chart Options   491

25 Normal Probability Plots   493

How to Obtain Normal Probability Plots   495
  Options   496

26 Sequence Charts   499

Plotting Health Care Stock   499

Seasonal Trends   500

Forecasting   501

Examining the Errors   502

How to Obtain Sequence Charts   502
  Time Axis Reference Lines   504
  Formatting Options   505

27 Autocorrelation and Cross-Correlation   507

The Autocorrelation Function   507

The Partial Autocorrelation Function   509

The Cross-Correlation Function   510

How to Obtain Autocorrelation and Partial Autocorrelation Charts   512
  Options   513

How to Obtain Cross-Correlation Charts   514
  Options   515

Bibliography   517

Index   521

1
Data Transformations

In an ideal situation, your raw data are perfectly suitable for the type of analysis you want to perform, and any relationships between variables are either conveniently linear or neatly orthogonal. Unfortunately, this is rarely the case. Preliminary analysis may reveal inconvenient coding schemes or coding errors, or data transformations may be required in order to coax out the true relationship between variables.

With SPSS, you can perform data transformations ranging from simple tasks, such as collapsing categories for analysis, to creating new variables based on complex equations and conditional statements.

Computing Values

To compute values for a variable based on numeric transformations of other variables, from the menus choose:

Transform
 Compute...

This opens the Compute Variable dialog box, as shown in Figure 1.1.

Figure 1.1 Compute Variable dialog box

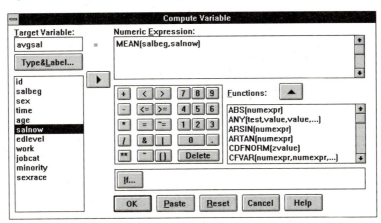

Target Variable. The name of the variable that receives the computed value. The target variable can be an existing variable or a new one. New variable names must begin with a letter and cannot exceed eight characters. (See the *SPSS Base System User's Guide, Part 1* for complete variable naming rules.) By default, new computed variables are numeric (see "Variable Type and Label" on p. 8 for information on computing new string variables).

Numeric Expression. The expression used to compute the value of the target variable. The expression can use existing variable names, constants, arithmetic operators, and functions. You can type and edit the expression in the text box just like text in a syntax or output window (see the *SPSS Base System User's Guide, Part 1*). You can also use the calculator pad, variable list, and function list to paste elements into the expression.

Calculator Pad

The calculator pad contains numbers, arithmetic operators, relational operators, and logical operators (Table 1.1). You can use it like a calculator (using the mouse to point and click on keys) or simply as a reference for the correct symbols to use for various operators.

Table 1.1   Calculator pad operators

Arithmetic Operators		Relational Operators		Logical Operators	
+	Addition	<	Less than	&	And. Both relations must be true.
−	Subtraction	>	Greater than		
*	Multiplication	<=	Less than or equal to	|	Or. Either relation can be true.
/	Division	>=	Greater than or equal to		
**	Exponentiation	=	Equal to	~	Not. Reverses the true/false outcome of the expression.
( )	Order of operations	~=	Not equal to		

Arithmetic Operators

Since fairly complex expressions are possible, it is important to keep in mind the order in which operations are performed. Functions are evaluated first, followed by exponentiation, then multiplication and division, and finally addition and subtraction. You can control the order of operations by enclosing the operation you want executed first in parentheses. You can use the ( ) key on the calculator pad to enclose a highlighted portion of the expression in parentheses.

Relational Operators

A relation is a logical expression that compares two values using a relational operator. They are primarily used in conditional transformations (see "Relational and Logical Operators in Conditional Expressions" on p. 8).

Logical Operators

You can use logical operators to join two relations or reverse the true/false outcome of a conditional expression. They are primarily used in conditional transformations (see "Relational and Logical Operators in Conditional Expressions" on p. 8).

Functions

The function list contains over 70 built-in functions, including:

- Arithmetic functions
- Statistical functions
- Distribution functions
- Logical functions
- Date and time aggregation and extraction functions
- Missing-value functions
- Cross-case functions
- String functions

The following sections provide descriptions of some of the more commonly used functions. A complete list of functions is provided in the *SPSS Base System Syntax Reference Guide*.

Arithmetic Functions

ABS(numexpr). Absolute value. If the value of variable *scale* is –4.7 , ABS(scale) results in a value of 4.7, and ABS(scale – 5) results in a value of 9.7.

RND(numexpr). Round to the nearest integer. If the value of *scale* is 4.7, RND(scale) results in a value of 5, and RND(scale + 5) results in a value of 10.

TRUNC(numexpr). Truncate to an integer. If the value of *scale* is 4.7, TRUNC(scale) results in a value of 4, and TRUNC(scale + 5) results in a value of 9.

MOD(numexpr,modulus). Remainder of the first argument (numexpr) divided by the second argument (modulus). If the value of *year* is 1983, MOD(year, 100) results in a value of 83. The two arguments must be separated by a comma.

SQRT(numexpr). Square root. If *scale* is 4.7, SQRT(scale) results in a value of 2.17, and SQRT(scale − 0.7) results in a value of 2.

EXP(numexpr). Exponential. e is raised to the power of the argument (numexpr). If the value of *scale* is 2, EXP(scale) results in a value of 7.39.

LG10(numexpr). Base 10 logarithm. If the value of *scale* is 4.7, LG10(scale) results in a value of 0.67.

LN(numexpr). Natural or Naperian logarithm (base e). If the value of *scale* is 10, LN(scale) results in a value of 2.3.

ARSIN(numexpr). Arcsine. The result is expressed in radians.

ARTAN(numexpr). Arctangent. The result is given in radians.

SIN(radians). Sine. The argument must be specified in radians.

COS(radians). Cosine. The argument must be specified in radians.

All arithmetic functions except MOD have a single argument enclosed in parentheses. MOD has two arguments that must be separated by a comma. Arguments can be variables, constants, or expressions.

Statistical Functions

SUM(numexpr,numexpr,...). Sum of the values across the argument list. For example, SUM(var1, var2, var3) computes the sum of the three variables.

MEAN(numexpr, numexpr,...). Mean of the values across the argument list. For example, MEAN(var1, var2, 5) computes the mean of the two variables and the constant 5.

SD(numexpr, numexpr,...). Standard deviation of the values across the argument list. For example, SD(var1, var2, var3**2) computes a standard deviation based on the values of *var1* and *var2* and the squared value of *var3*.

VARIANCE(numexpr,numexpr,...). Variance of the values across the argument list.

CFVAR(numexpr,numexpr,...). Coefficient of variance of the values across the argument list.

MIN(value,value,...). Minimum value across the argument list.

MAX(value,value,...). Maximum value across the argument list.

All statistical functions have at least two arguments enclosed in parentheses. Arguments must be separated by commas. Arguments can be numeric variables, constants, or expressions.

Logical Functions

RANGE(test,lo,hi...). True if the value of the first argument is within the inclusive range(s) defined by the remaining arguments. The first argument (test) is usually a variable name. The other arguments are pairs of values defining ranges. You can have more than one pair of low and high values. For example, RANGE(year, 1900, 1949, 1960, 1999) is true if the value of *year* is between 1900 and 1949 or between 1960 and 1999, and it is false for the values 1950 through 1959.

ANY(test,value,value...). True if the value of the first argument matches the value of any of the remaining arguments on the list. The first argument (test) is usually a variable name, as in ANY(year, 1951, 1958, 1986, 1987).

Random Number Functions

NORMAL(stddev). Each case is assigned a pseudo-random number from a normal distribution with a mean of 0 and a user-specified standard deviation.

UNIFORM (max). Each case is assigned a pseudo-random number from a uniform distribution with a minimum of 0 and a user-specified maximum.

Distribution Functions

SPSS provides a variety of cumulative, inverse cumulative, and random number generator distribution functions. Cumulative distribution functions (CDF) are available for continuous, discrete, and noncentral distributions. Inverse cumulative distribution functions (inverse CDF) are available only for continuous distributions. Random number generator distribution functions (RNG) are available for continuous and discrete distributions. Table 1.2 lists the types of distribution functions available.

Table 1.2   Distribution functions

Continuous*	Discrete†	Noncentral‡
Beta	Bernoulli	Beta
Cauchy	Binomial	Chi-square
Chi-square	Geometric	F
Exponential	Hypergeometric	Student's t
F	Negative Binomial	
Gamma	Poisson	
Laplace		
Logistic		
Lognormal		
Normal		

Table 1.2 Distribution functions (Continued)

Continuous*	Discrete†	Noncentral‡
Pareto		
Student's t		
Uniform		
Weibull		

*CDF, inverse CDF, and RNG

†CDF and inverse CDF

‡CDF only

See the *SPSS Base System Syntax Reference Guide* for a complete list of distribution functions and the required arguments.

Nested Functions

A function can be used as an argument in another function, as in

`MEAN(RND(var1),TRUNC(var2))`

or even

`MEAN(RND(SD(var1)),TRUNC(SQRT(var2)))`

Missing Values with Functions

Functions and simple arithmetic expression treat missing values in different ways. In the expression,

`(var1+var2+var3)/3`

the result is missing if a case has a missing value for *any* of the three variables. However, in the expression,

`MEAN(var1, var2, var3)`

the result is missing only if the case has missing values for *all* three variables. For statistical functions, you can specify the minimum number of arguments that must have nonmissing values. To do so, type a period and the number after the function name (before the argument list), as in

`MEAN.2(var1, var2, var3)`

In this example, at least two of the three variables on the argument list must contain a nonmissing value for the function to return a nonmissing result.

Pasting and Editing Functions

Pasting a Function into an Expression. To paste a function into an expression:

1. Position the cursor in the expression at the point where you want the function to appear.
2. Double-click on the function on the Functions list (or select the function and click on the ▲ pushbutton).

The function is inserted in the expression. If you highlight part of the expression and then insert the function, the highlighted portion of the expression is used as the first argument in the function.

Editing a Function in an Expression. The function isn't complete until you enter the **arguments**, represented by question marks in the pasted function. The number of question marks indicates the minimum number of arguments required to complete the function. To edit a function:

1. Highlight the question mark(s) in the pasted function.
2. Enter the arguments. If the arguments are variable names, you can paste them from the source variable list.

Conditional Expressions

You can use **conditional expressions** (also called logical expressions) to apply transformations to selected subsets of cases. A conditional expression returns a value of true, false, or missing for each case. If the result of a conditional expression is true, the transformation is applied to that case. If the result is false or missing, the transformation is not applied to the case.

To specify a conditional expression, click on If... in the Compute Variable dialog box. This opens the If Cases dialog box, as shown in Figure 1.2.

Figure 1.2   If Cases dialog box

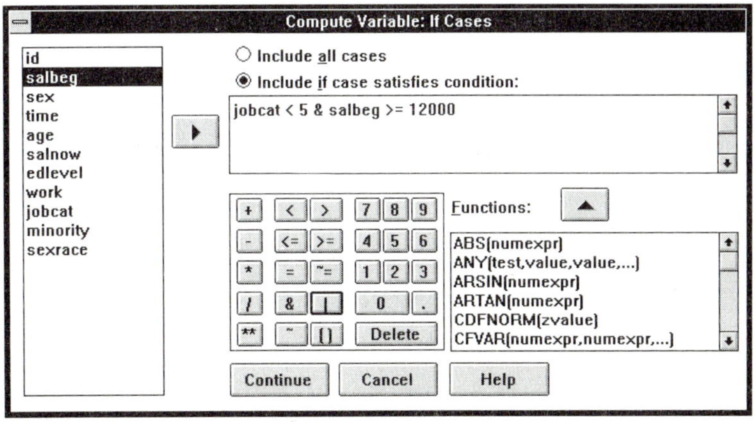

You can choose one of the following alternatives:

- **Include all cases**. This is the default. Values are calculated for all cases, and any conditional expressions are ignored.
- **Include if case satisfies condition**. Enter the conditional expression in the text box. The expression can include variable names, constants, arithmetic operators, numeric and other functions, logical variables, and relational operators.

Calculator Pad and Function List

These are identical to those described for the Compute Variable dialog box. See "Calculator Pad" on p. 2 and "Functions" on p. 3.

Relational and Logical Operators in Conditional Expressions

Most conditional expressions contain at least one relational operator, as in

```
age>=21
```

or

```
salary*3<100000
```

In the first example, only cases with a value of 21 or greater for *age* are selected. In the second, *salary* multiplied by 3 must be less than 100,000 for a case to be selected.

You can also link two or more conditional expressions using logical operators, as in

```
age>=21 | educat=1
```

or

```
salary*3<100000 & jobcat~=5
```

In the first example, cases that meet either the *age* condition or the *educat* condition are selected. In the second, both the *salary* and *jobcat* conditions must be met for a case to be selected.

Variable Type and Label

By default, new computed variables are numeric. To compute new string variables or assign descriptive variable labels, click on **Type & Label....** in the Compute Variable dialog box. This opens the Type and Label dialog box, as shown in Figure 1.3.

Figure 1.3 Type and Label dialog box

![Compute Variable: Type and Label dialog box with Label and Type options]

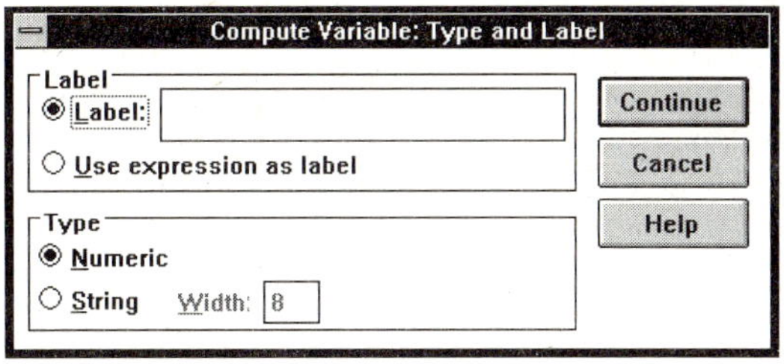

Label. Descriptive variable label. You can choose one of the following alternatives:

○ **Label**. Enter a label up to 120 characters long.

○ **Use expression as label**. The first 110 characters of the expression are used as the label.

Type. Variable format type. You can choose one of the following alternatives:

○ **Numeric**. This is the default setting.

○ **String**. Alphanumeric string.

Width. Enter the maximum width. A width specification is required for string variables.

Syntax Rules for Expressions

Items selected from the calculator pad, function list, and source variable list are pasted with correct syntax. If you type an expression in the text box or edit part of it (such as arguments for a function), remember the following simple syntax rules:

- String variable values must be enclosed in apostrophes or quotation marks, as in NAME='Fred'. If the string value includes an apostrophe, enclose the string in quotation marks.
- The argument list for a function must be enclosed in parentheses. You can insert a space between the argument name and the parentheses, but none is required.
- Multiple arguments in a function must be separated by commas. You can insert spaces between arguments, but none is required.
- Each relation in a complex expression must be complete by itself. For example, age>=18 & age<35 is correct, while age>=18 & <35 generates an error.
- A period (.) is the only valid decimal indicator in expressions, regardless of your Windows international settings.

Random Number Seed

Computations or conditional expressions that include random numbers (for example, the NORM and UNIFORM distribution functions) use the SPSS pseudo-random number generator, which begins with a **seed**, a very large integer value. Within a session, SPSS uses a different seed each time you generate a set of random numbers, producing different results. If you want to duplicate the same random numbers, you can reset the seed value. From the menus, choose:

Transform
  Random Number Seed...

This opens the Random Number Seed dialog box, as shown in Figure 1.4.

Figure 1.4   Random Number Seed dialog box

The seed can be any positive integer value up to 999,999,999. SPSS resets the seed to the specified value each time you open the dialog box and click on OK.

To duplicate the same series of random numbers, you should set the seed *before* you generate the series for the first time. Since SPSS resets the seed as it generates a series of random numbers, it is virtually impossible to determine what seed value was used previously unless you specified the value yourself.

Counting Occurrences

To count occurrences of the same value(s) across a list of variables within cases, from the menus choose:

Transform
  Count Occurrences...

This opens the Count Occurrences dialog box, as shown in Figure 1.5.

Figure 1.5 Count Occurrences dialog box

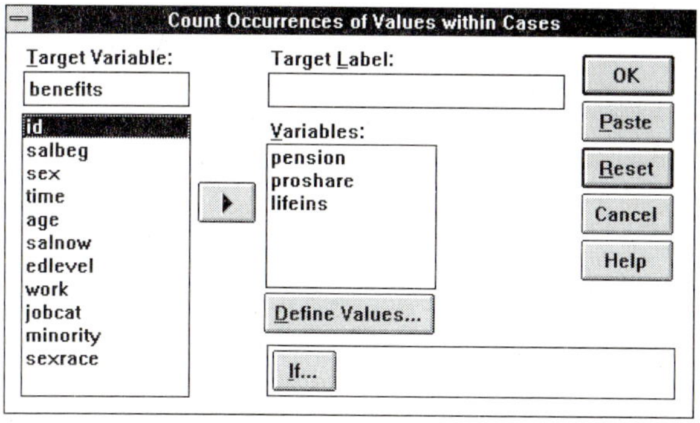

Target Variable. The name of the variable that receives the counted value. The target variable can be an existing numeric variable or a new one. New variable names must begin with a letter and cannot exceed eight characters. (See the *SPSS Base System User's Guide, Part 1* for complete variable naming rules.) The target variable must be numeric.

Target Label. Descriptive variable label for the target variable. The label can be up to 120 characters. If the target variable already exists, the current label (if any) is displayed.

Variables. The selected numeric or string variables from the source list for which you want to count occurrences of certain values. The list cannot contain both numeric and string variables.

Defining Values to Count

To specify the values to count, highlight a variable on the selected variables list and click on **Define Values...** in the Count Occurrences dialog box. This opens the Values to Count dialog box, as shown in Figure 1.6.

Figure 1.6 Values to Count dialog box

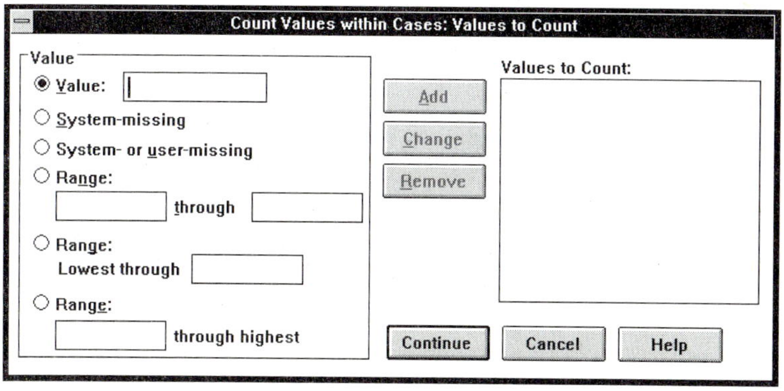

You can specify a single value, a range, or a combination of the two. To build a list of values to count, make selections from the Value alternatives and click on **Add** after each selection. Each occurrence of any value on the list across the variable list is counted.

Value. You can choose one of the following alternatives:

- **Value**. Counts occurrences of the value you have specified.
- **System-missing**. Counts occurrences of the system-missing value. This appears as SYSMIS on the Values to Count list. Not available for string variables.
- **System- or user-missing**. Counts occurrences of any missing values, both system-missing and user-missing values. This appears as MISSING on the Values to Count list.
- **Range**. Counts occurrences of values within the specified range. Not available for string variables.
- **Range: Lowest through n.** Counts occurrences of any value from the lowest observed value to the specified value. Not available for string variables.
- **Range: n through highest**. Counts occurrences from the specified value to the highest observed value. Not available for string variables.

All range specifications include any user-specified missing values that fall within the range.

Selecting Subsets of Cases

You can count occurrences of values for selected subsets of cases using conditional expressions. To specify a conditional expression, click on If... in the Count Occurrences dialog box. This opens the If Cases dialog box, as shown in Figure 1.2. (See "Conditional Expressions" on p. 7 for a description of this dialog box and instructions on how to specify conditional expressions. See "Calculator Pad" on p. 2, "Functions" on p. 3, and "Syntax Rules for Expressions" on p. 9 for additional information.)

Recoding Values

You can modify data values by recoding them. This is particularly useful for collapsing or combining categories. You can recode the values within existing variables or you can create new variables based on the recoded values of existing variables.

Recode into Same Variables

To recode the values of an existing variable, from the menus choose:

Transform
  Recode▶
    Into Same Variables...

This opens the Recode into Same Variables dialog box, as shown in Figure 1.7.

Figure 1.7   Recode into Same Variables dialog box

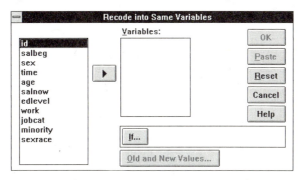

The source variable list contains the numeric and string variables in the data file. Select one or more variables for recoding. If you select multiple variables, they must all be the same type. You cannot recode numeric and string variables together.

Defining Values to Recode

To define the values to recode, click on Old and New Values... in the Recode into Same Variables dialog box. This opens the Old and New Values dialog box, as shown in Figure 1.8.

Figure 1.8   Old and New Values dialog box

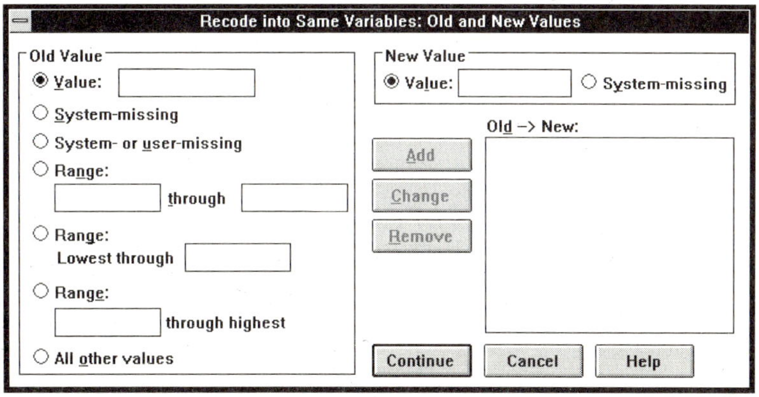

For each value (or range) that you want to recode, specify the old value and the new value, and then click on Add. You can recode multiple old values into a single new value. You cannot, however, recode a single old value into multiple new values.

Old Value. The current values for the variable that you want to recode into new values. You can choose one of the following alternatives:

- **Value**. Enter a single value. String values are automatically enclosed in apostrophes or quotes when they appear on the value list. If you enter quotation marks or apostrophes, they are considered part of the string value.
- **System-missing**. The system-missing value. This appears as SYSMIS on the value list. Not available for string variables.
- **System- or user-missing**. All missing values, including user-missing values. This appears as MISSING on the value list.
- **Range**. Enter an inclusive range of values. Not available for string variables.
- **Range: Lowest through n.** Any value from the lowest observed value to the specified value. Not available for string variables.
- **Range: n through highest**. Any value from the specified value to the highest observed value. Not available for string variables.
- **All other values**. Any remaining values not previously specified. This appears as ELSE on the value list.

New Value. The recoded value. You can choose one of the following alternatives:

- **Value**. Enter a value. String values are automatically enclosed in apostrophes or quotes when they appear on the value list. If you enter quotation marks or apostrophes, they are considered part of the string value.
- **System-missing**. The system-missing value. This appears as SYSMIS on the value list. Not available for string variables.

You can use the same new value with multiple old value specifications. This is particularly useful for combining noncontiguous categories that can't be defined in a range.

Recode Order

Recode specifications are automatically sorted on the value list, based on the old value specification, using the following order:

- Single values
- Missing values
- Ranges
- All other values

If you change a recode specification on the list, SPSS automatically re-sorts the list, if necessary, to maintain this order.

Selecting Subsets of Cases

You can recode values for selected subsets of cases using conditional expressions. To specify a conditional expression, click on If... in the Recode into Same Variables dialog box. This opens the If Cases dialog box, as shown in Figure 1.2. (See "Conditional Expressions" on p. 7 for a description of this dialog box and instructions on how to specify conditional expressions. See "Calculator Pad" on p. 2, "Functions" on p. 3, and "Syntax Rules for Expressions" on p. 9 for additional information.)

Recode into Different Variables

To create new variables based on the recoded values of existing variables, from the menus choose:

Transform
  Recode ▶
    Into Different Variables...

This opens the Recode into Different Variables dialog box, as shown in Figure 1.9.

Figure 1.9   Recode into Different Variables dialog box

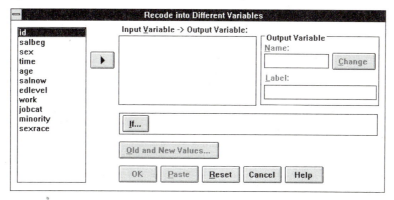

The source variable list contains the numeric and string variables in the data file. Select one or more variables for recoding. If you select multiple variables, they must all be the same type. You cannot recode numeric and string variables together.

Input Variable –> Output Variable. Selected variables from the source list appear in the input variable column. (The word Input changes to Numeric or String depending on the type of variables selected.) A question mark in the output variable column indicates that a name needs to be supplied for the output variable. You must provide output variable names for all selected input variables.

Output Variable. The new variable that receives the recoded values.

Name. An output variable name is required for each input variable. Highlight the input variable on the selected variable list and then type a name for the corresponding output variable. Variable names must start with a letter and cannot exceed eight characters. (See the *SPSS Base System User's Guide, Part 1* for complete variable naming rules).

Label. Optional descriptive variable label, up to 120 characters long.

After entering the output variable name and the optional label, click on **Change** to put the name on the output variable list, next to the corresponding input variable name.

Defining Values to Recode

To define the values to recode, click on **Old and New Values...** in the Recode into Different Variables dialog box. This opens the Old and New Values dialog box, as shown in Figure 1.10.

Figure 1.10 Old and New Values dialog box

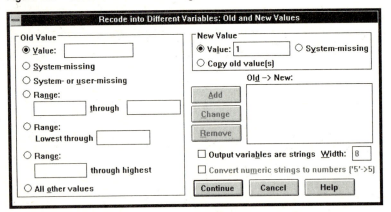

For each value (or range) that you want to recode, specify the old value from the input variable and the new value for the output variable, and then click on **Add**. You can recode multiple old values into a single new value. You cannot, however, recode a single old value into multiple new values.

Old Value. The values for the input variable that you want to recode for the output variable. You can choose one of the following alternatives:

- **Value**. Enter a value. String values are automatically enclosed in apostrophes or quotes when they appear on the value list. If you enter quotation marks or apostrophes, they are considered part of the string value.
- **System-missing**. The system-missing value. This appears as SYSMIS on the value list. Not available for string variables.
- **System- or user-missing**. All missing values, including user-missing values. This appears as MISSING on the value list.
- **Range**. Enter an inclusive range of values. Not available for string variables.
- **Range: Lowest through n.** Any value from the lowest observed value to the specified value. Not available for string variables.
- **Range: n through highest**. Any value from the specified value to the highest observed value. Not available for string variables.
- **All other values**. Any remaining values not previously specified. This appears as ELSE on the value list.

New Value. The recoded value for the output variable. You can choose one of the following alternatives:

- **Value**. Enter a value. String values are automatically enclosed in apostrophes or quotes when they appear on the value list. If you enter quotation marks or apostrophes, they are considered part of the string value.
- **System-missing**. The system-missing value. This appears as SYSMIS on the value list. Not available for string variables.
- **Copy old value(s)**. Retains the input variable value.

You can use the same new value with multiple old value specifications. This is particularly useful for combining noncontiguous categories that can't be defined in a range.

For string variables, there are two additional parameters:

- **Output variables are strings**. Select this item if your new output variables are string variables. This is required for new string variables.

  Width. Enter an integer between 1 and 255 for the maximum width of the string.

- **Convert numeric strings to numbers**. Valid values are numbers with an optional leading sign (+ or –) and a single period for a decimal point. Alphanumeric strings are assigned the system-missing value.

Missing Values

Any unspecified old values for the input variable are undefined for the new output variable and are assigned the system-missing value. To make sure unspecified old values for the input variable receive a nonmissing value for the output variable, do the following:

1. For the old value, select **All other values**.

2. For the new value, select **Copy old value(s)**.

3. Click on **Add**.

ELSE –> COPY appears on the value list. Any unspecified values for the input variable are retained for the output variable.

Selecting Subsets of Cases

You can recode values for selected subsets of cases using conditional expressions. To specify a conditional expression, click on **If...** in the Recode into Different Variables dialog box. This opens the If Cases dialog box, as shown in Figure 1.2. (See "Conditional Expressions" on p. 7 for a description of this dialog box and instructions on how to specify conditional expressions. See "Calculator Pad" on p. 2, "Functions" on p. 3, and "Syntax Rules for Expressions" on p. 9 for additional information.)

Ranking Data

To compute ranks, normal and savage scores, or classify cases into groups based on percentile values, from the menus choose:

Transform
  Rank Cases...

This opens the Rank Cases dialog box, as shown in Figure 1.11.

Figure 1.11 Rank Cases dialog box

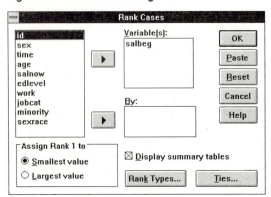

The numeric variables in the data file are displayed on the source variable list. Select one or more variables for which you want to compute ranks. To obtain the default simple ranking in ascending order with the mean rank assigned to ties, click on OK. SPSS creates a new variable that contains the rankings. The original variable is unaffected.

Optionally, you can organize rankings into subgroups by selecting one or more **grouping variables** for the By list. Ranks are computed within each group. Groups are defined by the combination of values of the grouping variables. For example, if you select *sex* and *minority* as grouping variables, ranks are computed for each combination of *sex* and *minority*.

Assign Rank 1 to. There are two options for the order in which values are ranked:

- **Smallest value.** Assigns ranks by ascending order, with the smallest value receiving a rank of 1. This is the default.
- **Largest value.** Assigns ranks by descending order, with the largest value receiving a rank of 1.

SPSS automatically creates a new variable name and a descriptive variable label for each variable ranked and each ranking method (see "Ranking Method," below). The following option is available for displaying a summary table of new variable names:

- **Display summary tables.** Displays a table of new variable names and labels that describe the variable ranked, ranking method, and any grouping variables. This is displayed by default. Deselect this item to suppress the summary table.

Ranking Method

Simple ranks are computed by default. To choose other ranking methods, click on Rank Types... in the Rank Cases dialog box. This opens the Rank Types dialog box, as shown in Figure 1.12.

Figure 1.12 Rank Types dialog box

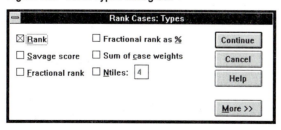

You can select multiple methods. A separate ranking variable is created for each method. You can choose one or more of the following methods:

- **Rank.** Simple rank. This is the default.
- **Savage score.** Scores based on an exponential distribution.
- **Fractional rank.** Each rank is divided by the number of cases with valid values or by the sum of any weighting variables (see Chapter 2).
- **Fractional rank as %.** Each rank is divided by the number of cases with valid values and multiplied by 100.
- **Sum of case weights.** The value of the variable is a constant for cases in the same group.
- **Ntiles.** A user-specified number of percentiles, each with approximately the same number of cases.

Proportion Estimates and Normal Scores

To create new ranking variables based on proportion estimates and normal scores, click on More>> in the Rank Types dialog box. The dialog box expands, as shown in Figure 1.13.

Figure 1.13 Expanded Rank Types dialog box

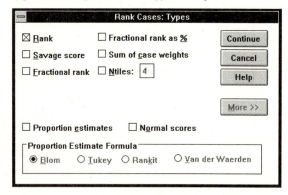

You can choose one or both of the following:

- **Proportion estimates.** The estimate of the cumulative proportion (area) of the distribution corresponding to a particular rank.
- **Normal scores.** The new variable contains the Z scores from the standard normal distribution that correspond to the estimated cumulative proportion. For example, if the estimated cumulative proportion is 0.50, the normal score is 0.

Proportion Estimate Formula. You can choose one of the following formula methods:

○ **Blom**. Blom's transformation, defined by the formula $(r - 3/8) / (w + 1/4)$, where w is the number of observations and r is rank, ranging from 1 to w (Blom, 1958). This is the default.

○ **Tukey**. Tukey's transformation, defined by the formula $(r - 1/3) / (w + 1/3)$, where w is the sum of case weights and r is the rank, ranging from 1 to w (Tukey, 1962).

○ **Rankit**. Uses the formula $(r - 1/2) / w$, where w is the number of observations and r is the rank, ranging from 1 to w (Chambers et al., 1983).

○ **Van der Waerden**. Van der Waerden's transformation, defined by the formula $r / (w + 1)$, where w is the sum of case weights and r is the rank, ranging from 1 to w (Lehmann, 1975).

Rank Ties

By default, cases with the same values for a variable are assigned the average (mean) of the ranks for the tied values. To choose an alternate method for handling ties, click on Ties... in the Rank Cases dialog box. This opens the Rank Ties dialog box, as shown in Figure 1.14.

Figure 1.14   Rank Ties dialog box

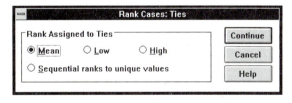

Rank Assigned to Ties. You can choose one of the following alternatives for assigning ranks to tied values:

○ **Mean**. Average rank assigned to tied values. This is the default.

○ **Low**. Lowest rank assigned to tied values.

○ **High**. Highest rank assigned to ties.

○ **Sequential ranks to unique values**. Ranks are assigned from 1 to D, where D is the number of unique values. Cases with the same value receive the same rank.

Table 1.3 shows the effects of each method on a group of data values.

Table 1.3 Alternatives for ranking ties

Value	Mean	Low	High	Sequential
10	1	1	1	1
15	3	2	4	2
15	3	2	4	2
15	3	2	4	2
16	5	5	5	3
20	6	6	6	4

Creating Consecutive Integers from Numeric and String Values

When category codes are not sequential, the resulting empty cells reduce performance and increase memory requirements for many SPSS procedures. Additionally, some procedures cannot use long string variables, and some require consecutive integer values for factor levels.

To recode string and numeric variables into consecutive integers, from the menus choose:

Transform
  Automatic Recode...

This opens the Automatic Recode dialog box, as shown in Figure 1.15.

Figure 1.15 Automatic Recode dialog box

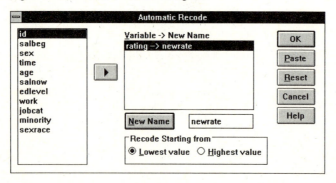

The variables in the working data file are displayed on the source variable list. Select one or more variables for which you want to recode values into consecutive integers. SPSS creates new variables containing the recoded values. The original variables are not affected. Any existing variable or value labels are retained for the new variables. If the original value doesn't have a value label, the original value is used as the value label for the recoded value.

Variable –> New Name. You must specify a new variable name to receive the recoded values for each selected variable. To specify a new variable name, highlight the original variable on the selected list, enter the new variable name in the text box, and click on New Name. The new variable name is displayed next to the original variable name. Variable names must begin with a letter and cannot exceed eight characters. (See the *SPSS Base System User's Guide, Part 1* for complete variable naming rules.)

Recode Starting from. There are two alternatives for the order in which new values are assigned:

○ **Lowest value**. Assigns values by ascending order, with the lowest value receiving a recoded value of 1. This is the default.

○ **Highest value**. Assigns values by descending order, with the highest value receiving a recoded value of 1.

String values are recoded in alphabetical order, with uppercase letters preceding their lowercase counterparts. Missing values are recoded into missing values higher than any nonmissing values, with their order preserved. For example, if the original variable has 10 nonmissing values, the lowest missing value would be recoded to 11, and the value 11 would be a missing value for the new variable.

Time Series Data Transformations

SPSS provides several data transformations that are useful in time series analysis:
- Generate date variables to establish periodicity, and distinguish between historical, validation, and forecasting periods.
- Create new time series variables as functions of existing time series variables.
- Replace system- and user-missing values with estimates based on one of several methods.

A **time series** is obtained by measuring a variable (or set of variables) regularly over a period of time. Time series data transformations assume a data file structure in which each case (row) represents a set of observations at a different time, and the length of time between cases is uniform.

Generating Date Variables

The observations in a time series occur at equally spaced intervals. The actual date of each observation does not matter in the analysis but is useful for establishing periodicity, labeling output, or specifying a portion of the time series that you want to analyze.

To generate date variables, from the menus choose:

Data
  Define Dates...

This opens the Define Dates dialog box, as shown in Figure 1.16.

Figure 1.16 Define Dates dialog box

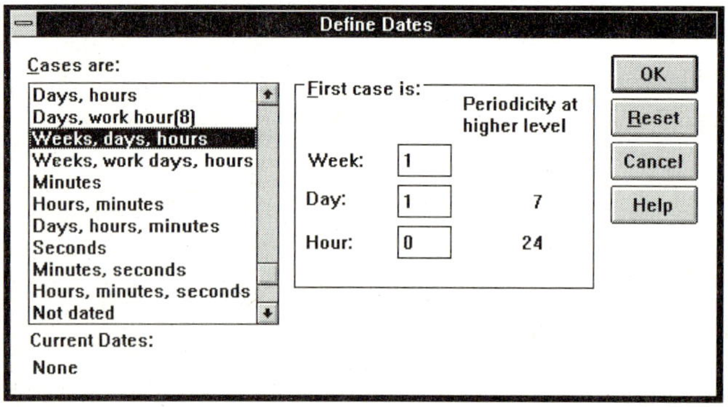

Cases Are: Defines the time interval used to generate dates.

First Case Is: Defines the starting date value, which is assigned to the first case. Sequential values, based on the time interval, are assigned to subsequent cases. All values must be positive integers.

> **Periodicity at higher level**. Indicates the repetitive cyclical variation, such as the number of months in a year or the number of days in a week. The value displayed indicates the maximum value you can enter.

For each component that is used to define the date, SPSS creates a new numeric variable. The new variable names end with an underscore. A descriptive string variable, *date_*, is also created from the components. For example, in Figure 1.16, four new variables would be created: *week_*, *day_*, *hour_*, and *date_*.

If date variables have already been defined, they are replaced when you define new date variables. Variables with the following names are removed from the working data file and replaced with the new date variables: *year_*, *quarter_*, *month_*, *week_*, *day_*, *hour_*, *minute_*, *second_*, and *date_*.

Table 1.4 and Table 1.5 indicate the range of valid starting values for each date component.

Table 1.4 Dates involving years, quarters, and months

Cases Are:	Year	Quarter	Month
Years	0–9999		
Years, quarters	0–9999	1–4	
Years, months	0–9999		1–12
Years, quarters, months	0–9999	1–4	1–12

Table 1.5 Dates involving weeks, days, hours, minutes, and seconds

Cases Are:	Week	Day	Hour	Minute	Second
Days		0–9999			
Weeks, days	0–9999	1–7			
Weeks, work days (5)	0–9999	1–5			
Weeks, work days (6)	0–9999	1–6			
Hours			0–9999		
Days, hours		0–9999	0–23		
Days, work hours (8)		0–9999	0–7		
Weeks, days, hours	0–9999	1–7	0–23		
Weeks, work days, hours	0–9999	1–5	0–7		
Minutes				0–9999	
Hours, minutes			0–9999	0–59	
Days, hours, minutes		0–9999	0–23	0–59	
Seconds					0–9999
Minutes, seconds				0–9999	0–59
Hours, minutes, seconds			0–9999	0–59	0–59

The following alternatives are also available:

Not dated. Removes any previously defined date variables. Any variables with the following names are deleted: *year_*, *quarter_*, *month_*, *week_*, *day_*, *hour_*, *minute_*, *second_*, and *date_*.

Custom. Indicates the presence of custom date variables created with command syntax (for example, a four-day work week). This item merely reflects the current state of the working data file. Selecting it from the list has no effect. (See the *SPSS Base System Syntax Reference Guide* for information on using the DATE command to create custom date variables.)

Creating Time Series Variables

You can create new time series variables based on functions of existing time series variables. (Any variable measured regularly over a period of time is a **time series variable**.)

To create new time series variables, from the menus choose:

Transform
 Create Time Series...

This opens the Create Time Series dialog box, as shown in Figure 1.17.

Figure 1.17   Create Time Series dialog box

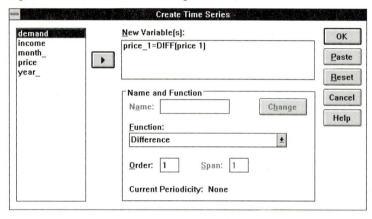

The numeric variables in the working data file are displayed on the source variable list.

New Variable(s). Displays new variable names and the functions based on existing variables that will be used to create them.

Name and Function. You can change the name and/or function used to create new time series variables. Enter a new name and/or select a different function and click on Change.

Name. Default new variable names are the first six characters of the existing variable used to create it, followed by an underscore and a sequential number. To override the default name, enter a new name. Variable names cannot exceed eight characters (see the *SPSS Base System User's Guide, Part 1* for complete variable naming rules).

▼ **Function**. You can choose one of the following alternatives:

Difference. Nonseasonal difference between successive values in the series.

Order. The number of previous values used to calculate the difference. Since one observation is lost for each order of difference, system-missing values appear at the beginning of the series. For example, if the difference order is 2, the first two cases will have the system-missing value for the new variable.

Seasonal difference. Difference between series values a constant span apart. The span is based on the currently defined periodicity. To compute seasonal differences, you must have defined date variables that include a periodic component (such as months of the year). See "Generating Date Variables" on p. 24 for information on creating date variables and changing the periodicity.

> **Order.** The number of seasonal periods used to compute the difference. The number of cases with the system-missing value at the beginning of the series is equal to the periodicity multiplied by the order. For example, if the current periodicity is 12 and the order is 2, the first 24 cases will have the system-missing value for the new variable.

Centered moving average. Average of a span of series values surrounding and including the current value.

> **Span.** The number of series values used to compute the average. If the span is even, the moving average is computed by averaging each pair of uncentered means. The number of cases with the system-missing value at the beginning and at the end of the series for a span of n is equal to $n/2$ for even span values and $(n-1)/2$ for odd span values. For example, if the span is 5, the number of cases with the system-missing value at the beginning and at the end of the series is 2.

Prior moving average. Average of the span of series values preceding the current value.

> **Span.** The number of preceding series values used to compute the average. The number of cases with the system-missing value at the beginning of the series is equal to the span value.

Running median. Median of a span of series values surrounding and including the current value.

> **Span.** The number of series values used to compute the median. If the span is even, the median is computed by averaging each pair of uncentered medians. The number of cases with the system-missing value at the beginning and at the end of the series for a span of n is equal to $n/2$ for even span values and $(n-1)/2$ for odd span values. For example, if the span is 5, the number of cases with the system-missing value at the beginning and at the end of the series is 2.

Cumulative sum. Cumulative sum of series values up to and including the current value.

Lag. Value of a previous case, based on the specified lag order.

Order. The number of cases prior to the current case from which the value is obtained. The number of cases with the system-missing value at the beginning of the series is equal to the order value.

Lead. Value of a subsequent case, based on the specified lead order.

Order. The number of cases after the current case from which the value is obtained. The number of cases with the system-missing value at the end of the series is equal to the order value.

Smoothing. New series values based on a compound data smoother. The smoother starts with a running median of 4, which is centered by a running median of 2. It then resmoothes these values by applying a running median of 5, a running median of 3, and hanning (running weighted averages). Residuals are computed by subtracting the smoothed series from the original series. This whole process is then repeated on the computed residuals. Finally, the smoothed residuals are computed by subtracting the smoothed values obtained the first time through the process. This is sometimes referred to as T4253H smoothing.

Missing Values

If the original time series contains missing values, the following rules apply:

- **Difference and Seasonal difference**: If either of a pair of values involved in a difference computation is missing, the result is set to system-missing in the new series.
- **Centered moving average, Prior moving average, Running median**: If any value within the span is missing, the result is set to system-missing in the new series.
- **Cumulative sum**. Cases with missing values are assigned the system-missing value in the new series.
- **Lag and Lead**: If the lag or lead case value is missing, the result is set to system-missing in the new series.
- **Smoothing**: Cases with missing values are not allowed, and all cases in the new series are assigned the system-missing value.

Replacing Missing Values

Missing observations can be problematic in time series analysis, and some time series measures cannot be computed if there are missing values in the series. To circumvent problems with missing values, you can replace missing values with estimates computed with one of several methods.

To create new time series variables that replace missing values in existing series, from the menus choose:

Transform
 Replace Missing Values...

This opens the Replace Missing Values dialog box, as shown in Figure 1.18.

Figure 1.18 Replace Missing Values dialog box

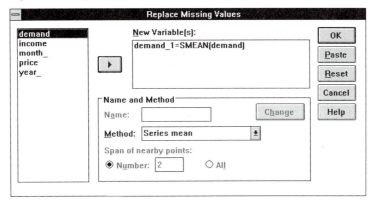

The numeric variables in the working data file are displayed on the source variable list.

New Variable(s). Displays new variable names and the functions based on existing variables that will be used to create them.

Name and Method. You can change the name and/or method used to create new time series variables. Enter a new name and/or select a different method and click on **Change**.

>   **Name.** Default new variable names are the first six characters of the existing variable used to create it, followed by an underscore and a sequential number. To override the default name, enter a new name. Variable names cannot exceed eight characters (see the *SPSS Base System User's Guide, Part 1* for complete variable naming rules).

Method. You can choose one of the following alternatives:

>   **Series mean.** Replaces missing values with the mean for the entire series.
>
>   **Mean of nearby points.** Replaces missing values with the mean of valid surrounding values.
>
>>   **Span of nearby points.** You can select one of two alternatives:
>>
>>   ○ **Number.** The number of valid values above and below the missing value used to compute the mean. The default is 2. Missing values near the beginning or end of the series will not be replaced if there are not enough valid values for the specified span. For example, if the second case has a missing value and the span is 2, the missing value for the case will not be replaced.
>>
>>   ○ **All.** Replaces missing values with the mean for the entire series. (This is equivalent to Series mean.)

Median of nearby points. Replaces missing values with the median of valid surrounding values.

Span of nearby points. You can select one of two alternatives:

○ **Number**. The number of valid values above and below the missing value used to compute the median. The default is 2. Missing values near the beginning or end of the series will not be replaced if there are not enough valid values for the specified span. For example, if the second case has a missing value and the span is 2, the missing value for the case will not be replaced.

○ **All**. Replaces missing values with the median for the entire series.

Linear interpolation. Replaces missing values using a linear interpolation. The last valid value before the missing value and the first valid value after the missing value are used for the interpolation. If the first or last case in the series has a missing value, the missing value is not replaced.

Linear trend at point. Replaces missing values with the linear trend for that point. The existing series is regressed on an index variable scaled 1 to n. Missing values are replaced with their predicted values.

Pending Transformations

To run pending transformations, from the menus choose:

Transform
  Run Pending Transforms

By default, data transformations are executed immediately. If you have a large number of transformations or you are working with a large data file, you can save processing time by changing your Preferences settings to delay the execution of transformations until SPSS encounters a command that requires a data pass (see the *SPSS Base System User's Guide, Part 1*). If you choose to delay the execution of data transformations, they are automatically executed as soon as you run any statistical procedure that requires a data pass. You can also run pending transformations at any time without running any statistical procedure.

2 File Handling and File Transformations

Data files are not always organized in the ideal form for your specific needs. You may want to combine data files, sort the data in a different order, select a subset of cases, or change the unit of analysis by grouping cases together. SPSS offers a wide range of file transformation capabilities, including the ability to:

- **Sort data**. You can sort cases based on the value of one or more variables.
- **Transpose cases and variables**. SPSS reads rows as cases and columns as variables. For data files in which this order is reversed, you can switch the rows and columns and read the data in the correct format.
- **Merge files**. You can merge two or more data files together. You can combine files with the same variables but different cases, or files with the same cases but different variables.
- **Select subsets of cases**. You can restrict your analysis to a subset of cases or perform simultaneous analyses on different subsets.
- **Aggregate data**. You can change the unit of analysis by aggregating cases based on the value of one or more grouping variables.
- **Weight data**. Weight cases for analysis based on the value of a weight variable.

Sorting Data

Sorting cases (sorting rows of the data file) is often useful—and sometimes necessary—in conjunction with merging files (see "Combining Data Files" on p. 33), split-file processing (see "Sorting Cases for Split-File Processing" on p. 49), and generating summary reports (see Chapter 19).

To reorder the sequence of cases in the data file based on the value of one or more sorting variables, from the menus choose:

Data
  Sort Cases...

This opens the Sort Cases dialog box, as shown in Figure 2.1

Figure 2.1 Sort Cases dialog box

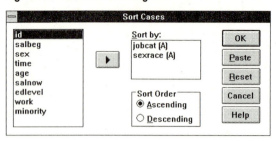

The variables in the data file appear on the source variable list. Select one or more sort variables. If you select multiple sort variables, the order in which they appear on the Sort list determines the order in which cases are sorted. For example, based on the Sort list in Figure 2.1, cases will be sorted by the value of *sexrace* within sorted categories of *jobcat*. For string variables, uppercase letters precede their lowercase counterparts in sort order (for example, the string value "Yes" comes before "yes" in sort order).

Sort Order. There are two alternatives for sort order:

❍ **Ascending.** Sort cases by ascending order of the values of the sort variable(s). This is the default.

❍ **Descending.** Sort case by descending order of the values of the sort variable(s).

Transposing Cases and Variables

SPSS assumes a file structure in which cases are represented in rows and variables are represented in columns. Sometimes, however, data are recorded in the opposite fashion. You might, for example, find this to be the case with spreadsheet data. To switch the columns and rows in the data file, from the menus choose:

Data
 Transpose...

This opens the Transpose dialog box, as shown in Figure 2.2.

Figure 2.2 Transpose dialog box

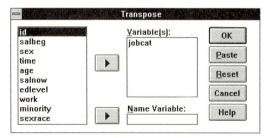

The variables in the data file appear on the source variable list. Select one or more variables. The selected variables become cases, and all cases become variables.

Name Variable. By default, SPSS assigns the new variable names *var001*, *var002*, and so on to the transposed data. Optionally, you can use the values of an existing variable in the untransposed file as the variable names for the transposed file. If the name variable is numeric, the new variable names begin with the letter *V* followed by the numeric values. If values exceed eight characters, they are truncated. If values are not unique, SPSS creates unique variable names by adding a sequential number to the end of the value. A table of the new variable names is displayed in the output window.

Missing Values in Transposed Data Files

Any user-missing values are converted to the system-missing value when the data file is transposed. If you want to retain the original data values in the transposed file, before transposing the file, change the variable definition so that there are no user-missing values (see the *SPSS Base System User's Guide, Part 1*).

Combining Data Files

With SPSS, you can combine data from two files in two different ways. You can:
- Merge files containing the same variables but different cases.
- Merge files containing the same cases but different variables.

Merging Files That Contain Different Cases

The Add Cases procedure merges two data files that contain the same variables but different cases. For example, you might record the same information for customers in two different sales regions and maintain the data for each region in separate files. The variables can be in any order in the two files. Variables are matched by name. The procedure also provides a facility to match variables that contain the same information but different variable names in the two files.

The Add Cases procedure adds cases to the working data file from a second, external SPSS data file. So, before you can merge the files, one of them must already be open.

To add cases to the working data file from an external SPSS data file, from the menus choose:

Data
 Merge Files ▶
  Add Cases...

This opens a standard dialog box for selecting files. Select the external data file you want to merge with the working data file. Select the variables you want to include in the new working file, using the Add Cases From dialog box, shown in Figure 2.3.

Figure 2.3   Add Cases From dialog box

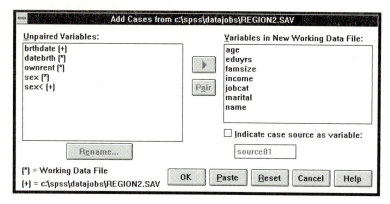

Unpaired Variables. Variables to be excluded from the new, merged data file. Variables from the working data file are identified with an asterisk (*). Variables from the external data file are identified with a plus sign (+). By default, this list contains:

- Variables from either data file that do not match a variable name in the other file. You can create pairs from unpaired variables and include them in the new, merged file (see below).
- Variables defined as numeric data in one file and string data in the other file. Numeric variables cannot be merged with string variables. For example, in Figure 2.3, *sex* is a numeric variable in the working data file, but it is a short string variable in the external data file.
- String variables of unequal width. The defined width of a string variable must be the same in both data files.

Variables in the New Working Data File. Variables to be included in the new, merged data file. By default, all the variables that match both name and data type (numeric or string) are included on the list. You can remove variables from the list if you don't want them included in the merged file.

The following option is also available:

❏ **Indicate case source as variable.** Creates an **indicator variable** that indicates the source data file for each case in the merged file. For cases from the working data file, the value of this variable is 0; for cases from the external data file, the value of this variable is 1. The default name of the variable is *source01*. You can enter a variable name up to eight characters long. The name cannot be the same as one of the variables on the list to be included in the merged file.

Selecting Variables

If the same information is recorded under different variable names in the two files, you can create a pair from the Unpaired Variables list. Select the two variables on the Unpaired Variables list and click on Pair. (Use the ctrl-click method to select noncontiguous pairs of variables.) Both variable names appear together on the same line on the list of variables to be included in the merged file, as shown in Figure 2.4. By default, the name of the variable in the working data file is used as the name of the variable in the merged file.

Figure 2.4   Selecting variable pairs

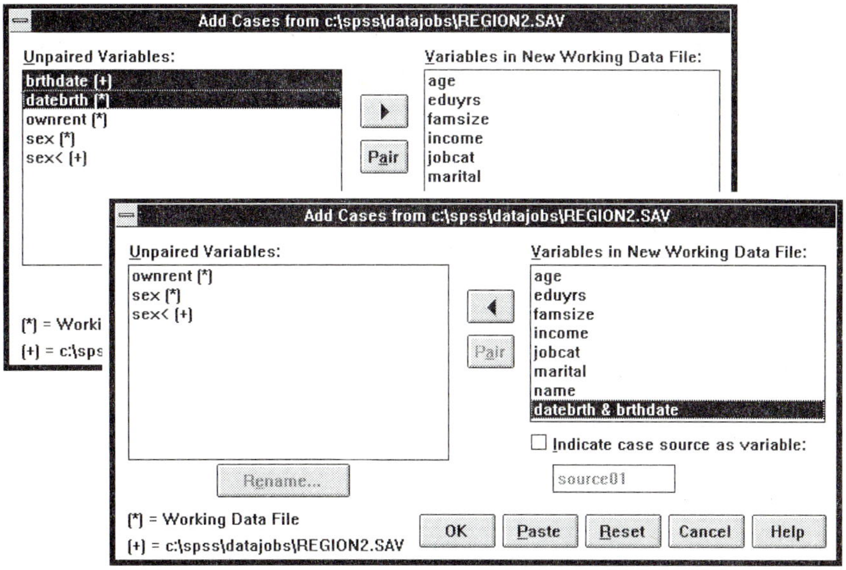

Macintosh: Use ⌘-click to select pairs of variables.

To include an unpaired variable from one file without pairing it with a variable from the other file, select the variable on the Unpaired Variables list and click on ▶ . Any unpaired variables included in the merged file will contain missing data for cases from the file that does not contain that variable. For example, the variable *ownrent* exists in the working data file but not in the external data file. If this variable is included in the merged file, cases from the external file will contain the system-missing value for this variable in the merged file.

Removing Variables

To remove a variable from the list of variables to be included in the merged file, select the variable on the list and click on ◄. The variable is moved to the Unpaired Variables list. The variable name is displayed twice on the Unpaired Variables list, once for the working data file and once for the external file. To move the variable back to the list of variables to be included in the merged file, select both variable names on the Unpaired Variables list and click on Pair.

Renaming Variables

You can rename variables from either the working data file or the external file before moving them from the Unpaired Variables list to the list of variables to be included in the merged data file. Renaming variables enables you to:

- Use the variable name from the external file rather than the name from the working data file for variable pairs—for example, to use *brthdate* instead of *datebrth* for the variable pair in Figure 2.6.
- Include two variables with the same name but of unmatched types or different string widths. For example, to include both the numeric variable *sex* from the working data file and the string variable *sex* from the external file, one of them must be renamed first.

To rename a variable on the Unpaired Variables list, highlight the variable and click on Rename... in the Add Cases From dialog box. This opens the Rename dialog box, as shown in Figure 2.5. The new variable name can be up to eight characters long. (See the *SPSS Base System User's Guide, Part 1* for complete variable naming rules.)

Figure 2.5   Rename dialog box

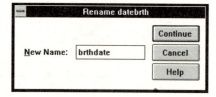

Both the original variable name and the new name are displayed on the Unpaired Variables list. If the new variable name is the same as the other variable in the pair, only one variable name appears on the list of variables to be included in the merged file, as shown in Figure 2.6.

Figure 2.6 Selecting renamed variables

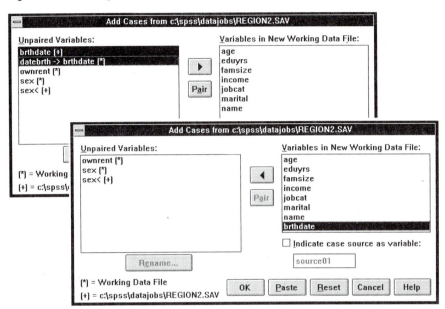

To undo variable renaming, simply go back to the Rename dialog box and delete the new variable name.

Dictionary Information

Any existing dictionary information (variable and value labels, user-missing values, display formats) in the working data file is applied to the merged data file. If any dictionary information for a variable is undefined in the working data file, dictionary information from the external data file is used.

If the working data file contains any defined value labels or user-missing values for a variable, any additional value labels or user-missing values for that variable in the external file are ignored.

Merging Files That Contain Different Variables

With the Add Variables procedure, you can:

- Merge two SPSS data files that contain the same cases but different variables.
- Use a table lookup file to add data to multiple cases in another file.

The two data files to be merged must meet the following requirements:
- Files must be in SPSS or SPSS/PC+ format.
- Cases must be sorted in the same order in both data files.
- If one or more key variables are used to match cases, the two data files must be sorted by ascending order of the key variable(s).

The Add Variables procedure merges the working data file with an external SPSS data file. Both files must be sorted in the same case order, so before you can merge the files, you must complete any necessary sorting. One of the files must already be open when you start the procedure (see "Sorting Data" on p. 31).

To add variables to the working data file from an external SPSS data file or to use data from a table lookup file, from the menus choose:

Data
  Merge Files ▶
    Add Variables...

This opens a standard dialog box for selecting files. Select the external data file you want to merge with the working data file. Select the variables you want to include in the new working file, using the Add Variables From dialog box, as shown in Figure 2.7.

Figure 2.7 Add Variables From dialog box

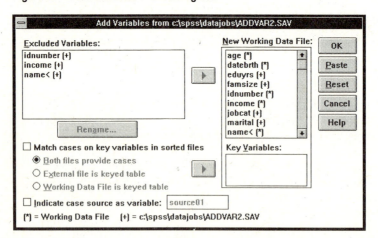

Excluded Variables. Variables to be excluded from the new, merged data file. By default, this list contains any variable names from the external data file that duplicate variable names in the working data file. If you want to include the variable with the duplicate name in the merged file, you can rename it and add it to the list of variables to be included (see "Renaming Variables" on p. 41). Variables from the working data file are identified with an asterisk (*). Variables from the external data file are identified with a plus sign (+).

New Working Data File. Variables to be included in the new, merged data file. By default, all unique variable names in both data files are included on the list.

The following options are also available:

❏ **Match cases on key variables in sorted files**. If some cases in one file do not have matching cases in the other file (that is, some cases are missing in one file), use **key variables** to identify and correctly match cases from the two files. You can also use key variables with table lookup files. The key variables must have the same names in both data files. Both data files must be sorted by ascending order of the key variables, and the order of variables on the Key Variables list must be the same as their sort sequence. Key variables are included in the new, merged file.

Cases that do not match on the key variables are included in the merged file but are not merged with cases from the other file. Unmatched cases contain values for only the variables in the file from which they are taken; variables from the other file contain the system-missing value.

You can choose one of the following alternatives for the key variable matching method:

○ **Both files provide cases**. Cases in one file correspond to cases in the other file on a one-to-one basis. This is the default. The key variables should uniquely identify each case. If two or more cases have the same values for all the key variables, SPSS merges those cases in sequential order and issues a warning message.

○ **External file is keyed table**. The external data file is a table lookup file.

○ **Working data file is keyed table**. The working data file is a table lookup file.

A **keyed table** or **table lookup file** is a file in which data for each "case" can be applied to multiple cases in the other data file. For example, if one file contains information on individual family members (for example, sex, age, education) and the other file contains overall family information (for example, total income, family size, location), you can use the file of family data as a table lookup file and apply the common family data to each individual family member in the merged data file.

The following option is also available:

❏ **Indicate case source as variable.** Creates an indicator variable that indicates the source data file for each case in the merged file. For cases from the working data file that are missing from the external file, the value of this variable is 0; for cases from the external data file that are missing from the working data file and cases present in both files, the value of this variable is 1. The default name of the variable is *source01*. You can enter a variable name up to eight characters long. The name cannot be the same as one of the variables on the list to be included in the merged file.

Selecting Key Variables

Key variables are selected from the Excluded Variables list. The key variables must be present in both data files. By default, any variables in the external file that duplicate variable names in the working data file are placed on the Excluded Variables list. For example, in Figure 2.8, *idnumber* and *name* are the key variables.

To select a key variable, highlight the variable on the Excluded Variables list, select Match cases on key variables in sorted files, and click on the ▶ pushbutton next to the Key Variables list. You can select multiple key variables. Both files must be sorted by ascending order of the key variables, and the order of variables on the Key Variables list must be the same as their sort sequence.

Key variables must have the same variable names in both data files. If the names differ, you can rename the variable in one file to match the variable name in the other file (see "Renaming Variables," below).

Figure 2.8 Selecting key variables

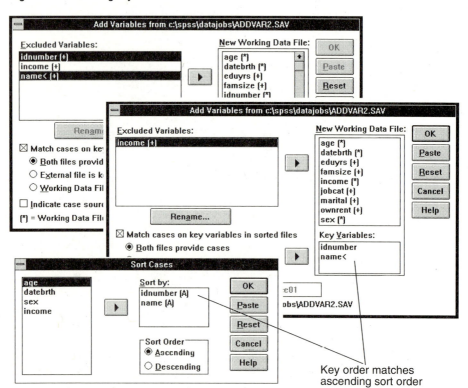

Renaming Variables

There are several reasons for renaming variables before merging two files that contain different variables:

- You want to include a variable from the external file that has the same name as a variable in the working data file but contains different data.
- You want to select a key variable that does not have the same name in both data files.
- You don't like a variable name and want to change it.

To rename a variable, highlight the variable on the Excluded Variables list and click on Rename... in the Add Variables From dialog box. This opens the Rename dialog box, as shown in Figure 2.9. The new variable name can be up to eight characters long. (See the *SPSS Base System User's Guide, Part 1* for complete variable naming rules.)

Figure 2.9　Rename dialog box

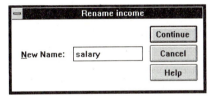

Both the original variable name and the new name are displayed on the Excluded Variables list. If you move the renamed variable to the New Working Data File list or the Key Variables list, only the new variable name is displayed, as shown in Figure 2.10.

To undo variable renaming, simply go back to the Rename dialog box and delete the new variable name.

Figure 2.10 Selecting renamed variables

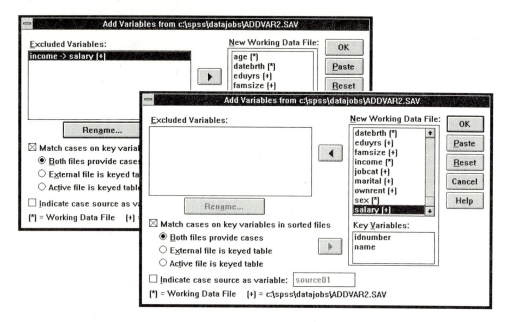

Applying a Data Dictionary

An SPSS data dictionary can contain extensive data definition information, including:
- Data type (numeric, string, etc.) and width
- Display format
- Descriptive variable and value labels
- User-missing value specifications

To apply the data dictionary information from another SPSS data file to the working data file, from the menus choose:

Data
  Apply Dictionary...

This opens a standard dialog box for selecting files. Dictionary information is applied based on matching variable names. The variables don't have to be in the same order in

both files, and variables that aren't present in both files are unaffected. The following rules apply:
- If the variable type (numeric or string) is the same in both files, all the dictionary information is applied.
- If the variable type is not the same for both files, or if it is a long string (more than eight characters), only the variable label is applied.
- Numeric, dollar, dot, comma, date, and time formats are all considered numeric, and all dictionary information is applied.
- String variable widths are not affected by the applied dictionary.
- For short string variables (eight characters or less), missing values and specified values for value labels are truncated if they exceed the defined width of the variable in the working data file.
- Any applied dictionary information overwrites existing dictionary information.

Weighted Files

The following rules apply to weighted files (see "Weighting Cases" on p. 54):
- If the working data file is weighted and the file containing the dictionary is unweighted, the working data file remains weighted.
- If the working data file is unweighted and the file containing the dictionary is weighted by a variable that exists in the working data file, the working data file is weighted by that variable.
- If both files are weighted but they are not weighted by the same variable, the weight is changed in the working data file if the weight variable in the file containing the dictionary also exists in the working data file.

The status bar at the bottom of the SPSS application window displays the message Weight on if weighting is in effect in the working data file.

Aggregating Data

You can aggregate cases based on the value of one or more grouping variables and create a new data file containing one case for each group. For example, you can aggregate county data by state and create a new data file in which state is the unit of analysis. To aggregate cases, from the menus choose:

Data
  Aggregate...

This opens the Aggregate Data dialog box, as shown in Figure 2.11.

Figure 2.11 Aggregate Data dialog box

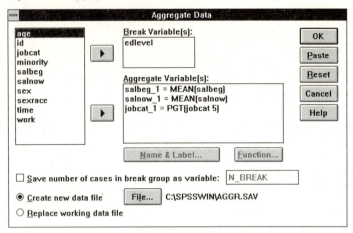

The variables in the data file appear on the source variable list. You must select at least one break variable and define at least one new variable based on an aggregate variable and an aggregate function.

Break Variable(s). Cases are grouped together based on the values of the break variables. Each unique combination of break variable values defines a group and generates one case in the new aggregated file. All break variables are saved in the new file with their existing names and dictionary information. The break variable can be either numeric or string.

Aggregate Variable(s). Variables are used with aggregate functions (see "Aggregate Functions" on p. 45) to create the new variables for the aggregated file. By default, SPSS creates new aggregate variable names using the first several characters of the source variable name followed by an underscore and a sequential two-digit number. For example, *salbeg* on the source list becomes *salbeg_01* on the Aggregate Variable(s) list. The aggregate variable name is followed by an optional variable label (see "New Variable Names and Labels" on p. 47) in quotes, the name of the aggregate function, and the source variable name in parentheses. Source variables for aggregate functions must be numeric.

To create a variable containing the number of cases in each break group, select:

❏ **Save number of cases in break group as variable.** You can create a variable containing the number of cases in each break group. The default variable name is *N_BREAK*. Enter a new name to override the default. Variable names must begin with a letter and cannot exceed eight characters.

To specify the filename and location of the aggregated data file, choose one of the following alternatives:

○ **Create new data file**. By default, a file is created in the current directory. To change the file name or directory, click on File... (see "Aggregate Filename and Location" on p. 47).

○ **Replace working data file**. Replaces the working data file with the new aggregated data file. This creates a temporary aggregated file unless you explicitly save the file.

Aggregate Functions

New variables in the aggregated file are created by applying aggregate functions to existing variables. By default, the mean of values across cases is used as the value of the new aggregated variable. To specify a different aggregate function, highlight the variable on the Aggregate Variable(s) list and click on Function... in the Aggregate Data dialog box. This opens the Aggregate Function dialog box, as shown in Figure 2.12.

Figure 2.12 Aggregate Function dialog box

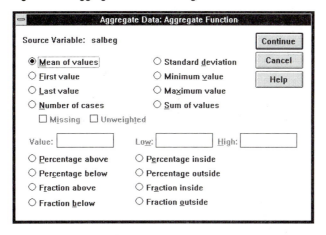

For each variable, you can choose one of the aggregate functions described below. When a function is performed, the resulting value is displayed on the Aggregate Variable(s) list in the Aggregate Data dialog box.

○ **Mean of values**. Mean across cases in the break group. This is displayed as MEAN.

○ **First value**. First nonmissing observed value in the break group. This is displayed as FIRST.

○ **Last value**. Last nonmissing observed value in the break group. This is displayed as LAST.

- **Number of cases**. Number of cases in the break group. This is displayed as N. You can also choose one or both of the following:
  - **Missing**. Number of missing cases in the break group. This is displayed as NMISS.
  - **Unweighted**. Number of unweighted cases in the break group. This is displayed as NU.

  If you select both Missing and Unweighted, the result is the number of unweighted missing values in the break group. This is displayed as NUMISS.
- **Standard deviation**. Standard deviation across cases in the break group. This is displayed as SD.
- **Minimum value**. Minimum value across cases in the break group. This is displayed as MIN.
- **Maximum value**. Maximum value across cases in the break group. This is displayed as MAX.
- **Sum of values**. Sum of values across cases in the break group. This is displayed as SUM.
- **Percentage above**. Percentage of cases in the break group greater than a user-specified value. This is displayed as PGT.
- **Percentage below**. Percentage of cases in the break group less than a user-specified value. This is displayed as PLT.
- **Fraction above**. Fraction of cases in the break group greater than a user-specified value. This is displayed as FGT.
- **Fraction below**. Fraction of cases in the break group less than a user-specified value. This is displayed as FLT.
- **Percentage inside**. Percentage of cases in the break group with values within the inclusive range defined by Low and High. This is displayed as PIN.
- **Percentage outside**. Percentage of cases in the break group with values outside the inclusive range defined by Low and High. This is displayed as POUT.
- **Fraction inside**. Fraction of cases in the break group with values within the inclusive range defined by Low and High. This is displayed as FIN.
- **Fraction outside**. Fraction of cases in the break group with values outside the inclusive range defined by Low and High. This is displayed as FOUT.

New Variable Names and Labels

SPSS provides default variable names for the variables in the new aggregated data file. To specify a different variable name and an optional descriptive label for a new variable, highlight the variable on the Aggregate Variable(s) list and click on **Name & Label...** in the Aggregate Data dialog box. This opens the Variable Name and Label dialog box, as shown in Figure 2.13.

Figure 2.13 Variable Name and Label dialog box

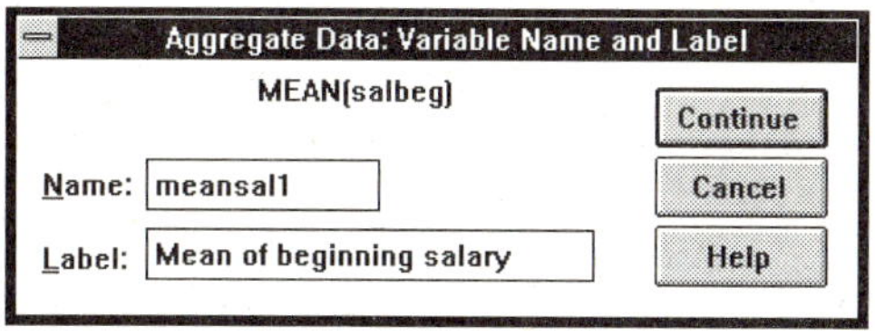

The aggregate function name, the original variable name, and any related value specifications are displayed for reference purposes. To specify a different aggregate function, return to the main dialog box and click on **Function...** (see "Aggregate Functions" on p. 45).

Name. Variable names must begin with a letter and cannot exceed eight characters. (See the *SPSS Base System User's Guide, Part 1* for complete variable naming rules.)

Label. Optional, descriptive variable label, up to 120 characters long.

Aggregate Filename and Location

By default, SPSS creates a new aggregated data file in the current directory. To specify a different filename or directory or to replace the working data file with the aggregated data file, click on **File...** in the Aggregate Data dialog box. This opens a standard dialog box for selecting files. You can choose to create a new data file or replace the working data file.

Split-File Processing

To split your data file into separate groups for analysis, from the menus choose:

Data
  Split File...

This opens the Split File dialog box, as shown in Figure 2.14.

Figure 2.14 Split File dialog box

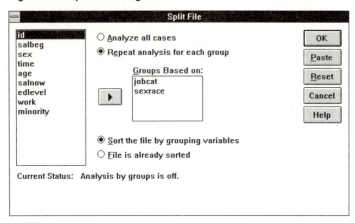

The numeric and short string variables in the data file appear on the source variable list. Select Repeat analysis for each group and choose one or more variables to use as grouping variables. The maximum number of grouping variables is eight. You can use numeric, short string, and long string variables as grouping variables. A separate analysis is performed for each subgroup.

If you select multiple grouping variables, the order in which they appear on the Groups list determines the manner in which cases are grouped. For example, based on the Groups list in Figure 2.14, cases will be grouped by the value of *sexrace* within categories of *jobcat*.

Turning Split-File Processing On and Off

Once you invoke split-file processing, it remains in effect for the rest of the session unless you turn it off. You can choose one of the following alternatives for the status of split-file processing:

- **Analyze all cases**. Split-file processing is off. All cases are analyzed together. Any split-file grouping variables are ignored. This is the default.
- **Repeat analysis for each group**. Split-file processing is on. A separate analysis is performed for each subgroup.

If split-file processing is in effect, the message Split File on appears on the status bar at the bottom of the SPSS application window.

Sorting Cases for Split-File Processing

The Split File procedure creates a new subgroup each time it encounters a different value for one of the grouping variables. Therefore, it is important to sort cases based on the values of the grouping variables before invoking split-file processing. You can choose one of the following alternatives for file sorting:

- **Sort the file by grouping variables**. This is the default. If the file isn't already sorted, this sorts the cases by the values of the grouping variables before splitting the file for analysis.
- **File is already sorted**. If the file is already sorted in the proper order, this alternative can save processing time.

Selecting Subsets of Cases

You can restrict your analysis to a specific subgroup based on criteria that include variables and complex expressions. You can also select a random sample of cases. The criteria used to define a subgroup can include:

- Variable values and ranges
- Date and time ranges
- Case (row) numbers
- Arithmetic expressions
- Logical expressions
- Functions

To select a subset of cases for analysis, from the menus choose:

Data
  Select Cases...

This opens the Select Cases dialog box, as shown in Figure 2.15.

Figure 2.15 Select Cases dialog box

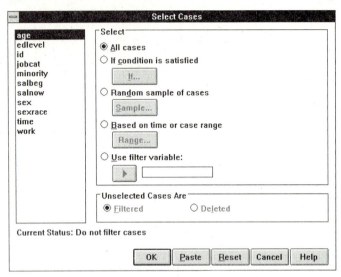

Select. You can choose one of the following alternatives for case selection:

- **All cases**. Use all cases in the data file. This is the default. If filtering (see below) is in effect, you can use this option to turn it off.

- **If condition is satisfied**. You can use conditional expressions to select cases. A **conditional expression** returns a value of true, false, or missing for each case. If the result of a conditional expression is true, the case is selected. If the result is false or missing, the case is not selected. (For information on how to use conditional expressions, see "Selecting Cases Based on Conditional Expressions" on p. 51.)

- **Random sample of cases**. You can select a percentage or an exact number of cases. (For more information on random samples, see "Selecting a Random Sample" on p. 52.)

- **Based on time or case range**. For time-series data with defined date variables (see Chapter 1), you can select a range of dates or times.

- **Use filter variable**. You can select a numeric variable from the data file to use to filter or delete cases. Cases with any value other than 0 or missing for the filter variable are selected.

Unselected Cases. You can choose one of the following alternatives for the treatment of unselected cases:

○ **Filtered**. Unselected cases are not included in the analysis but remain in the data file. You can use the unselected cases later in the session if you turn filtering off. If you select a random sample or if you select cases based on a conditional expression, this generates a variable named *filter_$* with a value of 1 for selected cases and a value of 0 for unselected cases.

○ **Deleted**. Unselected cases are deleted from the data file. By reducing the number of cases in the open data file, you can save processing time. The cases can be recovered if you close the data file without saving any changes and then reopen it. The deletion of cases is permanent only if you save the changes to the data file.

Current Status. Status of filtering. There are two possible states:

Do not filter cases. Filtering is off. If All cases is selected or if unselected cases are deleted, filtering is off.

Filter cases by values of [variable name]. Filtering is on. The variable is either a user-specified variable or the system-generated variable *filter_$*. If filtering is on, the message Filter on appears on the status bar.

Selecting Cases Based on Conditional Expressions

To select cases based on a conditional expression, select If condition is satisfied and click on If... in the Select Cases dialog box. This opens the Select Cases If dialog box, as shown in Figure 2.16.

Figure 2.16 Select Cases If dialog box

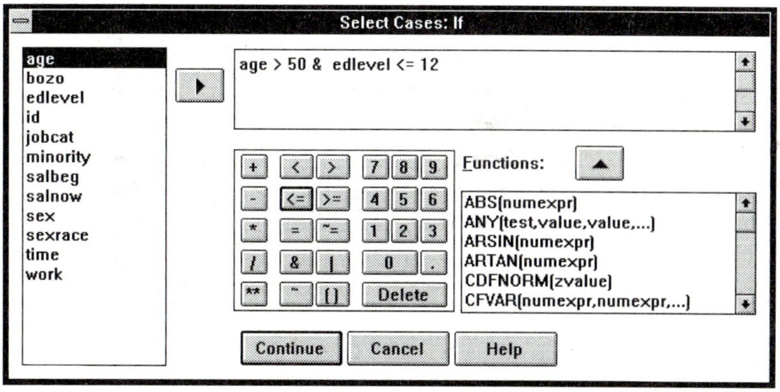

The conditional expression can use existing variable names, constants, arithmetic operators, logical operators, relational operators, and functions. You can type and edit the expression in the text box just like text in a syntax or output window (see the *SPSS Base*

System User's Guide, Part 1). You can also use the calculator pad, variable list, and function list to paste elements into the expression. See Chapter 1 for more information on working with conditional expressions.

Selecting a Random Sample

To obtain a random sample, choose Random sample of cases in the Select Cases dialog box and click on Sample... This opens the Random Sample dialog box, as shown in Figure 2.17.

Figure 2.17 Random Sample dialog box

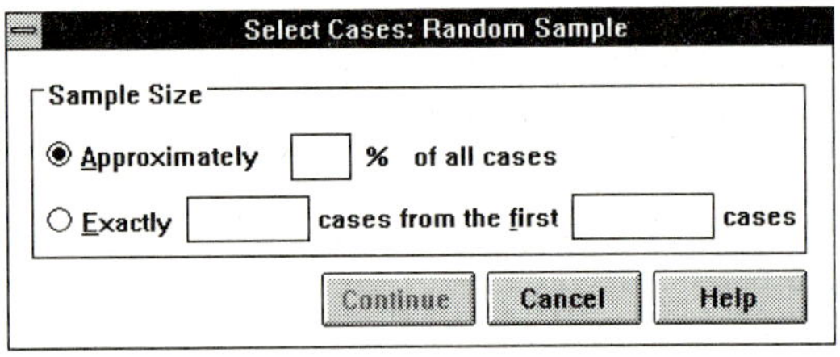

Sample Size. You can choose one of the following alternatives for sample size:

- **Approximately**. A user-specified percentage. SPSS generates a random sample of approximately the specified percentage of cases.
- **Exactly**. A user-specified number of cases. You must also specify the number of cases from which to generate the sample. This second number should be less than or equal to the total number of cases in the data file. If the number exceeds the total number of cases in the data file, the sample will contain proportionally fewer cases than the requested number.

Setting the Seed for Random Sampling

The SPSS pseudo-random number generator begins with a **seed**, a very large integer value. Within a session, SPSS uses a different seed each time you select a random sample, producing a different sample of cases. If you want to duplicate the same random sample, you can reset the seed value using the Random Number Seed dialog box. See Chapter 1 for more information.

Selecting a Range of Dates or Times

To select a range of dates and/or times (for time-series data in which each case represents a set of observations at a different time), select Based on time or case range and click on Range... in the Select Cases dialog box. This opens the Select Cases Range dialog box. If there are no defined date variables, the dialog box looks like Figure 2.18. If there are defined date variables, the dialog box provides a set of text entry boxes for each numeric date variable. For example, Figure 2.19 shows the Select Cases Range dialog box with date variables for year and month. To generate date variables for time-series data, use the Define Dates option on the Data menu. For more information on generating date variables, see Chapter 1.

Figure 2.18   Select Cases Range dialog box with no defined date variables

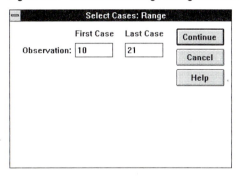

Figure 2.19   Select Cases Range dialog box with defined date variables

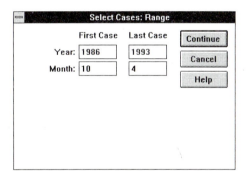

First Case. Enter the starting date and/or time values for the range. If no dates variables are defined, enter the starting observation number (row number in the Data Editor, unless Split File is on). If you don't specify a Last Case value, all cases from the starting date/time to the end of the time series are selected.

Last Case. Enter the ending date and/or time values for the range. If no date variables are defined, enter the ending observation number (row number in the Data Editor, unless Split File is on). If you don't specify a First Case value, all cases from the beginning of the time series up to the ending date/time are selected.

Case Selection Status

If you have selected a subset of cases but have not discarded unselected cases, unselected cases are marked in the Data Editor with a diagonal line through the row number, as shown in Figure 2.20.

Figure 2.20 Case selection status

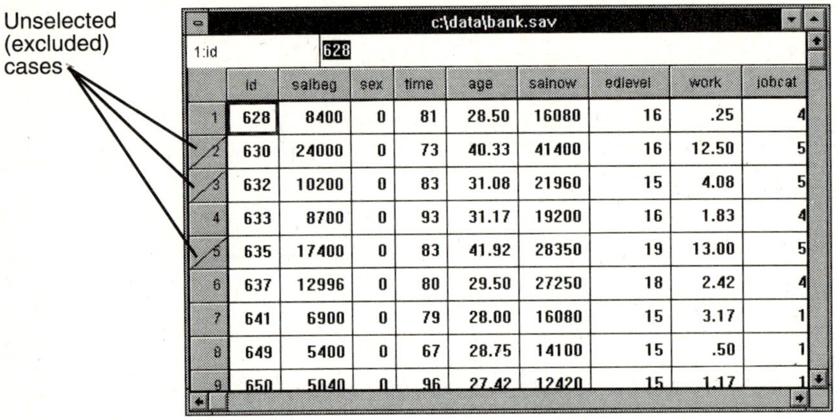

Unselected (excluded) cases →

id	salbeg	sex	time	age	salnow	edlevel	work	jobcat
628	8400	0	81	28.50	16080	16	.25	4
630	24000	0	73	40.33	41400	16	12.50	5
632	10200	0	83	31.08	21960	15	4.08	5
633	8700	0	93	31.17	19200	16	1.83	4
635	17400	0	83	41.92	28350	19	13.00	5
637	12996	0	80	29.50	27250	18	2.42	4
641	6900	0	79	28.00	16080	15	3.17	1
649	5400	0	67	28.75	14100	15	.50	1
650	5040	0	96	27.42	12420	15	1.17	1

Weighting Cases

If each record in the data file represents more than one case, you can specify the replication factor with the Weight procedure. To apply weights to cases based on the value of a weighting variable, from the menus choose:

Data
  Weight Cases...

This opens the Weight Cases dialog box, as shown in Figure 2.21.

Figure 2.21 Weight Cases dialog box

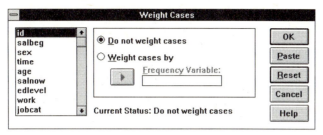

The numeric variables in the data file appear on the source variable list. Select **Weight cases by** and choose a single variable to use as a weight variable.

Turning Weights On and Off

Once you apply a weight variable, it remains in effect until you select another weight variable or turn weighting off. Cases with a negative value, 0, or a missing value for the weighting variable are excluded from all analyses. You can choose one of the following alternatives for the status of weighting:

- **Do not weight cases**. Weighting is off. Any selected weight variable is ignored. This is the default.
- **Weight cases by**. Weighting is on. Cases are weighted by the selected frequency variable.

The status bar at the bottom of the SPSS application window displays the message Weight on if weighting is in effect in the working data file.

Weights in Scatterplots and Histograms

Scatterplots and histograms have an option for turning case weights on and off, but this does not affect cases with a negative value, 0, or a missing value for the weight variable. These cases remain excluded from the chart even if you turn weighting off from within the chart.

3 Data Tabulation

Few people would dispute the effects of "rainy days and Mondays" on the body and spirit. It has long been known that more suicides occur on Mondays than other days of the week. An excess of cardiac deaths on Mondays has also been noted (Rabkin et al., 1980). In this chapter, using a study of coronary heart disease among male Western Electric employees (Paul et al., 1963), we will examine the day of death to see if an excess of deaths occurred on Mondays.

A Frequency Table

A first step in analyzing data about day of death might be to count the number of deaths occurring on each day of the week. Figure 3.1 contains this information.

Figure 3.1   Frequency of death by day of week

```
DAYOFWK    DAY OF DEATH

                                                     Valid      Cum
    Value Label              Value   Frequency  Percent  Percent  Percent
    SUNDAY                     1         19       7.9     17.3     17.3
    MONDAY                     2         11       4.6     10.0     27.3
    TUESDAY                    3         19       7.9     17.3     44.5
    WEDNESDAY                  4         17       7.1     15.5     60.0
    THURSDAY                   5         15       6.3     13.6     73.6
    FRIDAY                     6         13       5.4     11.8     85.5
    SATURDAY                   7         16       6.7     14.5    100.0
    MISSING                    9        130      54.2    Missing
                                      -------   -------  -------
                       Total            240     100.0    100.0

Valid cases     110    Missing cases    130
```

Each row of the frequency table describes a particular day of the week. The last row (labeled *MISSING*) represents cases for which the day of death is not known or death has not occurred. For the table in Figure 3.1, there are 110 cases for which day of death is known. The first column (*Value Label*) gives the name of the day, while the second column contains the **value**, which is the numeric or string value given to the computer to represent the day.

The number of people dying on each day (the **frequency**) appears in the third column. Monday is the least-frequent day of death, with 11 deaths. These 11 deaths represent 4.6% (11/240) of all cases. This **percentage** appears in the fourth column. However, of the 240 cases, 130 are **missing cases** (cases for which day of death is unknown or death has not occurred). The 11 deaths on Monday represent 10.0% of the total deaths for which day of death is known (11/110). This **valid percentage** appears in the fifth column.

The last column of the table contains the **cumulative percentage**. For a particular day, this percentage is the sum of the valid percentages of that day and of all other days that precede it in the table. For example, the cumulative percentage for Tuesday is 44.5, which is the sum of the percentage of deaths that occurred on Sunday, Monday, and Tuesday. It is calculated as

$$\frac{19}{110} + \frac{11}{110} + \frac{19}{110} = \frac{49}{110} = 44.5\%$$

Equation 3.1

Sometimes it is helpful to look at frequencies for a selected subset of cases. Figure 3.2 is a frequency table of day of death for a subset characterized by sudden cardiac death. This is a particularly interesting category, since it is thought that sudden death may be related to stressful events such as returning to the work environment. In Figure 3.2, deaths do not appear to cluster on any particular day. Twenty-two percent of deaths occurred on Sunday, while 8.3% occurred on Thursday. Since the number of sudden deaths in the table is small, the magnitude of the observed fluctuations is not very large.

Figure 3.2   Frequency of sudden cardiac death by day of week

```
DAYOFWK    DAY OF DEATH

                                                    Valid     Cum
  Value Label            Value   Frequency  Percent Percent   Percent
  SUNDAY                   1         8       22.2    22.2      22.2
  MONDAY                   2         4       11.1    11.1      33.3
  TUESDAY                  3         4       11.1    11.1      44.4
  WEDNESDAY                4         7       19.4    19.4      63.9
  THURSDAY                 5         3        8.3     8.3      72.2
  FRIDAY                   6         6       16.7    16.7      88.9
  SATURDAY                 7         4       11.1    11.1     100.0
                                   -------  -------  -------
                          Total     36      100.0   100.0

Valid cases      36     Missing cases     0
```

Visual Displays

While the numbers in the frequency table can be studied and compared, it is often useful to present results in a form that can be interpreted visually. Figure 3.3 is a pie chart of the data displayed in Figure 3.1. Each slice represents a day of the week. The size of the slice depends on the frequency of death for that day. Monday is represented by 10% of the pie chart, since 10.0% of the deaths for which the day is known occurred on Monday.

Figure 3.3   Pie chart of death by day of week

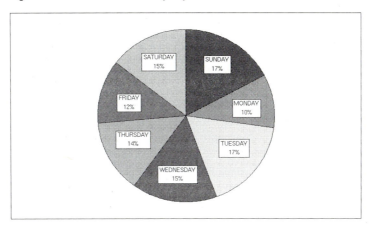

Another way to represent the data is with a bar chart, as shown in Figure 3.4. There is a bar for each day, and the height of the bar is proportional to the number of deaths observed on that day. The number of deaths, or frequency, is displayed at the top of each bar.

Figure 3.4   Bar chart of frequency of death by day of week

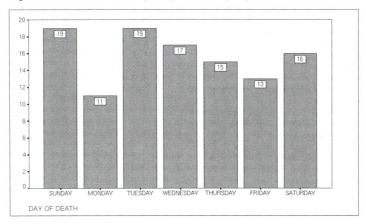

Only values that actually occur in the data are represented in the bar chart. For example, if no deaths occurred on Thursday, no space would be left for Thursday, and the bar for Wednesday would be followed by the bar for Friday. Likewise, if you charted the number of cars per family, the bar describing 6 cars might be next to the one for 25 cars if no family owned 7 to 24 cars. Therefore, you should pay attention to where categories with no cases may occur.

Although the basic information presented by frequency tables, pie charts, and bar charts is the same, the visual displays enliven the data. Differences among the days of the week are apparent at a glance, eliminating the need to pore over columns of numbers.

What Day?

Although the number of sudden cardiac deaths is small in this study, the data in Figure 3.2 indicate that the number of deaths on Mondays is not particularly large. In fact, the most deaths occurred on Sunday—slightly over 22%. A study of over 1000 sudden cardiac deaths in Rochester, Minnesota, also found a slightly increased incidence of death on weekends for men (Beard et al., 1982). The authors speculate that for men, this might mean that "the home environment is more stressful than the work environment." But you should be wary of explanations that are not directly supported by data. It is only too easy to find a clever explanation for any statistical finding.

Histograms

A frequency table or bar chart of all values for a variable is a convenient way of summarizing a variable that has a relatively small number of distinct values. Variables such as sex, country, and astrological sign are necessarily limited in the number of values they can have. For variables that can take on many different values, such as income to the penny or weight in ounces, a tally of the cases with each observed value may not be very informative. In the worst situation, when all cases have different values, a frequency table is little more than an ordered list of those values.

Variables that have many values can be summarized by grouping the values of the variables into intervals and counting the number of cases with values within each interval. For example, income can be grouped into $5,000 intervals such as 0–4999, 5000–9999, 10000–14999, and so forth, and the number of observations in each group can be tabulated. Such grouping should be done using SPSS during the actual analysis of the data. Whenever possible, the values for variables should be entered into the data file in their original, ungrouped form.

A histogram is a convenient way to display the distribution of such grouped values. Consider Figure 3.5, which is a histogram of body weight in pounds for the sample of 240 men from the Western Electric study. The numbers below the bars indicate the midpoint, or middle value, of each interval. Each bar represents the number of cases having values in the interval. Intervals that have no observations are included in the histogram, but no bars are printed. This differs from a bar chart, which does not leave space for the empty categories.

Figure 3.5 Histogram of body weight

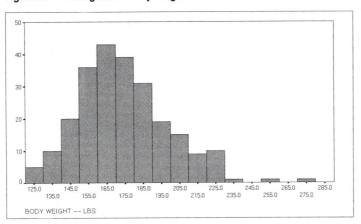

A histogram can be used whenever it is reasonable to group adjacent values. Histograms should not be used to display variables when there is no underlying order to the values. For example, if 100 different religions are arbitrarily assigned codes of 1 to 100, grouping values into intervals is meaningless. Either a bar chart or a histogram in which each interval corresponds to a single value should be used to display such data.

Percentiles

The information in a histogram can be further summarized by computing values above and below which a specified percentage of cases fall. Such values are called **percentiles**. For example, the 50th percentile, or median, is the value above and below which 50% (or half) of the cases fall. The 25th percentile is the value below which 25% and above which 75% of the cases fall.

Figure 3.6 contains values for the 25th, 50th, and 75th percentiles for the weight data shown in the histogram in Figure 3.5. You see that 25% of the men weigh less than 156 pounds, 50% weigh less than 171 pounds, and 75% weigh less than 187 pounds.

Figure 3.6 Percentiles for body weight

```
WT58       BODY WEIGHT -- LBS

Percentile     Value      Percentile     Value      Percentile     Value
  25.00       156.000        50.00      171.000        75.00      187.000

Valid cases       240     Missing cases       0
```

From these three percentiles, sometimes called **quartiles** (since they divide the distribution into four parts containing the same number of cases), you can tell that 50% of the men weigh between 156 and 187 pounds. (Remember that 25% of the men weigh less than 156 and 25% weigh more than 187. That leaves 50% of the men with weights between those two values.)

Screening Data

Frequency tables, bar charts, and histograms can serve purposes other than summarizing data. Unexpected codes in the tables may indicate errors in data entry or coding. Cases with day of death coded as 0 or 8 are in error if the numbers 1 through 7 represent the days of the week and 9 stands for unknown. Since errors in the data should be eliminated as soon as possible, it is a good idea to run frequency tables as the first step in analyzing data.

Frequency tables and visual displays can also help you identify cases with values that are unusual but possibly correct. For example, a tally of the number of cars in families may show a family with 25 cars. Although such a value is possible, especially if the survey did not specify cars in working condition, it raises suspicion and should be examined to ensure that it is really correct.

Incorrect data values distort the results of statistical analyses, and correct but unusual values may require special treatment. In either case, early identification is valuable.

How to Obtain Frequency Tables

The Frequencies procedure produces frequency tables, measures of central tendency and dispersion, histograms, and bar charts. You can sort frequency tables by value or by count, and you can display frequency tables in condensed format.

The minimum specification is one numeric or short string variable.

To get frequency tables, charts, and related statistics, from the menus choose:

Statistics
  Summarize ▶
    Frequencies...

This opens the Frequencies dialog box, as shown in Figure 3.7.

The numeric and short string variables are displayed on the source list. Select one or more variables for analysis. To get a standard frequency table showing counts, percentages, and valid and cumulative percentages, click on OK. The first 40 characters of any variable labels are shown in the output.

Figure 3.7 Frequencies dialog box

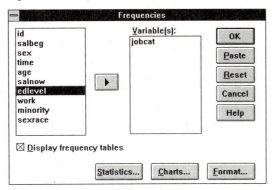

The following option is also available:

❏ **Display frequency tables**. By default, frequency tables are displayed. To suppress tables, deselect this item (for example, if you want to display only selected charts). If you suppress frequency tables without selecting any additional statistics or charts, only counts of cases with valid and missing values are shown.

Frequencies Statistics

To obtain optional descriptive and summary statistics for numeric variables, click on Statistics... in the Frequencies dialog box. This opens the Frequencies Statistics dialog box, as shown in Figure 3.8.

Figure 3.8 Frequencies Statistics dialog box

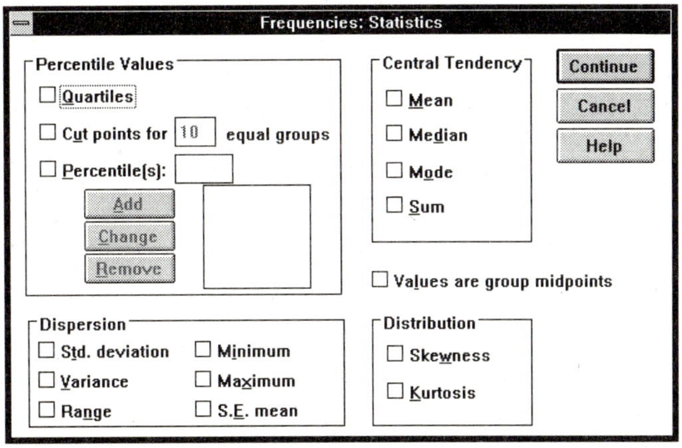

Percentile Values. You can choose one or more of the following:

- **Quartiles.** Displays the 25th, 50th, and 75th percentiles.
- **Cut points for n equal groups.** Displays percentile values that divide the sample into equal-size groups of cases. The default number of groups is 10. Optionally, you can request a different number of groups. Enter a positive integer between 2 and 100. For example, if you enter 4, quartiles are shown. The number of percentiles displayed is one fewer than the number of groups specified; you need only two values to divide a sample into three groups.
- **Percentile(s).** User-specified percentile values. Enter a percentile value between 0 and 100, and click on **Add**. Repeat this process for any other percentile values. Values appear in sorted order on the percentile list. To remove a percentile, highlight it on the list and click on **Remove**. To change a value, highlight it on the list, enter a new value, and click on **Change**.

If a requested percentile cannot be computed, SPSS displays a period (.) as the value associated with that percentile.

Dispersion. You can choose one or more of the following:

- **Std. deviation.** Standard deviation. A measure of how much observations vary from the mean, expressed in the same units as the data.
- **Variance.** A measure of how much observations vary from the mean, equal to the square of the standard deviation.
- **Range.** The difference between the largest (maximum) and smallest (minimum) values.
- **Minimum.** The smallest value.
- **Maximum.** The largest value.
- **S.E. mean.** Standard error of the mean. A measure of variability of the sample mean.

Central Tendency. You can choose one or more of the following:

- **Mean.** The arithmetic average.
- **Median.** The median is defined as the value below which half the cases fall. If there is an even number of cases, the median is the average of the two middle cases when the cases are sorted in ascending order. The median is not available if you request sorting by frequency counts (see "Frequencies Format" on p. 66).
- **Mode.** The most frequently occurring value. If several values are tied for the highest frequency, only the smallest value is displayed.
- **Sum.** The sum of all the values.

Distribution. You can choose one or more of the following:

- **Skewness.** An index of the degree to which a distribution is not symmetric. The standard error of the skewness statistic is also displayed.
- **Kurtosis.** A measure of the extent to which observations cluster around a central point. The standard error of the kurtosis statistic is also displayed.

For grouped or collapsed data, the following option is also available:

- **Values are group midpoints.** If the values represent midpoints of groups (for example, all people in their thirties are coded as 35), you can estimate percentiles for the original, ungrouped data, assuming that cases are uniformly distributed in each interval. Since this affects the values of the median and the percentiles for *all* variables, you should not select this option if any variable on the variable list contains ungrouped data.

Frequencies Charts

To get bar charts or histograms, click on Charts... in the Frequencies dialog box. This opens the Frequencies Charts dialog box, as shown in Figure 3.9.

Figure 3.9   Frequencies Charts dialog box

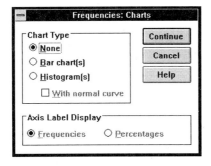

Chart Type. You can choose one of the following alternatives:

○ **None.** No charts. This is the default setting.
○ **Bar chart(s).** The scale is determined by the frequency count of the largest category plotted.
○ **Histogram(s).** Histograms are available for numeric variables only. The number of intervals plotted is 21 (or fewer if the range of values is less than 21).

- **With normal curve.** This option superimposes a normal curve over the histogram(s).

Axis Label Display. For bar charts, you can control labeling of the vertical axis. Choose one of the following alternatives:

- **Frequencies.** The axis is labeled with frequencies. This is the default setting.
- **Percentages.** The axis is labeled with percentages.

Frequencies Format

To modify the format of the frequency table output, select **Display frequency tables** in the Frequencies dialog box and click on **Format...** to open the Frequencies Format dialog box, as shown in Figure 3.10.

Figure 3.10 Frequencies Format dialog box

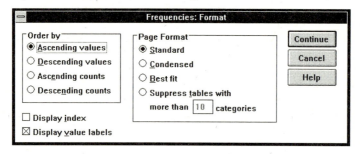

Order by. Order selection determines the order by which data values are sorted and displayed in a frequency table. You can choose one of the following alternatives:

- **Ascending values.** Sorts categories by ascending order of values. This is the default setting.
- **Descending values.** Sorts categories by descending order of values.
- **Ascending counts.** Sorts categories by ascending order of frequency counts.
- **Descending counts.** Sorts categories by descending order of frequency counts.

If you request a histogram or percentiles, categories of the frequency table are sorted by ascending order, regardless of your order selection.

Page Format. You can choose one of the following alternatives:

- **Standard.** Displays as many frequency tables on a page as will fit. This is the default.
- **Condensed.** Condensed format. This format displays frequency counts in three columns. It does not display value labels or percentages that include cases with missing values, and it rounds valid and cumulative percentages to integers.

○ **Best fit.** Conditional condensed format. If a table cannot fit on one page in default format, condensed format is used.

○ **Suppress tables with more than n categories.** Does not display tables for variables with more categories than specified. To override the default value of 10, enter an integer value greater than or equal to 1. This item is particularly useful if your variable list includes continuous variables for which summary statistics or histograms are requested, but for which a frequency table would be long and uninformative. For example, the frequency table that would accompany the histogram of weight in Figure 3.5 would have a separate entry for each one-pound weight increment.

The following additional format choices are also available:

❏ **Display index.** Displays a positional and alphabetic index of frequency tables. This is particularly useful if you have a large number of variables.

❏ **Display value labels.** The first 20 characters of the value labels are shown. This is the default setting. To suppress value labels, deselect this item. Value labels are automatically suppressed when condensed format is chosen.

Additional Features Available with Command Syntax

You can customize your frequencies if you paste your selections into a syntax window and edit the resulting FREQUENCIES command syntax. (For information on syntax windows, see the *SPSS Base System User's Guide, Part 1*.) Additional features include:

- The ability to exclude ranges of data values from analysis (with the VARIABLES subcommand).
- Additional formatting options, such as the ability to begin each frequency table on a new page, double-space tables, or write tables to a file (with the FORMAT subcommand).
- For bar charts, user-specified lower and upper data bounds and maximum scale axis value (with the BARCHART subcommand).
- For histograms, user-specified lower and upper data bounds, maximum horizontal axis value, and interval width (with the HISTOGRAM subcommand).
- Additional options for processing of grouped data (with the GROUPED subcommand).

See the *SPSS Base System Syntax Reference Guide* for complete FREQUENCIES command syntax.

4 Descriptive Statistics

Survey data that rely on voluntary information are subject to many sources of error. People fail to recall events correctly, deliberately distort the truth, or refuse to participate. Refusals influence survey results by failing to provide information about certain types of people—those who refuse to answer surveys at all and those who avoid certain questions. For example, if college graduates tend to be unwilling to answer polls, results of surveys will be biased.

One possible way to examine the veracity of survey responses is to compare them to similar data recorded in official records. Systematic differences between actual data and self-reported responses jeopardize the usefulness of the survey. Unfortunately, in many sensitive areas—illicit drug use, abortion history, or even income—official records are usually unavailable.

Wyner (1980) examined the differences between the actual and self-reported numbers of arrests obtained from 79 former heroin addicts enrolled in the Vera Institute of Justice Supported Employment Experiment. As part of their regular quarterly interviews, participants were asked about their arrest histories in New York City. The self-reported value was compared to arrest-record data coded from New York City Police Department arrest sheets. The goal of the study was not only to quantify the extent of error but also to identify factors related to inaccurate responses.

Examining the Data

Figure 4.1 shows histograms for the following three variables—actual number of arrests, self-reported number of arrests, and the difference of the two. From a histogram, it is possible to see the shape of the distribution; that is, how likely the different values are, how much spread, or **variability**, there is among the values, and where typical values are concentrated. Such characteristics are important because of the direct insight they provide into the data and because many statistical procedures are based on assumptions about the underlying distributions of variables.

Figure 4.1 Self-reported and actual arrests

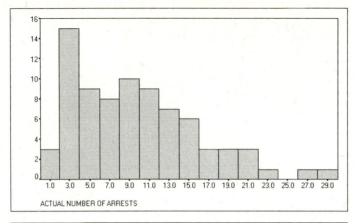
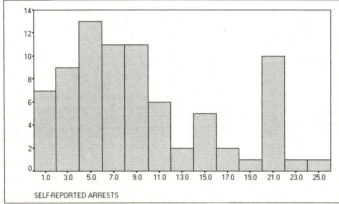
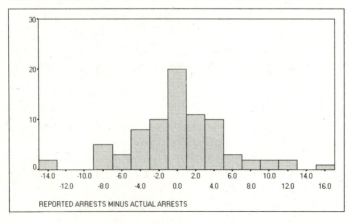

The distributions of the self-reported and actual number of arrests have a somewhat similar shape. Neither distribution has an obvious central value, although the self-reported values peak at 4 to 5 arrests, while the actual number of arrests peaks at 2 to 3 arrests. The distribution of self-reported arrests peaks again at 20 to 21 arrests. The peaks corresponding to intervals containing 5, 15, and 20 arrests arouse suspicion that people may be more likely to report their arrest records as round numbers. Examination of the actual number of arrests shows no corresponding peaks at multiples of five.

The distribution of the differences between reported and actual number of arrests is not as irregularly shaped as the two distributions from which it is derived. It has a peak at the interval with a midpoint of 0. Most cases cluster around the peak values, and cases far from these values are infrequent.

Summarizing the Data

Although frequency tables and bar charts are useful for summarizing and displaying data (see Chapter 3), further condensation and description is often desirable. A variety of summary measures that convey information about the data in single numbers can be computed. The choice of summary measure, or statistic, depends upon characteristics of both the data and the statistic. One important characteristic of the data that must be considered is the level of measurement of each variable being studied.

Levels of Measurement

Measurement is the assignment of numbers or codes to observations. **Levels of measurement** are distinguished by ordering and distance properties. A computer does not know what measurement underlies the values it is given. You must determine the level of measurement of your data and apply appropriate statistical techniques.

The traditional classification of levels of measurement into nominal, ordinal, interval, and ratio scales was developed by S. S. Stevens (1946). This remains the basic typology and is the one used throughout this manual. Variations exist, however, and issues concerning the statistical effect of ignoring levels of measurement have been debated (for example, see Borgatta & Bohrnstedt, 1980).

Nominal Measurement

The **nominal** level of measurement is the "lowest" in the typology because no assumptions are made about relations between values. Each value defines a distinct category and serves merely as a label or name (hence, *nominal* level) for the category. For example, the birthplace of an individual is a nominal variable. For most purposes, there is no inherent ordering among cities or towns. Although cities can be ordered according to size, density, or air pollution, as birthplaces they cannot be ordered or ranked against other cities. When numeric values are attached to nominal categories, they are merely identifiers. None of the properties of numbers, such as relative size, addition, or multiplication, can be applied to these numerically coded categories. Therefore, statistics that assume ordering or meaningful numerical distances between the values do not ordinarily give useful information about nominal variables.

Ordinal Measurement

When it is possible to rank or order all categories according to some criterion, the **ordinal** level of measurement is achieved. For example, classifying employees into clerical, supervisory, and managerial categories is an ordering according to responsibilities or skills. Each category has a position lower or higher than another category. Furthermore, knowing that supervisory is higher than clerical and that managerial is higher than supervisory automatically means that managerial is higher than clerical. However, nothing is known about how much higher; no distance is measured. Ordering is the sole mathematical property applicable to ordinal measurements, and the use of numeric values does not imply that any other property of numbers is applicable.

Interval Measurement

In addition to order, **interval** measurements have the property of meaningful distance between values. A thermometer, for example, measures temperature in degrees that are the same size at any point on the scale. The difference between 20°C and 21°C is the same as the difference between 5°C and 6°C. However, an interval scale does not have an inherently determined zero point. In the familiar Celsius and Fahrenheit systems, 0° is determined by an agreed-upon definition, not by the absence of heat. Consequently, interval-level measurement allows us to study differences between items but not their proportionate magnitudes. For example, it is incorrect to say that 80°F is twice as hot as 40°F.

Ratio Measurement

Ratio measurements have all the ordering and distance properties of an interval scale. In addition, a zero point can be meaningfully designated. In measuring physical distances between objects using feet or meters, a zero distance is naturally defined as the absence of any distance. The existence of a zero point means that ratio comparisons can be made. For example, it is quite meaningful to say that a 6-foot-tall adult is twice as tall as a 3-foot-tall child or that a 500-meter race is five times as long as a 100-meter race.

Because ratio measurements satisfy all the properties of the real number system, any mathematical manipulations appropriate for real numbers can be applied to ratio measures. However, the existence of a zero point is seldom critical for statistical analyses.

Summary Statistics

Figure 4.2 and Figure 4.3 contain a variety of summary statistics that are useful in describing the distributions of self-reported and actual numbers of arrests and their difference. The statistics can be grouped into three categories according to what they quantify: central tendency, dispersion, and shape.

Figure 4.2 was obtained with the Descriptives procedure; Figure 4.3, with the Frequencies procedure. If your computer has a math coprocessor, the Descriptives procedure is faster than the Frequencies procedure. However, the median and mode are not available with Descriptives.

Figure 4.2 Summary statistics from the Descriptives procedure

```
Variable   ACTUAL      ACTUAL NUMBER OF ARRESTS

Mean                  9.253            S.E. Mean         .703
Std Dev               6.248            Variance        39.038
Kurtosis               .597            S.E. Kurt         .535
Skewness               .908            S.E. Skew         .271
Range                28.000            Minimum              1
Maximum                  29            Sum            731.000

Valid observations -       79       Missing observations -        0
- - - - - - - - - - - - - - - - - - - - - - - - - - - - - - - - - -
Variable   SELF        SELF-REPORTED ARRESTS

Mean                  8.962            S.E. Mean         .727
Std Dev               6.458            Variance        41.704
Kurtosis              -.485            S.E. Kurt         .535
Skewness               .750            S.E. Skew         .271
Range                25.000            Minimum              0
Maximum                  25            Sum            708.000

Valid observations -       79       Missing observations -        0
- - - - - - - - - - - - - - - - - - - - - - - - - - - - - - - - - -
Variable   ERRORS      REPORTED ARRESTS MINUS ACTUAL ARRESTS

Mean                  -.291            S.E. Mean         .587
Std Dev               5.216            Variance        27.209
Kurtosis              1.102            S.E. Kurt         .535
Skewness               .125            S.E. Skew         .271
Range                29.000            Minimum        -14.000
Maximum                  15            Sum            -23.000

Valid observations -       79       Missing observations -        0
```

Figure 4.3 Summary statistics from the Frequencies procedure

```
ACTUAL     ACTUAL NUMBER OF ARRESTS

Mean           9.253    Std err        .703    Median        8.000
Mode           3.000    Std dev       6.248    Variance     39.038
Kurtosis        .597    S E Kurt       .535    Skewness       .908
S E Skew        .271    Range        28.000    Minimum       1.000
Maximum       29.000    Sum         731.000

Valid cases       79    Missing cases     0
- - - - - - - - - - - - - - - - - - - - - - - - - - - - - - - - - -
SELF       SELF-REPORTED ARRESTS

Mean           8.962    Std err        .727    Median        7.000
Mode           5.000    Std dev       6.458    Variance     41.704
Kurtosis       -.485    S E Kurt       .535    Skewness       .750
S E Skew        .271    Range        25.000    Minimum        .000
Maximum       25.000    Sum         708.000

Valid cases       79    Missing cases     0
- - - - - - - - - - - - - - - - - - - - - - - - - - - - - - - - - -
ERRORS     REPORTED ARRESTS MINUS ACTUAL ARRESTS

Mean           -.291    Std err        .587    Median         .000
Mode          -1.000    Std dev       5.216    Variance     27.209
Kurtosis       1.102    S E Kurt       .535    Skewness       .125
S E Skew        .271    Range        29.000    Minimum     -14.000
Maximum       15.000    Sum         -23.000

* Multiple modes exist.  The smallest value is shown.

Valid cases       79    Missing cases     0
```

Measures of Central Tendency

The mean, median, and mode are frequently used to describe the location of a distribution. The **mode** is the most frequently occurring value (or values). For the actual number of arrests, the mode is 3; for the self-reported values, it is 5. The distribution of the difference between the actual and self-reported values is multimodal. That is, it has more than one mode because the values −1 and 0 occur with equal frequency. SPSS, however, displays only one of the modes, the smaller value, as shown in Figure 4.3. The mode can be used for data measured at any level. It is not usually the preferred measure for interval and ordinal data, since it ignores much of the available information.

The **median** is the value above and below which one-half of the observations fall. For example, if there are 79 observations, the median is the 40th-largest observation. When there is an even number of observations, no unique center value exists, so the mean of the two middle observations is usually taken as the median value. For the arrest data, the median is 0 for the differences, 8 for the actual arrests, and 7 for the self-reported arrests. For ordinal data, the median is usually a good measure of central tendency, since it uses the ranking information. The median should not be used for nominal data, since ranking of the observations is not possible.

The **mean**, also called the arithmetic average, is the sum of the values of all observations divided by the number of observations. Thus,

$$\bar{X} = \sum_{i=1}^{N} \frac{X_i}{N}$$

Equation 4.1

where N is the number of cases and X_i is the value of the variable for the ith case. Since the mean utilizes the distance between observations, the measurements should be interval or ratio. Calculating the mean race, religion, and auto color provides no useful information. For dichotomous variables coded as 0 and 1, the mean has a special interpretation: it is the proportion of cases coded 1 in the data.

The three measures of central tendency need not be the same. For example, the mean number of actual arrests is 9.25, the median is 8, and the mode is 3. The arithmetic mean is greatly influenced by outlying observations, while the median is not. Adding a single case with 400 arrests would increase the mean from 9.25 to 14.1, but it would not affect the median. Therefore, if there are values far removed from the rest of the observations, the median may be a better measure of central tendency than the mean.

For symmetric distributions, the observed mean, median, and mode are usually close in value. For example, the mean of the differences between self-reported and actual arrest values is –0.291, the median is 0, and the modes are –1 and 0. All three measures give similar estimates of central tendency in this case.

Measures of Dispersion

Two distributions can have the same values for measures of central tendency and yet be very dissimilar in other respects. For example, if the actual number of arrests for five cases in two methadone clinics is 0, 1, 10, 14, and 20 for clinic A, and 8, 8, 9, 10, and 10 for clinic B, the mean number of arrests (9) is the same in both. However, even a cursory examination of the data indicates that the two clinics are different. In clinic B, all cases have fairly comparable arrest records, while in clinic A the records are quite disparate. A quick and useful index of dissimilarity, or dispersion, is the **range**. It is the difference between the maximum and minimum observed values. For clinic B, the range is 2, while for clinic A it is 20. Since the range is computed from only the minimum and maximum values, it is sensitive to extremes.

Although the range is a useful index of dispersion, especially for ordinal data, it does not take into account the distribution of observations between the maximum and minimum. A commonly used measure of variation that is based on all observations is the **variance**. For a sample, the variance is computed by summing the squared differences from the mean for all observations and then dividing by one less than the number of observations. In mathematical notation, this is

$$s^2 = \sum_{i=1}^{N} \frac{(X_i - \bar{X})^2}{N-1}$$

Equation 4.2

If all observations are identical—that is, if there is no variation—the variance is 0. The more spread out they are, the greater the variance. For the methadone clinic example above, the sample variance for clinic A is 73, while for clinic B it's 1.

The square root of the variance is termed the **standard deviation**. While the variance is expressed in squared units, the standard deviation is expressed in the same units of measurement as the observations. This is an appealing property, since it is much clearer to think of variability in terms of the number of arrests rather than the number of arrests squared.

The Normal Distribution

For many variables, most observations are concentrated near the middle of the distribution. As distance from the central concentration increases, the frequency of observation decreases. Such distributions are often described as "bell-shaped." An example is the **normal distribution** (see Figure 4.4). A broad range of observed phenomena in nature and in society is approximately normally distributed. For example, the distributions of variables such as height, weight, and blood pressure are approximately normal. The normal distribution is by far the most important theoretical distribution in statistics and serves as a reference point for describing the form of many distributions of sample data.

The normal distribution is symmetric: each half is a mirror image of the other. Three measures of central tendency—the mean, median, and mode—coincide exactly. As shown in Figure 4.4, 95% of all observations fall within two standard deviations (σ) of the mean (μ), and 68% fall within one standard deviation. The exact theoretical proportion of cases falling into various regions of the normal curve can be found in tables included in most introductory statistics textbooks.

Figure 4.4   Normal curve

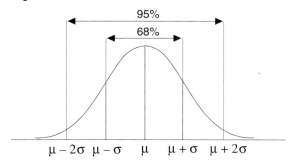

In SPSS, you can superimpose a normal distribution on a histogram. Consider Figure 4.5, a histogram of the differences in self-reported and actual arrests. The curved line indicates what the distribution of cases would be if the variable had a normal distribution with the same mean and variance. Tests for normality are available in the Explore procedure (see Chapter 5).

Figure 4.5   Histogram with normal curve superimposed

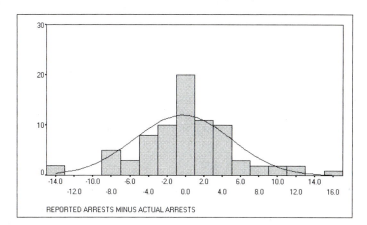

Measures of Shape

A distribution that is not symmetric but has more cases (more of a "tail") toward one end of the distribution than the other is said to be **skewed**. If the tail is toward larger values, the distribution is positively skewed, or skewed to the right. If the tail is toward smaller values, the distribution is negatively skewed, or skewed to the left.

Another characteristic of the form of a distribution is called **kurtosis**—the extent to which, for a given standard deviation, observations cluster around a central point. If cases within a distribution cluster more than those in the normal distribution (that is, the distribution is more peaked), the distribution is called **leptokurtic**. A leptokurtic distribution also tends to have more observations straggling into the extreme tails than does a normal distribution. If cases cluster less than in the normal distribution (that is, it is flatter), the distribution is termed **platykurtic**.

Although examination of a histogram provides some indication of possible skewness and kurtosis, it is often desirable to compute formal indexes that measure these properties. Values for skewness and kurtosis are 0 if the observed distribution is exactly normal. Positive values for skewness indicate a positive skew, while positive values for kurtosis indicate a distribution that is more peaked than normal. For samples from a normal distribution, measures of skewness and kurtosis typically will not be exactly 0 but will fluctuate around 0 because of sampling variation.

Standard Scores

It is often desirable to describe the relative position of an observation within a distribution. Knowing that a person achieved a score of 80 in a competitive examination conveys little information about performance. Judgment of performance would depend on whether 80 is the lowest, the median, or the highest score.

One way of describing the location of a case in a distribution is to calculate its **standard score**. This score, sometimes called the **Z score**, indicates how many standard deviations above or below the mean an observation falls. It is calculated by finding the difference between the value of a particular observation X_i and the mean of the distribution, and dividing this difference by the standard deviation:

$$Z_i = \frac{X_i - \bar{X}}{S} \qquad \text{Equation 4.3}$$

The mean of Z scores is 0 and the standard deviation is 1. For example, a participant with five actual arrests would have a Z score of $(5 - 9.25)/6.25$, or -0.68. Since the score is negative, the case had fewer arrests than the average for the individuals studied. Figure 4.6 shows summary statistics for Z scores based on the difference between actual and self-reported arrests.

Figure 4.6 Summary statistics for Z scores

```
Variable   ZERRORS    Zscore:  REPORTED ARRESTS MINUS ACTUAL

Mean                   .000         S.E. Mean        .113
Std Dev               1.000         Variance        1.000
Kurtosis              1.102         S.E. Kurt        .535
Skewness               .125         S.E. Skew        .271
Range                 5.560         Minimum      -2.62812
Maximum            2.93146          Sum              .000
```

Standardization permits comparison of scores from different distributions. For example, an individual with Z scores of −0.68 for actual arrests and 1.01 for the difference between self-reported and actual arrests had fewer arrests than the average but exaggerated more than the average.

When the distribution of a variable is approximately normal and the mean and variance are known or are estimated from large samples, the Z score of an observation provides more specific information about its location. For example, if actual arrests and response error were normally distributed, 75% of cases would have more arrests than the example individual, but only 16% would have exaggerated as much as the example individual (75% of a standard normal curve lies above a Z score of −0.68, and 16% lies above a score of 1.01).

Who Lies?

The distribution of the difference between self-reported and actual arrests indicates that response error exists. Although observing a mean close to 0 is comforting, misrepresentation is obvious. What, then, are the characteristics that influence willingness to be truthful?

Wyner identifies three factors that are related to inaccuracies: the number of arrests before 1960, the number of multiple-charge arrests, and the perceived desirability of being arrested. The first factor is related to a frequently encountered difficulty—the more distant an event in time, the less likely it is to be correctly recalled. The second factor, underreporting of multiple-charge arrests, is probably caused by the general social undesirability of serious arrests. Finally, persons who view arrest records as laudatory are likely to inflate their accomplishments.

How to Obtain Descriptive Statistics

The Descriptives procedure computes univariate summary statistics and saves standardized variables. Although it computes statistics also available in the Frequencies procedure, Descriptives computes descriptive statistics for continuous variables more efficiently because it does not sort values into a frequencies table.

The minimum specification is one or more numeric variables.

To obtain descriptive statistics and Z scores, from the menus choose:

Statistics
  Summarize ▶
    Descriptives...

This opens the Descriptives dialog box, as shown in Figure 4.7.

Figure 4.7 Descriptives dialog box

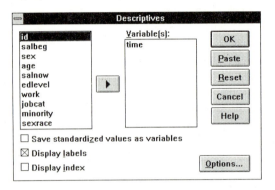

The numeric variables in your data file appear on the source list. Select one or more variables for which you want descriptive statistics. To obtain the default statistics (mean, standard deviation, minimum, and maximum) and display variable labels, click on **OK**.

You can also choose one or more of the following:

❑ **Save standardized values as variables.** Creates one Z-score variable for each variable. New variable names are created by prefixing the letter *z* to the first seven characters of original variable names. For example, *zsalnow* is the Z-score variable for *salnow*. If this naming convention would produce duplicate names, an alternate naming convention is used: first *zsc001* through *zsc099*, then *stdz01* through *stdz09*, then *zzzz01* through *zzzz09*, and then *zqzq01* through *zqzq09*.

Variable labels for Z-score variables are generated by prefixing *zscore* to the first 31 characters of the original variable label. If SPSS assigns a variable name that does not contain part of the original variable name, it prefixes *zscore(original variable name)* to the first 31 characters of the original variable's label. If the original variable has no label, it uses *zscore(original variable name)* for the label.

SPSS displays a table in the output showing the original variable name, the new variable name and its label, and the number of cases for which the Z score is computed.

❑ **Display labels.** Displays 40-character variable labels in the output. If requested statistics do not fit in the available page width, labels are truncated to 21 characters and then, if necessary, a serial output format is used. Labels are displayed by default.

❏ **Display index.** Displays a positional and alphabetical reference index showing the page location in the statistics output for each variable. The variables are listed by their position in the data file and alphabetically.

Descriptives Options

To obtain additional descriptive statistics or control the order in which variables appear in the output, click on Options... in the Descriptives dialog box. This opens the Descriptives Options dialog box, as shown in Figure 4.8.

Figure 4.8 Descriptives Options dialog box

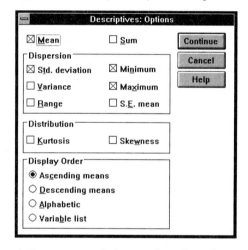

At least one statistic must be selected.

You can choose one or both of the following statistics:

❏ **Mean.** The arithmetic average. Displayed by default.

❏ **Sum.** The sum of all the values.

Dispersion. You can choose one or more of the following dispersion statistics:

❏ **Std. deviation.** Standard deviation. Displayed by default. A measure of how much observations vary from the mean, expressed in the same units as the data.

❏ **Variance.** A measure of how much observations vary from the mean, equal to the square of the standard deviation.

❏ **Range.** The difference between the largest (maximum) and smallest (minimum) values.

❏ **Minimum.** The smallest value. Displayed by default.

- **Maximum.** The largest value. Displayed by default.
- **S. E. mean.** Standard error of the mean. A measure of variability of the sample mean.

Distribution. You can choose one or both of the following distribution statistics:
- **Kurtosis.** A measure of the extent to which observations cluster around a central point, given their standard deviation. The standard error of the kurtosis statistic is also displayed.
- **Skewness.** An index of the degree to which a distribution is not symmetric. The standard error of the skewness statistic is also displayed.

Display Order. You can choose one of the following display options:
- **Ascending means.** Displays variables in order of ascending means. This is the default setting.
- **Descending means.** Displays variables in order of descending means.
- **Alphabetic.** Sorts the variables alphabetically by name.
- **Variable list.** Displays variables in the order they appear in the selected variables list.

Additional Features Available with Command Syntax

You can customize your descriptive statistics if you paste your selections into a syntax window and edit the resulting DESCRIPTIVES command syntax. (For information on syntax windows, see the *SPSS Base System User's Guide, Part 1*.) Additional features include:

- Z scores for a subset of variables (with the VARIABLES subcommand).
- User-specified names for Z-score variables (with the VARIABLES subcommand).
- Exclusion from the analysis of cases with missing values for any variable (with the MISSING subcommand).
- Additional display order options such as sorting by variance (with the SORT subcommand).

See the *SPSS Base System Syntax Reference Guide* for complete DESCRIPTIVES command syntax.

5 Exploring Data

The first step of data analysis should always be a detailed examination of the data. Whether the problem you're solving is simple or complex, or whether you're planning to do a *t* test or a multivariate repeated measures analysis of variance, you should first take a careful look at the data. In this chapter, we'll consider a variety of descriptive statistics and displays useful as a preliminary step in data analysis. Using the SPSS Explore procedure, you can screen your data, visually examine the distributions of values for various groups, and test for normality and homogeneity of variance.

Reasons for Exploring Data

There are several important reasons for examining your data carefully before you begin your analysis. Let's start with the simplest.

Identifying Mistakes

Data must make a hazardous journey before finding final rest in a computer file. First, a measurement is made or a response elicited, sometimes with a faulty instrument or by a careless experimenter. The result is then recorded, often barely legibly, in a lab notebook, medical chart, or personnel record. Often this information is not actually coded and entered onto a data form until much later. From this form, the numbers must find their way into their designated slot in the computer file. Then they must be properly introduced to a computer program. Their correct location and missing values must be specified.

Errors can be introduced at any step. Some errors are easy to spot. For example, forgetting to declare a value as missing, using an invalid code, or entering the value 701 for age will be apparent from a frequency table. Other errors, such as entering an age of 54 instead of 45, may be difficult, if not impossible, to spot. Unless your first step is to carefully check your data for mistakes, errors may contaminate all of your analyses.

Exploring the Data

After completing data acquisition, entry, and checking, it's time to look at the data—not to search haphazardly for statistical significance, but to examine the data systematically using simple exploratory techniques. Why bother, you might ask? Why not just begin your analysis?

Data analysis has often been compared to detective work. Before the actual trial of a hypothesis, there is much evidence to be gathered and sifted. Based on the clues, the hypothesis itself may be altered, or the methods for testing it may have to be changed. For example, if the distribution of data values reveals a gap—that is, a range where no values occur—we must ask why. If some values are extreme (far removed from the other values), we must look for reasons. If the pattern of numbers is strange (for example, if all values are even), we must determine why. If we see unexpected variability in the data, we must look for possible explanations; perhaps there are additional variables that may explain it.

Preparing for Hypothesis Testing

Looking at the distribution of the values is also important for evaluating the appropriateness of the statistical techniques we are planning to use for hypothesis testing or model building. Perhaps the data must be transformed so that the distribution is approximately normal or so that the variances in the groups are similar; or perhaps a nonparametric technique is needed.

Ways of Displaying Data

Now that we've established why it's important to look at data, we'll consider some of the techniques available for exploring data. One technique is to create a graphical representation of the data. To illustrate, we'll use data from a study of coronary heart disease among male employees of Western Electric and salary data from a study of employees of a bank engaged in Equal Employment Opportunity litigation.

The Histogram

The **histogram** is commonly used to represent data graphically. The range of observed values is subdivided into equal intervals, and the number of cases in each interval is obtained. Each bar in a histogram represents the number of cases with values within the interval.

Figure 5.1 is a histogram of diastolic blood pressure for a sample of 239 men from the Western Electric study. The values on the vertical axis indicate the number of cases. The values on the horizontal axis are midpoints of value ranges. For example, the midpoint of the first bar is 65, and the midpoint of the second bar is 75, indicating that each bar covers a value range of 10. Thus, the first bar contains cases with diastolic blood pressures in the 60's. Cases with diastolic blood pressures in the 70's go into the next bar, and so on.

Figure 5.1   Histogram of diastolic blood pressure

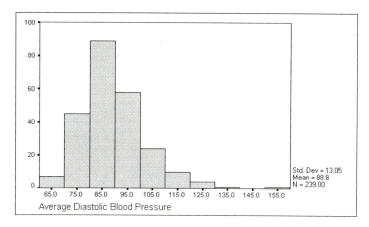

The Stem-and-Leaf Plot

A display closely related to the histogram is the stem-and-leaf plot. A **stem-and-leaf plot** provides more information about the actual values than does a histogram. Consider Figure 5.2, which is a stem-and-leaf plot of the diastolic blood pressures. As in a histogram, the length of each row corresponds to the number of cases that fall into a particular interval. However, a stem-and-leaf plot represents each case with a numeric value that corresponds to the actual observed value. This is done by dividing observed values into two components—the leading digit or digits, called the **stem**, and the trailing digit, called the **leaf**. For example, the value 75 has a stem of 7 and a leaf of 5.

Figure 5.2   Stem-and-leaf plot of diastolic blood pressure

```
Frequency     Stem &  Leaf

     .00       6  *
    7.00       6  .   5558889
   13.00       7  *   0000111223344
   32.00       7  .   55555555667777777777788888889999
   44.00       8  *   00000000000000000000011111222223333333334444
   45.00       8  .   555555555566666667777777777777788888999999999
   31.00       9  *   0000000001111111122222222333334
   27.00       9  .   556666667777777888888888899999
   13.00      10  *   0000122233333
   11.00      10  .   55555577899
    5.00      11  *   00003
    5.00      11  .   55789
    2.00      12  *   01
    4.00   Extremes      (125), (133), (160)

Stem width:      10
Each leaf:        1 case(s)
```

In this example, each stem is divided into two rows. The first row of each pair has cases with leaves of 0 through 4, while the second row has cases with leaves of 5 through 9. Consider the two rows that correspond to the stem of 11. In the first row, we can see that there are four cases with diastolic blood pressure of 110 and one case with a reading of 113. In the second row, there are two cases with a value of 115 and one case each with a value of 117, 118, and 119.

The last row of the stem-and-leaf plot is for cases with extreme values (values far removed from the rest). In this row, the actual values are displayed in parentheses. In the frequency column, we see that there are four extreme cases. Their values are 125, 133, and 160. Only distinct values are listed.

To identify cases with extreme values, you can generate a table identifying cases with the largest and smallest values. Figure 5.3 shows the five cases with the largest and smallest values for diastolic blood pressure. Values of a case-labeling variable can be used to identify cases. Otherwise, the sequence of the case in the data file is reported.

Figure 5.3   Cases with extreme values

```
                        Extreme Values
                        ------- ------

5    Highest    Case #              5    Lowest     Case #

     160        Case: 120                65        Case: 73
     133        Case: 56                 65        Case: 156
     125        Case: 163                65        Case: 157
     125        Case: 42                 68        Case: 153
     121        Case: 26                 68        Case: 175
```

Other Stems

In Figure 5.2, each stem was divided into two parts—one for leaves of 0 through 4, and the other for leaves of 5 through 9. When there are few stems, it is sometimes useful to subdivide each stem even further. Consider Figure 5.4, a stem-and-leaf plot of cholesterol levels for the men in the Western Electric study. In this figure, stems 2 and 3 are divided into five parts, each representing two leaf values. The first row, designated by an asterisk, is for leaves of 0 and 1; the next, designated by t, is for leaves of 2's and 3's; the third, designated by f, is for leaves of 4's and 5's; the fourth, designated by s, is for leaves of 6's and 7's; and the fifth, designated by a period, is for leaves of 8's and 9's. Rows without cases are not represented in the plot. For example, in Figure 5.4, the first two rows for stem 1 (corresponding to 0–1 and 2–3) are omitted.

This stem-and-leaf plot differs from the previous one in another way. Since cholesterol values have a wide range—from 106 to 515 in this example—using the first two digits for the stem would result in an unnecessarily detailed plot. Therefore, we will use only the hundreds digit as the stem, rather than the first two digits. The stem setting of 100 appears in the column labeled *Stem width*. The leaf is then the tens digit. The last digit is ignored. Thus, from this stem-and-leaf plot, it is not possible to determine the exact cholesterol level for a case. Instead, each case is classified by only its first two digits.

Figure 5.4 Stem-and-leaf plot of cholesterol levels

```
Frequency     Stem & Leaf

     1.00  Extremes    (106)
     2.00       1 f    55
     6.00       1 s    677777
    12.00       1 .    888889999999
    23.00       2 *    00000000000001111111111
    36.00       2 t    222222222222222223333333333333333333
    35.00       2 f    44444444444444444455555555555555555
    42.00       2 s    666666666666666666667777777777777777777777
    28.00       2 .    8888888888888889999999999999
    18.00       3 *    000000011111111111
    17.00       3 t    22222222222233333
     9.00       3 f    444445555
     6.00       3 s    666777
     1.00       3 .    8
     3.00  Extremes    (393), (425), (515)

Stem width:    100
Each leaf:     1 case(s)
```

The Boxplot

Both the histogram and the stem-and-leaf plot provide useful information about the distribution of observed values. We can see how tightly cases cluster together. We can see if there is a single peak or several peaks. We can determine if there are extreme values.

A display that further summarizes information about the distribution of the values is the boxplot. Instead of plotting the actual values, a **boxplot** displays summary statistics for the distribution. It plots the median, the 25th percentile, the 75th percentile, and values that are far removed from the rest.

Figure 5.5 shows an annotated sketch of a boxplot. The lower boundary of the box is the 25th percentile and the upper boundary is the 75th percentile. (These percentiles, sometimes called Tukey's hinges, are calculated a little differently from ordinary percentiles.) The horizontal line inside the box represents the median. Fifty percent of the cases have values within the box. The length of the box corresponds to the interquartile range, which is the difference between the 75th and 25th percentiles.

The boxplot includes two categories of cases with outlying values. Cases with values that are more than 3 box-lengths from the upper or lower edge of the box are called **extreme values**. On the boxplot, these are designated with an asterisk (*). Cases with values that are between 1.5 and 3 box-lengths from the upper or lower edge of the box are called **outliers** and are designated with a circle. The largest and smallest observed values that aren't outliers are also shown. Lines are drawn from the ends of the box to these values. (These lines are sometimes called **whiskers** and the plot is called a **box-and-whiskers plot**.)

Figure 5.5 Annotated sketch of a boxplot

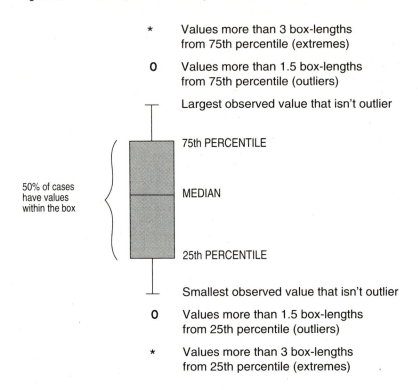

What can you tell about your data from a boxplot? From the median, you can determine the central tendency, or location. From the length of the box, you can determine the spread, or variability, of your observations. If the median is not in the center of the box, you know that the observed values are skewed. If the median is closer to the bottom of the box than to the top, the data are positively skewed. If the median is closer to the top of the box than to the bottom, the opposite is true: the distribution is negatively skewed. The length of the tail is shown by the whiskers and the outlying and extreme points.

Boxplots are particularly useful for comparing the distribution of values in several groups. For example, suppose you want to compare the distribution of beginning salaries for people employed in several different positions at a bank. Figure 5.6 contains boxplots of the bank salary data. From these plots, you can see that the first two job categories have similar distributions for salary, although the first category has several extreme values. The third job category has little variability; all 27 people in this category earn similar amounts of money. The last two groups have much higher median salaries than the other groups, and a larger spread as well.

Figure 5.6 Boxplots for bank salary data

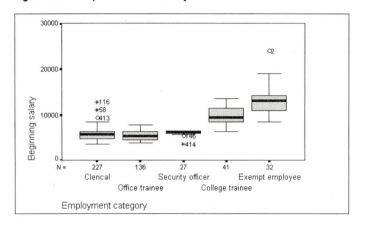

Evaluating Assumptions

Many statistical procedures, such as analysis of variance, require that all groups come from normal populations with the same variance. Therefore, before choosing a statistical hypothesis, we need to test the hypothesis that all the group variances are equal or that the samples come from normal populations. If it appears that the assumptions are violated, we may want to determine appropriate transformations.

The Levene Test

Numerous tests are available for evaluating the assumption that all groups come from populations with equal variances. Many of these tests, however, are heavily dependent on the data being from normal populations. Analysis-of-variance procedures, on the other hand, are reasonably robust to departures from normality. The **Levene test** is a homogeneity-of-variance test that is less dependent on the assumption of normality than most tests and thus is particularly useful with analysis of variance. It is obtained by computing, for each case, the absolute difference from its cell mean and performing a one-way analysis of variance on these differences.

From Figure 5.7, you can see that for the salary data, the null hypothesis that all group variances are equal is rejected. We should consider transforming the data if we plan to use a statistical procedure that requires equality of variance. Next we'll consider how to select a transformation.

Figure 5.7 The Levene test

```
Test of homogeneity of variance              df1       df2    Significance
Levene Statistic             28.9200           4       458          .0000
```

Spread-versus-Level Plots

Often there is a relationship between the average value, or level, of a variable and the variability, or spread, associated with it. For example, we can see in Figure 5.6 that as salaries increase, so does the variability.

One way of studying the relationship between spread and level is to plot the values of spread and level for each group. If there is no relationship, the points should cluster around a horizontal line. If this is not the case, we can use the observed relationship between the two variables to choose an appropriate transformation.

Determining the Transformation

A power transformation is frequently used to stabilize variances. A power transformation raises each data value to a specified power. For example, a power transformation of 2 squares all of the data values. A transformation of 1/2 calculates the square root of all the values. If the power is 0, the log of the numbers is used.

To determine an appropriate power for transforming the data, we can plot, for each group, the log of the median against the log of the interquartile range. Figure 5.8 shows such a plot for the salary data shown in Figure 5.6.

Figure 5.8 Spread-versus-level plot of bank data

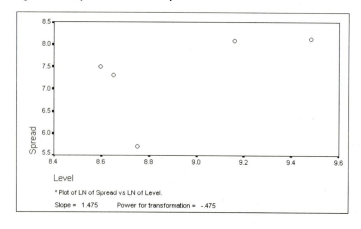

You see that there is a fairly strong linear relationship between spread and level. From the slope of the line, we can estimate the power value that will eliminate or lessen this relationship. The power is obtained by subtracting the slope from 1. That is,

Power = 1 − slope **Equation 5.1**

Although this formula can result in all sorts of powers, for simplicity and clarity we usually choose the closest powers that are multiples of 1/2. Table 5.1 shows the most commonly used transformations.

Table 5.1 Commonly used transformations

Power	Transformation
3	Cube
2	Square
1	No change
1/2	Square root
0	Logarithm
−1/2	Reciprocal of the square root
−1	Reciprocal

As shown in Figure 5.8, the slope of the least-squares line for the bank data is 1.475, so the power for the transformation is −0.475. Rounding to the nearest multiple of a half, we will use the reciprocal of the square root.

After applying the power transformation, it is wise to obtain a spread-versus-level plot for the transformed data. From this plot, you can judge the success of the transformation.

Tests of Normality

Since the normal distribution is very important to statistical inference, we often want to examine the assumption that our data come from a normal distribution. One way to do this is with a normal probability plot. In a **normal probability plot**, each observed value is paired with its expected value from the normal distribution. (The expected value from the normal distribution is based on the number of cases in the sample and the rank order of the case in the sample.) If the sample is from a normal distribution, we expect that the points will fall more or less on a straight line.

The first plot in Figure 5.9 is a normal probability plot of a sample of 200 points from a normal distribution. Note how the points cluster around a straight line. You can also plot the actual deviations of the points from a straight line. This is called a **detrended normal plot** and is shown in the second plot in Figure 5.9. If the sample is from a normal population, the points should cluster around a horizontal line through 0, and there should be no pattern. A striking pattern suggests departure from normality.

Figure 5.9   Normal plots for a normal distribution

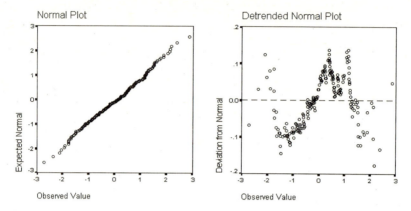

Figure 5.10 shows a normal probability plot and a detrended plot for data from a uniform distribution. The points do not cluster around a straight line, and the deviations from a straight line are not randomly distributed around 0.

Figure 5.10   Normal plots for a uniform distribution

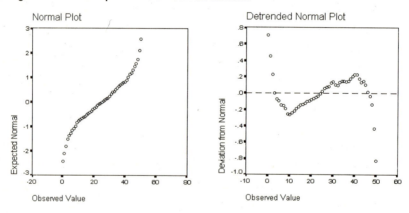

Although normal probability plots provide a visual basis for checking normality, it is often desirable to compute a statistical test of the hypothesis that the data are from a normal distribution. Two commonly used tests are the Shapiro-Wilks' test and the Lilliefors test. The **Lilliefors test**, based on a modification of the Kolmogorov-Smirnov test, is used when means and variances are not known but must be estimated from the data. The **Shapiro-Wilks' test** shows good power in many situations compared to other tests of normality (Conover, 1980).

Figure 5.11 contains normal probability plots and Figure 5.12 contains the Lilliefors test of normality for the diastolic blood pressure data. From the small observed significance levels, you see that the hypothesis of normality can be rejected. However, it is important to remember that whenever the sample size is large, almost any goodness-of-fit test will result in rejection of the null hypothesis. It is almost impossible to find data that are *exactly* normally distributed. For most statistical tests, it is sufficient that the data are approximately normally distributed. Thus, for large data sets, you should look not only at the observed significance level but also at the actual departure from normality.

Figure 5.11 Normal plots for diastolic blood pressure

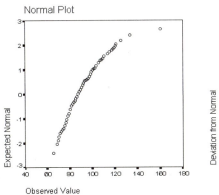
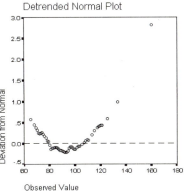

Figure 5.12 Normality test

```
                    Statistic        df       Significance
K-S (Lilliefors)      .0974          239         .0000
```

Estimating Location with Robust Estimators

We often use the arithmetic mean to estimate central tendency, or location. We know, however, that the mean is heavily influenced by outliers. One very large or very small value can change the mean dramatically. The median, on the other hand, is insensitive to outliers; addition or removal of extreme values has little effect on it. The median is called a **resistant measure**, since its value depends on the main body of the data and not on outliers. The advantages of resistant measures are obvious: their values are not unduly influenced by a few observations, and they don't change much if small amounts of data are added or removed.

Although the median is an intuitive, simple measure of location, there are better estimators of location if we are willing to make some assumptions about the population from which our data originate. Estimators that depend on simple, fairly nonrestrictive assumptions about the underlying distribution and are not sensitive to these assumptions are called **robust estimators**. In the following sections, we will consider some robust estimators of central tendency that depend only on the assumption that the data are from a symmetric population.

The Trimmed Mean

A simple robust estimator of location can be obtained by "trimming" the data to exclude values that are far removed from the others. For example, a 20% trimmed mean disregards the smallest 20% and the largest 20% of all observations. The estimate is based on only the 60% of data values that are in the middle. What is the advantage of a trimmed mean? Like the median, it results in an estimate that is not influenced by extreme values. However, unlike the median, it is not based solely on a single value, or two values, that are in the middle. It is based on a much larger number of middle values. (The median can be considered a 50% trimmed mean, since half of the values above and below the median are ignored.) In general, a trimmed mean makes better use of the data than does the median.

M-Estimators

When calculating a trimmed mean, we divide our cases into two groups: those included and those excluded from the computation of the mean. We can consider the trimmed mean as a weighted mean in which cases have weights of 0 or 1, depending on whether they are included or excluded from the computations. A weighted mean is calculated by assigning a weight to each case and then using the formula $\overline{X} = (\Sigma w_i x_i) / (\Sigma w_i)$. In calculating the trimmed mean, we treat observations that are far from most of the others by excluding them altogether. A less extreme alternative is to include them but give them smaller weights than cases closer to the center, which we can do using the **M-estimator**, or generalized *m*aximum-likelihood estimator.

Since many different schemes can be used to assign weights to cases, there are many different M-estimators. (The usual mean can be viewed as an M-estimator with all cases having a weight of 1.) All commonly used M-estimators assign weights so that they decrease as distance from the center of the distribution increases. Figure 5.13 through Figure 5.16 show the weights used by four common M-estimators.

Common M-Estimators

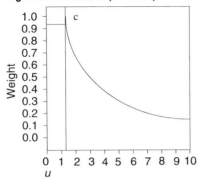

Figure 5.13 Huber's (c = 1.339)

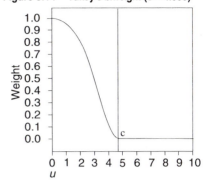

Figure 5.14 Tukey's biweight (c = 4.685)

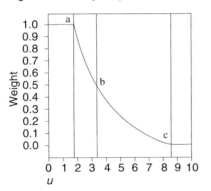

Figure 5.15 Hampel's (a = 1.7, b = 3.4, c = 8.5)

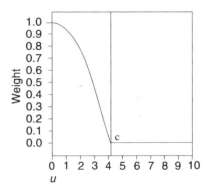

Figure 5.16 Andrew's (c = 1.339π)

Consider Figure 5.13, which shows Huber's M-estimator. The value on the horizontal axis is a standardized distance from the estimate of location. It is computed using the following formula:

$$u_i = \frac{|\text{value for } i\text{th case} - \text{estimate of location}|}{\text{estimate of spread}}$$

Equation 5.2

The estimate of spread used is the median of the absolute deviations from the sample median, commonly known as MAD. It is calculated by first finding the median for the sample and then computing for each case the absolute value of the deviation from the median. The MAD is then the median of these absolute values. Since the weights for cases depend on the value of the estimate of central location, M-estimators must be computed iteratively.

From Figure 5.13, you can see that cases have weights of 1 up to a certain critical point, labeled c. After the critical point, the weights decrease as u, the standardized distance from the location estimate, increases. The SPSS values for these critical points are given in parentheses in Figure 5.13 through Figure 5.16.

The four M-estimators in Figure 5.13 through Figure 5.16 differ from each other in the way they assign weights. The Tukey biweight (Figure 5.14) does not have a point at which weights shift abruptly from 1. Instead, weights gradually decline to 0. Cases with values greater than c standardized units from the estimate are assigned weights of 0.

Hampel's three-part redescending M-estimator (Figure 5.15) has a more complicated weighting scheme than the Huber or the Tukey biweight. It uses four schemes for assigning weights. Cases with values less than a receive a weight of 1, cases with values between a and b receive a weight of a/u, and cases between b and c receive a weight of

$$\frac{a}{u} \times \frac{c-u}{c-b}$$ Equation 5.3

Cases with values greater than c receive a weight of 0. With Andrew's M-estimator (Figure 5.16), there is no abrupt change in the assignment of weights. A smooth function replaces the separate pieces.

Figure 5.17 contains basic descriptive statistics and values for the M-estimators for the diastolic blood pressure data. As expected, the estimates of location differ for the various methods. The mean produces the largest estimate: 88.79. That's because we have a positively skewed distribution and the mean is heavily influenced by the large values. Of the M-estimators, the Huber and Hampel estimates have the largest values. They too are influenced by the large data values. The remaining two M-estimates are fairly close in value.

Figure 5.17 M-estimates for blood pressure variable

```
DBP58        AVERAGE DIAST BLOOD PRESS

Valid cases:        239.0    Missing cases:        1.0    Percent missing:        .4

Mean            88.7908   Std Err        .8441   Min         65.0000   Skewness       1.2557
Median          87.0000   Variance    170.3006   Max        160.0000   S E Skew        .1575
5% Trim         88.0065   Std Dev      13.0499   Range       95.0000   Kurtosis       3.5958
                                                 IQR         17.0000   S E Kurt        .3137

                                      M-Estimators
                                      ------------

Huber   (1.339)                   87.1219    Tukey  (4.685)              86.4269
Hampel  (1.700,3.400,8.500)       87.1404    Andrew (1.340 * pi)         86.4105
```

In summary, M-estimators are good alternatives to the usual mean and median. The Huber M-estimator is good if the distribution is close to normal but is not recommended if there are extreme values. For further discussion of robust estimators, see Hogg (1979) and Hoaglin et al. (1983).

How to Explore Your Data

The Explore procedure provides a variety of descriptive plots and statistics, including stem-and-leaf plots, boxplots, normal probability plots, and spread-versus-level plots. Also available are the Levene test for homogeneity of variance, Shapiro-Wilks' and Lilliefors tests for normality, and several robust maximum-likelihood estimators of location. Cases can be subdivided into groups and statistics can be obtained for each group.

The minimum specification is one or more numeric dependent variables.

To obtain exploratory plots and statistics, from the menus choose:

Statistics
 Summarize ▶
  Explore...

This opens the Explore dialog box, as shown in Figure 5.18.

Figure 5.18 Explore dialog box

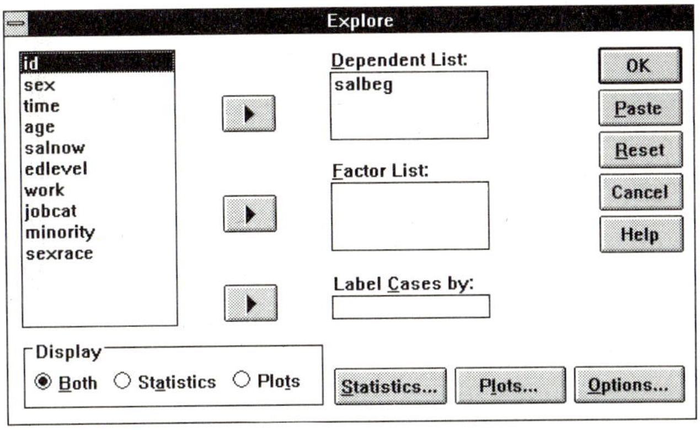

The variables in your data file appear on the source list. Select one or more numeric dependent variables and click on **OK** to get the default analysis, which includes boxplots, stem-and-leaf plots, and basic descriptive statistics for each variable. By default, cases with missing values for any dependent or factor variable are excluded from all summaries.

By default, output is produced for all cases. Optionally, you can obtain separate analyses for groups of cases based on their values for one or more numeric or short string

factor variables. (For example, *jobcat* is the factor variable in Figure 5.6.) If you select more than one factor variable, separate summaries of each dependent variable are produced for each factor variable.

When output is produced showing individual cases (such as outliers), cases are identified by default by their sequence in the data file. Optionally, you can label cases with their values for a variable, such as a case ID variable. It can be a long string, short string, or numeric variable. For long string variables, the first 15 characters are used.

Display. You can also choose one of the following display options:

- **Both.** Displays plots and statistics. This is the default.
- **Statistics.** Displays statistics only (suppresses all plots).
- **Plots.** Displays plots only (suppresses all statistics).

Explore Statistics

To obtain robust estimators or to display outliers, percentiles, or frequency tables, select Both or Statistics under Display and click on Statistics... in the Explore dialog box to open the Explore Statistics dialog box, as shown in Figure 5.19.

Figure 5.19 Explore Statistics dialog box

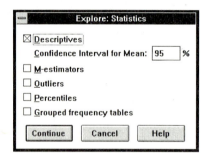

At least one statistic must be selected. You can choose one or more of the following statistics:

- **Descriptives.** Includes the mean and confidence intervals for the mean, median, 5% trimmed mean, standard error, variance, standard deviation, minimum, maximum, range, and interquartile range. Skewness and kurtosis and their standard errors are also shown. This is the default. Interquartile ranges are computed according to the HAVERAGE method.

  Confidence intervals for mean. By default, the 95% confidence interval for the mean is displayed. You can specify any confidence interval between 1 and 99.99%.

- **M-estimators**. Robust maximum-likelihood estimators of location. Displays Huber's M-estimator ($c = 1.339$), Andrew's wave estimator ($c = 1.34\pi$), Hampel's redescending M-estimator ($a = 1.7$, $b = 3.4$, and $c = 8.5$), and Tukey's biweight estimator ($c = 4.685$). (See "M-Estimators" on p. 94.)

- **Outliers**. Displays cases with the five largest and five smallest values. These are labeled *Extreme Values* in the output (See Figure 5.3.)

- **Percentiles**. Displays the following percentiles: 5, 10, 25, 50, 75, 90, and 95. The weighted average at $X_{(W+1)p}$ (HAVERAGE) is used to calculate percentiles, where W is the sum of the weights for all cases with nonmissing values, p is the percentile divided by 100, i is the rank of the case when cases are sorted in ascending order, and X_i is the value for the ith case. The percentile value is the weighted average of X_i and X_{i+1} using the formula $(1-f)X_i + fX_{i+1}$, where $(W+1)p$ is decomposed into an integer part i and fractional part f. Also displays Tukey's hinges (25th, 50th, and 75th percentiles).

- **Grouped frequency tables**. Displays tables for the total sample and broken down by any factor variables. Starting value and increment are selected on the basis of observed data values.

Explore Plots

To obtain histograms, normality plots and tests, or spread-versus-level plots with Levene's statistic, select Both or Plots under Display and click on Plots... in the Explore dialog box to open the Explore Plots dialog box, as shown in Figure 5.20.

Figure 5.20   Explore Plots dialog box

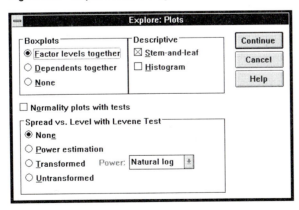

At least one plot must be selected.

Boxplots. You can choose one of the following boxplot display alternatives:

○ **Factor levels together**. For a given dependent variable, displays boxplots for each group side by side. This is the default. Select this display method when you want to compare groups for a variable. If no factor variable is selected, only a boxplot for the total sample is shown.

○ **Dependents together**. For a given group, displays boxplots for each dependent variable side by side. Select this display method when you want to compare variables for a particular group.

○ **None**. Suppresses boxplot.

Descriptive. You can choose one or both of the following descriptive plots:

❏ **Stem-and-leaf**. Displayed by default. Each observed value is divided into two components—the leading digits (stem) and trailing digits (leaf). To suppress stem-and-leaf plots, deselect this item.

❏ **Histogram**. The range of observed values is divided into equal intervals and the number of cases in each interval is displayed.

Spread vs. Level with Levene Test. For all spread-versus-level plots, the slope of the regression line and Levene's test for homogeneity of variance are displayed. Levene's test is based on the original data if no transformation is specified and on the transformed data if a transformation is specified. If no factor variable is selected, spread-versus-level plots are not produced.

You can choose one of the following alternatives:

○ **None**. Suppresses spread-versus-level plots and Levene's statistic. This is the default.

○ **Power estimation**. For each group, the natural log of the median is plotted against the log of the interquartile range. Estimated power is also displayed. Use this method to determine an appropriate transformation for your data.

○ **Transformed**. Data are transformed according to a user-specified power. The interquartile range and median of the transformed data are plotted. (See "Determining the Transformation" on p. 90.)

⬇ **Power**. To transform data, you must select a power for the transformation. You can choose one of the following alternatives:

Natural log. Natural log transformation. This is the default.

1/square root. For each data value, the reciprocal of the square root is calculated.

Reciprocal. Reciprocal transformation.

Square root. Square root transformation.

Square. Data values are squared.

Cube. Data values are cubed.

○ **Untransformed**. No transformation of the data is performed. (Power value is 1.)

The following option is available for normal probability and detrended probability plots:

❏ **Normality plots with tests**. Normal probability and detrended probability plots are produced, and the Shapiro-Wilks' statistic and the Kolmogorov-Smirnov statistic with a Lilliefors significance level for testing normality are calculated. The Shapiro-Wilks' statistic is not calculated if the sample size exceeds 50.

Explore Options

To modify the handling of missing values, click on Options... in the Explore dialog box. This opens the Explore Options dialog box, as shown in Figure 5.21.

Figure 5.21   Explore Options dialog box

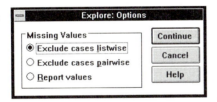

Missing Values. You can choose one of the following alternatives:

○ **Exclude cases listwise**. Cases with missing values for any dependent or factor variable are excluded from all analyses. This is the default.

○ **Exclude cases pairwise**. Cases with no missing values for variables in a cell are included in the analysis of that cell. The case may have missing values for variables used in other cells.

○ **Report values**. Missing values for factor variables are treated as a separate category. All output is produced for this additional category. Frequency tables include categories for missing values.

Additional Features Available with Command Syntax

You can customize your exploratory data analysis if you paste your selections into a syntax window and edit the resulting EXAMINE command syntax. (For information on syntax windows, see the *SPSS Base System User's Guide, Part 1*.) Additional features include:

- Output for cells formed by *combinations* of factor variables (using the keyword BY).
- User-specified number of outliers displayed (with the STATISTICS subcommand).

- User-specified starting and increment values for frequency tables (with the FREQUENCIES subcommand).
- Alternative methods of percentile estimation and user-specified percentiles (with the PERCENTILES subcommand).
- Additional user-specified power values for spread-versus-level plot transformations (with the PLOT subcommand).
- User-specified critical points for M-estimators (with the MESTIMATORS subcommand).

See the *SPSS Base System Syntax Reference Guide* for complete EXAMINE command syntax.

6 Crosstabulation and Measures of Association

Unfortunately, winning the lottery is but a dream for most of us. But who hasn't pondered the consequences: paying off the mortgage, junking the old clunker, vacationing in exotic warm locations... And then there's the question of what to tell the boss. Although some of us have repeatedly rehearsed the parting conversation, others may delude themselves into thinking that they will continue to work.

To determine whether most people see themselves as workers or nonworkers if they should suddenly become rich, let's consider data from the 1991 General Social Survey. (Davis, et al., 1991). The General Social Survey asked a national sample of working adults 18 and older whether they would continue working if they became rich.

Crosstabulation

To see whether the hypothetical work rate is similar for males and females, the responses must be tallied separately for each sex. Figure 6.1 is a **crosstabulation** of sex and response. The number of cases with each combination of values of the two variables is displayed in a **cell** in the table, together with various percentages. These cell entries provide information about relationships between the variables.

Figure 6.1 Crosstabulation of sex by response

```
SEX    RESPONDENTS SEX   by   RICHWORK   IF RICH, CONTINUE OR STOP WORKING

                       RICHWORK        Page 1 of 1
            Count    |
            Row Pct  |CONTINUE STOP WOR
            Col Pct  |WORKING  KING           Row
            Tot Pct  |    1        2         Total
    SEX              |
               1     |  234      89            323
       MALE          |  72.4     27.6          52.4
                     |  56.8     43.6
                     |  38.0     14.4
                     |
               2     |  178      115           293
       FEMALE        |  60.8     39.2          47.6
                     |  43.2     56.4
                     |  28.9     18.7

            Column      412       204          616
            Total       66.9      33.1        100.0

Number of Missing Observations:   901
```

In Figure 6.1, work status is called the **column variable**, since each status is displayed in a column of the table. Similarly, the sex of the respondent is called the **row variable**. With two categories of the column variable and two of the row, there are four cells in the table.

Cell Contents and Marginals

The first entry in the each cell is the number of cases, or **frequency**, in that cell. It is labeled as *Count* in the key displayed in the upper-left corner of the table. For example, 234 males would continue to work, and 89 males would stop working. The second entry in the table is the **row percentage** (*Row Pct*). It is the percentage of all cases in a row that fall into a particular cell. Of the 323 men, 72.4% would continue to work and 27.6% would not. Of the 293 women, 60.8% would continue to work and 39.2% would not.

The **column percentage** (*Col Pct*), the third item in each cell, is the percentage of all cases in a column that occur in a cell. For example, of the 412 people who would continue to work, 56.8% are men and 43.2% are women.

The last entry in the cell is the **table percentage** (*Tot Pct*). The number of cases in the cell is expressed as a percentage of the total number of cases in the table. For example, the 234 males who would continue to work represent 38% of the 616 respondents.

The numbers to the right and below the table are known as **marginals**. They are the counts and percentages for the row and column variables taken separately. In Figure 6.1, the column marginals show that 66.9% of the respondents would continue to work, while 33.1% would stop.

Choosing Percentages

Row, column, and table percentages convey different types of information, so it is important to choose carefully among them.

In this example, the column percentage indicates the distribution of males and females in each of the response categories. It conveys no direct information about whether males and females are equally likely to keep working. For example, if the number of males in the survey was twice the number of females, an identical work rate for both sexes would give column percentages of 66.7% and 33.3%. However, this does not indicate that the work rate is higher for males. There are just more of them.

The row percentage tells you the percentage of males who would continue working and the percentage of females who would continue working. By looking at row percentages, you can compare work rates for males and females. Interpretation of this comparison is not affected by unequal numbers of males and females in the study.

Since it is always possible to interchange the rows and columns of any table, general rules about when to use row and column percentages cannot be given. The percentages to use depend on the nature of the two variables. If one of the two variables is under experimental control, it is termed an **independent variable**. The independent variable is hypothesized to affect the response, or **dependent variable**. If variables can be classified as dependent and independent, the following guideline may be helpful: if the independent variable is the row variable, select row percentages; if the independent variable is the column variable, select column percentages. In this example the dependent variable is work status, whether a person would continue working or not. The sex of the respondent is the independent variable. Since the independent variable is the row variable in Figure 6.1, row percentages should be used for comparisons of work rates.

Adding a Control Variable

Figure 6.1 is an overall comparison of men's and women's responses. If you wanted to see whether particular groups of men and women differ, you would have to include additional variables in the crosstabulation table. For example, to see whether marital status affects the responses of men and women, you could crosstabulate sex and response for each of the marital status categories of interest. Figure 6.2 shows separate crosstabulations of sex and work plans for married people and for people who have never been married.

Figure 6.2 Crosstabulations of sex by response by marital status

```
SEX    RESPONDENTS SEX    by  RICHWORK   IF RICH, CONTINUE OR STOP WORKING
Controlling for..
MARITAL   MARITAL STATUS   Value = 1   MARRIED

                    RICHWORK        Page 1 of 1
            Count
            Row Pct  CONTINUE STOP WOR
                     WORKING  KING
                          1       2    Row
                                       Total
    SEX
              1         137      46     183
         MALE           74.9     25.1   56.1

              2          80      63     143
         FEMALE         55.9     44.1   43.9

         Column         217     109     326
         Total          66.6    33.4   100.0


         Chi-Square                Value           DF         Significance
         ----------                -----           --         ------------

Pearson                          12.91011          1            .00033
Continuity Correction            12.07404          1            .00051
Likelihood Ratio                 12.89133          1            .00033
Mantel-Haenszel test for         12.87051          1            .00033
    linear association

Minimum Expected Frequency -   47.813
```

```
SEX    RESPONDENTS SEX    by  RICHWORK   IF RICH, CONTINUE OR STOP WORKING
Controlling for..
MARITAL   MARITAL STATUS   Value = 5   NEVER MARRIED

                    RICHWORK        Page 1 of 1
            Count
            Row Pct  CONTINUE STOP WOR
                     WORKING  KING
                          1       2    Row
                                       Total
    SEX
              1          65      31      96
         MALE           67.7     32.3   59.6

              2          50      15      65
         FEMALE         76.9     23.1   40.4

         Column         115      46     161
         Total          71.4    28.6   100.0


         Chi-Square                Value           DF         Significance
         ----------                -----           --         ------------

Pearson                           1.61258          1            .20413
Continuity Correction             1.19266          1            .27479
Likelihood Ratio                  1.63897          1            .20047
Mantel-Haenszel test for          1.60256          1            .20554
    linear association

Minimum Expected Frequency -   18.571
```

These tables show interesting differences. Almost 75% of married men think they would continue to work, while only 56% of married women think they would continue to work. When you consider never-married respondents, however, the percentage of women who would continue to work (77%) increases substantially, surpassing the percentage of men (68%). Single women seem to be as attached to their work (or as willing to lie) as their male counterparts.

Graphical Representation of Crosstabulations

As with frequency tables, visual representation of a crosstabulation often simplifies the search for associations. Figure 6.3 is a **bar chart** of the crosstabulations shown in Figure 6.2. In a bar chart, the height of each bar represents the frequencies or percentages for each category of a variable. In Figure 6.3, the percentages plotted are the row percentages shown in Figure 6.2 for respondents who would continue to work. This chart clearly shows that the work rates differ quite a bit for married men and women, but not for those who have never married.

Figure 6.3 Bar chart

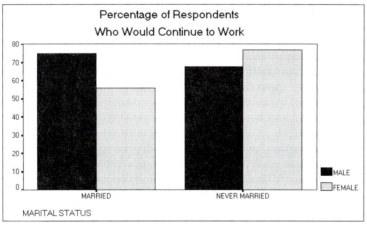

Using Crosstabulation for Data Screening

Errors and unusual values in data entry that cannot be spotted with frequency tables can sometimes be identified using crosstabulation. For example, a case coded as a male with a history of three pregnancies would not be identified as suspicious in frequency tables of sex and number of pregnancies. When considered separately, the code *male* is acceptable for sex and the value 3 is acceptable for number of pregnancies. The combination, however, is unexpected.

Whenever possible, crosstabulations of related variables should be obtained so that anomalies can be identified and corrected before further statistical analysis of the data.

Crosstabulation Statistics

Although examination of the various row and column percentages in a crosstabulation is a useful first step in studying the relationship between two variables, row and column percentages do not allow for quantification or testing of that relationship. For these purposes, it is useful to consider various indexes that measure the extent of association as well as statistical tests of the hypothesis that there is no association.

The Chi-Square Test of Independence

The hypothesis that two variables in a crosstabulation are independent of each other is often of interest. Two variables are **independent** if the probability that a case falls into a given cell is simply the product of the marginal probabilities of the two categories defining the cell.

In Figure 6.1, for example, if work status and sex are independent, the probability of a man continuing to work is the product of the probability of a male and the probability of continuing to work. From the table, 52.4% of the respondents were male and 66.9% of the respondents would continue to work. Thus, if sex and work status are independent, the probability of of a male cotinuing to work is estimated to be

$$P(\text{male})\, P(\text{continue work}) = 0.524 \times 0.669 = 0.35 \qquad \textbf{Equation 6.1}$$

The **expected** number of cases in that cell is 216, which is 35% of the 616 cases in the sample. From the table, the **observed** number of men who would continue to work is 234, 18 more than would be expected if the two variables are independent.

To construct a statistical test of the independence hypothesis, you repeat the above calculations for each cell in the table. The probability under independence of an observation falling into cell (*ij*) is estimated by

$$P(\text{row} = i \text{ and column} = j) = \left(\frac{\text{count in row } i}{N}\right)\left(\frac{\text{count in column } j}{N}\right) \qquad \textbf{Equation 6.2}$$

To obtain the expected number of observations in cell (ij), the probability is multiplied by the total sample size.

$$E_{ij} = N\left(\left(\frac{\text{count in row } i}{N}\right)\left(\frac{\text{count in column } j}{N}\right)\right)$$
$$= \frac{(\text{count in row } i)\,(\text{count in column } j)}{N}$$

Equation 6.3

Figure 6.4 contains the observed and expected frequencies and the **residuals**, which are the observed minus the expected frequencies for the data in Figure 6.1.

Figure 6.4 Observed, expected, and residual values

```
SEX    RESPONDENTS SEX  by   RICHWORK    IF RICH, CONTINUE OR STOP WORKING

                     RICHWORK      Page 1 of 1
              Count
              Exp Val  |CONTINUE STOP WOR
              Residual |WORKING  KING         Row
                       |    1        2      Total
     SEX            ---+------------------
                1  |    234       89      323
         MALE      |   216.0    107.0    52.4%
                   |    18.0    -18.0
                   +------------------
                2  |    178      115      293
         FEMALE    |   196.0     97.0    47.6%
                   |   -18.0     18.0
                   +------------------
            Column      412      204      616
             Total     66.9%    33.1%   100.0%

      Chi-Square                  Value        DF       Significance
   --------------------        -----------    ----      ------------

   Pearson                        9.48684       1          .00207
   Continuity Correction          8.96619       1          .00275
   Likelihood Ratio               9.49640       1          .00206
   Mantel-Haenszel test for       9.47144       1          .00209
       linear association

   Minimum Expected Frequency -    97.032


   Number of Missing Observations:   901
```

A statistic often used to test the hypothesis that the row and column variables are independent is the **Pearson chi-square**. It is calculated by summing over all cells the squared residuals divided by the expected frequencies.

$$\chi^2 = \sum_i \sum_j \frac{(O_{ij} - E_{ij})^2}{E_{ij}}$$

Equation 6.4

The calculated chi-square is compared to the critical points of the theoretical chi-square distribution to produce an estimate of how likely (or unlikely) this calculated value is if the two variables are in fact independent. Since the value of the chi-square depends on the number of rows and columns in the table being examined, you must know the **degrees of freedom** for the table. The degrees of freedom can be viewed as the number of cells of a table that can be arbitrarily filled when the row and column totals (marginals) are fixed. For an $r \times c$ table, the degrees of freedom are $(r-1) \times (c-1)$, since once $(r-1)$ rows and $(c-1)$ columns are filled, frequencies in the remaining row and column cells must be chosen so that marginal totals are maintained.

In this example, there is one degrees of freedom (1×1) and the Pearson chi-square value is 9.49 (see Figure 6.4). If sex and continuing to work are independent, the probability that a random sample would result in a chi-square value of at least that magnitude is 0.002. This probability is also known as the **observed significance level** of the test. If the probability is small enough (usually less than 0.05 or 0.01), the hypothesis that the two variables are independent is rejected.

Since the observed significance level in Figure 6.4 is very small, the hypothesis that sex and continuing to work are independent is rejected. When the chi-square test is calculated for married and never married persons separately (Figure 6.2), different results are obtained. The observed significance level for married respondents is 0.0003, so the independence hypothesis is rejected. For never-married people, the observed significance level is less than 0.204, and the hypothesis that sex and work status are independent is not rejected.

An alternative to the commonly used Pearson chi-square is the **likelihood-ratio chi-square** (see Figure 6.4). This test is based on maximum-likelihood theory and is often used in the analysis of categorical data. For large samples, the Pearson and likelihood-ratio chi-square statistics give very similar results. (The Mantel-Haenszel test is discussed in "Ordinal Measures" on p. 118.)

The chi-square test is a test of independence; it provides little information about the strength or form of the association between two variables. The magnitude of the observed chi-square depends not only on the goodness of fit of the independence model but also on the sample size. If the sample size for a particular table increases n-fold, so does the chi-square value. Thus, large chi-square values can arise in applications where residuals are small relative to expected frequencies but where the sample size is large.

Certain conditions must be met for the chi-square distribution to be a good approximation of the distribution of the statistic in the equation given above. The data must be random samples from multinomial distributions and the expected values must not be too small. While it has been recommended that all expected frequencies be at least 5, studies indicate that this is probably too stringent and can be relaxed (Everitt, 1977). SPSS/PC+ displays the number of cells with expected frequencies less than 5 and the minimum expected cell value.

To improve the approximation for a 2×2 table, **Yates' correction for continuity** is sometimes applied. Yates' correction for continuity involves subtracting 0.5 from positive differences between observed and expected frequencies (the residuals) and adding 0.5 to negative differences before squaring. For a discussion of the controversy over the merits of this correction, see Conover (1974) and Mantel (1974).

Fisher's exact test, based on the hypergeometric distribution, is an alternative test for the 2×2 table. It calculates exact probabilities of obtaining the observed results if the two variables are independent and the marginals are fixed. It is most useful when the total sample size and the expected values are small. SPSS/PC+ calculates Fisher's exact test if any expected cell value in a 2×2 table is less than 5.

Measures of Association

In many research situations, it is the strength and nature of the dependence of the variables that is of central concern. Indexes that attempt to quantify the relationship between variables in a crosstabulation are called **measures of association**. No single measure adequately summarizes all possible types of association. Measures vary in their interpretation and in the way they define perfect and intermediate association. These measures also differ in the way they are affected by various factors such as marginals. For example, many measures are "margin sensitive" in that they are influenced by the marginal distributions of the rows and columns. Such measures reflect information about the marginals along with information about association.

A particular measure may have a low value for a given table, not because the two variables are not related but because they are not related in the way to which the measure is sensitive. No single measure is best for all situations. The type of data, the hypothesis of interest, and the properties of the various measures must all be considered when selecting an index of association for a given table. It is not, however, reasonable to compute a large number of measures and then to report the most impressive as if it were the only one examined.

The measures of association available with crosstabulation in SPSS/PC+ are computed only from bivariate tables. For example, if three dichotomous variables are specified in the table, two sets of measures are computed, one for each subtable produced by the values of the controlling variable. In general, if relationships among more than two variables are to be studied, examination of bivariate tables is only a first step. For an extensive discussion of more sophisticated multivariate procedures for the analysis of qualitative data, see Fienberg (1977), Everitt (1977), and Haberman (1978).

Nominal Measures

Consider measures that assume only that both variables in the table are nominally measured. As such, these measures can provide only some indication of the strength of association between variables; they cannot indicate direction or anything about the nature of the relationship. The measures provided are of two types: those based on the chi-square statistic and those that follow the logic of proportional reduction in error, denoted PRE.

Chi-Square-Based Measures

As explained above, the chi-square statistic itself is not a good measure of the degree of association between two variables. But its widespread use in tests of independence has encouraged the use of measures of association based upon it. Each of these measures based on the chi-square attempts to modify the chi-square statistic to minimize the influence of sample size and degrees of freedom as well as to restrict the range of values of the measure to those between 0 and 1. Without such adjustments, comparison of chi-square values from tables with varying dimensions and sample sizes is meaningless.

The **phi coefficient** modifies the Pearson chi-square by dividing it by the sample size and taking the square root of the result:

$$\phi = \sqrt{\frac{\chi^2}{N}} \qquad \text{Equation 6.5}$$

For a 2×2 table only, the phi coefficient is equal to the Pearson correlation coefficient, so the sign of phi matches that of the correlation coefficient. For tables in which one dimension is greater than 2, phi may not lie between 0 and 1, since the chi-square value can be greater than the sample size. To obtain a measure that must lie between 0 and 1, Pearson suggested the use of

$$C = \sqrt{\frac{\chi^2}{\chi^2 + N}} \qquad \text{Equation 6.6}$$

which is called the **coefficient of contingency**. Although the value of this measure is always between 0 and 1, it cannot generally attain the upper limit of 1. The maximum value possible depends upon the number of rows and columns. For example, in a 4×4 table, the maximum value of C is 0.87.

Cramér introduced the following variant:

$$V = \sqrt{\frac{\chi^2}{N(k-1)}} \qquad \text{Equation 6.7}$$

where k is the smaller of the number of rows and columns. This statistic, known as **Cramér's V**, can attain the maximum of 1 for tables of any dimension. If one of the table dimensions is 2, V and phi are identical.

Figure 6.5 shows the values of the chi-square-based measures for the strike-it-rich data. The test of the null hypothesis that a measure is 0 is based on the Pearson chi-square probability. Since the observed significance level is very small, you can reject the null hypothesis that the chi-squared based measures are zero.

Figure 6.5 Chi-square-based measures

```
SEX   RESPONDENTS SEX   by   RICHWORK   IF RICH, CONTINUE OR STOP WORKING

                RICHWORK        Page 1 of 1
        Count  |
               |CONTINUE STOP WOR
               |WORKING  KING
               |       1|       2|  Row
SEX            |        |        | Total
            1  |   234  |    89  |  323
    MALE       |        |        |  52.4
               |--------|--------|
            2  |   178  |   115  |  293
    FEMALE     |        |        |  47.6
               |--------|--------|
       Column      412      204     616
        Total      66.9     33.1   100.0


                                                                Approximate
         Statistic                 Value      ASE1    Val/ASE0  Significance
         ---------                 -----      ----    --------  ------------

Phi                                .12410                         .00207 *1
Cramer's V                         .12410                         .00207 *1
Contingency Coefficient            .12315                         .00207 *1


*1 Pearson chi-square probability

Number of Missing Observations:  901
```

The chi-square-based measures are hard to interpret. Although when properly standardized they can be used to compare strength of association in several tables, the strength of association being compared is not easily related to an intuitive concept of association.

Proportional Reduction in Error

Common alternatives to chi-square-based measurements are those based on the idea of **proportional reduction in error (PRE)**, introduced by Goodman and Kruskal (1954). With PRE measures, the meaning of association is clearer. These measures are all essentially ratios of a measure of error in predicting the values of one variable based on knowledge of that variable alone and the same measure of error applied to predictions based on knowledge of an additional variable.

For example, Figure 6.6 is a crosstabulation of depth of hypnosis and success in treatment of migraine headaches by suggestion (Cedercreutz, 1978). The best guess of the results of treatment when no other information is available is the outcome category with the largest proportion of observations (the modal category).

Figure 6.6 Depth of hypnosis and success of treatment

```
HYPNOSIS   DEPTH OF HYPNOSIS   by   MIGRAINE    OUTCOME

                       MIGRAINE                           Page 1 of 1
             Count
             Col Pct   CURED      BETTER     NO
             Tot Pct                         CHANGE       Row
                       1.00       2.00       3.00        Total
HYPNOSIS
             1.00      13         5                      18
     DEEP              56.5       15.6                   18.0
                       13.0       5.0

             2.00      10         26         17          53
   MEDIUM              43.5       81.3       37.8        53.0
                       10.0       26.0       17.0

             3.00                 1          28          29
    LIGHT                         3.1        62.2        29.0
                                  1.0        28.0

           Column      23         32         45          100
           Total       23.0       32.0       45.0        100.0


                                                                       Approximate
         Statistic                    Value        ASE1    Val/ASE0   Significance
-----------------------------         --------     ------  --------   ------------

Lambda :
    symmetric                         .35294       .11335   2.75267
    with HYPNOSIS dependent           .29787       .14702   1.72276
    with MIGRAINE dependent           .40000       .10539   3.07580
Goodman & Kruskal Tau :
    with HYPNOSIS dependent           .29435       .06304              .00000   *2
    with MIGRAINE dependent           .34508       .04863              .00000   *2


*2 Based on chi square approximation

Number of Missing Observations:  0
```

In Figure 6.6, *no change* is the largest outcome category, with 45% of the subjects. The estimate of the probability of incorrect classification is 1 minus the probability of the modal category:

$$P(1) = 1 - 0.45 = 0.55 \qquad \text{Equation 6.8}$$

Information about the depth of hypnosis can be used to improve the classification rule. For each hypnosis category, the outcome category that occurs most frequently for that hypnosis level is predicted. Thus, *no change* is predicted for participants achieving a light level of hypnosis, *better* for those achieving a medium level, and *cured* for those achieving a deep level. The probability of error when depth of hypnosis is used to predict outcome is the sum of the probabilities of all the cells that are not row modes:

$$P(2) = 0.05 + 0.10 + 0.17 + 0.01 = 0.33 \qquad \text{Equation 6.9}$$

Goodman and Kruskal's **lambda**, with outcome as the predicted (dependent) variable, is calculated as

$$\lambda_{outcome} = \frac{P(1) - P(2)}{P(1)} = \frac{0.55 - 0.33}{0.55} = 0.40 \qquad \text{Equation 6.10}$$

Thus, a 40% reduction in error is obtained when depth of hypnosis is used to predict outcome.

Lambda always ranges between 0 and 1. A value of 0 means the independent variable is of no help in predicting the dependent variable. A value of 1 means that the independent variable perfectly specifies the categories of the dependent variable (perfection can occur only when each row has at most one non-zero cell). When the two variables are independent, lambda is 0; but a lambda of 0 need not imply statistical independence. As with all measures of association, lambda is constructed to measure association in a very specific way. In particular, lambda reflects the reduction in error when values of one variable are used to predict values of the other. If this particular type of association is absent, lambda is 0. Other measures of association may find association of a different kind even when lambda is 0. A measure of association sensitive to every imaginable type of association does not exist.

For a particular table, two different lambdas can be computed, one using the row variable as the predictor and the other using the column variable. The two do not usually have identical values, so care should be taken to specify which is the dependent variable; that is, the variable whose prediction is of primary interest. In some applications, dependent and independent variables are not clearly distinguished. In those instances, a symmetric version of lambda, which predicts the row variable and column variable with equal frequency, can be computed. When the lambda statistic is requested, SPSS displays the symmetric lambda as well as the two asymmetric lambdas.

Goodman and Kruskal's Tau

When lambda is computed, the same prediction is made for all cases in a particular row or column. Another approach is to consider what happens if the prediction is randomly made in the same proportion as the marginal totals. For example, if you're trying to predict migraine outcome without any information about the depth of the hypnosis, you can use the marginal distributions in Figure 6.6 instead of the modal category to guess *cured* for 23% of the cases, *better* for 32% of the cases, and *no change* for 45% of the cases.

Using these marginals, you would expect to correctly classify 23% of the 23 cases in the *cured* category, 32% of the 32 cases in the *better* category, and 45% of the 45 cases in the *no change* category. This results in the correct classification of 35.78 out of 100 cases. When additional information about the depth of hypnosis is incorporated into the prediction rule, the prediction is based on the probability of the different outcomes for each depth of hypnosis. For example, for those who experienced deep hypnosis, you would predict *cure* 72% of the time (13/18) and *better* 28% of the time (5/18). Similarly, for those with light hypnosis, you would predict *better* 3% of the time and *no change* 97% of the time. This results in correct classification for about 58 of the cases.

Goodman and Kruskal's tau is computed by comparing the probability of error in the two situations. In this example, when predicting only from the column marginal totals, the probability of error is 0.64. When predicting from row information, the probability of error is 0.42. Thus,

tau (migraine | hypnosis) = (0.64 − 0.42) / 0.64 = 0.34   **Equation 6.11**

By incorporating information about the depth of hypnosis, we have reduced our error of prediction by about 34%.

A test of the null hypothesis that tau is 0 can be based on the value of $(N-1)(c-1)$ tau (col | row), which has a chi-square distribution with $(c-1) \times (r-1)$ degrees of freedom. In this example, the observed significance level for tau is very small, and you can reject the null hypothesis that tau is 0. The asymptotic standard error for the statistic is shown in the column labeled *ASE1*. The asymptotic standard error can be used to construct confidence intervals.

Measuring Agreement

Measures of agreement allow you to compare the ratings of two observers for the same group of objects. For example, consider the data reported in Bishop et al. (1975), shown in Figure 6.7.

Figure 6.7 Student teachers rated by supervisors

```
SUPRVSR1  Supervisor 1  by  SUPRVSR2  Supervisor 2

              SUPRVSR2                       Page 1 of 1
       Count
       Tot Pct  Authorit Democrat Permissi
                arian    ic       ve         Row
                   1.00     2.00     3.00  Total
SUPRVSR1
          1.00      17        4        8     29
   Authoritarian  23.6      5.6     11.1   40.3

          2.00       5       12               17
      Democratic   6.9     16.7            23.6

          3.00      10        3       13     26
      Permissive  13.9      4.2     18.1   36.1

        Column      32       19       21     72
         Total    44.4     26.4     29.2  100.0


                                                        Approximate
     Statistic              Value      ASE1   Val/ASE0  Significance
     ---------              -----      ----   --------  ------------

Kappa                      .36227    .09075    4.32902

Number of Missing Observations:  0
```

Two supervisors rated the classroom style of 72 teachers. You are interested in measuring the agreement between the two raters. The simplest measure that comes to mind is just the proportion of cases for which the raters agree. In this case, it is 58.3%. The disadvantage of this measure is that no correction is made for the amount of agreement expected by chance. That is, you would expect the supervisors to agree sometimes even if they were assigning ratings by tossing dice.

To correct for chance agreement, you can compute the proportion of cases that you would expect to be in agreement if the ratings are independent. For example, supervisor 1 rated 40.3% of the teachers as authoritarian, while supervisor 2 rated 44.4% of the teachers as authoritarian. If their rankings are independent, you would expect that 17.9% ($40.3\% \times 44.4\%$) of the teachers would be rated as authoritarian by both. Similarly, 6.2% ($23.6\% \times 26.4\%$) would be rated as democratic and 10.5% ($36.1\% \times 29.2\%$) as permissive. Thus, 34.6% of all the teachers would be classified the same merely by chance.

The difference between the observed proportion of cases in which the raters agree and that expected by chance is 0.237 (0.583 – 0.346). **Cohen's kappa** (Cohen, 1960) normalizes this difference by dividing it by the maximum difference possible for the marginal totals. In this example, the largest possible "non-chance" agreement is 1 – 0.346 (the chance level). Therefore,

kappa = 0.237 / (1 – 0.346) = 0.362   **Equation 6.12**

The test of the null hypothesis that kappa is 0 can be based on the ratio of the measure to its standard error, assuming that the null hypothesis is true. (See Benedetti and Brown, 1978, for further discussion of standard errors for measures of association.) This asymptotic error is not the one shown on the output. The asymptotic standard error on the output, *ASE1*, does not assume that the true value is 0.

Since the kappa statistic measures agreement between two raters, the two variables that contain the ratings must have the same range of values. If this is not true, SPSS will not compute kappa.

Ordinal Measures

Although relationships among ordinal variables can be examined using nominal measures, other measures reflect the additional information available from ranking. Consideration of the kind of relationships that may exist between two ordered variables leads to the notion of direction of relationship and to the concept of **correlation**. Variables are positively correlated if cases with low values for one variable also tend to have low values for the other, and cases with high values on one also tend to be high on the other. Negatively correlated variables show the opposite relationship: the higher the first variable, the lower the second tends to be.

The **Spearman correlation coefficient** is a commonly used measure of correlation between two ordinal variables. For all of the cases, the values of each of the variables are ranked from smallest to largest, and the Pearson correlation coefficient is computed on the ranks. The **Mantel-Haenszel chi-square** is another measure of linear association between the row and column variables in a crosstabulation. It is computed by multiplying the square of the Pearson correlation coefficient by the number of cases minus 1. The resulting statistic has one degree of freedom (Mantel & Haenszel, 1959). (Although the Mantel-Haenszel statistic is displayed whenever chi-square is requested, it should not be used for nominal data.)

Ordinal Measures Based on Pairs

For a table of two ordered variables, several measures of association based on a comparison of the values of both variables for all possible *pairs* of cases or observations are available. Cases are first compared to determine if they are concordant, discordant, or tied. A pair of cases is **concordant** if the values of both variables for one case are higher (or both are lower) than the corresponding values for the other case. The pair is **discordant** if the value of one variable for a case is larger than the corresponding value for the other case, and the direction is reversed for the second variable. When the two cases have identical values on one or on both variables, they are **tied**.

Thus, for any given pair of cases with measurements on variables X and Y, the pair may be concordant, discordant, or tied in one of three ways: they may be tied on X but not on Y, they may be tied on Y but not on X, or they may be tied on both variables. When data are arranged in crosstabulated form, the number of concordant, discordant, and tied pairs can be easily calculated since all possible pairs can be conveniently determined.

If the preponderance of pairs is concordant, the association is said to be positive: as ranks of variable X increase (or decrease), so do ranks of variable Y. If the majority of pairs is discordant, the association is negative: as ranks of one variable increase, those of the other tend to decrease. If concordant and discordant pairs are equally likely, no association is said to exist.

The ordinal measures presented here all have the same numerator: the number of concordant pairs (P) minus the number of discordant pairs (Q) calculated for all distinct pairs of observations. They differ primarily in the way in which $P - Q$ is normalized. The simplest measure involves subtracting Q from P and dividing by the total number of pairs. If there are no pairs with ties, this measure (**Kendall's tau-a**) is in the range from -1 to $+1$. If there are ties, the range of possible values is narrower; the actual range depends on the number of ties. Since all observations within the same row are tied, so also are those in the same column, and the resulting tau-a measures are difficult to interpret.

A measure that attempts to normalize $P - Q$ by considering ties on each variable in a pair separately but not ties on both variables in a pair is **tau-b**:

$$\tau_b = \frac{P - Q}{\sqrt{(P + Q + T_X)(P + Q + T_Y)}} \qquad \text{Equation 6.13}$$

where T_X is the number of pairs tied on X but not on Y, and T_Y is the number of pairs tied on Y but not on X. If no marginal frequency is 0, tau-b can attain $+1$ or -1 only for a square table.

A measure that can attain, or nearly attain, $+1$ or -1 for any $r \times c$ table is **tau-c**:

$$\tau_c = \frac{2m(P - Q)}{N^2(m - 1)} \qquad \text{Equation 6.14}$$

where m is the smaller of the number of rows and columns. The coefficients tau-b and tau-c do not differ much in value if each margin contains approximately equal frequencies.

Goodman and Kruskal's gamma is closely related to the tau statistics and is calculated as

$$G = \frac{P - Q}{P + Q} \qquad \text{Equation 6.15}$$

Gamma can be thought of as the probability that a random pair of observations is concordant minus the probability that the pair is discordant, assuming the absence of ties. The absolute value of gamma is the proportional reduction in error between guessing the concordant and discordant ranking of each pair depending on which occurs more often and guessing the ranking according to the outcome of a fair toss of a coin. Gamma is 1 if all observations are concentrated in the upper left to lower right diagonal of the table. In the case of independence, gamma is 0. However, the converse (that a gamma of 0 necessarily implies independence) need not be true except in the 2×2 table.

In the computation of gamma, no distinction is made between the independent and dependent variables; the variables are treated symmetrically. Somers (1962) proposed an asymmetric extension of gamma that differs only in the inclusion of the number of pairs not tied on the independent variable (X) in the denominator. **Somers' d** is

$$d_Y = \frac{P - Q}{P + Q + T_Y}$$

Equation 6.16

The coefficient d_Y indicates the proportionate excess of concordant pairs over discordant pairs among pairs not tied on the independent variable. The symmetric variant of Somers' d uses for the denominator the average value of the denominators of the two asymmetric coefficients.

These ordinal measures for the migraine data are shown in Figure 6.8. All of the measures indicate that there is a fairly strong positive association between the two variables.

Figure 6.8 Ordinal measures

```
HYPNOSIS   DEPTH OF HYPNOSIS   by   MIGRAINE   OUTCOME
Number of valid observations = 100


                                                                Approximate
         Statistic                Value      ASE1     Val/ASE0  Significance
    ------------------            -------    -------  --------  ------------

Kendall's Tau-b                    .67901    .04445   11.96486
Kendall's Tau-c                    .63360    .05296   11.96486
Gamma                              .94034    .02720   11.96486
Somers' D :
    symmetric                      .67866    .04443   11.96486
    with HYPNOSIS dependent        .65774    .05440   11.96486
    with MIGRAINE dependent        .70096    .03996   11.96486

Pearson's R                        .71739    .04484   10.19392   .00000 *4
Spearman Correlation               .72442    .04317   10.40311   .00000 *4


*4 T-value and significance based on a normal approximation
```

Measures Involving Interval Data

If the two variables in the table are measured on an interval scale, various coefficients that make use of this additional information can be calculated. A useful symmetric coefficient that measures the strength of the *linear* relationship is the **Pearson correlation coefficient** (r). It can take on values from -1 to $+1$, indicating negative or positive linear correlation.

The **eta coefficient** is appropriate for data in which the dependent variable is measured on an interval scale and the independent variable on a nominal or ordinal scale. When squared, eta can be interpreted as the proportion of the total variability in the dependent variable that can be accounted for by knowing the values of the independent variable. The measure is asymmetric and does not assume a linear relationship between the variables.

Estimating Risk in Cohort Studies

Often you want to identify variables that are related to the occurrence of a particular event. For example, you may want to determine if smoking is related to heart disease. A commonly used index that measures the strength of the association between presence of a factor and occurrence of an event is the **relative risk ratio**. It is estimated as the ratio of two incidence rates; for example, the incidence rate of heart disease in those who smoke and the incidence rate of heart disease in those who do not smoke.

For example, suppose you observe for five years 1000 smokers without a history of heart disease and 1000 nonsmokers without a history of heart disease, and you determine how many of each group develop heart disease during this time period. (Studies in which a group of disease-free people are studied to see who develops the disease are called **cohort** or **prospective studies**.) Figure 6.9 contains hypothetical results from such a cohort study.

Figure 6.9   Hypothetical cohorts

```
SMOKING   Smoking   by   HDISEASE    Heart Disease

                 HDISEASE         Page 1 of 1
        Count
                 Yes       No
                                         Row
                    1.00     2.00      Total
SMOKING
                  100      900        1000
          1.00                         50.0
   Yes

                   50      950        1000
          2.00                         50.0
   No

        Column    150     1850        2000
        Total     7.5     92.5       100.0


      Statistic                    Value         95% Confidence Bounds
--------------------               -------       ----------------------
Relative Risk Estimate (SMOKING 1.0 / SMOKING 2.0) :
    case control                   2.11111       1.48544        3.00032
    cohort (HDISEASE 1.0 Risk)     2.00000       1.44078        2.77628
    cohort (HDISEASE 2.0 Risk)      .94737        .92390         .97143

Number of Missing Observations:   0
```

The five-year incidence rate for smokers is 100/1000, while the incidence rate for nonsmokers is 50/1000. The relative risk ratio is 2 (100/1000 divided by 50/1000). This indicates that, in the sample, smokers are twice as likely to develop heart disease as nonsmokers.

The estimated relative risk and its 95% confidence interval are in the row labeled *cohort (HDISEASE 1.0 Risk)* in Figure 6.9. In SPSS, the ratio is always computed by taking the incidence in the first row and dividing it by the incidence in the second row. Since either column can represent the event, separate estimates are displayed for each column. The 95% confidence interval does not include the value of 1, so you can reject the null hypothesis that the two incidence rates are the same.

Estimating Risk in Case-Control Studies

In the cohort study described above, we took a group of disease-free people (the cohort) and watched what happened to them. Another type of study that is commonly used is called a **retrospective**, or **case-control study**. In this type of study, we take a group of people with the disease of interest (the cases) and a comparable group of people without the disease (the controls) and see how they differ. For example, we could take 100 people with documented coronary heart disease and 100 controls without heart disease and establish how many in each group smoked. The hypothetical results are shown in Figure 6.10.

Figure 6.10 Hypothetical smoking control

```
GROUP    by   SMOKING

                        SMOKING         Page 1 of 1
              Count
              Row Pct  Yes         No
                                                     Row
                          1.00        2.00          Total
GROUP
              1.00         30          70            100
    Cases                 30.0        70.0           50.0

              2.00         10          90            100
    Control                10.0        90.0          50.0

              Column       40         160            200
              Total        20.0       80.0           100.0


         Statistic                  Value        95% Confidence Bounds
------------------------           --------      ---------------------
Relative Risk Estimate (GROUP 1.0 / GROUP 2.0) :
    case control                    3.85714        1.76660      8.42156
    cohort (SMOKING 1.0 Risk)       3.00000        1.55083      5.80335
    cohort (SMOKING 2.0 Risk)        .77778         .67348       .89823

Number of Missing Observations:  0
```

From a case-control study, we cannot estimate incidence rates. Thus, we cannot compute the relative risk ratio. Instead, we estimate relative risk using what is called an **odds ratio**. We compute the odds that a case smokes and divide it by the odds that a control smokes.

For example, from Figure 6.10, the odds that a case smokes are 30/70. The odds that a control smokes are 10/90. The odds ratio is then 30/70 divided by 10/90, or 3.85. The odds ratio and its confidence interval are in the row labeled *case control* in Figure 6.10. SPSS expects the cases to be in the first row and the controls in the second. Similarly, the event of interest must be in the first column. For further discussion of measures of risk, see Kleinbaum et al. (1982).

How to Obtain Crosstabulations

The Crosstabs procedure produces two-way to *n*-way crosstabulations and related statistics for numeric and short string variables. In addition to cell counts, you can obtain cell percentages, expected values, and residuals.

The minimum specifications are:
- One numeric or short string row variable.
- One numeric or short string column variable.

To obtain crosstabulations and related statistics as well as measures of association, from the menus choose:

Statistics
  Summarize ▶
    Crosstabs...

This opens the Crosstabs dialog box, as shown in Figure 6.11.

Figure 6.11 Crosstabs dialog box

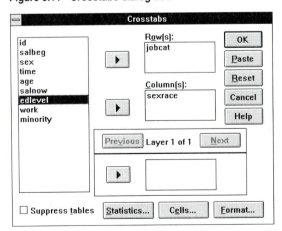

The numeric and short string variables in your data file are displayed on the source variable list. Select the variables you want to use as the row and column variables. A crosstabulation is produced for each combination of row and column variables. For example, if there are four variables on the Row(s) list and three variables on the Column(s) list, you will get 12 crosstabulations. To get a crosstabulation in default format (cell counts only and no measures of association), click on **OK**.

Optionally, you can select one or more layers of control variables. A separate crosstabulation is produced for each category of each control variable. For example, if you have one row variable, one column variable, and one control variable with two categories, you will get two crosstabulations, as in Figure 6.2.

You can add additional layers of control variables by clicking on **Next**. Each layer divides the crosstabulation into smaller subgroups. For example, if *jobcat* is the row variable, *sexrace* is the column variable, *edlevel* is the layer 1 control variable, and *age* is the layer 2 control variable, you will get separate crosstabulations of *jobcat* and *sexrace* for each category of *age* within each category of *edlevel*. If *age* and *edlevel* each have six categories, you will get 36 crosstabulations (probably not what you want).

You can add up to eight layers of control variables. Use **Next** and **Previous** to move between the control variables for the different layers.

The following option is also available:

❑ **Suppress tables.** If you are interested in crosstabulation statistical measures but don't want to display the actual tables, you can choose **Suppress tables**. However, if you haven't selected any statistics from the Crosstabs Statistics dialog box, no output will be generated.

Crosstabs Statistics

To obtain statistics and measures of association, click on **Statistics...** in the Crosstabs dialog box. This opens the Crosstabs Statistics dialog box, as shown in Figure 6.12.

Figure 6.12 Crosstabs Statistics dialog box

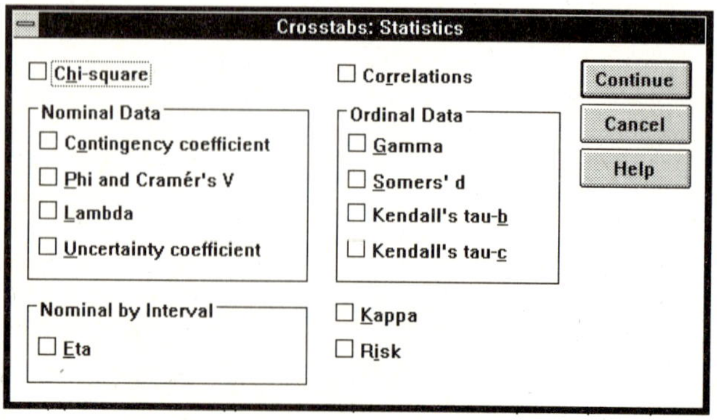

You can choose one or more of the following statistics:

- **Chi-square.** Pearson chi-square, likelihood-ratio chi-square, and Mantel-Haenszel linear association chi-square. For 2×2 tables, Fisher's exact test is computed when a table that does not result from missing rows or columns in a larger table has a cell with an expected frequency of less than 5. Yates' corrected chi-square is computed for all other 2×2 tables.
- **Correlations.** Pearson's *r* and Spearman's correlation coefficient. These are available for numeric data only.
- **Kappa.** Cohen's kappa. The kappa coefficient can only be computed for square tables in which the row and column values are identical (Kraemer, 1982).
- **Risk.** Relative risk ratio. This can only be calculated for 2×2 tables (Kleinbaum et al., 1982).

Nominal Data. Nominal measures assume that variables have values with no intrinsic order (such as *Catholic, Protestant, Jewish*). You can choose one or more of the following:

- **Contingency coefficient.**
- **Phi and Cramér's V.**
- **Lambda.** Symmetric and asymmetric lambda, and Goodman and Kruskal's tau.
- **Uncertainty coefficient.** Symmetric and asymmetric uncertainty coefficient.

Nominal by Interval. It is assumed that one variable is measured on a nominal scale, and the other is measured on an interval scale.

- **Eta.** Eta is not available for short string variables. The nominal variable must be coded numerically. Two eta values are computed: one treats the column variable as the nominal variable; the other treats the row variable as the nominal variable.

Ordinal Data. Ordinal measures assume that variables have values with some intrinsic order (such as *None, Some, A lot*). You can choose one or more of the following:

- **Gamma.** Zero-order gammas are displayed for 2-way tables, and conditional gammas are displayed for 3-way to 10-way tables.
- **Somers' d.** Symmetric and asymmetric Somers' *d*.
- **Kendall's tau-b.**
- **Kendall's tau-c.**

Crosstabs Cell Display

The default crosstabulation displays only the number of cases in each cell. You can also display row, column, and total percentages, expected values, and residuals. To change the cell display, click on Cells... in the Crosstabs dialog box. This opens the Crosstabs Cell Display dialog box, as shown in Figure 6.13.

Figure 6.13 Crosstabs Cell Display dialog box

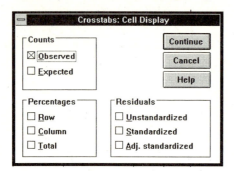

You can choose any combination of cell displays. For example, Figure 6.1 was produced by selecting row, column, and total percentages, in addition to the default observed count. At least one item must be selected.

Counts. You can choose one or more of the following:

- **Observed.** Observed frequencies. This is the default. To suppress observed frequencies, deselect this item.
- **Expected.** Expected frequencies. The number of cases expected in each cell if the two variables in the subtable are statistically independent.

Percentages. You can choose one or more of the following:

- **Row.** The number of cases in each cell expressed as a percentage of all cases in that row.
- **Column.** The number of cases in each cell expressed as a percentage of all cases in that column.
- **Total.** The number of cases in each cell expressed as a percentage of all cases in the subtable.

Residuals. You can choose one or more of the following:

- **Unstandardized.** The value of the observed cell count minus the expected value.

- **Standardized.** Standardized residuals (Haberman, 1978).
- **Adj. standardized.** Adjusted standardized residuals (Haberman, 1978).

Crosstabs Table Format

You can modify the table format by clicking on Format... in the Crosstabs dialog box. This opens the Crosstabs Table Format dialog box, as shown in Figure 6.14.

Figure 6.14 Crosstabs Table Format dialog box

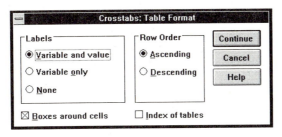

Labels. You can choose one of the following alternatives:

- **Variable and value.** Displays both variable and value labels for each table. This is the default. Only the first 16 characters of the value labels are used. Value labels for the columns are displayed on two lines with eight characters per line.
- **Variable only.** Displays variable labels but suppresses value labels.
- **None.** Suppresses both variable and value labels.

Row Order. You can choose one of the following alternatives:

- **Ascending.** Displays row variable values in ascending order from lowest to highest. This is the default.
- **Descending.** Displays row variable values in descending order from highest to lowest.

The following format choices are also available:

- **Boxes around cells.** This is the default. To produce tables without boxes, deselect this item.
- **Index of tables.** The index lists all crosstabulations produced and the page number on which each table begins.

Additional Features Available with Command Syntax

You can customize your crosstabulation if you paste your selections to a syntax window and edit the resulting CROSSTABS command syntax. An additional feature is the option of using integer mode (with the VARIABLES subcommand). Integer mode, although not significantly faster, conserves memory when variables are coded as adjacent integers and allows you to display cells containing missing data. See the *SPSS Base System Syntax Reference Guide* for complete CROSSTABS command syntax.

7 Describing Subpopulation Differences

The 1964 Civil Rights Act prohibits discrimination in the workplace based on sex or race; employers who violate the act are liable to prosecution. Since passage of this legislation, women, blacks, and other groups have filed numerous lawsuits charging unfair hiring or advancement practices.

The courts have ruled that statistics can be used as *prima facie* evidence of discrimination, and many lawsuits depend heavily on complex statistical analyses to demonstrate that similarly qualified individuals are not treated equally. Identifying and measuring all variables that legitimately influence promotion and hiring is difficult, if not impossible, especially for nonroutine jobs. Years of schooling and prior work experience can be quantified, but what about the more intangible attributes, such as enthusiasm and creativity? How are they to be objectively measured so as not to become convenient smoke screens for concealing discrimination?

Searching for Discrimination

In this chapter, we analyze employee records for 474 individuals hired between 1969 and 1971 by a bank engaged in Equal Employment Opportunity litigation. Two types of unfair employment practices are of particular interest: shunting (placing some employees in lower job categories than other employees with similar qualifications) and salary and promotion inequities.

Although extensive and intricate statistical analyses are usually involved in studies of this kind (Roberts, 1980), the discussion here is necessarily limited. The SPSS Means procedure is used to calculate average salaries for groups of employees based on race and sex. Additional grouping variables are introduced to help "explain" some of the observed variability in salary.

Who Does What?

Figure 7.1 is a crosstabulation of job category at the time of hiring by sex and race characteristics. The first three job classifications contain 64% of white males (adding column percentages), 94% of both minority males and white females, and 100% of minority females. Among white males, 17% are in the college trainee program, compared with 4% of white females.

Figure 7.1   Crosstabulation of job category by sex–race

```
JOBCAT    EMPLOYMENT CATEGORY   by   SEXRACE   SEX & RACE CLASSIFICATION

                          SEXRACE                              Page 1 of 1
           Count
           Col Pct  WHITE MA  MINORITY  WHITE FE  MINORITY
           Tot Pct  LES       MALES     MALES     FEMALES   Row
                        1         2         3         4     Total
JOBCAT              ─────────────────────────────────────
              1        75        35        85        32      227
   CLERICAL          38.7      54.7      48.3      80.0     47.9
                    15.8       7.4      17.9       6.8

              2        35        12        81         8      136
   OFFICE TRAINEE   18.0      18.8      46.0      20.0     28.7
                     7.4       2.5      17.1       1.7

              3        14        13                           27
   SECURITY OFFICER  7.2      20.3                           5.7
                     3.0       2.7

              4        33         1         7                 41
   COLLEGE TRAINEE  17.0       1.6       4.0                 8.6
                     7.0        .2       1.5

              5        28         2         2                 32
   EXEMPT EMPLOYEE  14.4       3.1       1.1                 6.8
                     5.9        .4        .4

              6         3         1         1                  5
   MBA TRAINEE       1.5       1.6        .6                 1.1
                      .6        .2        .2

              7         6                                      6
   TECHNICAL         3.1                                     1.3
                     1.3

          Column     194        64       176        40       474
          Total     40.9      13.5      37.1       8.4     100.0

Number of Missing Observations:  0
```

Although these observations are interesting, they do not imply discriminatory placement into beginning job categories because the qualifications of the various groups are not necessarily similar. If women and nonwhites are more qualified than white males in the same beginning job categories, discrimination may be suspected.

Level of Education

One easily measured employment qualification is years of education. Figure 7.2 shows the average years of education for the entire sample (labeled *For Entire Population*) and then for each of the two sexes (labeled *SEX, MALES* or *FEMALES*) and then for each of the two race categories within each sex category (labeled *MINORITY, WHITE* or *NONWHITE*).

Figure 7.2 Education by sex and race

```
           - - Description of Subpopulations - -

Summaries of        EDLEVEL      EDUCATIONAL LEVEL
By levels of        SEX          SEX OF EMPLOYEE
                    MINORITY     MINORITY CLASSIFICATION


Variable            Value    Label                Mean      Std Dev    Cases

For Entire Population                           13.4916     2.8848      474

SEX                   0      MALES              14.4302     2.9793      258
    MINORITY          0      WHITE              14.9227     2.8484      194
    MINORITY          1      NONWHITE           12.9375     2.8888       64

SEX                   1      FEMALES            12.3704     2.3192      216
    MINORITY          0      WHITE              12.3409     2.4066      176
    MINORITY          1      NONWHITE           12.5000     1.9081       40

Total Cases = 474
```

The entire sample has an average of 13.49 years of education. Males have more years of education than females—an average of 14.43 years compared with 12.37. White males have the highest level of education, almost 15 years, which is 2 years more than non-white males and approximately 2.5 years more than either group of females.

In Figure 7.3, the cases are further subdivided by their combined sex–race characteristics and by their initial job category. For each cell in the table, the average years of education, the standard deviation, and number of cases are displayed. White males have the highest average years of education in all job categories except MBA trainees, where the single minority male MBA trainee has 19 years of education. From this table, it does not appear that females and minorities are overeducated when compared to white males in similar job categories. However, it is important to note that group means provide information about a particular class of employees. While discrimination may not exist for a class as a whole, some individuals within that class may be victims (or beneficiaries) of discrimination.

Figure 7.3 Education by sex–race and job category

```
- - Description of Subpopulations - -

Summaries of       EDLEVEL       EDUCATIONAL LEVEL
By levels of       JOBCAT        EMPLOYMENT CATEGORY
                   SEXRACE       SEX & RACE CLASSIFICATION

Variable          Value   Label                      Mean      Std Dev    Cases

For Entire Population                              13.4916     2.8848      474

JOBCAT              1     CLERICAL                 12.7753     2.5621      227
  SEXRACE           1     WHITE MALES              13.8667     2.3035       75
  SEXRACE           2     MINORITY MALES           13.7714     2.3147       35
  SEXRACE           3     WHITE FEMALES            11.4588     2.4327       85
  SEXRACE           4     MINORITY FEMALES         12.6250     2.1213       32

JOBCAT              2     OFFICE TRAINEE           13.0221     1.8875      136
  SEXRACE           1     WHITE MALES              13.8857     1.4095       35
  SEXRACE           2     MINORITY MALES           12.5833     2.6097       12
  SEXRACE           3     WHITE FEMALES            12.8148     1.9307       81
  SEXRACE           4     MINORITY FEMALES         12.0000      .0000        8

JOBCAT              3     SECURITY OFFICER         10.1852     2.2194       27
  SEXRACE           1     WHITE MALES              10.2857     2.0542       14
  SEXRACE           2     MINORITY MALES           10.0769     2.4651       13

JOBCAT              4     COLLEGE TRAINEE          17.0000     1.2845       41
  SEXRACE           1     WHITE MALES              17.2121     1.3407       33
  SEXRACE           2     MINORITY MALES           17.0000       .            1
  SEXRACE           3     WHITE FEMALES            16.0000      .0000        7

JOBCAT              5     EXEMPT EMPLOYEE          17.2813     1.9713       32
  SEXRACE           1     WHITE MALES              17.6071     1.7709       28
  SEXRACE           2     MINORITY MALES           14.0000     2.8284        2
  SEXRACE           3     WHITE FEMALES            16.0000      .0000        2

JOBCAT              6     MBA TRAINEE              18.0000     1.4142        5
  SEXRACE           1     WHITE MALES              18.3333     1.1547        3
  SEXRACE           2     MINORITY MALES           19.0000       .            1
  SEXRACE           3     WHITE FEMALES            16.0000       .            1

JOBCAT              7     TECHNICAL                18.1667     1.4720        6
  SEXRACE           1     WHITE MALES              18.1667     1.4720        6

Total Cases = 474
```

Beginning Salaries

The average beginning salary for the 474 persons hired between 1969 and 1971 is $6,806. The distribution by the four sex–race categories is shown in Figure 7.4.

Figure 7.4 Beginning salary by sex–race

```
- - Description of Subpopulations - -

Summaries of       SALBEG        BEGINNING SALARY
By levels of       SEXRACE       SEX & RACE CLASSIFICATION

Variable          Value   Label                      Mean      Std Dev    Cases

For Entire Population                              6806.4346   3148.2553    474

SEXRACE             1     WHITE   MALES            8637.5258   3871.1017    194
SEXRACE             2     MINORITY MALES           6553.5000   2228.1436     64
SEXRACE             3     WHITE   FEMALES          5340.4886   1225.9605    176
SEXRACE             4     MINORITY FEMALES         4780.5000    771.4188     40

Total Cases = 474
```

White males have the highest beginning salaries—an average of $8,638—followed by minority males. Because males are in higher job categories than females, this difference is not surprising.

Figure 7.5 shows beginning salaries subdivided by race, sex, and job category. For most of the job categories, white males have higher beginning salaries than the other groups. There is a $1,400 salary difference between white males and white females in the clerical jobs and a $1,000 difference in the general office trainee classification. In the college trainee program, white males averaged over $3,000 more than white females. However, Figure 7.3 shows that white females in the college trainee program had only an undergraduate degree, while white males had an average of 17.2 years of schooling.

Figure 7.5 Beginning salary by sex–race and job category

```
                    - - Description of Subpopulations - -
Summaries of      SALBEG      BEGINNING SALARY
By levels of      JOBCAT      EMPLOYMENT CATEGORY
                  SEXRACE     SEX & RACE CLASSIFICATION


Variable            Value   Label                      Mean

For Entire Population                               6806.4346

JOBCAT                1     CLERICAL                 5733.9471
   SEXRACE            1     WHITE MALES              6553.4400
   SEXRACE            2     MINORITY MALES           6230.7429
   SEXRACE            3     WHITE FEMALES            5147.3176
   SEXRACE            4     MINORITY FEMALES         4828.1250

JOBCAT                2     OFFICE TRAINEE           5478.9706
   SEXRACE            1     WHITE MALES              6262.2857
   SEXRACE            2     MINORITY MALES           5610.0000
   SEXRACE            3     WHITE FEMALES            5208.8889
   SEXRACE            4     MINORITY FEMALES         4590.0000

JOBCAT                3     SECURITY OFFICER         6031.1111
   SEXRACE            1     WHITE MALES              6102.8571
   SEXRACE            2     MINORITY MALES           5953.8462

JOBCAT                4     COLLEGE TRAINEE          9956.4878
   SEXRACE            1     WHITE MALES             10467.6364
   SEXRACE            2     MINORITY MALES          11496.0000
   SEXRACE            3     WHITE FEMALES            7326.8571

JOBCAT                5     EXEMPT EMPLOYEE         13258.8750
   SEXRACE            1     WHITE MALES             13255.2857
   SEXRACE            2     MINORITY MALES          15570.0000
   SEXRACE            3     WHITE FEMALES           10998.0000

JOBCAT                6     MBA TRAINEE             12837.6000
   SEXRACE            1     WHITE MALES             14332.0000
   SEXRACE            2     MINORITY MALES          13992.0000
   SEXRACE            3     WHITE FEMALES            7200.0000

JOBCAT                7     TECHNICAL               19996.0000
   SEXRACE            1     WHITE MALES             19996.0000

Total Cases = 474
```

Introducing More Variables

The differences in mean beginning salaries between males and females are somewhat suspect. It is, however, unwise to conclude that salary discrimination exists, since several important variables, such as years of prior experience, have not been considered. It is necessary to **control** (or adjust statistically) for other relevant variables. **Cross-classifying** cases by the variables of interest and comparing salaries across the subgroups is one way of achieving control. However, as the number of variables increases, the number of cases in each cell rapidly diminishes, making statistically meaningful comparisons difficult. To circumvent these problems, you can use regression methods, which achieve control by specifying certain statistical relations that may describe what is happening. Regression methods are described in Chapter 15.

How to Obtain Subgroup Means

The Means procedure calculates subgroup means and related univariate statistics for dependent variables within categories of one or more independent variables. Optionally, you can also obtain one-way analysis of variance, eta, and a test of linearity.

The minimum specifications are:
- One numeric dependent variable.
- One numeric or short string independent variable.

To obtain subgroup means and related univariate statistics, from the menus choose:

Statistics
  Compare Means ▶
    Means...

This opens the Means dialog box, as shown in Figure 7.6.

Figure 7.6   Means dialog box

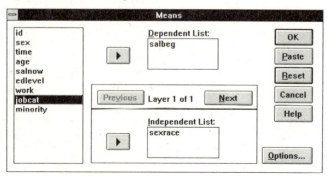

The numeric and short string variables in your data file appear on the source variable list. Select one or more numeric variables for the Dependent list, and select one or more numeric or short string variables for the Independent list. To obtain the default table of means and number of cases, click on OK. Subgroup means for each dependent variable are calculated for each category of each independent variable, as in Figure 7.4.

Optionally, you can specify additional **layers** of independent variables. Each layer further subdivides the sample. For example, Figure 7.2 was produced by using *edlevel* as the dependent variable, *sex* as the layer 1 independent variable, and *minority* as the layer 2 independent variable. Subgroup means of *edlevel* are calculated for each category of *minority* within each category of *sex*.

You can specify up to five layers of independent variables. Use Next and Previous to move between the independent variable lists for the different layers.

Means Options Dialog Box

To obtain additional univariate statistics, control the display of variable and value labels, or generate an analysis of variance for the first layer, click on Options... in the Means dialog box. This opens the Means Options dialog box, as shown in Figure 7.7.

Figure 7.7 Means Options dialog box

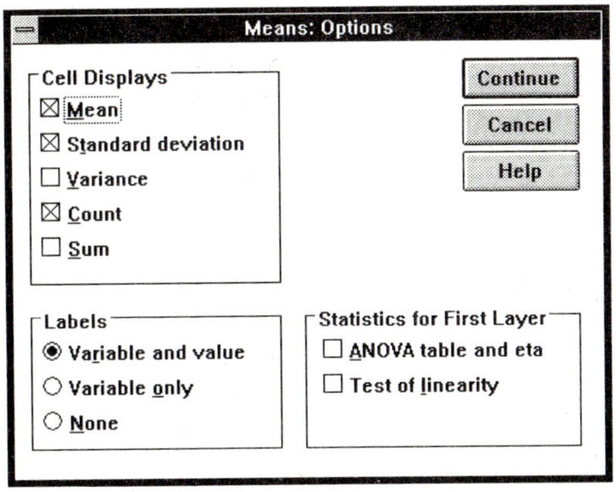

Cell Displays. You can choose one or more of the following subgroup statistics for the dependent variable(s) within each category (cell) of each independent variable:

❑ **Mean.** The arithmetic mean. Displayed by default.

❑ **Standard deviation.** A measure of how much observations vary from the mean, expressed in the same units as the data. Displayed by default.

- **Variance.** A measure of how much observations vary from the mean, equal to the square of the standard deviation. The units are the square of those of the variable itself.
- **Count.** The number of cases in each subgroup. Displayed by default.
- **Sum.** The sum of all the values in each subgroup.

Labels. You can choose one of the following alternatives:
- **Variable and value.** Displays variable and value labels. This is the default.
- **Variable only.** Displays variable labels but suppresses value labels.
- **None.** Suppresses both variable and value labels.

Statistics for First Layer. For subgroups based on categories of the independent variables in the first layer only, you can choose one or more of the following additional statistics:
- **ANOVA table and eta.** Displays a one-way analysis-of-variance table and calculates eta and eta^2 for each independent variable in the first layer.
- **Test of linearity.** Calculates the sums of squares, degrees of freedom, and mean square associated with linear and nonlinear components, as well as the F ratio, R, and R^2. Linearity is not calculated if the independent variable is a short string.

Additional Features Available with Command Syntax

You can customize the Means procedure if you paste your selections into a syntax window and edit the resulting MEANS command syntax. (For information on syntax windows, see the *SPSS Base System User's Guide, Part 1*.) An additional feature is the option to generate output in crosstabular format (with the CROSSBREAK subcommand). See the *SPSS Base System Syntax Reference Guide* for complete MEANS command syntax.

8 Multiple Response Analysis

Introduction to Multiple Response Data

The example in this section illustrates the use of multiple response items in a market research survey. The data in these tables are fictitious and should not be interpreted as real.

An airline might survey passengers flying a particular route to evaluate competing carriers. In this example, American Airlines wants to know about its passengers' use of other airlines on the Chicago–New York route and the relative importance of schedule and service in selecting an airline. The flight attendant hands each passenger a brief questionnaire upon boarding similar to the one shown in Figure 8.1. The first question is a multiple response question because the passenger can circle more than one response. However, this question cannot be coded directly because an SPSS variable can have only one value for each case. You must use several variables to map responses to the question. There are two ways to do this. One is to define a variable corresponding to each of the choices (for example, American, United, TWA, Eastern, and Other). If the passenger circles United, the variable *united* is assigned a code of 1—otherwise, 0. This is the **multiple dichotomy method** of mapping variables.

Figure 8.1 An in-flight questionnaire

```
Circle all airlines that you have flown at least one time
in the last six months on this route:


   American   United   TWA   Eastern   Other:_____


Which is more important in selecting a flight?
   Schedule              Service
(Circle only one.)


Thank you for your cooperation.
```

The other way to map the responses is the **multiple category method**, in which you estimate the maximum number of possible responses to the question and set up the same number of variables, with codes used to specify the airline flown. By perusing a sample of the questionnaires, you might discover that no user has flown more than 3 different airlines on this route in the last six months. Further, you find that due to the deregulation of airlines, 10 other airlines are named in the *Other* category. Using the multiple response method, you would define 3 variables, coded as 1 = *american*, 2 = *united*, 3 = *twa*, 4 = *eastern*, 5 = *republic*, 6 = *usair*, and so on. If a given passenger circles American and TWA, the first variable has a code of 1, the second has a code of 3, and the third has some missing-value code. Another passenger might have circled American and entered USAir. Thus, the first variable has a code of 1, the second a code of 6, and the third a missing-value code. If you use the multiple dichotomy method, on the other hand, you end up with 14 separate variables. Although either method of mapping is feasible for this survey, the method you choose depends on the distribution of responses.

Set Definition

Each SPSS variable created from the survey question is an elementary variable. To analyze a multiple response item, you must combine the variables into one of two types of multiple response sets: a multiple dichotomy set or a multiple category set. For example, if the airline survey asked about only three airlines (American, United, and TWA) and you used dichotomous variables to account for multiple responses, the separate frequency tables would resemble Table 8.1. When you define a **multiple dichotomy set**, each of the three variables in the set becomes a category of the group variable. The counted values represent the *Have flown* category of each elementary variable. Table 8.2 shows the frequencies for this multiple dichotomy set. The 75 people using American Airlines are the 75 cases with code 1 for the variable representing American Airlines in Table 8.1. Because some people circled more than one response, 120 responses are recorded for 100 respondents.

Table 8.1 Dichotomous variables tabulated separately

American

Category Label	Code	Frequency	Relative Frequency
Have flown	1	75	75.0
Have not flown	0	25	25.0
	Total	100	100.0

United

Category Label	Code	Frequency	Relative Frequency
Have flown	1	30	30.0
Have not flown	0	70	70.0
	Total	100	100.0

TWA

Category Label	Code	Frequency	Relative Frequency
Have flown	1	15	15.0
Have not flown	0	85	85.0
	Total	100	100.0

Table 8.2 Dichotomous variables tabulated as a group

Airlines

Variable	Frequency	Relative Frequency
American	75	62.5
United	30	25.0
TWA	15	12.5
Total	120	100.0

If you discover that no respondent mentioned more than two airlines, you could create two variables, each having three codes, one for each airline. The frequency tables for these elementary variables would resemble Table 8.3. When you define a **multiple category set**, the values are tabulated by adding the same codes in the elementary variables together. The resulting set of values is the same as those for each of the elementary variables. Table 8.4 shows the frequencies for this multiple category set. For example, the 30 responses for United are the sum of the 25 United responses for airline 1 and the five United responses for airline 2.

Table 8.3 Multiple response items tabulated separately

Airline 1

Category Label	Code	Frequency	Relative Frequency
American	1	75	75.0
United	2	25	25.0
	Total	100	100.0

Airline 2

Category Label	Code	Frequency	Relative Frequency
United	2	5	5.0
TWA	3	15	15.0
Missing	99	80	80.0
	Total	100	100.0

Table 8.4 Multiple response items tabulated as a group

Airlines

Category Label	Code	Frequency	Relative Frequency
American	1	75	62.5
United	2	30	25.0
TWA	3	15	12.5
	Total	120	100.0

Crosstabulations

Both multiple dichotomy and multiple category sets can be crosstabulated with other variables in the SPSS Multiple Response Crosstabs procedure. In the airline passenger survey, the airline choices can be crosstabulated with the question asking why people chose different airlines. If you have organized the first question into dichotomies as in Table 8.1, the three crosstabulations of the dichotomous variables with the schedule/service question would resemble Figure 8.2. If you had chosen the multiple category set method and created two variables, the two crosstabulations would resemble Figure 8.3 (cases with missing values are omitted from the table for airline 2). With either method, the crosstabulation of the elementary variable and the group variable would resemble Figure 8.4. Each row in Figure 8.4 represents the *Have flown* information for the three dichotomous variables. Like codes are added together for the multiple category set. For example, 21 respondents have flown United and think schedule is the most important consideration in selecting a flight. The 21 cases are a combination of 20 people who flew

United as airline 1 and circled *Schedule* plus one person who flew United as airline 2 and circled *Schedule*.

Figure 8.2 Dichotomous variables crosstabulated separately

```
   AMERICAN
by SELECT
```

	Count	SELECT Schedule 0	Service 1	Row Total
AMERICAN				
Have not flown	0	20	5	25 25.0
Have flown	1	41	34	75 75.0
Column Total		61 61.0	39 39.0	100 100.0

```
   UNITED
by SELECT
```

	Count	SELECT Schedule 0	Service 1	Row Total
UNITED				
Have not flown	0	40	30	70 70.0
Have flown	1	21	9	30 30.0
Column Total		61 61.0	39 39.0	100 100.0

```
   TWA
by SELECT
```

	Count	SELECT Schedule 0	Service 1	Row Total
TWA				
Have not flown	0	53	32	85 85.0
Have flown	1	8	7	15 15.0
Column Total		61 61.0	39 39.0	100 100.0

Figure 8.3 Multiple response variables crosstabulated separately

```
    AIRLINE1
 by SELECT
```

	Count	SELECT Schedule Service		Row Total
		0	1	
AIRLINE1 American	1	41	34	75 75.0
United	2	20	5	25 25.0
Column Total		61 61.0	39 39.0	100 100.0

```
    AIRLINE2
 by SELECT
```

	Count	SELECT Schedule Service		Row Total
		0	1	
AIRLINE2 United	2	1	4	5 25.0
TWA	3	8	7	15 75.0
Column Total		9 45.0	11 55.0	20 100.0

Figure 8.4 A group crosstabulated

```
    AIRLINES (group)
 by SELECT
```

	Count	SELECT Schedule Service		Row Total
		0	1	
AIRLINES American	1	41	34	75 62.5
United	2	21	9	30 25.0
TWA	3	8	7	15 12.5
Column Total		70 58.3	50 41.7	120 100.0

Analyzing Multiple Response Data

Two procedures are available for analyzing multiple dichotomy and multiple category sets (see "Introduction to Multiple Response Data" on p. 137). The Multiple Response Frequencies procedure displays frequency tables. The Multiple Response Crosstabs procedure displays two- and three-dimensional crosstabulations. Before using either procedure, you must first define your multiple response sets.

How to Define Multiple Response Sets

The Define Multiple Response Sets procedure groups elementary variables into multiple dichotomy and multiple category sets, for which you can obtain frequency tables and crosstabulations.

The minimum specifications are:
- Two or more numeric variables.
- Value(s) to be counted.
- A name for the multiple response set.

To define one or more multiple response sets, from the menus choose:

Statistics
 Multiple Response ▶
  Define Sets...

This opens the Define Multiple Response Sets dialog box, as shown in Figure 8.5.

Figure 8.5 Define Multiple Response Sets dialog box

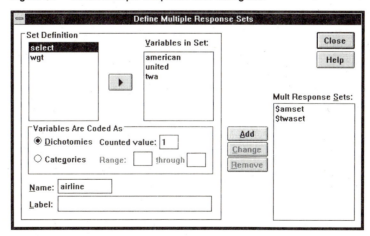

The numeric variables in your data file appear on the source list. To define a multiple response set, select two or more variables, indicate how variables are coded, and supply a set name; then click on **Add** to add the multiple response set to the list of defined sets. You can use the same variables in more than one set. After you define each set, all selected variables move back to the source variable list.

Variables Are Coded As. You can choose one of the following alternatives:

- **Dichotomies**. Elementary variables having two categories. This is the default. Select this item to create a multiple dichotomy set. Enter an integer value for **Counted** value. Each variable having at least one occurrence of the counted value becomes a category of the multiple dichotomy set.

- **Categories**. Elementary variables having more than two categories. Select this item to create a multiple category set having the same range of values as the component variables. Enter integer values for the minimum and maximum values of the range for categories of the multiple category set. SPSS totals each distinct integer value in the inclusive range across all component variables. Empty categories are not tabulated.

Name. The name for the multiple response set. Enter up to seven characters for the name. SPSS prefixes a dollar sign ($) to the name you assign. You cannot use the following reserved names: *casenum*, *sysmis*, *jdate*, *date*, *time*, *length*, and *width*. The name of the multiple response set exists only for use in multiple response procedures. You cannot refer to multiple response set names in other procedures.

Label. Enter an optional descriptive variable label for the multiple response set. The label can be up to 40 characters long.

You can define up to 20 multiple response sets. Each set must have a unique name. To remove a set, highlight it on the list of multiple response sets and click on **Remove**. To change a set, highlight it on the list, modify any set definition characteristics, and click on **Change**.

How to Obtain Multiple Response Frequencies

The Multiple Response Frequencies procedure produces frequency tables for multiple response sets.

The minimum specification is one or more defined multiple response sets.

To obtain multiple response frequencies for defined multiple response sets, you must first define one or more multiple response sets (see "How to Define Multiple Response Sets" on p. 143). Then, from the menus choose:

Statistics
  Multiple Response ▶
    Frequencies...

This opens the Multiple Response Frequencies dialog box, as shown in Figure 8.6.

Figure 8.6  Multiple Response Frequencies dialog box

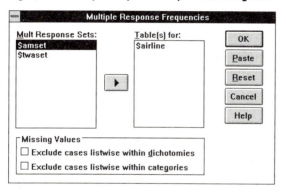

The currently defined multiple response sets appear on the source list. Select one or more sets for frequency tables. Click on **OK** to get the default frequency tables showing counts and percentages. Cases with missing values are excluded on a table-by-table basis.

For multiple dichotomy sets, category names shown in the output come from variable labels defined for elementary variables in the group. If variable labels are not defined, variable names are used as labels. For multiple category sets, category labels come from the value labels of the first variable in the group. If categories missing for the first variable are present for other variables in the group, define a value label for the missing categories.

Missing Values. You can choose one or both of the following:

❑ **Exclude cases listwise within dichotomies**. Excludes cases with missing values for any variable from the tabulation of the multiple dichotomy set. This applies only to multiple response sets defined as dichotomy sets. By default, a case is considered missing for a multiple dichotomy set if none of its component variables contains the counted value. Cases with missing values for some but not all variables are included in tabulations of the group if at least one variable contains the counted value.

❑ **Exclude cases listwise within categories**. Excludes cases with missing values for any variable from tabulation of the multiple category set. This applies only to multiple response sets defined as category sets. By default, a case is considered missing for a multiple category set only if none of its components has valid values within the defined range.

Additional Features Available with Command Syntax

You can customize your multiple response frequencies if you paste your selections into a syntax window and edit the resulting MULT RESPONSE command syntax. (For information on syntax windows, see the *SPSS Base System User's Guide, Part 1*.) Additional features include output format options such as suppression of value labels (with the FORMAT subcommand). See the *SPSS Base System Syntax Reference Guide* for complete MULT RESPONSE command syntax.

How to Crosstabulate Multiple Response Sets

The Multiple Response Crosstabs procedure crosstabulates defined multiple response sets, elementary variables, or a combination. You can also obtain cell percentages based on cases or responses, modify the handling of missing values, or get paired crosstabulations.

The minimum specifications are:

- One numeric variable or multiple response set for each dimension of the crosstabulation.
- Category ranges for any elementary variables.

To obtain crosstabulation tables for multiple response sets, you must first define one or more multiple response sets (see "How to Define Multiple Response Sets" on p. 143). Then, from the menus choose:

Statistics
 Multiple Response ▶
  Crosstabs...

This opens the Multiple Response Crosstabs dialog box, as shown in Figure 8.7.

Figure 8.7 Multiple Response Crosstabs dialog box

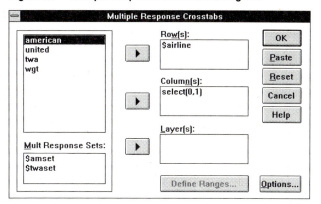

The numeric elementary variables in your data file appear on the source list. The currently defined multiple response sets appear on the list of multiple response sets. Select row and column items for the crosstabulation. A table is produced for each combination of row and column items.

After defining the value ranges of any elementary variables (see "Define Value Ranges," below), click on **OK** to get the default tables displaying cell counts. Cases with missing values are excluded on a table-by-table basis.

For multiple dichotomy sets, category names shown in the output come from variable labels defined for elementary variables in the group. If variable labels are not defined, variable names are used as labels. For multiple category sets, category labels come from the value labels of the first variable in the group. If categories missing for the first variable are present for other variables in the group, define a value label for the missing categories. SPSS displays category labels for columns on three lines, with up to eight characters per line. To avoid splitting words, you can reverse row and column items or redefine labels.

Optionally, you can obtain a two-way crosstabulation for each category of a control variable or multiple response set. Select one or more items for the Layer(s) list.

Define Value Ranges

Value ranges must be defined for any elementary variables in the crosstabulation. To define value ranges for an elementary variable, highlight the variable on the Row(s), Column(s), or Layer(s) list and click on **Define Ranges...** in the Multiple Response

Crosstabs dialog box. This opens the Multiple Response Crosstabs Define Variable Ranges dialog box, as shown in Figure 8.8.

Figure 8.8 Multiple Response Crosstabs Define Variable Ranges dialog box

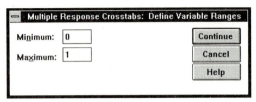

Enter integer minimum and maximum category values that you want to tabulate. Categories outside the range are excluded from analysis. Values within the inclusive range are assumed to be integers (non-integers are truncated).

Options

To obtain cell percentages, control the computation of percentages, modify the handling of missing values, or get a paired crosstabulation, click on Options... in the Multiple Response Crosstabs dialog box. This opens the Multiple Response Crosstabs Options dialog box, as shown in Figure 8.9.

Figure 8.9 Multiple Response Crosstabs Options dialog box

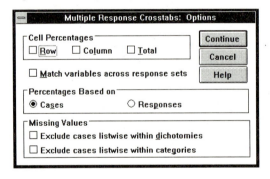

Cell Percentages. Cell counts are always displayed. You can also choose one or more of the following:

❑ **Row.** Displays row percentages.

❑ **Column.** Displays column percentages.

❑ **Total.** Displays two-way table total percentages.

Percentages Based on. You can choose one of the following alternatives:

- **Cases**. Bases cell percentages on cases, or respondents. This is the default. This item is not available if you select matching of variables across multiple category sets.

- **Responses**. Bases cell percentages on responses. For multiple dichotomy sets, the number of responses is equal to the number of counted values across cases. For multiple category sets, the number of responses is the number of values in the defined range (see "Define Value Ranges" on p. 147).

Missing Values. You can choose one or both of the following:

- **Exclude cases listwise within dichotomies**. Excludes cases with missing values for any variable from the tabulation of the multiple dichotomy set. This applies only to multiple response sets defined as dichotomy sets. By default, a case is considered missing for a multiple dichotomy set only if none of its elementary variables contains the counted value.

- **Exclude cases listwise within categories**. Excludes cases with missing values for any component variable from tabulation of the multiple category set. This applies only to multiple response sets defined as category sets. By default, a case is considered missing for a multiple category set only if none of its elementary variables has valid values falling within the defined range.

By default, when crosstabulating two multiple category sets, SPSS tabulates each variable in the first group with each variable in the second group and sums the counts for each cell. So, some responses can appear more than once in a table. You can choose the following option:

- **Match variables across response sets.** Pairs the first variable in the first group with the first variable in the second group, the second variable in the first group with the second variable in the second group, etc. If you select this option, SPSS bases cell percentages on responses rather than respondents. Pairing is not available for multiple dichotomy sets or elementary variables.

Additional Features Available with Command Syntax

You can customize your multiple response crosstabulation if you paste your selections into a syntax window and edit the resulting MULTIPLE RESPONSE command syntax. Additional features include:

- Crosstabulation tables with up to five dimensions (with the BY subcommand).
- Output formatting options, including suppression of value labels (with the FORMAT subcommand).

See the *SPSS Base System Syntax Reference Guide* for complete MULTIPLE RESPONSE command syntax.

9 One-Sample T Test

We are constantly bombarded by statistics which purport to describe us and our environment. We are told (World Almanac, 1994) that the "typical" American male has a life expectancy at birth of 72 years, while the "typical" female has a life expectancy of 79 years. Americans own 2 radios per person, three quarters of a television set, half a telephone. We've grown up knowing that the typical work week for full time employees is 40 hours. That's still the implicit standard by which we judge our work habits. Of course it's possible that "norms" such as the number of hours in the typical work week have changed with time, or were never really true.

In this chapter you'll test the hypothesis that the average work week for full time employees is 40 hours. You'll use data from the 1993 General Social Survey. The statistical technique that you'll use is called the one-sample *t* test. It's useful in many situations when you have a standard or norm and want to test whether it's reasonably to believe that the norm is true for the population from which your sample has been selected. The norm is a known value. It's not one you estimate from a sample. For example, if you want to test whether 16 oz. cereal boxes really weigh 16 ounces, the norm is 16 ounces. It's the claim made by the manufacturer. You shouldn't use the one-sample *t* test if you have two samples and want to test whether they are from populations with the same mean. For example, if you want to test whether men and women have the same average work week you should use the two sample *t* test described in Chapter 10 or one of the nonparametric tests described in Chapter 17. If you have more than two groups whose means you want to compare you may want to use the one-way analysis of variance described in Chapter 11 or the Kruskal-Wallis test described in Chapter 17.

Summary Statistics

Each year staff from the General Social Survey interview a representative sample of the US adult population. They ask people a wide variety of questions: are they happy? How often do they pray? How satisfied are they with their lives? Their jobs? They also obtain more mundane information such as a person's status in the labor force, and the number of hours worked the previous week.

Figure 9.1 contains descriptive information on the number of hours worked last week for the 741 people employed full time. You see that the average work week is 46.29 hours. The standard deviation is 11.27 hours. It's also always a good idea to examine a histogram or stem and leaf plot of the data values. From these you can see whether there are outlying observations which may affect the results. You'll also get an idea of what the distribution of values looks like. Is it symmetric? Does it have a single peak? Is it approximately normal? These are important considerations for choosing an appropriate statistical technique for analyzing the data.

Figure 9.1   Summary statistics

Variable		Number of Cases	Mean	SD	SE of Mean
HRS1	NUMBER OF HOURS WORK	741	46.2888	11.269	.414

Based on these summary statistics in Figure 9.1 what can you conclude about the 40 hour work week? It's certainly true that the 741 full-time workers in the sample do not work an average of 40 hours a week. Their average work week is 6.3 hours longer than the mythical 40 hours. You know that for a fact. You will certainly be correct if you conclude that your sample of 741 full time workers does not have an average work week of 40 hours.

But is that really the conclusion that you want to draw? There's nothing special about the 741 people in the sample. They just happened to be randomly selected for inclusion in the General Social Survey. What is noteworthy about them is that they have been randomly selected from the entire US adult population and that's the population about which you want to draw conclusions. You want to be able to say that on the basis of the results obtained from the sample of 741 people you believe (or do not believe) the statement that the average full time worker in the US population works a forty-hour work week.

Results from Samples

If you took another random sample of 741 people from the US adult population, do you think that their average work week would be exactly the same as that of the first sample? Of course not. Different samples from the same population give different results. To get some idea of how much sample means from the same sample vary, look at Figure 9.2, a histogram of 500 sample means. Each mean is based on a random sample of 741 cases from a normal population with a mean of 40 and a standard deviation of 11. This is what you would expect to see if the average work week in the US population is 40 hours, with a standard deviation of 11, and you take a random sample of 741 people, calculate their mean hours worked, and then repeat the same procedure 500 times.

You see that the distribution of sample means in Figure 9.2 clusters around 40, the population value. As you expect, the means of all the samples are not exactly 40. That's because the results you obtain from a random sample of the population are not identical to what you would obtain if you had values for the entire population. You see from Figure 9.2 that about half of the samples have average work weeks greater than 40, and half have average work weeks less than 40. The spread of possible sample values depends on how much variability there is in the population from which you select the sample, and also on how large the sample is. For example, if everyone in the population works between 39 and 41 hours per week, sample means will vary little. However, if the hours worked in the population vary from 10 to 90 hours per week, sample means will vary quite a bit. Similarly, if you take 10 cases from a population you expect that the sample results will vary more than if you take 100 cases from the same population. The larger the sample size, the less the sample means from the same population vary.

Figure 9.2   Histogram of 500 sample means

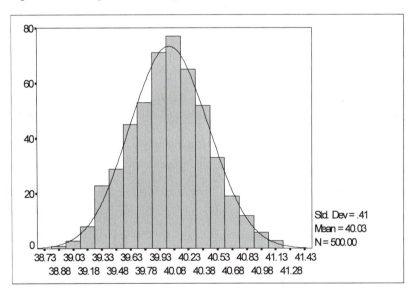

You can calculate how much sample means from the same population vary by dividing the population standard deviation by the square root of the sample size. This is called the standard error of the mean. The **standard error of the mean** is nothing more than the standard deviation of the distribution of all possible means from the same population. Look at Figure 9.2 again. You see the distribution of 500 means. If you find the standard deviation of the 500 means you have an estimate of the standard error of the mean. Fortunately, you don't have to take all of those samples to calculate the standard error of the mean. All you need to know is the population standard deviation and the sample size. If you don't know what the real population standard deviation is you can use the sample standard deviation as an estimate. It's your best guess for the population value. Then you can estimate the standard error of the mean by dividing the sample standard deviation by the square root of the sample size. From Figure 9.3 you see that the estimated standard error of the mean for this example is

$$\frac{11.269}{\sqrt{741}} = 0.414 \qquad \text{Equation 9.1}$$

Are the Sample Results Unlikely?

If the distribution of sample means is normal—or if your sample size is sufficiently large—you can calculate the likelihood of obtaining various sample results. (In Chapter 10 you'll see that under many conditions the distribution of sample means is approximately normal, even if the sample isn't from a normal population.) For example, you know that 95% of the values in a normal distribution fall within plus or minus two standard deviations of the mean. Assuming that the true population mean is 40, and the standard error of the mean is 0.41, you expect approximately 95% of the sample means to be between 39.18 hours and 40.82 hours. Does your sample mean fall in this range? Not by a long shot. The observed sample mean of 46.29 is not only not in the interval, but (if you look at Figure 9.2) it doesn't even appear in the histogram. The observed sample mean is very different from those in Figure 9.2.

You can calculate a standard score for the observed mean by subtracting the observed sample mean from the population mean, and dividing by the standard deviation of the sample mean (which is what we have called the standard error of the mean). The standard score is 15.1. This tells you that your observed sample mean is more than 15 standard deviation units above the population value of 40. In a normal distribution 99% of the cases have standard scores between +2.58 and −2.58. A value of 15 is really off the scale. What can you conclude from all of this? You can conclude that it's unlikely that the observed sample mean is coming from a population with a mean value of 40. If the true mean is 40 in the population, it's very, very unlikely that you would observe a sample mean of 46.29 based on 741 cases.

Is it possible that the population mean is 40? Yes, it's possible, but as you've seen the likelihood is extremely small. To evaluate this likelihood you have to determine how often you would expect to obtain standard scores less than −15.1 or greater than 15.1.

The One-Sample T Test

You can use the One-Sample T Test procedure to test the hypothesis that your sample comes from a population with a specified mean.

Figure 9.3 shows the results from the one-sample t test. You specify the value of 40 for your *test value* since you want to test the hypothesis that your sample is coming from a population with a mean value of 40. You can see from the entry labeled *Mean Difference* that the difference between the sample mean and the hypothesized population value is 6.29 hours. The entry labeled *t-value* is the standard score for your observed mean. You calculate it by dividing the mean difference by the standard error of the mean.

Figure 9.3   One-Sample T Test results

```
One Sample t-test
```

Variable		Number of Cases	Mean	SD	SE of Mean
HRS1	NUMBER OF HOURS WORK	741	46.2888	11.269	.414

Test Value = 40

Mean Difference	95% CI Lower	Upper	t-value	df	2-Tail Sig
6.29	5.476	7.102	15.19	740	.000

The probability that you see a sample mean with a standard score of −15.1 or less or a standard score of +15.1 or more is shown in the entry labeled *2-Tail Sig*. This probability is called the observed significance level. The modifier "2-Tail" says that the probability is calculated based on differences in both directions. That is, the probability of a standard score less than −15.1 and the probability of a standard score greater than 15.1 are combined. (See Chapter 10 for a discussion of "one-tail" versus "two-tail" tests.) The value 0.000 is displayed if the observed significance level is less than 0.0005. From the observed significance level in Figure 9.3 you know the chances are less than 5 in 10,000 (0.0005) that you would see a discrepancy at least as large as the one you've observed, if in fact the population value is 40. A commonly used rule is that you reject the hypothesis that your sample comes from a population with the specified mean, if the observed significance level for the t value is less than 0.05.

The observed significance level is calculated from the t distribution. For sample sizes larger than 30, the t distribution looks very much like the normal distribution. The reason the t distribution is used instead of the normal distribution is that the standard deviation of the population is not known, but is estimated from the sample. That introduces additional variability into the standard score. If you know the population standard deviation, you know the true value for the standard error of the mean and you can calculate an exact standard score. If you estimate the population standard deviation, then the standard score depends on how close your sample standard deviation is to the population standard deviation. For large sample sizes the effect of estimating the standard deviation is negligible. For small sample sizes it makes a difference. A *t* value of 2 has a two tailed observed significance level of 0.10 if there are only 6 cases in your sample. The same *t* value has an observed significance level of 0.05 if there are 60 cases in the sample. That's why the *t* distribution that's used for calculating the observed significance level is indexed by what are called the degrees of freedom. For this example, the degrees of freedom, labeled *df* in Figure 9.3, are just the number of cases in the sample minus 1.

Confidence Intervals

When you calculate the mean difference between the sample mean and the hypothetical population value you don't expect the result to be exactly 0. In fact, the differences will have a distribution, just as the sample means do. The distribution of sample differences is also approximately normal, and it has the same standard deviation as the distribution of sample means. That's because all you've done is to subtract the hypothetical population value from all of the sample means. Adding or subtracting the same number from the values of a variable for all of the cases doesn't change the standard deviation. It just changes the mean. We'll use this fact to calculate what's called a **confidence interval** for the difference.

Based on the observed significance level you've rejected the notion that the average work week for full time workers is 40 hours. But you now probably want to know how much longer or shorter than 40 hours the true work week is. Based on the evidence at hand, your best guess is certainly the difference that you've observed, 6.29 hours. However it's most unlikely that you would obtain the same mean difference if you asked every eligible person in the US for the number of hours they worked last week. The mean difference you observe depends on the people actually included in your sample.

It would be helpful if you could identify a range of possible values for the true population difference. Then you would have a reasonable idea of how large the difference might be. That's what a confidence interval does. It provides a range of values, which (with a designated likelihood) includes the true population value. A confidence interval is based on the fact that you know what percentage of values fall where in a normal distribution. For example, you know that 95% of the sample means should be within about 2 standard errors (1.96 to be exact) of the population mean. That means that if you take a sample mean, add and subtract from it 2 times the standard error, 95% of the time the resulting interval should include the unknown population value. For small sample sizes instead of using the cutoff of 2 (or 1.96) from the normal distribution, you use the corresponding value from the *t* distribution.

From Figure 9.33, the 95% confidence interval for the population mean difference is from 5.48 to 7.10 hours. That means that the observed sample results are compatible with the true population difference being as small as 5.48 hours or as large as 7.10 hours. You still don't know what the true difference from 40 hours is, but at least you have an idea of what it might reasonably be. The shorter the length of the confidence interval, the more informative it is. For example, if your confidence interval for the difference went from 2 to 10 hours, you'd much a much broader range of plausible values for the difference. You couldn't pinpoint the difference as well as you can with the first interval.

A confidence interval is based on the idea of what happens in the long run. For example, you don't know whether the confidence interval you just computed does or does not include the true population difference. All you know is that when you compute 95% confidence intervals, 95% of them include the unknown population value. A particular interval either includes or does or does not include the unknown population value. Unfortunately you don't know whether your interval is one of the unlucky 5% which don't include the true population value. But you're 95% "confident" that it does.

Note that the 95% confidence interval you computed does not include the value of 0. That's because whenever your observed significance level is less than 0.05 (indicating that your observed results are not compatible with the population value) the corresponding 95% confidence interval for the population difference will not include 0. Similarly, if the observed significance level is greater than 0.05 (indicating that your results are compatible with the hypothesized value) the corresponding 95% confidence interval for the difference will include 0.

You can compute confidence intervals for many different types of statistics. For example, you can compute a confidence interval for the population value for the average work week. All you do is add and subtract two times the standard error of the mean from the observed sample mean. Since the observed sample mean is 46.29 and 1.96 times the standard error is 0.81, the 95% confidence interval is from 45.48 to 47.10 hours. That means that you're reasonably confident that the true number of hours full time employees work is between 45.48 and 47.10 (You can also arrive at this answer by adding 40 to the confidence interval for the mean difference, since the mean difference and the average work week have the same standard error.)

Hypothesis Testing

In this chapter you used the one-sample t test to test whether it appears plausible that your sample comes from a population with a known mean. You did this by seeing how likely or unlikely your observed results are if in fact your sample is from a population with the specified mean. If on the basis of the t statistic you found your sample results to be incompatible with the population value, you concluded that your sample was probably not from a population with the specified mean. On the other hand, if your sample results didn't appear unlikely, you did not dispute that they might come from a population with the specified mean. Chapter 10 formalizes many of the ideas introduced in this chapter. You should read that to learn more about testing a hypothesis.

How to Obtain a One-Sample T Test

The One-Sample T Test procedure computes Student's *t* statistic for testing the significance of a difference between the mean of a sample and a constant value.

The minimum specifications are:
- One or more numeric test variables.
- A test value.

To obtain a one-sample *t* test, from the menus choose:

Statistics
  Compare Means ▶
    One-Sample T Test...

This opens the One-Sample T Test dialog box, as shown in Figure 9.4.

Figure 9.4 One-Sample T Test dialog box

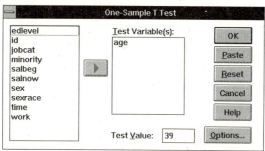

The numeric variables in your data file appear in the source list. Select one or more numeric test variables. Each test variable produces one *t* test. Enter a test value and click on **OK** to obtain the default one-sample *t* test with a two-tailed probability and a 95% confidence interval. To obtain a one-tailed probability, divide the *t* probability by 2.

One-Sample T Test Options

To change confidence interval bounds or control the handling of cases with missing values, click on **Options** in the One-Sample T Test dialog box. This opens the One-Sample T Test Options dialog box, as shown in Figure 9.5.

Figure 9.5 One-Sample T Test Options dialog box

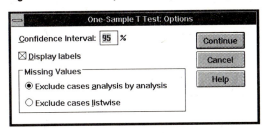

Confidence Interval. A 95% confidence interval for the difference in means is displayed by default. Optionally, you can request a different confidence level by entering a value between 1 and 99. For example, to obtain a 99% confidence interval, enter 99.

Missing Values. You can choose one of the following:

- **Exclude cases analysis-by-analysis.** Cases with missing values for either the grouping variable or the test variable are excluded from the analysis of that variable. This is the default.

- **Exclude cases listwise.** Cases with missing values for any test variable are excluded from all analyses.

You can also choose the following display option:

- **Display labels.** By default, any variable labels are displayed in the output. To suppress labels, deselect this option.

10 Testing Hypotheses about Differences in Means

Would you buy a disposable raincoat, vegetables in pop-top cans, or investment counseling via closed-circuit television? These products and 17 others were described in questionnaires administered to 100 married couples (Davis & Ragsdale, 1983). Respondents were asked to rate on a scale of 1 (definitely want to buy) to 7 (definitely do not want to buy) their likelihood of buying the product. Of the 100 couples, 50 received questionnaires with pictures of the products and 50 received questionnaires without pictures. In this chapter, we will examine whether pictures affect consumer preferences and whether husbands' and wives' responses differ.

Testing Hypotheses

The first part of the table in Figure 10.1 contains basic descriptive statistics for the buying scores of couples receiving questionnaires with and without pictures. A couple's buying score is simply the sum of all ratings assigned to products by the husband and wife individually. Low scores indicate buyers, while high scores indicate reluctance to buy. The 50 couples who received questionnaires without pictures (group 1) had a mean score of 168, while the 48 couples who received forms with pictures had an average score of 159. (Two couples did not complete the questionnaire and are not included in the analysis.) The standard deviations show that scores for the second group were somewhat more variable than those for the first.

If you are willing to restrict the conclusions to the 98 couples included in the study, it is safe to say that couples who received forms with pictures indicated a greater willingness to purchase the products than couples who received forms without pictures. However, this statement is not very satisfying. What is needed is some type of statement about the effect of the two questionnaire types for all couples—or at least some larger group of couples—not just those actually studied.

Figure 10.1 Family buying scores by questionnaire type

```
                        Number
    Variable            of Cases    Mean        SD          SE of Mean

    FAMSCORE    FAMILY BUYING SCORE

    NO PICTURES         50          168.0000    21.787      3.081
    PICTURES            48          159.0833    27.564      3.979


    Mean Difference = 8.9167

    Levene's Test for Equality of Variances:  F= 1.382   P= .243


           t-test for Equality of Means                    95%
    Variances  t-value   df      2-Tail Sig   SE of Diff   CI for Diff

    Equal      1.78      96      .078         5.008        (-1.027, 18.860)
    Unequal    1.77      89.43   .080         5.032        (-1.084, 18.918)
```

Samples and Populations

The totality of cases about which conclusions are desired is called the **population**, while the cases actually included in the study constitute the **sample**. The couples in this experiment can be considered a sample from the population of couples in the United States.

The field of statistics helps us draw inferences about populations based on observations obtained from **random samples**, or samples in which the characteristics and relationships of interest are independent of the probabilities of being included in the sample. The necessity of a good research design cannot be overemphasized. Unless precautions are taken to ensure that the sample is from the population of interest and that the cases are chosen and observed without bias, the results obtained from statistical analyses may be misleading. For example, if a sample contains only affluent suburban couples, conclusions about all couples may be unwarranted.

If measurements are obtained from an entire population, the population can be characterized by the various measures of central tendency, dispersion, and shape described in Chapter 4. The results describe the population exactly. If, however, you obtain information from a random sample—the usual case—the results serve as **estimates** of the unknown population values. Special notation is used to identify population values, termed **parameters**, and to distinguish them from sample values, termed **statistics**. The mean of a population is denoted by μ, and the variance by σ^2. The symbols $\bar{X}$ and S^2 are reserved for the mean and variance of samples.

Sampling Distributions

The observations actually included in a study are just one of many random samples that could have been selected from a population. For example, if the population consists of married couples in the United States, the number of different samples that could be chosen for inclusion in a study is mind-boggling. The estimated value of a population parameter depends on the particular sample chosen. Different samples usually produce different estimates.

Figure 10.2 is a histogram of 400 means produced by the SPSS Frequencies procedure. Each mean is calculated from a random sample of 25 observations from a population that has a normal distribution with a mean value of 0 and a standard deviation of 1. The estimated means are not all the same. Instead, they have a distribution. Most sample means are fairly close to 0, the population mean. The mean of the 400 means is 0, and the standard deviation of these means is 0.2. In fact, the distribution of the means appears approximately normal.

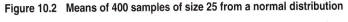

Figure 10.2   Means of 400 samples of size 25 from a normal distribution

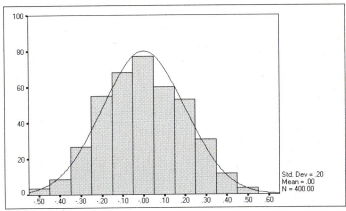

Although Figure 10.2 gives some idea of the appearance of the distribution of sample means of size 25 from a standard normal population, it is only an approximation since all possible samples of size 25 have not been taken. If the number of samples taken is increased to 1000, an even better picture of the distribution could be obtained. As the number of samples of a fixed size increases, the observed (or empirical) distribution of the means approaches the underlying or theoretical distribution.

The theoretical distribution of all possible values of a statistic obtained from a population is called the **sampling distribution** of the statistic. The mean of the sampling distribution is called the **expected value** of the statistic. The standard deviation is termed the **standard error**. The sampling distributions of most commonly used statistics calculated from random samples are tabulated and readily accessible. Knowing the sampling distribution of a statistic is very important for hypothesis testing, since from it you can calculate the probability of obtaining an observed sample value if a particular hypothesis is true. For example, from Figure 10.2, it appears quite unlikely that a sample mean based on a sample of size 25 from a standard normal distribution would be greater than 0.5 if the population mean were 0.

Sampling Distribution of the Mean

Since hypotheses about population means are often of interest, the sampling distribution of the mean is particularly important. If samples are taken from a normal population, the sampling distribution of the sample mean is also normal. As expected, the observed distribution of the 400 means in Figure 10.2 is approximately normal. The theoretical distribution of the sample mean, based on all possible samples of size 25, is exactly normal.

Even when samples are taken from a non-normal population, the distribution of the sample means will be approximately normal for sufficiently large samples. This is one reason for the importance of the normal distribution in statistical inference. Consider Figure 10.3, which shows a sample from a uniform distribution. In a uniform distribution, all values of a variable are equally likely; hence, the proportion of cases in each bin of the histogram is roughly the same.

Figure 10.3 Values from a uniform distribution

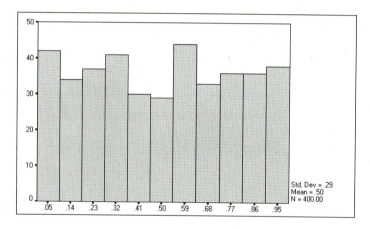

Figure 10.4 is a histogram of 400 means calculated from samples of size 25 from a uniform distribution. Note that the observed distribution is approximately normal even though the distribution from which the samples were taken is markedly non-normal.

Both the size of a sample and the shape of the distribution from which samples are taken affect the shape of the sampling distribution of the mean. If samples are small and come from distributions that are far from normal, the distribution of the means will not be even approximately normal. As the size of the sample increases, the sampling distribution of the mean will approach normality.

Figure 10.4 Distribution of 400 means from samples of size 25 from a uniform distribution

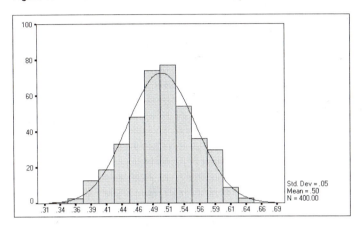

The mean of the theoretical sampling distribution of the means of samples of size N is μ, the population mean. The standard error, which is another name for the standard deviation of the sampling distribution of the mean, is

$$\sigma_{\bar{X}} = \frac{\sigma}{\sqrt{N}} \qquad \text{Equation 10.1}$$

where σ is the standard deviation of the population and N is the sample size.

The standard deviation of the observed sampling distribution of means in Figure 10.2 is 0.20. This is the same as the value of the standard error for the theoretical distribution, which, from the previous formula, is $1/5$, or 0.20.

Usually, the value of the standard error is unknown and is estimated from a single sample using

$$S_{\bar{X}} = \frac{S}{\sqrt{N}} \qquad \text{Equation 10.2}$$

where S is the *sample* standard deviation. The estimated standard error is displayed in the SPSS Frequencies procedure and is also part of the output shown in Figure 10.1. For example, for group 1 the estimated standard error of the mean is

$$\frac{21.787}{\sqrt{50}} = 3.081 \qquad \text{Equation 10.3}$$

This value is displayed in the column labeled *SE of Mean* in Figure 10.1.

The standard error of the mean depends on both the sample standard deviation and the sample size. For a fixed standard deviation, as the size of a sample increases, the standard error decreases. This is intuitively clear, since the more data are gathered, the more confident you can be that the sample mean is not too far from the population mean. Also, as the standard deviation of the observations decreases, the standard error decreases as well. Small standard deviations occur when observations are fairly homogeneous. In this case, means based on different samples should also not vary much.

The Two-Sample T Test

Consider again whether there is evidence that the type of form administered influences couples' buying decisions. The question is not whether the two sample means are equal, but whether the two population means are equal.

To test the hypothesis that, in the population, buying scores for the two questionnaire types are the same, the following statistic can be calculated:

$$t = \frac{\bar{X}_1 - \bar{X}_2}{\sqrt{\frac{S_1^2}{N_1} + \frac{S_2^2}{N_2}}}$$

Equation 10.4

where $\bar{X}_1$ is the sample mean of group 1, S_1^2 is the variance, and N_1 is the sample size.

Based on the sampling distribution of the above statistic, you can calculate the probability that a difference at least as large as the one observed would occur if the two population means (μ_1 and μ_2) are equal. This probability is called the **observed significance level**. If the observed significance level is small enough (usually less than 0.05, or 0.01), the hypothesis that the population means are equal is rejected.

The *t* value and its associated probability are given in Figure 10.1 in the row labeled *Unequal*. The *t* value is

$$t = \frac{168.0 - 159.08}{\sqrt{\frac{21.787^2}{50} + \frac{27.564^2}{48}}} = 1.77$$

Equation 10.5

If $\mu_1 = \mu_2$, the probability of observing a difference at least as large as the one in the sample is estimated to be about 0.08. Since this probability is greater than 0.05, the hypothesis that mean buying scores in the population are equal for the two types of forms is not rejected. The entry under *df* in Figure 10.1 is a function of the sample size in the two groups and is used together with the *t* value in establishing the observed significance level.

Another statistic based on the *t* distribution can be used to test the equality of means hypothesis. This statistic, known as the **pooled-variance t test**, is based on the assumption that the population variances in the two groups are equal and is obtained using a pooled estimate of that common variance. The test statistic is identical to the equation for t given previously except that the individual group variances are replaced by a pooled estimate, S_p^2. That is,

$$t = \frac{\bar{X}_1 - \bar{X}_2}{\sqrt{\dfrac{S_p^2}{N_1} + \dfrac{S_p^2}{N_2}}}$$

Equation 10.6

where S_p^2, the pooled variance, is a weighted average of the individual variances and is calculated as

$$S_p^2 = \frac{(N_1 - 1) S_1^2 + (N_2 - 1) S_2^2}{N_1 + N_2 - 2}$$

Equation 10.7

From the output in Figure 10.1, the pooled t test value for the study is 1.78. The degrees of freedom for the pooled t test are 96, the sum of the sample sizes in both groups minus 2. If the pooled-variance t test is used when the population variances are not equal, the probability level associated with the statistic may be in error. The amount of error depends on the inequality of the sample sizes and of the variances. However, using the separate-variance t value when the population variances are equal will usually result in an observed significance level somewhat larger than it should be. For large samples, the discrepancy between the two methods is small. In general, it is a good idea to use the separate-variance t test whenever you suspect that the variances are unequal.

Levene's test is used to test the hypothesis that the two population variances are equal. This test is less dependent on the assumption of normality than most tests of equality of variance. It is obtained by computing for each case the absolute difference from its group mean and then performing a one-way analysis of variance on these differences. In Figure 10.1, the value of the Levene statistic is 1.382. If the observed significance level for this test is small, the hypothesis that the population variances are equal is rejected and the separate-variance t test for means should be used. In this example, the significance level for the Levene statistic is large, and thus the pooled-variance t test is appropriate.

Significance Levels

The commonsense interpretation of a small observed significance level is straightforward: it appears unlikely that the two population means are equal. Of course, there is a possibility that the means are equal and the observed difference is due to chance. The observed significance level is the probability that a difference at least as large as the one observed would have arisen if the means were really equal.

When the observed significance level is too large to reject the equality hypothesis, the two population means may indeed be equal, or they may be unequal, but the difference cannot be detected. Failure to detect can be due to a true difference that is very small. For example, if a new cancer drug prolongs survival time by only one day when compared to the standard treatment, it is unlikely that such a difference will be detected, especially if survival times vary substantially and the additional day represents a small increment.

There are other reasons why true differences may not be found. If the sample sizes in the two groups are small or the variability large, even substantial differences may not be detected. Significant t values are obtained when the numerator of the t statistic is large compared to the denominator. The numerator is the difference between the sample means, and the denominator depends on the standard deviations and sample sizes of the two groups. For a given standard deviation, the larger the sample size, the smaller the denominator. Thus, a difference of a given magnitude may be significant if obtained with a sample size of 100 but not significant with a sample size of 25.

One-Tailed versus Two-Tailed Tests

A two-tailed test is used to detect a difference in means between two populations regardless of the direction of the difference. For example, in the study of buying scores presented in this chapter, we are interested in whether buying scores without pictures are larger *or* smaller than buying scores with pictures. In applications where you are interested in detecting a difference in one direction—such as whether a new drug is better than the current treatment—a so-called one-tailed test can be performed. The procedure is the same as for the two-tailed test, but the resulting probability value is divided by 2, adjusting for the fact that the equality hypothesis is rejected only when the difference between the two means is sufficiently large and in the direction of interest. In a two-tailed test, the equality hypothesis is rejected for large positive or negative values of the statistic.

What's the Difference?

It appears that the questionnaire type has no significant effect on couples' willingness to purchase products. Overall buying scores for the two conditions are similar. Pictures of the products do not appear to enhance their perceived desirability. In fact, the pictures actually appear to make several products somewhat less desirable. However, since the purpose of the questionnaires is to ascertain buying intent, including a picture of the actual product may help gauge true product response. Although the concept of disposable raincoats may be attractive, if they make the owner look like a walking trash bag, their appeal may diminish considerably.

Using Crosstabulation to Test Hypotheses

The SPSS Independent-Samples T Test procedure is used to test hypotheses about the equality of two means for variables measured on an interval or ratio scale. Crosstabulation and the Pearson chi-square statistic can be used to test hypotheses about a dichotomous variable, such as purchase of a particular product.

Figure 10.5 is an SPSS crosstabulation showing the number of husbands who would definitely want to buy vegetables in pop-top cans when shown a picture and when not shown a picture of the product (value 1 of variable *H2S*). The vegetables in pop-top cans were chosen by 6.0% of the husbands who were tempted with pictures and 16.0% of the husbands who were not shown pictures. The chi-square statistic provides a test of the hypothesis that the proportion of husbands selecting the vegetables in pop-top cans is the same for the picture and no-picture forms.

Figure 10.5 Preference of husbands for vegetables in pop-top cans

```
H2S  POP-TOP CANS HUSB SELF   by  VISUAL   PICTURE ACCOMPANIED QUESTION

                    VISUAL           Page 1 of 1
            Count
            Col Pct  NO PICTU PICTURES
                     RES                    Row
                         0        1       Total
H2S
          1              8        3         11
    DEFINITELY        16.0      6.0       11.0

          2             42       47         89
    VERY LIKELY       84.0     94.0       89.0

       Column           50       50        100
        Total         50.0     50.0      100.0

      Chi-Square                Value         DF       Significance
      ----------                -----        ----      ------------

Pearson                         2.55363        1         .11004
Continuity Correction           1.63432        1         .20111
Likelihood Ratio                2.63933        1         .10425
Mantel-Haenszel test for        2.52809        1         .11184
    linear association

Minimum Expected Frequency -    5.500
```

The probability of 0.11 associated with the Pearson chi-square in Figure 10.5 is the probability that a difference at least as large as the one observed would occur in the sample if in the population there were no difference in the selection of the product between the two formats. Since the probability is large, the hypothesis of no difference between the two formats is not rejected.

Independent versus Paired Samples

Several factors contribute to the observed differences in response between two groups. Part of the observed difference in scores between the picture and no-picture formats may be attributable to form type. Another component is due to differences between individuals. Not all couples have the same buying desires, so even if the type of form does not affect buying, differences between the two groups will probably be observed due to differences between the couples within the two groups.

One method of minimizing the influence of individual variation is to choose the two groups so that the couples within them are comparable on characteristics that can influence buying behavior, such as income, education, family size, and so forth.

It is sometimes possible to obtain pairs of subjects, such as twins, and assign one member of each pair to each of the two treatments. Another frequently used experimental design is to expose the same individual to both types of conditions. (In this design, care must be taken to ensure that the sequential administration of treatments does not influence response by providing practice, decreasing attention span, or affecting the second treatment in other ways.) In both designs, subject-to-subject variability has substantially less effect. These designs are called **paired-samples designs**, since for each subject there is a corresponding pair in the other group. In the second design, a person is paired with himself or herself. In an **independent-samples design**, there is no pairing of cases; all observations are independent.

Analysis of Paired Data

Although the interpretation of the significance of results from paired experiments is the same as those from the two independent samples discussed previously, the actual computations are different. For each pair of cases, the difference in the responses is calculated. The statistic used to test the hypothesis that the mean difference in the population is 0 is

$$t = \frac{\bar{D}}{S_D/\sqrt{N}} \qquad \text{Equation 10.8}$$

where $\bar{D}$ is the observed difference between the two means and S_D is the standard deviation of the differences of the paired observations. The sampling distribution of t, if the differences are normally distributed with a mean of 0, is Student's t with $N-1$ degrees of freedom, where N is the number of pairs. If the pairing is effective, the standard error of the difference will be smaller than the standard error obtained if two independent samples with N subjects each were chosen. However, if the variables chosen for pairing do not affect the responses under study, pairing may result in a test that is less powerful since true differences can be detected less frequently.

For example, to test the hypothesis that there is no difference between husbands' and wives' buying scores, a paired *t* test should be calculated. A paired test is appropriate since husbands and wives constitute matched observations. Including both members of a couple helps control for nuisance effects such as socioeconomic status and age. The observed differences are more likely to be attributable to differences in sex.

Figure 10.6 contains output from the paired *t* test. The entry under *Number of pairs* is the number of pairs of observations. The mean difference is the difference between the mean scores for males and females. The *t* value is the mean difference divided by the standard error of the difference ($0.55/1.73 = 0.32$). The two-tailed probability for this test is 0.75, so there is insufficient evidence to reject the null hypothesis that married males and females have similar mean buying scores.

Figure 10.6 Husbands' versus wives' buying scores

```
                     - - - t-tests for paired samples - - -

                      Number of        2-tail
Variable                 pairs   Corr    Sig       Mean        SD     SE of Mean
HSSCALE  HUSBAND SELF SCALE                      82.0918    14.352     1.450
                          98    .367    .000
WSSCALE  WIFE SELF SCALE                         81.5408    15.942     1.610


         Paired Differences
  Mean       SD       SE of Mean        t-value     df    2-tail Sig
  .5510    17.095       1.727              .32      97       .750
  95% CI (-2.877, 3.979)
```

The correlation coefficient between husbands' and wives' scores is 0.367. A positive correlation indicates that pairing has been effective in decreasing the variability of the mean difference. The larger the correlation coefficient, the greater the benefit of pairing.

Hypothesis Testing: A Review

The purpose of hypothesis testing is to help draw conclusions about population parameters based on results observed in a random sample. The procedure remains virtually the same for tests of most hypotheses.

- A hypothesis of no difference (called a **null hypothesis**) and its alternative are formulated.
- A test statistic is chosen to evaluate the null hypothesis.
- For the sample, the test statistic is calculated.
- The probability, if the null hypothesis is true, of obtaining a test value at least as extreme as the one observed is determined.
- If the observed significance level is judged small enough, the null hypothesis is rejected.

The Importance of Assumptions

In order to perform a statistical test of any hypothesis, it is necessary to make certain assumptions about the data. The particular assumptions depend on the statistical test being used. Some procedures require stricter assumptions than others. For parametric tests, some knowledge about the distribution from which samples are selected is required.

The assumptions are necessary to define the sampling distribution of the test statistic. Unless the distribution is defined, correct significance levels cannot be calculated. For the equal-variance t test, the assumption is that the observations are random samples from normal distributions with the same variance.

For many procedures, not all assumptions are equally important. Moderate violation of some assumptions may not always be serious. Therefore, it is important to know for each procedure not only what assumptions are needed but also how severely their violation may influence results.

The responsibility for detecting violations of assumptions rests with the researcher. Unlike the chemist who ignores laboratory safety procedures, the investigator who does not comply with good statistical practice is not threatened by explosions. However, from a research viewpoint, the consequences can be just as severe.

Wherever possible, **tests of assumptions**—often called diagnostic checks of the model—should be incorporated as part of the hypothesis-testing procedures. Throughout SPSS, attempts have been made to provide facilities for examining assumptions. For example, in the Explore procedure, there are several tests for normality. Discussions of other such diagnostics are included with the individual procedures.

How to Obtain an Independent-Samples T Test

The Independent-Samples T Test procedure computes Student's t statistic for testing the significance of a difference in means for independent samples. Both equal- and unequal-variance t values are provided, as well as the Levene test for equality of variances.

The minimum specifications are:
- One or more numeric test variables.
- One numeric or short string grouping variable.
- Group values for the grouping variable.

To obtain an independent-samples t test, from the menus choose:

Statistics
  Compare Means ▶
    Independent-Samples T Test...

This opens the Independent-Samples T Test dialog box, as shown in Figure 10.7.

Figure 10.7 Independent-Samples T Test dialog box

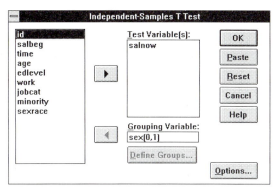

The numeric and short string variables in your data file appear on the source list. Select one or more numeric test variables. Each test variable produces one *t* test. Choose one numeric or short string grouping variable, which splits your file into two groups. After defining the categories of your grouping variable, you can click on **OK** to get the default independent-samples *t* test with two-tailed probabilities and a 95% confidence interval. (See Figure 10.1.) To obtain one-tailed probabilities, divide the *t* probabilities by 2.

Define Groups for Numeric Variables

You must define the two groups for the grouping variable. The procedure to follow for defining groups depends on whether your grouping variable is string or numeric. For both string and numeric variables, *t* tests are not performed if there are fewer than two non-empty groups.

To define groups, highlight the grouping variable and click on **Define Groups...** in the Independent-Samples T Test dialog box. For numeric variables, this opens the Define Groups dialog box, as shown in Figure 10.8.

Figure 10.8 Define Groups dialog box for numeric variables

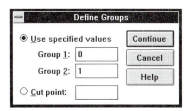

You can choose one of the following:

- **Use specified values.** User-specified group values. This is the default. Enter a group 1 value and a group 2 value that correspond to the two categories of the grouping variable. Cases with other values are excluded from the analysis.
- **Cut point.** User-specified cut point. All cases with values greater than or equal to the specified value are assigned to one group, and the remaining cases are assigned to the other group.

Define Groups for String Variables

The Define Groups dialog box for string variables is shown in Figure 10.9. Enter a group 1 value and a group 2 value that correspond to the two categories of the grouping variable. Cases with other values are excluded from the analysis.

Figure 10.9 Define Groups dialog box for string variables

Independent-Samples T Test Options

To change confidence interval bounds or control the handling of cases with missing values, click on Options... in the Independent-Samples T Test dialog box. This opens the Independent-Samples T Test Options dialog box, as shown in Figure 10.10.

Figure 10.10 Independent-Samples T Test Options dialog box

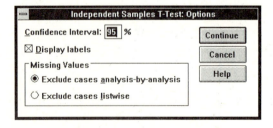

Confidence Interval. A 95% confidence interval for the difference in means is displayed by default. Optionally, you can request a different confidence level by entering a value between 1 and 99. For example, to obtain a 99% confidence interval, enter 99.

Missing Values. You can choose one of the following:

- **Exclude cases analysis by analysis.** Cases with missing values on either the grouping variable or the test variable are excluded from the analysis of that variable. This is the default.
- **Exclude cases listwise.** Cases with missing values on either the grouping variable or any test variable are excluded from all analyses.

You can also choose the following display option:

- **Display labels.** By default, any variable labels are displayed in the output. To suppress labels, deselect this setting.

How to Obtain a Paired-Samples T Test

The Paired-Samples T Test procedure computes Student's *t* statistic for testing the significance of a difference in means for paired samples.

The minimum specification is a pair of numeric variables.

To obtain a paired-samples *t* test, from the menus choose:

Statistics
 Compare Means ▶
  Paired-Samples T Test...

This opens the Paired-Samples T Test dialog box, as shown in Figure 10.11.

Figure 10.11 Paired-Samples T Test dialog box

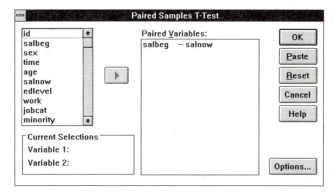

The numeric variables in your data file appear on the source list. Select one or more pairs of variables you want to use in the paired-samples tests. To select a pair:

1. Click on one of the variables. It appears as the first variable under Current Selections.

2. Click on another variable. It appears as the second variable. To remove a variable from Current Selections, click on it again.

3. Click on ▶ to move the pair to the Paired Variables list.

Repeat this process if you have more than one pair of variables.

To obtain the default test for paired samples with two-tailed probabilities and a 95% confidence interval for the mean difference, click on OK. To obtain one-tailed probabilities, divide the *t* probabilities by 2.

Macintosh: Use ⌘-click to select pairs of variables.

Paired-Samples T Test Options

To change confidence interval bounds or control the handling of cases with missing values, click on Options... in the Paired-Samples T Test dialog box. This opens the Paired-Samples T Test Options dialog box, as shown in Figure 10.12.

Figure 10.12 Paired-Samples T Test Options dialog box

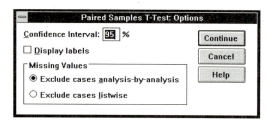

Confidence Interval. A 95% confidence interval for the mean difference is displayed by default. Optionally, you can request a different confidence level. Enter a value between 1 and 99. For example, to obtain a 99% confidence interval, enter 99.

Missing Values. You can choose one of the following:

○ **Exclude cases analysis by analysis.** Cases with missing values for either variable in a given pair are excluded from the analysis of that pair. This is the default.

○ **Exclude cases listwise.** Cases with missing values for any pair variable are excluded from all analyses.

You can also choose the following display option:

- **Display labels.** Displays any variable labels in output. This is the default setting.

Additional Features Available with Command Syntax

You can customize your paired-samples *t* tests if you paste your selections to a syntax window and edit the resulting T-TEST command syntax. (For information on syntax windows, see the *SPSS Base System User's Guide, Part 1*.) An additional feature is the ability to test a variable against each variable on a list (with the PAIRS subcommand). See the *SPSS Base System Syntax Reference Guide* for complete T-TEST command syntax.

11

One-Way Analysis of Variance

Which of four brands of paper towels is the strongest? Do six models of intermediate-size cars get the same average gasoline mileage? Do graduates of the top ten business schools receive the same average starting salaries? There are many situations in which you want to compare the means of several independent samples and, based on them, draw conclusions about the populations from which they were selected. Consider, for example, the following problem.

You are a manufacturer of paper used for making grocery bags. You suspect that the tensile strength of the bags depends on the pulp hardwood concentration. You currently use 10% hardwood concentration in the pulp and produce paper with an average tensile strength of about 15 pounds per square inch (psi). You want to see what happens if you vary the concentration of the pulp.

In consultation with the process engineer, you decide on four concentrations: 5%, 10%, 15%, and 20%. You measure the tensile strength of six samples at each of the four concentrations. You want to test the null hypothesis that all four concentrations result in the same average tensile strength of the paper.

Examining the Data

As always, before you embark on any statistical analysis, you should look at the distribution of data values to make sure that there is nothing unusual. You can use the Explore procedure (see Chapter 5) to make a boxplot for each group.

From the plots in Figure 11.1, you see that the medians for the four groups differ. It appears that as the concentration increases, so does the tensile strength. The vertical length of the boxes, a measure of the spread or variability of the data values, also seems to differ for the concentrations, but not in any systematic fashion. There are no outlying or extreme values.

Figure 11.1 Boxplots for the four concentration groups

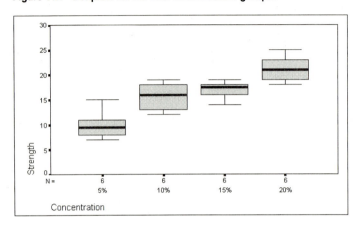

Sample Means and Confidence Intervals

The sample mean for a group provides the single best guess for the unknown population value μ_i. However, it is unlikely that the value of the sample mean is exactly equal to the population value. Instead, it is probably not too different. Based on the sample mean, you can calculate a range of values that, with a designated likelihood, includes the population value. Such a range is called a **confidence interval**. For example, as shown in Figure 11.2, the 95% confidence interval for the average tensile strength for a concentration of 10% is 12.72 to 18.61. This means that if you repeated the experiment under the same conditions and with the same sample sizes in each group, and each time calculated 95% confidence intervals, 95% of these intervals would contain the unknown population parameter value. Since the parameter value is not known, you don't know whether a particular interval contains the population value.

Figure 11.2 also shows descriptive statistics for the tensile strengths for the four concentrations. You see that as the concentration of hardwood increases, so does the mean strength. For a concentration of 5%, the average tensile strength is 10, while for a concentration of 20%, the average strength is 21.17. The group with a hardwood concentration of 15% has the smallest standard deviation. The others differ somewhat.

Figure 11.2   Sample means and confidence intervals for the four concentration groups

```
      Variable  STRENGTH
   By Variable  CONCENT

                         Standard    Standard
  Group   Count    Mean  Deviation      Error    Minimum    Maximum    95 Pct Conf Int for Mean
   5%        6  10.0000     2.8284     1.1547     7.0000    15.0000      7.0318  TO    12.9682
  10%        6  15.6667     2.8048     1.1450    12.0000    19.0000     12.7233  TO    18.6100
  15%        6  17.0000     1.7889      .7303    14.0000    19.0000     15.1227  TO    18.8773
  20%        6  21.1667     2.6394     1.0775    18.0000    25.0000     18.3968  TO    23.9366

  Total     24  15.9583     4.7226      .9640     7.0000    25.0000     13.9642  TO    17.9525
```

Testing the Null Hypothesis

The boxplots in Figure 11.1 and the means in Figure 11.2 suggest that the four concentrations result in different tensile strengths. Now you need to determine if the observed differences in the four sample means can be attributed to just the natural variability among sample means from the same population or whether it's reasonable to believe that the four concentrations come from populations that have different means. You must determine the probability of seeing results as remote as the ones you've observed when, in fact, all population means are equal.

The statistical technique you'll use to test the null hypothesis that several population means are equal is called **analysis of variance** (abbreviated ANOVA). This technique examines the variability of the observations within each group as well as the variability between the group means. Based on these two estimates of variability, you draw conclusions about the population means.

SPSS for Windows contains two different analysis-of-variance procedures: One-Way ANOVA and Simple Factorial ANOVA. This chapter discusses the One-Way ANOVA procedure. One-way analysis of variance is needed when only one variable is used to classify cases into the different groups. In the example on the tensile strength of paper, cases are assigned to groups based on their values for one variable: hardwood concentration. When two or more variables are used to form the groups, the Simple Factorial ANOVA procedure is required (see Chapter 12).

Note that you can use the One-Way ANOVA procedure only when your groups are independent. If you observe the same person under several conditions, you cannot use this procedure. You need a special class of procedures called *repeated measures analysis of variance*, available in the SPSS Advanced Statistics option.

Assumptions Needed for Analysis of Variance

Analysis-of-variance procedures require the following assumptions:
- Each of the groups is an independent random sample from a normal population.
- In the population, the variances of the groups are equal.

One way to check these assumptions is to use the Explore procedure to make stem-and-leaf plots or histograms for each group and calculate the variances. You can also use formal statistical tests to check the assumptions of normality and equal variances. See Chapter 5 for more information on stem-and-leaf plots and tests for normality.

The Levene Test

To test the null hypothesis that the groups come from populations with the same variance, you can use the **Levene test** (shown in Figure 11.3), which can be obtained with the One-Way ANOVA procedure. If the observed significance level is small, you can reject the null hypothesis that all variances are equal. In this example, since the observed significance level (0.583) is large, you can't reject the null hypothesis. This means you don't have sufficient evidence to suspect that the variances are unequal, confirming what you saw in the plot.

Figure 11.3 Levene test

```
Levene Test for Homogeneity of Variances
   Statistic      df1      df2     2-tail Sig.
      .6651        3       20         .583
```

Analyzing the Variability

Now you're ready to perform the analysis-of-variance test. In analysis of variance, the observed variability in the sample is divided, or partitioned, into two parts: variability of the observations within a group (that is, the variability of the observations around their group mean) and the variability among the group means.

If the null hypothesis is true, the population means for the four groups are equal and the observed data can be considered to be four samples from the same population. In this case, you should be able to estimate how much the four sample means should vary. If your observed sample means vary more than you expect, you have evidence to reject the null hypothesis. The analysis-of-variance table is shown in Figure 11.4.

Figure 11.4 One-way analysis-of-variance table

```
   Variable   STRENGTH
By Variable   CONCENT

                        Analysis of Variance

                          Sum of        Mean          F         F
       Source     D.F.   Squares       Squares       Ratio     Prob.

Between Groups     3     382.7917      127.5972      19.6052   .0000
Within Groups     20     130.1667        6.5083
Total             23     512.9583
```

Between-Groups Variability

In Figure 11.4, the row labeled *Between Groups* contains an estimate of the variability of the observations based on the variability of the group means. To calculate the entry labeled *Sum of Squares,* start by subtracting the overall mean (the mean of all the observations) from each group mean (the overall and group means are listed in Figure 11.2). Then square each difference and multiply the square by the number of observations in its group. Finally, add the results together. For this example, the between-groups sum of squares is

$$6 \times (10 - 15.96)^2 + 6 \times (15.67 - 15.96)^2 + 6 \times (17 - 15.96)^2$$
$$+ 6 \times (21.17 - 15.96)^2 = 382.79$$

Equation 11.1

The column labeled *D.F.* contains the degrees of freedom. To calculate the degrees of freedom for the between-groups sum of squares, subtract 1 from the number of groups. In this example, there are four concentrations, so there are three degrees of freedom.

To calculate the between-groups mean square, divide the between-groups sum of squares by its degrees of freedom:

$$\frac{382.79}{3} = 127.60$$

Equation 11.2

Within-Groups Variability

The row labeled *Within Groups* contains an estimate of the variability of the observations based on how much the observations vary from their group means. The within-groups sum of squares is calculated by multiplying each of the group variances (the square of the standard deviation) by the number of cases in the group minus 1 and then adding up the results. In this example, the within-groups sum of squares is

$$5 \times 8.0000 + 5 \times 7.8667 + 5 \times 3.2000 + 5 \times 6.9667 = 130.17 \quad \text{Equation 11.3}$$

To calculate the degrees of freedom for the within-groups sums of squares, take the number of cases in all groups combined and subtract the number of groups. In this example, there are 24 cases and 4 groups, so there are 20 degrees of freedom. The mean square is then calculated by dividing the sum of squares by the degrees of freedom:

$$\frac{130.17}{20} = 6.51 \quad \text{Equation 11.4}$$

Calculating the F Ratio

You now have two estimates of the variability in the population: the within-groups mean square and the between-groups mean square. The within-groups mean square is based on how much the observations within each group vary. The between-groups mean square is based on how much the group means vary among themselves. If the null hypothesis is true, the two numbers should be close to each other. If you divide one by the other, the ratio should be close to 1.

The statistical test for the null hypothesis that all groups have the same mean in the population is based on this ratio, called an *F* statistic. You take the between-groups mean square and divide it by the within-groups mean square. For this example,

$$F = \frac{127.6}{6.51} = 19.6 \quad \text{Equation 11.5}$$

This number appears in Figure 11.4 in the column labeled *F ratio*. It certainly doesn't appear to be close to 1. Now you need to obtain the observed significance level. You obtain the observed significance level by comparing the calculated *F* value to the **F distribution** (the distribution of the *F* statistic when the null hypothesis is true). The significance level is based on both the actual *F* value and the degrees of freedom for the two mean squares. In this example, the observed significance level is less than 0.00005, so you can reject the null hypothesis that the four concentrations of pulp result in paper with the same average tensile strength.

Multiple Comparison Procedures

A significant *F* value tells you only that the population means are probably not all equal. It doesn't tell you which pairs of groups appear to have different means. You reject the null hypothesis that all population means are equal if *any two* means are unequal. You need to use special tests called **multiple comparison procedures** to determine which means are significantly different from each other.

You might wonder why you can't just compare all possible pairs of means using a *t* test. The reason is that when you make many comparisons involving the same means, the probability that one comparison will turn out to be statistically significant increases. For example, if you have 5 groups and compare all pairs of means, you're making 10 comparisons. When the null hypothesis is true, the probability that at least one of the 10 observed significance levels will be less than 0.05 is about 0.29. The more comparisons you make, the more likely it is that you'll find one or more pairs to be statistically different, even if all population means are equal.

By adjusting for the number of comparisons you're making, multiple comparison procedures protect you from calling too many differences significant. The more comparisons you make, the larger the difference between pairs of means must be for a multiple comparison procedure to find it significant. When you use a multiple comparison procedure, you can be more confident that you are finding true differences.

Many multiple comparison procedures are available. They differ in how they adjust the observed significance level. One of the simplest is the **Bonferroni test**. It adjusts the observed significance level based on the number of comparisons you are making. For example, if you are making 5 comparisons, the observed significance level for the original comparison must be less than 0.05/5, or 0.01, for the difference to be significant at the 0.05 significance level. For further discussion of multiple comparison techniques, see Winer et al. (1991).

Figure 11.5 shows a portion of the Bonferroni test results obtained with the One-Way ANOVA procedure. At the bottom, you see a table that orders the group means from smallest to largest in both the rows and columns. (In this example, the order happens to be the same as the order of the group code numbers.) An asterisk marks a pair of means that are different at the 0.05 level after the Bonferroni correction is made. Differences are marked only once, in the lower diagonal of the table. If the significance level is greater than 0.05, the space is left blank.

Figure 11.5 Bonferroni multiple comparisons

```
      Variable   STRENGTH
   By Variable   CONCENT

Multiple Range Tests:  Modified LSD (Bonferroni) test with significance
                       level .05

The difference between two means is significant if
  MEAN(J)-MEAN(I)   >= 1.8039 * RANGE * SQRT(1/N(I) + 1/N(J))
  with the following value(s) for RANGE: 4.14

  (*) Indicates significant differences which are shown in the lower triangle

                              1  1  2
                           5  0  5  0
                           %  %  %  %
     Mean        CONCENT

    10.0000       5%
    15.6667      10%       *
    17.0000      15%       *
    21.1667      20%       *  *
```

In this example, the asterisks in the first column indicate that the mean of the 5% hardwood concentration group is significantly different from every other group. In the second column, the 10% group is different from the 20% group, but not from the 15% group. There are no asterisks in the third column. Thus, you see that all pairs of means are significantly different from each other except for the 10% and 15% groups.

The formula above the table indicates how large an observed difference must be for the multiple comparison procedure to call it significant. If no pairs are found to be significantly different, the table is omitted and a message is printed.

When the sample sizes in all of the groups are the same, you can also use the output of homogeneous subsets to identify subsets of means that are not different from each other. Figure 11.6 shows the homogeneous subsets output.

Figure 11.6 Homogeneous subsets

```
Subset 1

Group        5%

Mean       10.0000
- - - - - - - - - - - -
Subset 2

Group       10%           15%

Mean       15.6667       17.0000
- - - - - - - - - - - - - - - - - - -
Subset 3

Group       15%           20%

Mean       17.0000       21.1667
- - - - - - - - - - - - - - - - - - -
```

Groups that appear in the same subset are not significantly different from each other. In this example, the 10% and 15% hardwood concentration groups are in the same subset, as are the 15% and 20% groups. The 5% group is in a subset of its own, since it is significantly different from all of the other means.

How to Obtain a One-Way Analysis of Variance

The One-Way ANOVA procedure produces a one-way analysis of variance for an interval-level dependent variable by a single factor (independent) variable. You can test for trends across categories, specify contrasts, and use a variety of range tests.

The minimum specifications are:

- One numeric dependent variable. The variable is assumed to be measured on an interval scale.
- One numeric factor variable. Factor variable values should be integers.
- A defined range for the factor variable.

To obtain a one-way analysis of variance, from the menus choose:

Statistics
  Compare Means ▶
    One-Way ANOVA...

This opens the One-Way ANOVA dialog box, as shown in Figure 11.7.

Figure 11.7 One-Way ANOVA dialog box

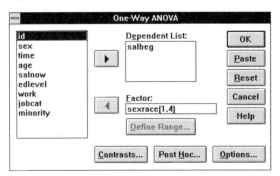

The numeric variables in your data file are displayed on the source variable list. Select your dependent variable(s) and a single factor (independent) variable. After defining a range for the factor variable (see "One-Way ANOVA Define Range," below), click on OK to obtain the default one-way analysis-of-variance table containing the F ratio, F probability, and sum of squares and mean squares for between groups and within groups. (See Figure 11.2.) A separate analysis-of-variance table is generated for each dependent variable.

One-Way ANOVA Define Range

A value range is required for the factor (independent) variable. To define the range, click on Define Range... in the One-Way ANOVA dialog box. This opens the One-Way ANOVA Define Range dialog box, as shown in Figure 11.8.

Figure 11.8 One-Way ANOVA Define Range dialog box

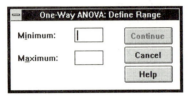

The minimum and maximum values must be integers. If any of the intervening values are non-integers, they are truncated in the analysis. Any empty categories are deleted from the analysis. If there are more than 50 categories of the factor variable, multiple comparison tests are not available.

One-Way ANOVA Contrasts

To partition the between-groups sum of squares into trend components or specify *a priori* contrasts, click on Contrasts... in the One-Way ANOVA dialog box. This opens the One-Way ANOVA Contrasts dialog box, as shown in Figure 11.9.

Figure 11.9 One-Way ANOVA Contrasts dialog box

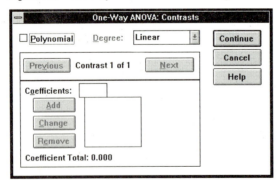

❏ **Polynomial.** Partitions the between-groups sum of squares into trend components. When you choose this option with balanced designs, SPSS computes the sum of squares for each order polynomial from weighted polynomial contrasts, using the group code as the metric. These contrasts are orthogonal; hence, the sum of squares for each order polynomial is statistically independent. If the design is unbalanced and there is equal spacing between groups, SPSS also computes sums of squares using the unweighted polynomial contrasts, which are not orthogonal. The deviation sums of squares are always calculated from the weighted sums of squares (Speed, 1976).

⬇ **Degree.** You can choose one of the following alternatives for the polynomial degree:

Linear. 1st-degree polynomial.

Quadratic. 2nd-degree polynomial.

Cubic. 3rd-degree polynomial.

4th. 4th-degree polynomial.

5th. 5th-degree polynomial.

Coefficients. User-specified *a priori* contrasts to be tested by the t statistic. Enter a coefficient value for each group (category) of the factor variable and click on **Add** after each entry. Each new value is added at the bottom of the coefficient list. To change a value on the list, highlight it, enter the new value in the text box, and click on **Change**. To remove a value, highlight it and click on **Remove**. To specify additional sets of contrasts, click on **Next**. You can specify up to 10 sets of contrasts and up to 50 coefficients for each set. Use **Next** and **Previous** to move between sets of contrasts.

The sequential order of the coefficients is important since it corresponds to the ascending order of the category values of the factor variable. The first coefficient on the list corresponds to the lowest group value of the factor variable, and the last coefficient corresponds to the highest value. For example, if there are six categories of the factor variable, the coefficient list –1, –1, –1, –1, 2, 2 contrasts the combination of the first four groups with the combination of the last two groups.

You can also specify fractional coefficients and exclude groups by assigning a coefficient of zero. For example, the coefficient list –1, 0, 0, 0, 0.5, 0.5 contrasts the first group with the combination of the fifth and sixth groups.

For most applications, the coefficients should sum to 0. Sets that do not sum to 0 can also be used, but a warning message is displayed.

Output for each contrast list includes the value of the contrast, the standard error of the contrast, the t statistic, the degrees of freedom for t, and the two-tailed probability of t. Both pooled- and separate-variance estimates are displayed.

One-Way ANOVA Post Hoc Multiple Comparisons

To produce post hoc multiple comparison tests, click on Post Hoc... in the One-Way ANOVA dialog box. This opens the One-Way ANOVA Post Hoc Multiple Comparisons dialog box, as shown in Figure 11.10.

Figure 11.10 One-Way ANOVA Post Hoc Multiple Comparisons dialog box

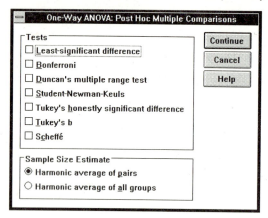

Tests. These tests always produce multiple comparisons between all groups. Non-empty group means are sorted by ascending order. Asterisks in the matrix indicate significantly different group means at an alpha level of 0.05. In addition to this output, homogeneous subsets are calculated for balanced designs if you also choose Harmonic average of all groups. You can choose one or more of the following tests:

- **Least-significant difference.** This is equivalent to doing multiple t tests between all pairs of groups. No "multiple comparisons" protection is provided.
- **Bonferroni.** The Bonferroni test is a modified least-significant-difference test.
- **Duncan's multiple range test.**
- **Student-Newman-Keuls.**
- **Tukey's honestly significant difference.**
- **Tukey's b.** Tukey's alternate procedure.
- **Scheffé.** This test is conservative for pairwise comparisons of means and requires larger differences between means for significance than the other multiple comparison tests.

Sample Size Estimate. You can choose one of the following alternatives:

- **Harmonic average of pairs.** If the sample sizes are not equal in all groups, a separate harmonic mean is computed for each pair of groups being compared. This is the default.

○ **Harmonic average of all groups.** If the sample sizes are not equal in all groups, a single harmonic mean is computed for all groups. If you choose this alternative, homogeneous subsets are calculated for all multiple comparison tests.

One-Way ANOVA Options

To obtain additional statistics, change the treatment of missing values, or use value labels to identify groups in output, click on Options... in the One-Way ANOVA dialog box. This opens the One-Way ANOVA Options dialog box, as shown in Figure 11.11.

Figure 11.11 One-Way ANOVA Options dialog box

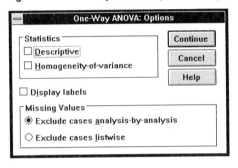

Statistics. You can choose one or more of the following:

❏ **Descriptive.** Calculates the number of cases, mean, standard deviation, standard error, minimum, maximum, and 95% confidence interval for each dependent variable for each group.

❏ **Homogeneity of variance.** Calculates the Levene statistic.

Missing Values. You can choose one of the following alternatives:

○ **Exclude cases analysis by analysis.** A case with a missing value for either the dependent variable or factor variable for a given analysis is not used in that analysis. Also, a case outside the range specified for the factor variable is not used. This is the default.

○ **Exclude cases listwise.** Cases with missing values for the factor variable or for *any* dependent variable included on the dependent list in the main dialog box are excluded from all analyses. If you have not specified multiple dependent variables, this has no effect.

The following labeling option is also available:

❑ **Display labels.** Uses the first eight characters from the value labels of the factor variable for group labels. By default, groups are labeled *GRP1*, *GRP2*, *GRP3*, etc., where the number indicates the value of the factor variable.

Additional Features Available with Command Syntax

You can customize your one-way analysis of variance if you paste your dialog box selections into a syntax window and edit the resulting ONEWAY command syntax. (For information on syntax windows, see the *SPSS Base System User's Guide, Part 1*.) Additional features include:

- Fixed- and random-effects statistics. Standard deviation, standard error, and 95% confidence intervals for the fixed-effects model. Standard error, 95% confidence intervals, and estimate of between-component variance for the random-effects model (using STATISTICS=EFFECTS).
- User-specified alpha levels for the least-significant difference, Bonferroni, Duncan, and Scheffé multiple comparisons tests (with the RANGES subcommand).
- Matrix facility to write a matrix of means, standard deviations, and frequencies or to read a matrix of means, frequencies, pooled variances, and degrees of freedom for the pooled variances. These matrixes can be used in place of raw data to obtain a one-way analysis of variance (with the MATRIX subcommand).

See the *SPSS Base System Syntax Reference Guide* for complete ONEWAY command syntax.

12 Analysis of Variance

Despite constitutional guarantees, any mirror will testify that all citizens are not created equal. The consequences of this inequity are pervasive. Physically attractive individuals are generally perceived as more desirable social partners, more persuasive communicators, and more likeable and competent. Even cute children and attractive burglars are disciplined more leniently than their homely counterparts (Sigall & Ostrove, 1975).

Much research on physical attractiveness focuses on its impact on heterosexual relationships and evaluations. Its effect on same-sex evaluations has received less attention. Anderson and Nida (1978) examined the influence of attractiveness on the evaluation of writing samples by college students. In the study, 144 male and 144 female students were asked to appraise essays purportedly written by college freshmen. As supplemental information, a slide of the "author" was projected during the evaluation. Half of the slides were of authors of the same sex as the rater; the other half were of authors of the opposite sex. Each author had previously been determined to be of high, medium, or low attractiveness. Each rater evaluated one essay for creativity, ideas, and style. The three scales were combined to form a composite measure of performance.

Descriptive Statistics

Figure 12.1 contains average composite scores for the essays, subdivided by the three categories of physical attractiveness and the two categories of sex similarity. The table is similar to the summary table shown for the one-way analysis of variance in Chapter 11. The difference here is that there are two independent (or grouping) variables: attractiveness and sex similarity. The first mean displayed (25.11) is for the entire sample. The number of cases (288) is shown in parentheses. Then, for each of the independent variables, mean scores are displayed for each of the categories. The attractiveness categories are ordered from low (coded 1) to high (coded 3). Evaluations in which the rater and author are of the same sex are coded as 1, while opposite-sex evaluations are coded as 2. The possible combinations of the values of the two variables result in six cells. Finally, a table of means is displayed for cases classified by both grouping variables. Attractiveness is the row variable, and sex is the column variable. Each mean is based on the responses of 48 subjects.

Figure 12.1 Table of group means

```
                        * * *  C E L L    M E A N S  * * *
                SCORE        COMPOSITE SCORE
             BY ATTRACT      ATTRACTIVENESS LEVEL
                SEX          SEX SIMILARITY

    TOTAL POPULATION

         25.11
       (   288)

    ATTRACT
            1           2           3

          22.98       25.78       26.59
       (    96)    (    96)    (    96)

    SEX
            1           2

          25.52       24.71
       (   144)    (   144)


                   SEX
                    1           2
    ATTRACT
            1     22.79       23.17
               (    48)    (    48)

            2     28.63       22.92
               (    48)    (    48)

            3     25.13       28.04
               (    48)    (    48)
```

The overall average score is 25.11. Highly attractive individuals received the highest average score (26.59), while those rated low in physical appeal had the lowest score (22.98). There doesn't appear to be much difference between the average scores (across attractiveness levels) assigned by same-sex (25.52) and opposite-sex (24.71) evaluators. However, highly attractive individuals received an average rating of 25.13 when evaluated by people of the same sex and 28.04 when evaluated by people of the opposite sex.

Analysis of Variance

Three questions are of interest in the study: Does attractiveness relate to the composite scores? Does sex similarity relate to the scores? Is there an interaction between the effects of attractiveness and sex? The statistical technique used to evaluate these questions is an extension of the one-way analysis of variance outlined in Chapter 11. The same assumptions are needed for correct application; that is, the observations should be independently selected from normal populations with equal variances. Again, discussion here is limited to instances in which both grouping variables are considered **fixed**; that is, they constitute the populations of interest.

The total observed variation in the scores is subdivided into four components: the sums of squares due to attractiveness, sex, their interaction, and the residual. This can be expressed as

$$\text{Total SS} = \text{Attractiveness SS} + \text{Sex SS} + \text{Interaction SS} + \text{Residual SS}$$

Equation 12.1

Figure 12.2 is the analysis-of-variance table for this study. The first column lists the sources of variation. The sums of squares attributable to each of the components are given in the second column. The sums of squares for each independent variable alone are sometimes termed the **main effect** sums of squares. The **explained** sum of squares is the total sum of squares for the main effect and interaction terms in the model.

The degrees of freedom for sex and attractiveness, listed in the third column, are one fewer than the number of categories. For example, since there are three levels of attractiveness, there are two degrees of freedom. Similarly, sex has one degree of freedom. Two degrees of freedom are associated with the interaction term (the product of the degrees of freedom of each of the individual variables). The degrees of freedom for the residual are $N - 1 - k$, where k equals the degrees of freedom for the explained sum of squares.

Figure 12.2 Analysis-of-variance table

```
          * * *  A N A L Y S I S   O F   V A R I A N C E  * * *

              SCORE      COMPOSITE SCORE
         by   ATTRACT    ATTRACTIVENESS LEVEL
              SEX        SEX SIMILARITY

                              Sum of                  Mean                    Sig
Source of Variation           Squares      DF         Square         F        of F

Main Effects                  733.700       3         244.567       3.276     .022
    ATTRACT                   686.850       2         343.425       4.600     .011
    SEX                        46.850       1          46.850       0.628     .429

2-Way Interactions            942.350       2         471.175       6.311     .002
    ATTRACT   SEX             942.350       2         471.175       6.311     .002

Explained                    1676.050       5         355.210       4.490     .000

Residual                    21053.140     282          74.656

Total                       22729.190     287          79.196
```

The mean squares shown in the fourth column in Figure 12.2 are obtained by dividing each sum of squares by its degrees of freedom. Hypothesis tests are based on the ratios of the mean squares of each source of variation to the mean square for the residual. When the assumptions are met and the true means are in fact equal, the distribution of the ratio is an F with the degrees of freedom for the numerator and denominator terms.

Testing for Interaction

The *F* value associated with the attractiveness and sex interaction is 6.311, as shown in Figure 12.2. The observed significance level is approximately 0.002. Therefore, it appears that there is an interaction between the two variables. What does this mean?

Consider Figure 12.3, which is a plot of the cell, or group, means in Figure 12.1. Notice how the mean scores relate not only to the attractiveness of the individual and to the sex of the rater, but also to the particular combination of the values of the variables. Opposite-sex raters assign the highest scores to highly attractive individuals. Same-sex raters assign the highest scores to individuals of medium attractiveness. Thus, the ratings for each level of attractiveness depend on the sex variable. If there were no interaction between the two variables, a plot similar to the one shown in Figure 12.4 might result, in which the difference between the two types of raters is the same for the three levels of attractiveness.

Figure 12.3 Cell means

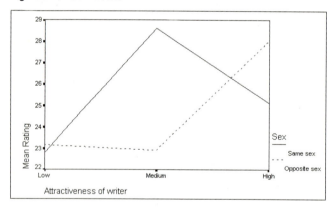

Figure 12.4 Cell means with no interaction

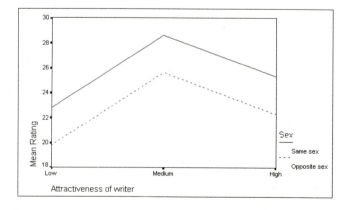

Tests for Sex and Attractiveness

Once the presence of interaction has been established, it is not particularly useful to continue hypothesis testing, since the two variables *jointly* affect the dependent variable. If there is no significant interaction, the grouping variables can be tested individually. The F value associated with attractiveness would provide a test of the hypothesis that attractiveness does not affect the rating. Similarly, the F value associated with sex would test the hypothesis that sex has no main effect on evaluation.

Note that the small F value associated with sex does not indicate that response is unaffected by sex, since sex is included in the significant interaction term. Instead, it shows that when response is averaged over attractiveness levels, the two sex-category means are not significantly different.

Explanations

Several explanations are consistent with the results of this study. Since people generally identify with individuals most like themselves, and since most people consider themselves moderately attractive, the highest degree of identification should be with same-sex individuals of moderate attractiveness. The higher empathy may result in the higher scores. An alternate theory is that moderately attractive individuals are generally perceived as more desirable same-sex friends; they have more favorable personality profiles and don't encourage unfavorable comparisons. Their writing scores may benefit from their perceived popularity.

Although we may not want friends who outshine us, attractive dates can reflect favorably on us and enhance our status. Physical beauty is generally advantageous for heterosexual relationships but may not be for same-sex friendships. This prejudice may affect all evaluations of highly attractive members of the opposite sex.

Extensions

Analysis-of-variance techniques can be used with any number of grouping variables. For example, the data in Figure 12.1 originated from a more complicated experiment than described here. There were four factors—essay quality, physical attractiveness, sex of writer, and sex of subject. The original data were analyzed with a $3 \times 3 \times 2 \times 2$ ANOVA table. (The numbers indicate how many categories each grouping variable has.) The conclusions from our simplified analysis are the same as those from the more elaborate analysis.

Each of the cells in our experiment had the same number of subjects. This greatly simplifies the analysis and its interpretation. When unequal sample sizes occur in the cells, the total sum of squares cannot be partitioned into nice components that sum to the total. Various techniques are available for calculating sums of squares in such **nonor-**

thogonal designs. The methods differ in the way they adjust the sums of squares to account for other effects in the model. Each method results in different sums of squares and tests different hypotheses. However, when all cell frequencies are equal, the methods yield the same results. For discussion of various procedures for analyzing designs with unequal cell frequencies, see Kleinbaum and Kupper (1978) and Overall and Klett (1972).

How to Obtain a Simple Factorial Analysis of Variance

The Simple Factorial ANOVA procedure tests the hypothesis that the group, or cell, means of the dependent variable are equal.

The minimum specifications are:
- One or more interval-level dependent variables.
- One or more categorical factor variables.
- Minimum and maximum group values for each factor variable.

To obtain a simple factorial ANOVA and optional statistics, from the menus choose:

Statistics
  ANOVA Models ▶
    Simple Factorial...

This opens the Simple Factorial ANOVA dialog box, as shown in Figure 12.5.

Figure 12.5 Simple Factorial ANOVA dialog box

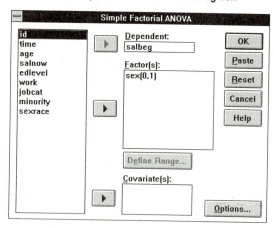

The numeric variables in your data file appear on the source list. Select an interval-level dependent variable. Choose one or more categorical variables, or factors, which split your file into two or more groups. After defining the range of the factor variable(s), click on **OK** to get the default analysis of variance using unique sums of squares. Cases with missing values for any variable are excluded from the analysis.

If there are five or fewer factors, the default model is **full factorial**, meaning that all factor-by-factor interaction terms are included. If you specify more than five factors, only interaction terms up to order five are included.

Optionally, you can select one or more continuous explanatory variables, or covariates, for the analysis.

Simple Factorial ANOVA Define Range

You must indicate the range of categories for each factor variable. To define categories, highlight a variable or group of variables on the Factor(s) list and click on **Define Range...** in the Simple Factorial ANOVA dialog box. This opens the Simple Factorial ANOVA Define Range dialog box, as shown in Figure 12.6.

Figure 12.6   Simple Factorial ANOVA Define Range dialog box

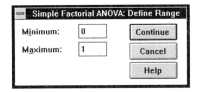

Enter values for minimum and maximum that correspond to the lowest and highest categories of the factor variable. Both values must be positive integers, and the minimum value you specify must be less than the maximum value. Cases with values outside the bounds are excluded. For example, if you specify a minimum value of 0 and a maximum value of 3, only the values 0, 1, 2, and 3 are used.

Repeat this process for each factor variable.

Simple Factorial ANOVA Options

To choose an alternate method for decomposing sums of squares, control the order of entry of covariates, obtain summary statistics, or suppress interaction terms, click on **Options...** in the Simple Factorial ANOVA dialog box. This opens the Simple Factorial ANOVA Options dialog box, as shown in Figure 12.7.

Figure 12.7 Simple Factorial ANOVA Options dialog box

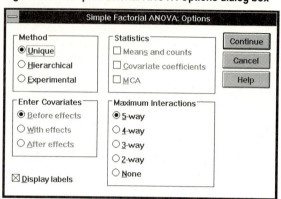

Method. Method selection controls how the effects are assessed. You can choose one of the following alternatives:

○ **Unique.** All effects are assessed simultaneously for their contribution. That is, each effect is adjusted for all other covariates, main effects, and interaction terms in the model. This is the default.

○ **Hierarchical.** Factor main effects and covariate effects are assessed hierarchically. If the default treatment of covariates is in effect, covariates are adjusted only for covariates that precede them on the Covariate(s) list. Main effects are adjusted for all covariates and for factors that precede them on the Factor(s) list. Interactions are not processed hierarchically; they are adjusted for all covariates, factors, and other interactions of the same and lower orders, just as in the experimental approach. Thus, the hierarchical method differs from the experimental method only in the treatment of covariates and main effects.

○ **Experimental.** If the default treatment of covariates (covariates entered before main effects) is in effect, effects are assessed in the following order: covariates, main effects, two-way interactions, three-way interactions, four-way interactions, and five-way interactions. This means that covariates are not adjusted for any other terms in the model except for other covariates; main effects are adjusted only for covariates and other main effects; and interactions are adjusted for all interactions of the same and lower order, as well as for all main effects and covariates. The effects within each type are adjusted for all other effects of that type and also for the effects of prior types. For example, all two-way interactions are adjusted for other two-way interactions and for all main effects and covariates.

Enter Covariates. Operation of the experimental and hierarchical methods depends on the order of entry of any covariates. If you want to select a covariate entry alternative, there must be at least one covariate on the Covariate(s) list. In addition, the experimental or hierarchical method must be specified (with the unique method, covariates are always entered concurrently with all other effects). You can choose one of the following alternatives:

○ **Before effects.** Processes covariates before main effects for factors. This is the default.

○ **With effects.** Processes covariates concurrently with main effects for factors.

○ **After effects.** Processes covariates after main effects for factors.

For example, if the experimental method is selected but you choose **After effects**, main effects are entered first and adjusted only for other main effects, and covariates are entered after the main effects and adjusted for other covariates and main effects. If, instead, you select the experimental method and **With effects**, covariates are entered together with main effects. This means that all covariates and main effects are adjusted for each other.

Statistics. You can choose one or more of the following:

❑ **Means and counts.** Requests means and counts for each dependent variable for groups defined for each factor and each combination of factors up to the fifth level. Means and counts are not available if you select unique sums of squares.

❑ **Covariate coefficients.** Unstandardized regression coefficients for the covariate(s). The coefficients are computed at the point where the covariates are entered into the model. Thus, their values depend on the method you specify. If you want covariate coefficients, there must be at least one covariate on the Covariate(s) list.

❑ **MCA.** Multiple classification analysis. In the MCA table, effects are expressed as deviations from the grand mean. The table includes a listing of unadjusted category effects for each factor, category effects adjusted for other factors, category effects adjusted for all factors and covariates, and eta and beta values. The MCA table is not available if you specify unique sums of squares.

Maximum Interactions. You can control the effects of various orders of interactions. Any interaction effects that are not computed are pooled into the residual sums of squares. You can choose one of the following alternatives:

○ **5-way.** Displays all interaction terms up to and including the fifth order. This is the default.

○ **4-way.** Displays all interaction effects up to and including the fourth order.

○ **3-way.** Displays all two- and three-way interaction effects.

○ **2-way.** Displays two-way interaction effects.

○ **None.** Deletes all interaction terms from the model. Only main effects and covariate effects appear in the ANOVA table.

You can also choose the following display option:

❏ **Display labels.** Displays any value and variable labels in the output. This is the default. To suppress labels, deselect this item.

Additional Features Available with Command Syntax

You can customize your analysis of variance if you paste your dialog box selections into a syntax window and edit the resulting ANOVA command syntax. (For information on syntax windows, see the *SPSS Base System User's Guide, Part 1*.) An additional feature is the ability to specify more than one dependent variable. See the *SPSS Base System Syntax Reference Guide* for complete ANOVA command syntax.

13 Measuring Linear Association

Youthful lemonade-stand entrepreneurs as well as executives of billion-dollar corporations share a common concern—how to increase sales. Hand-lettered signs affixed to neighborhood trees, television campaigns, siblings and friends canvassing local playgrounds, and international sales forces are known to be effective marketing tactics. However, it can be difficult to measure the effectiveness of specific marketing techniques when they are part of an overall marketing strategy, so businesses routinely conduct market research to determine exactly what makes their products sell.

Churchill (1979) describes a study undertaken by the manufacturer of Click ballpoint pens to determine the effectiveness of the firm's marketing efforts. A random sample of 40 sales territories is selected, and sales, amount of advertising, and number of sales representatives are recorded. This chapter looks at the relationship between sales and these variables.

Examining Relationships

A scatterplot can reveal various types of associations between two variables. Some commonly encountered patterns are illustrated in Figure 13.1. In the first example, there appears to be no discernible relationship between the two variables. In the second example, the variables are related exponentially; that is, Y increases very rapidly for increasing values of X. In the third example, the relationship between the two variables is U-shaped. Small and large values of the X variable are associated with large values of the Y variable.

Figure 13.1 Scatterplots showing common relationships

Figure 13.2 is a scatterplot showing the amount of sales and the number of television spots in each of 40 territories from the study. From the figure, it appears that there is a positive association between sales and advertising. That is, as the amount of advertising increases, so does the number of sales. The relationship between sales and advertising may be termed **linear**, since the observed points cluster more or less around a straight line.

Figure 13.2 Scatterplot showing a linear relationship

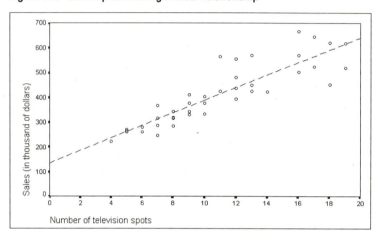

The Correlation Coefficient

Although a scatterplot is an essential first step in studying the association between two variables, it is often useful to quantify the strength of the association by calculating a summary index. One commonly used measure is the **Pearson correlation coefficient**, denoted by r. It is defined as

$$r = \frac{\sum_{i=1}^{N}(X_i - \bar{X})(Y_i - \bar{Y})}{(N-1)S_X S_Y}$$

Equation 13.1

where N is the number of cases and S_X and S_Y are the standard deviations of the two variables. The absolute value of r indicates the strength of the linear relationship. The largest possible absolute value is 1, which occurs when all points fall exactly on the line. When the line has a positive slope, the value of r is positive, and when the slope of the line is negative, the value of r is negative (see Figure 13.3).

Figure 13.3 Scatterplots with correlation coefficients of +1 and −1

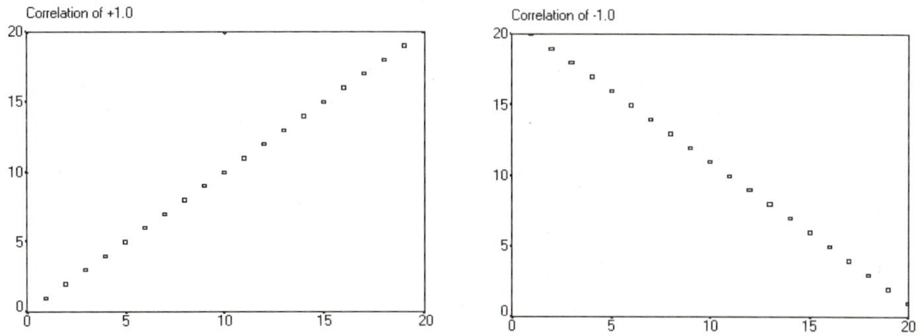

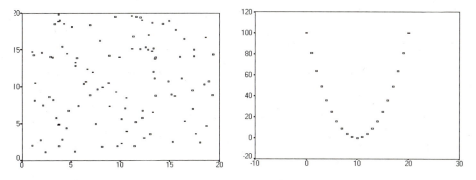

A value of 0 indicates no *linear* relationship. Two variables can have a strong association but a small correlation coefficient if the relationship is not linear. Figure 13.4 shows two plots with correlation coefficients of 0.

Figure 13.4 Scatterplots with correlation coefficients of 0

It is important to examine correlation coefficients together with scatterplots, since the same coefficient can result from very different underlying relationships. The variables plotted in Figure 13.5 have a correlation coefficient greater than 0.8, as do the variables plotted in Figure 13.2. But note how different the relationships are between the two sets of variables. In Figure 13.5, there is a strong positive linear association for only part of the graph. The relationship between the two variables is basically nonlinear. The scatterplot in Figure 13.2 is very different. The points cluster more or less around a line. Thus, the correlation coefficient should be used only to summarize the strength of linear association.

Figure 13.5 Scatterplot showing nonlinear relationship

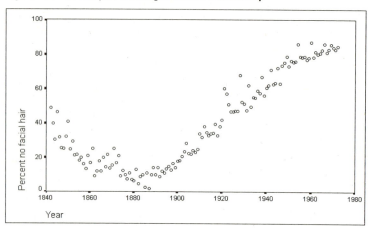

Some Properties of the Correlation Coefficient

A common mistake in interpreting the correlation coefficient is to assume that correlation implies causation. No such conclusion is automatic. While sales are highly correlated with advertising, they are also highly correlated with other variables, such as the number of sales representatives in a territory. Advertising alone does not necessarily result in increased sales. For example, territories with high sales may simply have more money to spend on TV spots, regardless of whether the spots are effective.

The correlation coefficient is a **symmetric measure**, since interchanging the two variables X and Y in the formula does not change the results. The correlation coefficient is not expressed in any units of measure, and it is not affected by linear transformations such as adding or subtracting constants or multiplying or dividing all values of a variable by a constant.

Calculating Correlation Coefficients

Figure 13.6 is a table of correlation coefficients for the number of television spots, number of sales representatives, and amount of sales. The entry in each cell is the correlation coefficient. For example, the correlation coefficient between advertising and sales is 0.8802. This value indicates that there is a fairly strong linear association between the two variables, as shown in Figure 13.2. The table is symmetric, since the correlation between X and Y is the same as the correlation between Y and X. The correlation values on the diagonal are all 1, since a variable is perfectly related to itself.

Figure 13.6 Correlation coefficients

```
     - -  Correlation Coefficients  - -

              ADVERTIS      REPS        SALES

ADVERTIS       1.0000      .7763**     .8802**
REPS            .7763**   1.0000       .8818**
SALES           .8802**    .8818**    1.0000

 * - Signif. LE .05     ** - Signif. LE .01      (2-tailed)

 " . " is printed if a coefficient cannot be computed
```

Hypothesis Tests about the Correlation Coefficient

Although the correlation coefficient is sometimes used only as a summary index to describe the observed strength of the association, in some situations description and summary are but a first step. The primary goal may be to test hypotheses about the unknown population correlation coefficient—denoted as ρ—based on its estimate, the sample correlation coefficient r. In order to test such hypotheses, certain assumptions must be made about the underlying joint distribution of the two variables. A common assumption is that independent random samples are taken from a distribution in which the two variables together are distributed normally. If this condition is satisfied, the test that the population coefficient is 0 can be based on the statistic

$$t = r\sqrt{\frac{N-2}{1-r^2}}$$

Equation 13.2

which, if $\rho = 0$, has a Student's t distribution with $N-2$ degrees of freedom. Either one- or two-tailed tests can be calculated. If nothing is known in advance, a two-tailed test is appropriate. That is, the hypothesis that the coefficient is 0 is rejected for both extreme positive and extreme negative values of t. If the direction of the association can be specified in advance, the hypothesis is rejected only for t values that are of sufficient magnitude and in the direction specified.

In SPSS, you can request that coefficients with two-tailed observed significance levels less than 0.05 be identified with a single asterisk and those with two-tailed significance levels less than 0.01 be identified with two asterisks. From Figure 13.6, the probability that a correlation coefficient of at least 0.88 in absolute value is obtained when there is no linear association in the population between sales and advertising is less than 0.01. Care should be exercised when examining the significance levels for large tables. Even if there is no association between the variables, if many coefficients are computed, some would be expected to be statistically significant by chance alone.

Special procedures must be employed to test more general hypotheses of the form $\rho = \rho_0$, where ρ_0 is a constant. If the assumptions of bivariate normality appear to be unreasonable, nonparametric measures such as Spearman's rho and Kendall's tau-*b* can be calculated. These coefficients make limited assumptions about the underlying distributions of the variables. (See "The Rank Correlation Coefficient" on p. 209.)

Correlation Matrices and Missing Data

For a variety of reasons, data files frequently contain incomplete observations. Respondents in surveys scrawl illegible responses or refuse to answer certain questions. Laboratory animals die before experiments are completed. Patients fail to keep scheduled clinic appointments.

Analysis of data with missing values is troublesome. Before even considering possible strategies, you should determine whether there is evidence that the missing-value pattern is not random. That is, are there reasons to believe that missing values for a variable are related to the values of that variable or other variables? For example, people with low incomes may be less willing to report their financial status than more affluent people. This may be even more pronounced for people who are poor but highly educated.

One simple method of exploring such possibilities is to subdivide the data into two groups—those observations with missing data for a variable and those with complete data—and examine the distributions of the other variables in the file across these two groups. The SPSS crosstabulation and independent-samples t test procedures are particularly useful for this. For a discussion of more sophisticated methods for detecting nonrandomness, see Frane (1976).

If it appears that the data are not missing randomly, use great caution in attempting to analyze the data. It may be that no satisfactory analysis is possible, especially if there are only a few cases.

If you are satisfied that the missing data are random, several strategies are available. First, if the same few variables are missing for most cases, exclude those variables from the analysis. Since this luxury is not usually available, alternately you can keep all variables but eliminate the cases with missing values. This is termed **listwise** missing-value treatment, since a case is eliminated if it has a missing value for any variable on the list. If many cases have missing data for some variables, listwise missing-value treatment can eliminate too many cases and leave you with a very small sample. One common technique is to calculate the correlation coefficient between a pair of variables based on all cases with complete information for the two variables, regardless of whether the cases have missing data for any other variable. For example, if a case has values for variables 1, 3, and 5 only, it is used in computations involving only variable pairs 1 and 3, 1 and 5, and 3 and 5. This is **pairwise** missing-value treatment.

Choosing Pairwise Missing-Value Treatment

Several problems can arise with pairwise matrices, one of which is inconsistency. There are some relationships between coefficients that are clearly impossible but may seem to occur when different cases are used to estimate different coefficients. For example, if age and weight and age and height have high positive correlations, it is impossible in the same sample for height and weight to have a high negative correlation. However, if the same cases are not used to estimate all three coefficients, such an anomaly can occur.

There is no single sample size that can be associated with a pairwise matrix, since each coefficient can be based on a different number of cases. Significance levels obtained from analyses based on pairwise matrices must be viewed with caution, since little is known about hypothesis testing in such situations.

It should be emphasized that missing-value problems should not be treated lightly. You should base your decision on careful examination of the data and not leave the choices up to system defaults.

The Rank Correlation Coefficient

The Pearson product-moment correlation is appropriate only for data that attain at least an interval level of measurement, such as the sales and advertising data used in this chapter. Normality is also assumed when testing hypotheses about this correlation coefficient. For ordinal data or interval data that do not satisfy the normality assumption, another measure of the linear relationship between two variables, **Spearman's rank correlation coefficient**, is available.

The rank correlation coefficient is the Pearson correlation coefficient based on the ranks of the data if there are no ties (adjustments are made if some of the data are tied). If the original data for each variable have no ties, the data for each variable are first ranked, and then the Pearson correlation coefficient between the ranks for the two variables is computed. Like the Pearson correlation coefficient, the rank correlation ranges between -1 and $+1$, where -1 and $+1$ indicate a perfect linear relationship between the ranks of the two variables. The interpretation is therefore the same except that the relationship between *ranks*, and not values, is examined.

Figure 13.7 shows the matrix of rank correlation coefficients for the sales and advertising data. SPSS displays a lower-triangular matrix in which redundant coefficients and the diagonal are omitted. As expected, these coefficients are similar in sign and magnitude to the Pearson coefficients shown in Figure 13.6.

Figure 13.7 Rank correlation coefficients

```
- - - S P E A R M A N   C O R R E L A T I O N   C O E F F I C I E N T S - - -

REPS           .7733
         N(     40)
         SIG  .000

SALES          .9182           .8636
         N(     40)      N(     40)
         SIG  .000       SIG  .000

             ADVERTIS          REPS
```

" . " is printed if a coefficient cannot be computed.

How to Obtain Bivariate Correlations

The Bivariate Correlations procedure computes Pearson product-moment and two rank-order correlation coefficients, Spearman's rho and Kendall's tau-*b*, with their significance levels. Optionally, you can obtain univariate statistics, covariances, and cross-product deviations.

The minimum specification is two or more numeric variables.

To obtain bivariate correlations, from the menus choose:

Statistics
  Correlate ▶
    Bivariate...

This opens the Bivariate Correlations dialog box, as shown in Figure 13.8.

Figure 13.8 Bivariate Correlations dialog box

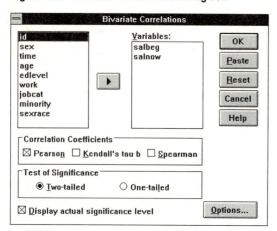

The numeric variables in your data file appear on the source list. Select two or more variables for analysis. To obtain the default Pearson correlations using two-tailed tests of significance, click on **OK**. If all cases have a missing value for one or both of a given pair of variables, or if they all have the same value for a variable, the coefficient cannot be computed and a period is displayed instead.

Correlation Coefficients. At least one type of correlation must be selected. You can choose one or more of the following:

- **Pearson.** This is the default setting. Displays a square correlation matrix. The correlation of a variable with itself is always 1.0 and can be found on the diagonal of the matrix. Each variable appears twice in the matrix with identical coefficients, and the upper and lower triangles of the matrix are mirror images.
- **Kendall's tau-b.** A rank-order coefficient. Displays the correlations of each variable with every other variable in a lower-triangular matrix. The correlation of a variable with itself (the diagonal) and redundant coefficients are not displayed.
- **Spearman.** Spearman's rho. A rank-order coefficient. Displays a lower-triangular matrix.

Test of Significance. You can choose one of the following:

- **Two-tailed.** This test is appropriate when the direction of the relationship cannot be determined in advance, as is often the case in exploratory data analysis. This is the default. See "Hypothesis Tests about the Correlation Coefficient" on p. 207.
- **One-tailed.** This test is appropriate when the direction of the relationship between a pair of variables can be specified in advance of the analysis.

The following display option is also available:

- **Display actual significance level.** By default, actual significance levels are displayed. Deselect this item to indicate significance levels with asterisks. Correlation coefficients significant at the 0.05 level are identified with a single asterisk, and those significant at the 0.01 level are identified with two asterisks.

Bivariate Correlations Options

To obtain optional statistics for Pearson correlations or modify the treatment of cases with missing values, click on **Options...** in the Bivariate Correlations dialog box. This opens the Bivariate Correlations Options dialog box, as shown in Figure 13.9.

Figure 13.9 Bivariate Correlations Options dialog box

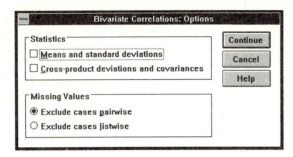

Statistics. For Pearson correlations, you can choose one or both of the following:

❏ **Means and standard deviations.** Displayed for each variable. The number of cases with nonmissing values is also shown. Missing values are handled on a variable-by-variable basis regardless of your missing values setting (see "Missing Values," below).

❏ **Cross-product deviations and covariances.** Displayed for each pair of variables. The cross-product deviation is equal to the sum of the products of mean-corrected variables. This is the numerator of the Pearson correlation coefficient, shown in Equation 13.1. The covariance is an unstandardized measure of the relationship between two variables, equal to the cross-product deviation divided by $N-1$.

Missing Values. You can choose one of the following alternatives:

❍ **Exclude cases pairwise.** Cases with missing values for one or both of a pair of variables for a correlation coefficient are excluded from the analysis. This is the default setting. Since each coefficient is based on all cases that have valid codes on that particular pair of variables, the maximum information available is used in every calculation. This can result in a set of coefficients based on a varying number of cases.

❍ **Exclude cases listwise.** Cases with missing values for any variable are excluded from all analyses.

Additional Features Available with Command Syntax

You can customize your correlations if you paste your selections into a syntax window and edit the resulting CORRELATIONS (Pearson correlations) or NONPAR CORR (Spearman or Kendall correlations) command syntax. (For information on syntax windows, see the *SPSS Base System User's Guide, Part 1*.) Additional features include:

- For Pearson correlations, a matrix facility to write a correlation matrix that can be used in place of raw data to obtain other analyses such as factor analysis (with the MATRIX subcommand).
- Correlations of each variable on a list with each variable on a second list (using the keyword WITH on the VARIABLES subcommand).

See the *SPSS Base System Syntax Reference Guide* for complete CORRELATIONS and NONPAR CORR command syntax.

14 Partial Correlation Analysis

Whenever you examine the relationship between two variables, you must be concerned with the effects of other variables on the relationship of interest. For example, if you are studying the relationship between education and income, you must worry about controlling for the effects of age and work experience. It may be that a small observed relationship between education and income is due to younger people being more highly educated but less experienced in the work force. If you control for job experience and age, the relationship between education and income may appear to be stronger.

The **partial correlation coefficient**, a technique closely related to multiple linear regression, provides us with a single measure of linear association between two variables while adjusting for the linear effects of one or more additional variables. Properly used, partial correlation is a useful technique for uncovering spurious relationships, identifying intervening variables, and detecting hidden relationships.

Computing a Partial Correlation Coefficient

Consider the steps involved in computing a partial correlation coefficient between salary and education, controlling for age. First, two regression equations must be estimated. The first equation predicts salary from age, and the second predicts education from age. For each of the regression equations, we compute the residuals for each case. The partial correlation coefficient between salary and education, controlling for age, is simply the usual Pearson correlation coefficient between the two sets of residuals.

In our example, the first regression equation removes the linear effects of age from salary. The residuals represent salary after the adjustment for age. The second regression equation removes the linear effects of age from education. The residuals represent education after the adjustment for age. The partial correlation coefficient estimates the linear association between the two variables after the effects of age are removed.

Because we used linear regression analysis to control for the age variable, we had to make the assumption that the relationships of interest are linear. If there is reason to suspect that the variables are related in a nonlinear way, the partial correlation coefficient is not an appropriate statistical technique to use.

The Order of the Coefficient

In the previous example, we controlled for the effect of only one variable, age. However, partial correlation analysis is not limited to a single control variable. The same procedure can be applied to several control variables.

The number of control variables determines the order of the partial correlation coefficient. If there is one control variable, the partial correlation coefficient is a **first-order partial**. If there are five control variables, it is a fifth-order partial. Sometimes the ordinary correlation coefficient is called a **zero-order correlation**, since there are no control variables.

(In fact, it is not necessary to keep computing regression equations, since partial correlation coefficients of a particular order can be computed recursively from coefficients of a lower order.)

Tests of Statistical Significance

The assumption of multivariate normality is required to test the null hypothesis that the population partial coefficient is 0. The test statistic is

$$t = r\sqrt{\frac{N - \theta - 2}{1 - r^2}}$$

Equation 14.1

where θ is the order of the coefficient and r is the partial correlation coefficient. The degrees of freedom for t are $N - \theta - 2$, where N is the number of cases.

Detecting Spurious Relationships

Partial correlation analysis can be used to detect spurious correlations between two variables. A **spurious correlation** is one in which the correlation between two variables results solely from the fact that one of the variables is correlated with a third variable that is the true predictor.

Consider the following example described by Kendall and Stuart (1973). Figure 14.1 is the correlation matrix between four variables measured in 16 large cities: crime rate, percentage of church membership, percentage of foreign-born males, and number of children under 5 per 1000 women between ages 15 and 44.

You can see that the correlation coefficient between crime rate (*CRIME*) and church membership (*CHURCH*) is negative (−0.14). The simplest conclusion is that church membership is a deterrent to crime. Although such a conclusion is no doubt comforting to theologians, let's examine the observed relationship further.

Figure 14.1 Zero-order correlation matrix

```
Zero Order Partials

             CRIME       CHURCH      PCTFRNM     UNDER5

CRIME        1.0000      -.1400      -.3400      -.3100
            (    0)     (   14)     (   14)     (   14)
            P= .        P= .605     P= .198     P= .243

CHURCH       -.1400      1.0000      .3300       .8500
            (   14)     (    0)     (   14)     (   14)
            P= .605     P= .        P= .212     P= .000

PCTFRNM      -.3400      .3300       1.0000      .4400
            (   14)     (   14)     (    0)     (   14)
            P= .198     P= .212     P= .        P= .088

UNDER5       -.3100      .8500       .4400       1.0000
            (   14)     (   14)     (   14)     (    0)
            P= .243     P= .000     P= .088     P= .
```

(Coefficient / (D.F.) / 2-tailed Significance)

" . " is printed if a coefficient cannot be computed

From Figure 14.1, you see that the crime rate is negatively correlated with the percentage of foreign-born males (*PCTFRNM*) and with the number of children per woman (*UNDER5*). Both of these variables are positively correlated with church membership. That is, both foreigners and women with many children tend to be church members.

Let's see what happens to the relationship between crime and church membership when we control for the linear effects of being foreign born and having many children. Figure 14.2 shows the partial correlation coefficient between crime and church membership when the percentage of foreign-born males is held constant. Note that the correlation coefficient, −0.03, is now close to 0.

Figure 14.2 First-order partials, controlling for percentage of foreign-born males

```
Controlling for..    PCTFRNM

             CRIME       CHURCH

CRIME        1.0000      -.0313
            (    0)     (   13)
            P= .        P= .912

CHURCH       -.0313      1.0000
            (   13)     (    0)
            P= .912     P= .
```

(Coefficient / (D.F.) / 2-tailed Significance)

" . " is printed if a coefficient cannot be computed

Similarly, Figure 14.3 is the partial correlation coefficient between crime and church membership when the number of young children per woman is held constant. The partial correlation coefficient, 0.25, is now positive.

Figure 14.3 First-order partials, controlling for number of children

```
Controlling for..    UNDER5
                CRIME       CHURCH
CRIME          1.0000        .2466
              (     0)      (    13)
               P= .          P= .376

CHURCH          .2466       1.0000
              (    13)      (     0)
               P= .376       P= .

(Coefficient / (D.F.) / 2-tailed Significance)

" . " is printed if a coefficient cannot be computed
```

The second-order partial correlation coefficient controlling for both foreign-born males and number of children is shown in Figure 14.4. The relationship between church membership and crime, 0.23, is now positive.

Figure 14.4 Second-order partial correlations

```
Controlling for..    PCTFRNM    UNDER5
                CRIME       CHURCH
CRIME          1.0000        .2321
              (     0)      (    12)
               P= .          P= .425

CHURCH          .2321       1.0000
              (    12)      (     0)
               P= .425       P= .

(Coefficient / (D.F.) / 2-tailed Significance)

" . " is printed if a coefficient cannot be computed
```

From examination of the partial coefficients, it appears that the original negative relationship between church membership and crime may be due to the presence of law-abiding foreigners with large families. In 1935, when the study was done, foreigners were less likely to commit crimes and more likely to be church members than the general population. These relationships cause the overall coefficient between the two variables to be negative. However, when these two variables are controlled for, the relationship between church membership and crime changes drastically.

Detecting Hidden Relationships

Theory or intuition sometimes suggests that there should be a relationship between two variables even though the data indicate no correlation. In this situation, it is possible that one or more additional variables are suppressing the expected relationship. For example, it may be that *A* is not correlated with *B* because *A* is negatively related to *C*, which is positively related to *B*.

For example, assume that a marketing research company wants to examine the relationship between the need for transmission-rebuilding kits and the intent to purchase such a kit. Initial examination of the data reveals almost no correlation (0.01) between need for such a kit and intent to buy. However, the data show a *negative* relationship (−0.5) between income and need to buy and a *positive* relationship (0.6) between income and intent to buy. If we control for the effect of income using a partial correlation coefficient, the first-order partial between need and intent, controlling for income, is 0.45. Thus, income hid the relationship between need and intent to buy.

Interpreting the Results of Partial Correlation Analysis

Proper interpretation of partial correlation analysis requires knowledge about the way the variables may be related. You must know, for example, the nature of the relationship between need for a transmission and family income; that is, does income influence need, or does need influence income? If you assume that need for a transmission influences family income, then need is specified as the control variable. One way of codifying the requisite assumptions in using partials in multivariate analysis is known as **path analysis** (Wright, 1960; Duncan, 1966).

How to Obtain Partial Correlations

The Partial Correlations procedure computes partial correlation coefficients that describe the linear relationship between two variables while controlling for the effects of one or more additional variables. The procedure calculates a matrix of zero-order coefficients and bases the partial correlations on this matrix.

The minimum specifications are:
- Two or more numeric variables for which partial correlations are to be computed.
- One or more numeric control variables.

To obtain a partial correlation analysis, from the menus choose:

Statistics
  Correlate ▶
    Partial...

This opens the Partial Correlations dialog box, as shown in Figure 14.5.

Figure 14.5 Partial Correlations dialog box

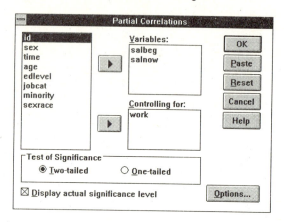

The numeric variables in your data file appear on the source list. Select two or more variables to be correlated and at least one control variable. To obtain the default partial correlation analysis with two-tailed probabilities, click on OK. SPSS produces a square matrix of the highest-order partial correlations. Cases with missing values for any of the variables are excluded from all analyses.

Test of Significance. You can choose one of the following alternatives:

- ○ **Two-tailed.** Two-tailed probabilities. This is the default.
- ○ **One-tailed.** One-tailed probabilities.

The following display option is also available:

- ❏ **Display actual significance level.** By default, the probability and degrees of freedom are shown for each coefficient. If you deselect this item, coefficients significant at the 0.05 level are identified with a single asterisk, coefficients significant at the 0.01 level are identified with a double asterisk, and degrees of freedom are suppressed. This setting affects both partial and zero-order correlation matrices.

Partial Correlations Options

To obtain optional univariate summary statistics or zero-order correlations, or to modify the handling of missing values, click on Options... in the Partial Correlations dialog box. This opens the Partial Correlations Options dialog box, as shown in Figure 14.6.

Figure 14.6 Partial Correlations Options dialog box

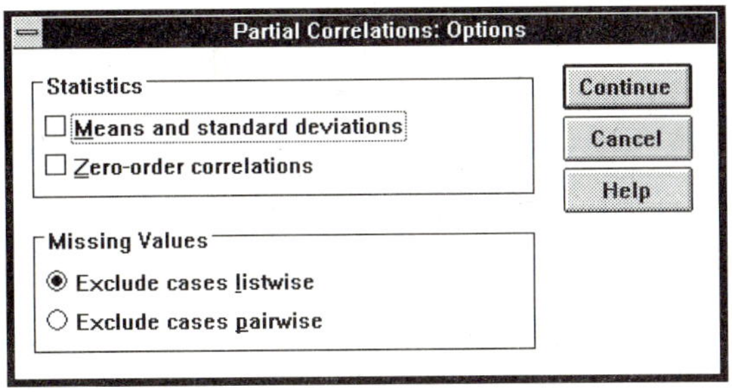

Statistics. You can choose one or both of the following:

- **Means and standard deviations.** Displayed for each variable. The number of cases with nonmissing values is also shown.
- **Zero-order correlations.** A matrix of simple correlations between all variables, including control variables, is displayed (see "The Order of the Coefficient" on p. 216).

Missing Values. You can choose one of the following alternatives:

- **Exclude cases listwise.** Cases having missing values for any variable, including a control variable, are excluded from all computations. This is the default.
- **Exclude cases pairwise.** For computation of the zero-order correlations on which the partial correlations are based, a case having missing values for one or both of a pair of variables is not used. Pairwise deletion uses as much of the data as possible. However, the number of cases may differ across coefficients. When pairwise deletion is in effect, the degrees of freedom for a particular partial coefficient are based on the smallest number of cases used in the calculation of any of the zero-order correlations.

Additional Features Available with Command Syntax

You can customize your partial correlations if you paste your selections into a syntax window and edit the resulting PARTIAL CORR command syntax. (For information on syntax windows, see the *SPSS Base System User's Guide, Part 1*.) Additional features include:

- Matrix facility to read a zero-order correlation matrix or to write a partial correlation matrix (with the MATRIX subcommand).
- Partial correlations between two lists of variables (using the keyword WITH on the VARIABLES subcommand).
- Multiple analyses (with multiple VARIABLES subcommands).

- User-specified order values to request, for example, both first- and second-order partial correlations when you have two control variables (with the VARIABLES subcommand).
- The ability to suppress redundant coefficients (with the FORMAT subcommand).
- An option to display a matrix of simple correlations when some coefficients cannot be computed (with the STATISTICS subcommand).

See the *SPSS Base System Syntax Reference Guide* for complete PARTIAL CORR command syntax.

15 Multiple Linear Regression Analysis

The 1964 Civil Rights Act prohibits discrimination in the workplace based on sex or race; employers who violate the act are liable to prosecution. Since passage of the Civil Rights Act, women, blacks, and other groups have filed numerous lawsuits charging unfair hiring or advancement practices.

The courts have ruled that statistics can be used as *prima facie* evidence of discrimination. Many lawsuits depend heavily on complex statistical analyses to demonstrate that similarly qualified individuals are not treated equally (Roberts, 1980). In this chapter, employee records for 474 individuals hired between 1969 and 1971 by a bank engaged in Equal Employment Opportunity litigation are analyzed. A mathematical model is developed that relates beginning salary and salary progression to employee characteristics such as seniority, education, and previous work experience. One objective is to determine whether sex and race are important predictors of salary.

The technique used to build the model is linear regression analysis, one of the most versatile data analysis procedures. Regression can be used to summarize data as well as to study relations among variables.

Linear Regression

Before examining a model that relates beginning salary to several other variables, consider the relationship between beginning salary and current (as of March, 1977) salary. For employees hired during a similar time period, beginning salary should serve as a reasonably good predictor of salary at a later date. Although superstars and underachievers might progress differently from the group as a whole, salary progression should be similar for the others. The scatterplot of beginning salary and current salary shown in Figure 15.1 supports this hypothesis.

A scatterplot may suggest what type of mathematical functions would be appropriate for summarizing the data. Many functions, including parabolas, hyperbolas, polynomials, and trigonometric functions, are useful in fitting models to data. The scatterplot in Figure 15.1 shows current salaries tending to increase linearly with increases in beginning salary. If the plot indicates that a straight line is not a good summary measure of the relationship, you should consider other methods of analysis, including transforming the data to achieve linearity (see "Coaxing a Nonlinear Relationship to Linearity" on p. 246).

Figure 15.1 Scatterplot of beginning and current salaries

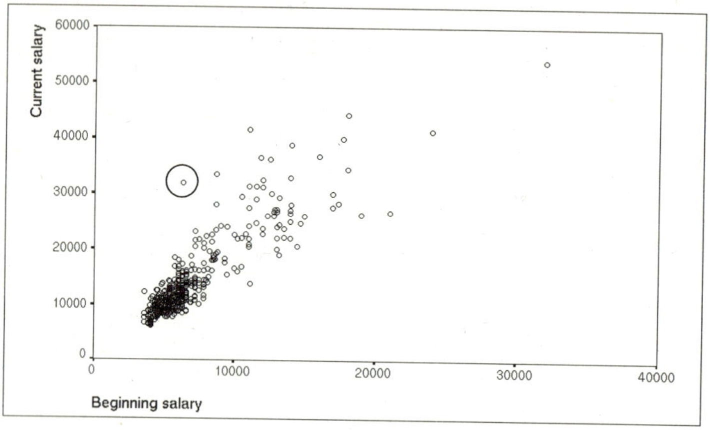

Outliers

A plot may also indicate the presence of points suspiciously different from the others. Examine such observations, termed **outliers**, carefully to see if they result from errors in gathering, coding, or entering data. The circled point in Figure 15.1 appears to be an outlier. Though neither the value of beginning salary ($6,300) nor the value of current salary ($32,000) is unique, jointly they are unusual.

The treatment of outliers can be difficult. If the point is incorrect due to coding or entry problems, you should correct it and rerun the analysis. If there is no apparent explanation for the outlier, consider interactions with other variables as a possible explanation. For example, the outlier may represent an employee who was hired as a low-paid clerical worker while pursuing an MBA degree. After graduation, the employee rose rapidly to a higher position; in this instance, the variable for education explains the unusual salary characteristics.

Choosing a Regression Line

Since current salary tends to increase linearly with beginning salary, a straight line can be used to summarize the relationship. The equation for the line is

$$\text{predicted current salary} = B_0 + B_1 (\text{beginning salary})$$

Equation 15.1

The **slope** (B_1) is the change (in dollars) in the fitted current salary for a change in the beginning salary. The **intercept** (B_0) is the theoretical estimate of current salary for a beginning salary of 0.

However, the observed data points do not all fall on a straight line, they cluster around it. Many lines can be drawn through the data points; the problem is to select among the possible lines. The method of **least squares** results in a line that minimizes the sum of squared vertical distances from the observed data points to the line. Any other line has a larger sum. Figure 15.2 shows the least-squares line superimposed on the salary scatterplot. Some vertical distances from points to the line are also shown.

Figure 15.2 Regression line for beginning and current salaries

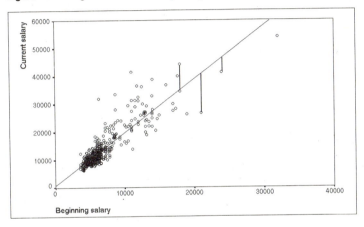

You can use SPSS to calculate the least-squares line. For the data in Figure 15.1, that line is

predicted current salary = 771.28 + 1.91 (beginning salary)   **Equation 15.2**

The slope and intercept values are shown in the column labeled B in the output shown in Figure 15.3.

Figure 15.3 Statistics for variables in the equation

```
------------------ Variables in the Equation ------------------

Variable              B          SE B       Beta         T     Sig T

SALBEG           1.909450      .047410    .880117    40.276    .0000
(Constant)     771.282303   355.471941                2.170    .0305
```

The Standardized Regression Coefficient

The **standardized regression coefficient**, labeled *Beta* in Figure 15.3, is defined as

$$\text{beta} = B_1 \frac{S_X}{S_Y} \qquad \text{Equation 15.3}$$

Multiplying the regression coefficient (B_1) by the ratio of the standard deviation of the independent variable (S_X) to the standard deviation of the dependent variable (S_Y) results in a dimensionless coefficient. In fact, the beta coefficient is the slope of the least-squares line when both X and Y are expressed as Z scores. The beta coefficient is discussed further in "Beta Coefficients" on p. 254.

From Samples to Populations

Generally, more is sought in regression analysis than a description of observed data. You usually want to draw inferences about the relationship of the variables in the population from which the sample was taken. How are beginning and current salaries related for all employees, not just those included in the sample? Inferences about population values based on sample results are based on the following assumptions:

Normality and Equality of Variance. For any fixed value of the independent variable X, the distribution of the dependent variable Y is normal, with mean $\mu_{Y/X}$ (the mean of Y for a given X) and a constant variance of σ^2 (see Figure 15.4). This assumption specifies that not all employees with the same beginning salary have the same current salary. Instead, there is a normal distribution of current salaries for each beginning salary. Though the distributions have different means, they have the same variance: σ^2.

Figure 15.4 Regression assumptions

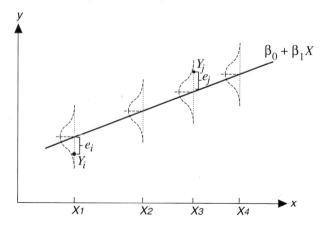

Independence. The Y's are statistically independent of each other; that is, observations are in no way influenced by other observations. For example, observations are *not* independent if they are based on repeated measurements from the same experimental unit. If three observations are taken from each of four families, the twelve observations are not independent.

Linearity. The mean values $\mu_{Y/X}$ all lie on a straight line, which is the population regression line. This is the line drawn in Figure 15.4. An alternative way of stating this assumption is that the linear model is correct.

When there is a single independent variable, the model can be summarized by

$$Y_i = \beta_0 + \beta_1 X_i + e_i \qquad \text{Equation 15.4}$$

The population parameters (values) for the slope and intercept are denoted by β_1 and β_0. The term e_i, usually called the **error**, is the difference between the observed value of Y_i and the subpopulation mean at the point X_i. The e_i are assumed to be normally distributed, independent, random variables with a mean of 0 and variance of σ^2 (see Figure 15.4).

Estimating Population Parameters

Since β_0 and β_1 are unknown population parameters, they must be estimated from the sample. The least-squares coefficients B_0 and B_1, discussed in "Choosing a Regression Line" on p. 224, are used to estimate the population parameters.

However, the slope and intercept estimated from a single sample typically differ from the population values and vary from sample to sample. To use these estimates for inference about the population values, the sampling distributions of the two statistics are needed. When the assumptions of linear regression are met, the sampling distributions of B_0 and B_1 are normal, with means of β_0 and β_1.

The standard error of B_0 is

$$\sigma_{B_0} = \sigma \sqrt{\frac{1}{N} + \frac{\bar{X}^2}{(N-1) S_X^2}} \qquad \text{Equation 15.5}$$

where S_X^2 is the sample variance of the independent variable. The standard error of B_1 is

$$\sigma_{B_1} = \frac{\sigma}{\sqrt{(N-1) S_X^2}} \qquad \text{Equation 15.6}$$

Since the population variance of the errors, σ^2, is not known, it must also be estimated. The usual estimate of σ^2 is

$$S^2 = \frac{\sum_{i=1}^{N}(Y_i - B_0 - B_1 X_i)^2}{N-2}$$
Equation 15.7

The positive square root of S^2 is termed the **standard error of the estimate**, or the standard deviation of the residuals. (The reason for this name is discussed in "Predicting a New Value" on p. 234.) The estimated standard errors of the slope and intercept are displayed in the third column (labeled *SE B*) in Figure 15.3.

Testing Hypotheses

A frequently tested hypothesis is that there is no linear relationship between X and Y—that the slope of the population regression line is 0. The statistic used to test this hypothesis is

$$t = \frac{B_1}{S_{B_1}}$$
Equation 15.8

The distribution of the statistic, when the assumptions are met and the hypothesis of no linear relationship is true, is Student's t distribution with $N-2$ degrees of freedom. The statistic for testing the hypothesis that the intercept is 0 is

$$t = \frac{B_0}{S_{B_0}}$$
Equation 15.9

Its distribution is also Student's t with $N-2$ degrees of freedom.

These t statistics and their two-tailed observed significance levels are displayed in the last two columns of Figure 15.3. The small observed significance level (less than 0.00005) associated with the slope for the salary data supports the hypothesis that beginning salary and current salary have a linear association.

Confidence Intervals

A statistic calculated from a sample provides a point estimate of the unknown parameter. A point estimate can be thought of as the single best guess for the population value. While the estimated value from the sample is typically different from the value of the unknown population parameter, the hope is that it isn't too far away. Based on the sample estimate, it is possible to calculate a range of values that, within a designated likelihood, includes the population value. Such a range is called a **confidence interval**. For example, as shown in Figure 15.5, the 95% confidence interval for β_1, the population slope, is 1.816 to 2.003.

Figure 15.5 Confidence intervals

```
---- Variables in the Equation -----

Variable          95% Confdnce Intrvl B

SALBEG          1.816290    2.002610
(Constant)     72.778982 1469.785624
```

Ninety-five percent confidence means that if repeated samples are drawn from a population under the same conditions and 95% confidence intervals are calculated, 95% of the intervals will contain the unknown parameter β_1. Since the parameter value is unknown, it is not possible to determine whether a particular interval contains it.

Goodness of Fit

An important part of any statistical procedure that builds models from data is establishing how well the model actually fits, or its **goodness of fit**. This includes the detection of possible violations of the required assumptions in the data being analyzed.

The R-squared Coefficient

A commonly used measure of the goodness of fit of a linear model is R^2, or the **coefficient of determination**. It can be thought of in a variety of ways. Besides being the square of the correlation coefficient between variables X and Y, it is the square of the correlation coefficient between Y (the observed value of the dependent variable) and $\hat{Y}$ (the predicted value of Y from the fitted line). If you compute the predicted salary for each employee (based on the coefficients in the output in Figure 15.3) as follows

predicted current salary = 771.28 + 1.91 (beginning salary)   **Equation 15.10**

and then calculate the square of the Pearson correlation coefficient between predicted current salary and observed current salary, you will get R^2. If all the observations fall on the regression line, R^2 is 1. If there is no linear relationship between the dependent and independent variables, R^2 is 0.

Note that R^2 is a measure of the goodness of fit of a particular model and that an R^2 of 0 does not necessarily mean that there is no association between the variables. Instead, it indicates that there is no *linear* relationship.

In the output in Figure 15.6, R^2 is labeled *R Square* and its square root is labeled *Multiple R*. The sample R^2 tends to be an optimistic estimate of how well the model fits the population. The model usually does not fit the population as well as it fits the sample from which it is derived. The statistic adjusted R^2 attempts to correct R^2 to more closely reflect the goodness of fit of the model in the population. Adjusted R^2 is given by

$$R_a^2 = R^2 - \frac{p(1-R^2)}{N-p-1}$$

Equation 15.11

where p is the number of independent variables in the equation (1 in the salary example).

Figure 15.6 Summary statistics for the equation

```
Multiple R          .88012
R Square            .77461
Adjusted R Square   .77413
Standard Error   3246.14226
```

Analysis of Variance

To test the hypothesis that there is no linear relationship between X and Y, several equivalent statistics can be computed. When there is a single independent variable, the hypothesis that the population R^2 is 0 is identical to the hypothesis that the population slope is 0. The test for $R_{pop}^2 = 0$ is usually obtained from the analysis-of-variance table (see Figure 15.7).

Figure 15.7 Analysis-of-variance table

```
Analysis of Variance
                 DF      Sum of Squares       Mean Square
Regression        1    17092967800.01978   17092967800.0198
Residual        472     4973671469.79454      10537439.55465

F =    1622.11776       Signif F =   .0000
```

The total observed variability in the dependent variable is subdivided into two components—that which is attributable to the regression (labeled *Regression*) and that which is not (labeled *Residual*). Consider Figure 15.8. For a particular point, the distance from Y_i to $\bar{Y}$ (the mean of the Y's) can be subdivided into two parts:

$$Y_i - \bar{Y} = \left(Y_i - \hat{Y}_i\right) + \left(\hat{Y}_i - \bar{Y}\right)$$

Equation 15.12

The distance from Y_i (the observed value) to $\hat{Y}_i$ (the value predicted by the regression line), or $Y_i - \hat{Y}_i$, is called the **residual from the regression**. It is zero if the regression line passes through the point. The second component $(\hat{Y}_i - \bar{Y})$ is the distance from the regression line to the mean of the Y's. This distance is "explained" by the regression in

Figure 15.8 Components of variability

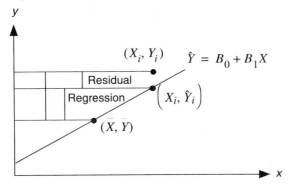

that it represents the improvement in the estimate of the dependent variable achieved by the regression. Without the regression, the mean of the dependent variable $\bar{Y}$ is used as the estimate. It can be shown that

$$\sum_{i=1}^{N}\left(Y_i - \bar{Y}\right)^2 = \sum_{i=1}^{N}\left(Y_i - \hat{Y}_i\right)^2 + \sum_{i=1}^{N}\left(\hat{Y}_i - \bar{Y}\right)^2 \qquad \text{Equation 15.13}$$

The first quantity following the equals sign is called the **residual sum of squares** and the second quantity is the **regression sum of squares**. The sum of these is called the **total sum of squares**.

The analysis-of-variance table in Figure 15.7 displays these two sums of squares under the heading *Sum of Squares*. The *Mean Square* for each entry is the sum of squares divided by the degrees of freedom (*DF*). If the regression assumptions are met, the ratio of the mean square regression to the mean square residual is distributed as an *F* statistic with p and $N - p - 1$ degrees of freedom. *F* serves to test how well the regression model fits the data. If the probability associated with the *F* statistic is small, the hypothesis that $R^2_{pop} = 0$ is rejected. For this example, the *F* statistic is

$$F = \frac{\text{mean square regression}}{\text{mean square residual}} = 1622 \qquad \text{Equation 15.14}$$

The observed significance level (*Signif F*) is less than 0.00005.

The square root of the *F* value (1622) is 40.28, which is the value of the *t* statistic for the slope in Figure 15.3. The square of a *t* value with *k* degrees of freedom is an *F* value with 1 and *k* degrees of freedom. Therefore, either *t* or *F* values can be computed to test that $\beta_i = 0$. Another useful summary statistic is the standard error of the estimate, S, which can also be calculated as the square root of the residual mean square (see "Predicting a New Value" on p. 234).

Another Interpretation of R-squared

Partitioning the sum of squares of the dependent variable allows another interpretation of R^2. It is the proportion of the variation in the dependent variable "explained" by the model:

$$R^2 = 1 - \frac{\text{residual sum of squares}}{\text{total sum of squares}} = 0.775 \qquad \text{Equation 15.15}$$

Similarly, adjusted R^2 is

$$R_a^2 = 1 - \frac{\text{residual sum of squares}/(N-p-1)}{\text{total sum of squares}/(N-1)} \qquad \text{Equation 15.16}$$

where p is the number of independent variables in the equation (1 in the salary example).

Predicted Values and Their Standard Errors

By comparing the observed values of the dependent variable with the values predicted by the regression equation, you can learn a good deal about how well a model and the various assumptions fit the data (see the discussion of residuals beginning with "Searching for Violations of Assumptions" on p. 236). Predicted values are also of interest when the results are used to predict new data. You may wish to predict the mean Y for all cases with a given value of X (denoted X_0) or to predict the value of Y for a single case. For example, you can predict either the mean salary for all employees with a beginning salary of $10,000 or the salary for a particular employee with a beginning salary of $10,000. In both situations, the predicted value

$$\hat{Y}_0 = B_0 + B_1 X_0 = 771 + 1.91 \times 10{,}000 = 19{,}871 \qquad \text{Equation 15.17}$$

is the same. What differs is the standard error.

Predicting Mean Response

The estimated standard error for the predicted mean Y at X_0 is

$$S_{\hat{Y}} = S\sqrt{\frac{1}{N} + \frac{(X_0 - \bar{X})^2}{(N-1)S_X^2}}$$

Equation 15.18

The equation for the standard error shows that the smallest value occurs when X_0 is equal to $\bar{X}$, the mean of X. The larger the distance from the mean, the greater the standard error. Thus, the mean of Y for a given X is better estimated for central values of the observed X's than for outlying values. Figure 15.9 is a plot of the standard errors of predicted mean salaries for different values of beginning salary (obtained by saving the standard error as a new variable in the Linear Regression procedure and then using the Scatter option on the Graphs menu).

Figure 15.9 Standard errors for predicted mean responses

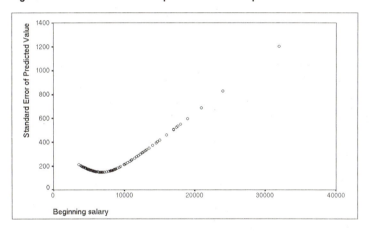

Prediction intervals for the mean predicted salary are calculated in the standard way. The 95% confidence interval at X_0 is

$$\hat{Y} \pm t_{\left(1 - \frac{\alpha}{2}, N - 2\right)} S_{\hat{Y}}$$

Equation 15.19

Figure 15.10 shows a typical 95% confidence band for predicted mean responses. It is narrowest at the mean of X and widens as the distance from the mean $(X_0 - \bar{X})$ increases.

Figure 15.10   95% confidence band for mean prediction

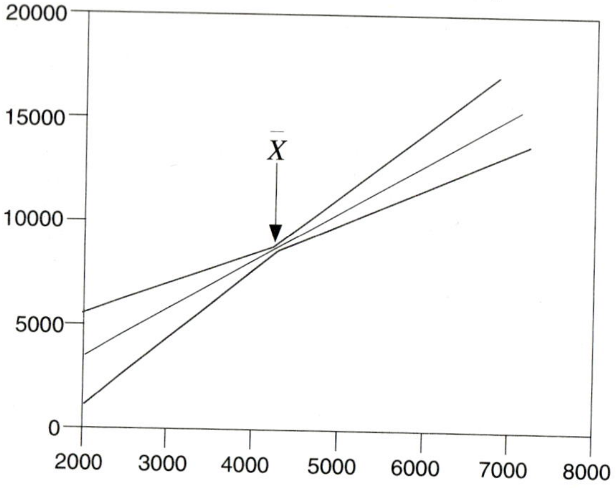

Predicting a New Value

Although the predicted value for a single new observation at X_0 is the same as the predicted value for the mean at X_0, the standard error is not. The two sources of error when predicting an individual observation are:

1. The individual value may differ from the population mean of Y for X_0.

2. The estimate of the population mean at X_0 may differ from the population mean.

The sources of error are illustrated in Figure 15.11.

Figure 15.11   Sources of error in predicting individual observations

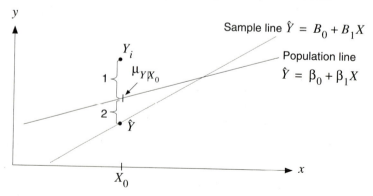

When estimating the mean response, only the second error component is considered. The variance of the individual prediction is the variance of the mean prediction plus the variance of Y_i for a given X. This can be written as

$$S^2_{\text{ind}\hat{Y}} = S^2_{\hat{Y}} + S^2 = S^2 \left[1 + \frac{1}{N} + \frac{(X_0 - \bar{X})^2}{(N-1) S^2_X} \right] \qquad \text{Equation 15.20}$$

Prediction intervals for the new observation are obtained by substituting $S_{\text{ind}\hat{Y}}$ for $S_{\hat{Y}}$ in Equation 15.19. If the sample size is large, the terms $1/N$ and

$$\frac{(X_0 - \bar{X})^2}{(N-1) S^2_X} \qquad \text{Equation 15.21}$$

are negligible. In that case, the standard error is simply S, which explains the name standard error of the estimate for S (see "Estimating Population Parameters" on p. 227). You can obtain plots of confidence intervals for predicted values using the Scatter option on the Graphs menu.

Reading the Casewise Plot

Figure 15.12 shows the output from the beginning and end of a plot of the salary data. The sequential number of the case is listed first, followed by the plot of standardized residuals, the observed (*SALNOW*), predicted (**PRED*), and residual (**RESID*) values. In SPSS, you can save predicted values and confidence intervals for the mean responses and for individual responses and use the List Cases procedure to display these values for all cases or for a subset of cases (see Chapter 18).

Figure 15.12   Casewise plot with predicted values

```
Casewise Plot of Standardized Residual

*: Selected    M: Missing

          -3.0         0.0         3.0
Case #     O:...........:...........:O      SALNOW      *PRED       *RESID
  1        .           *.          .         16080    16810.6600    -730.6600
  2        .    *      .           .         41400    46598.0758   -5198.0758
  3        .           .   *       .         21960    20247.6695    1712.3305
  4        .           .  *        .         19200    17383.4949    1816.5051
  5        .  *        .           .         28350    33995.7076   -5645.7076
  6        .           .   *       .         27250    25586.4910    1663.5090
  7        .           .   *       .         16080    13946.4854    2133.5146
  8        .           .       *   .         14100    11082.3108    3017.6892
  9        .           .    *      .         12420    10394.9089    2025.0911
 10        .          *.           .         12300    12800.8156    -500.8156
 11        .           .     *     .         15720    12800.8156    2919.1844
 12        .      *    .           .          8880    12227.9807   -3347.9807
 ..
 ..
 ..
470        .           *           .          9420     9592.9401    -172.9401
471        .           .*          .          9780     9134.6721     645.3279
472        .       *   .           .          7680     9249.2391   -1569.2391
473        .        *  .           .          7380     8561.8372   -1181.8372
474        .         * .           .          8340    10738.6099   -2398.6099
Case #     O:...........:...........:O      SALNOW      *PRED       *RESID
          -3.0         0.0         3.0
```

Searching for Violations of Assumptions

You usually don't know in advance whether a model such as linear regression is appropriate. Therefore, it is necessary to conduct a search focused on residuals to look for evidence that the necessary assumptions are violated.

Residuals

In model building, a **residual** is what is left after the model is fit. It is the difference between an observed value and the value predicted by the model:

$$E_i = Y_i - B_0 - B_1 X_i = Y_i - \hat{Y}_i \qquad \text{Equation 15.22}$$

In regression analysis, the true errors, e_i, are assumed to be independent normal values with a mean of 0 and a constant variance of σ^2. If the model is appropriate for the data, the observed residuals, E_i, which are estimates of the true errors, e_i, should have similar characteristics.

If the intercept term is included in the equation, the mean of the residuals is always 0, so the mean provides no information about the true mean of the errors. Since the sum of the residuals is constrained to be 0, the residuals are *not* strictly independent. However, if the number of residuals is large when compared to the number of independent variables, the dependency among the residuals can be ignored for practical purposes.

The relative magnitudes of residuals are easier to judge when they are divided by estimates of their standard deviations. The resulting **standardized residuals** are expressed in standard deviation units above or below the mean. For example, the fact that a particular residual is −5198.1 provides little information. If you know that its standardized form is −3.1, you know not only that the observed value is less than the predicted value but also that the residual is larger than most in absolute value.

Residuals are sometimes adjusted in one of two ways. The standardized residual for case i is the residual divided by the sample standard deviation of the residuals. Standardized residuals have a mean of 0 and a standard deviation of 1. The **Studentized residual** is the residual divided by an estimate of its standard deviation that varies from point to point, depending on the distance of X_i from the mean of X. Usually standardized and Studentized residuals are close in value, but not always. The Studentized residual reflects more precisely differences in the true error variances from point to point.

Linearity

For the bivariate situation, a scatterplot is a good means for judging how well a straight line fits the data. Another convenient method is to plot the residuals against the predicted values. If the assumptions of linearity and homogeneity of variance are met, there should be no relationship between the predicted and residual values. You should be suspicious of any observable pattern.

For example, fitting a least-squares line to the data in the plots shown in Figure 15.13 yields the residual plots shown in Figure 15.14. The two residual plots show patterns, since straight lines do not fit the data well. Systematic patterns between the predicted values and the residuals suggest possible violations of the assumption of linearity. If the assumption were met, the residuals would be randomly distributed in a band clustered around the horizontal line through 0, as shown in Figure 15.15.

Figure 15.13 Scatterplots of cubic and quadratic relationships

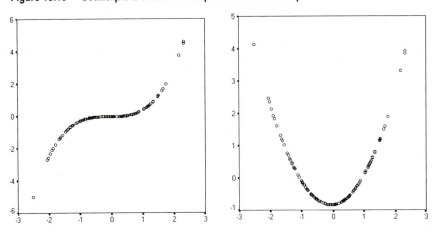

Figure 15.14 Standardized residuals scatterplots—cubic and quadratic relationships

Figure 15.15 Randomly distributed residuals

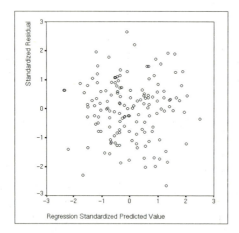

Residuals can also be plotted against individual independent variables by saving them in the Linear Regression procedure and then using the Scatter option on the Graphs menu. Again, if the assumptions are met, you should see a horizontal band of residuals. Consider as well plotting the residuals against independent variables not in the equation. If the residuals are not randomly distributed, you may want to include the variable in the equation for a multiple regression model (see "Multiple Regression Models" on p. 250).

Equality of Variance

You can also use the previously described plots to check for violations of the equality-of-variance assumption. If the spread of the residuals increases or decreases with values of the independent variables or with predicted values, you should question the assumption of constant variance of Y for all values of X.

Figure 15.16 is a plot of the Studentized residuals against the predicted values for the salary data. The spread of the residuals increases with the magnitude of the predicted values, suggesting that the variability of current salaries increases with salary level. Thus, the equality-of-variance assumption appears to be violated.

Figure 15.16   Unequal variance

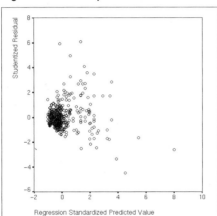

Independence of Error

Whenever the data are collected and recorded sequentially, you should plot residuals against the sequence variable. Even if time is not considered a variable in the model, it could influence the residuals. For example, suppose you are studying survival time after surgery as a function of complexity of surgery, amount of blood transfused, dosage of medication, and so forth. In addition to these variables, it is also possible that the surgeon's skill increased with each operation and that a patient's survival time is influenced by the number of prior patients treated. The plot of standardized residuals corresponding to the order in which patients received surgery shows a shorter survival time for earlier patients than for later patients (see Figure 15.17). If sequence and the residual are independent, you should not see a discernible pattern.

Figure 15.17   Serial plot

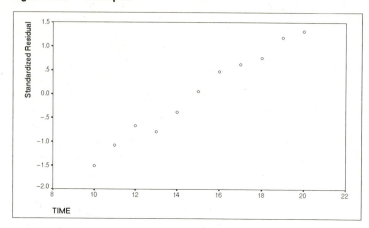

The **Durbin-Watson statistic**, a test for serial correlation of adjacent error terms, is defined as

$$d = \frac{\sum_{t=2}^{N} (E_t - E_{t-1})^2}{\sum_{t=1}^{N} E_t^2}$$ **Equation 15.23**

The possible values of the statistic range from 0 to 4. If the residuals are not correlated with each other, the value of d is close to 2. Values less than 2 mean that adjacent residuals are positively correlated. Values greater than 2 mean that adjacent residuals are negatively correlated. Consult tables of the d statistic for bounds upon which significance tests can be based.

Normality

The distribution of residuals may not appear to be normal for reasons other than actual non-normality: misspecification of the model, nonconstant variance, a small number of residuals actually available for analysis, etc. Therefore, you should pursue several lines of investigation. One of the simplest is to construct a histogram of the residuals, such as the one for the salary data shown in Figure 15.18.

Figure 15.18 Histogram of standardized residuals

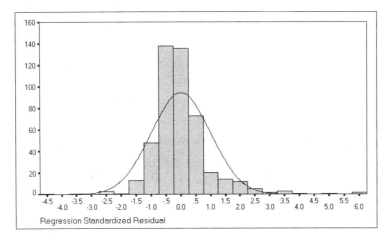

A normal distribution is superimposed on a histogram of observed frequencies (indicated by the bars). It is unreasonable to expect the observed residuals to be exactly normal—some deviation is expected because of sampling variation. Even if the errors are normally distributed in the population, sample residuals are only approximately normal.

In the histogram in Figure 15.18, the distribution does not seem normal, since there is an exaggerated clustering of residuals toward the center and a straggling tail toward large positive values. Thus, the normality assumption may be violated.

Another way to compare the observed distribution of residuals to the expected distribution under the assumption of normality is to plot the two cumulative distributions against each other for a series of points. If the two distributions are identical, a straight line results. By observing how points scatter about the expected straight line, you can compare the two distributions.

Figure 15.19 is a cumulative probability plot of the salary residuals. Initially, the observed residuals are above the "normal" line, since there is a smaller number of large negative residuals than expected. Once the greatest concentration of residuals is reached, the observed points are below the line, since the observed cumulative proportion exceeds the expected. Tests for normality are available using the Explore procedure (see Chapter 5).

Figure 15.19   Normal probability (P–P) plot

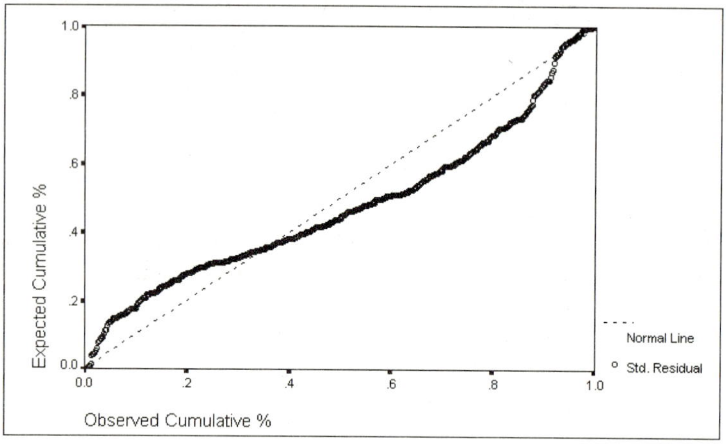

Locating Outliers

You can spot outliers readily on residual plots, since they are cases with very large positive or negative residuals. In general, standardized residual values greater than an absolute value of 3 are considered outliers. Since you usually want more information about outliers, you can use the casewise plotting facility to display identification numbers and a variety of other statistics for cases having residuals beyond a specified cutoff point.

Figure 15.20 displays information for the nine cases with standardized residuals greater than the absolute value of 3. Only two of these nine cases have current salaries less than those predicted by the model (cases 67 and 122). The others all have larger salaries, an average of $33,294, than the average for the sample, only $13,767. Thus, there is some evidence that the model may not fit well for the highly paid cases.

Figure 15.20   Casewise plot of residuals outliers

```
Casewise Plot of Standardized Residual

Outliers = 3.       *: Selected    M: Missing

              -6.      -3.     3.       6.
    Case #    0:.......:       :.......:O   SALNOW      *PRED        *RESID
       24     .             ..*          .     28000    17383.4949    10616.5051
       60     .             ..         *.      32000    12800.8156    19199.1844
       67     .           *..            .     26400    37043.1894   -10643.1894
      114     .             .. *         .     38800    27511.2163    11288.7837
      122     .    *        ..           .     26700    40869.7266   -14169.7266
      123     .             .. *         .     36250    24639.4039    11610.5961
      129     .             ..       *   .     33500    17383.4949    16116.5051
      149     .             ,..         *      41500    21782.8671    19717.1329
      177     .             ..   *      .      36500    23295.1513    13204.8487
```

Other Unusual Observations: Mahalanobis Distance

In the section "Outliers" on p. 224, one case was identified as an outlier because the combination of values for beginning and current salaries was atypical. This case (case 60) also appears in Figure 15.20, since it has a large value for the standardized residual. Another unusual case (case 56) has a beginning salary of $31,992. Since the average beginning salary for the entire sample is only $6,806 and the standard deviation is 3148, the case is eight standard deviations above the mean. But since the standardized residual is not large, this case does not appear in Figure 15.20.

However, cases that have unusual values for the independent variables can have a substantial impact on the results of analysis and should be identified. One measure of the distance of cases from average values of the independent variables is **Mahalanobis distance**. In the case of a regression equation with a single independent variable, it is the square of the standardized value of X:

$$D_i = \left(\frac{X_i - \bar{X}}{S_X}\right)^2 \qquad \textbf{Equation 15.24}$$

When there is more than one independent variable—where Mahalanobis distance is most valuable—the computations are more complex.

You can save Mahalanobis distances with SPSS and display cases with the five highest and lowest values using the Explore procedure (see Chapter 5). As shown in Figure 15.21, the Mahalanobis distance for case 56 is 64 (8^2).

Figure 15.21 Mahalanobis distances

```
                      Extreme Values
                      -------  ------

  5   Highest     Case #              5   Lowest      Case #

      63.99758    Case: 56                .00011      Case: 78
      29.82579    Case: 2                 .00075      Case: 448
      20.32559    Case: 122               .00088      Case: 302
      14.99121    Case: 67                .00088      Case: 192
      12.64145    Case: 55                .00088      Case: 203
```

Influential Cases: Deleted Residuals and Cook's Distance

Certain observations in a set of data can have a large influence on estimates of the parameters. Figure 15.22 shows such a point. The regression line obtained for the data is quite different if the point is omitted. However, the residual for the circled point is not particularly large when the case (case 8) is included in the computations and does not therefore arouse suspicion (see the column labeled *RES_1* in Figure 15.23).

Figure 15.22 Influential observation

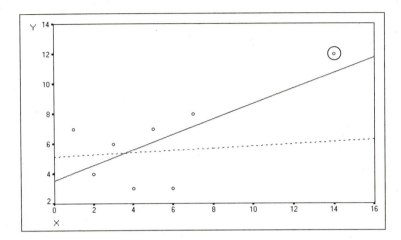

One way to identify an influential case is to compare the residuals for a case when the suspected case is included in the equation and when it is not. The **adjusted predicted value** for case *i* when it is not included in the computation of the regression line is

$$\hat{Y}_i^{(i)} = B_0^{(i)} + B_1^{(i)} X_i \qquad \text{Equation 15.25}$$

where the superscript *(i)* indicates that the *i*th case is excluded. The change in the predicted value when the *i*th case is deleted is

$$\hat{Y}_i - \hat{Y}_i^{(i)} \qquad \text{Equation 15.26}$$

The residual calculated for a case when it is not included is called the **deleted residual**, computed as

$$Y_i - \hat{Y}_i^{(i)} \qquad \text{Equation 15.27}$$

The deleted residual can be divided by its standard error to produce the **Studentized deleted residual**.

Although the difference between the deleted residual and ordinary residual for a case is useful as an index of the influence of that case, this measure does not reflect changes in residuals of other observations when the *i*th case is deleted. **Cook's distance** does consider changes in all residuals when case *i* is omitted (Cook, 1977). It is defined as

$$C_i = \frac{\sum_{j=1}^{N}\left(\hat{Y}_j^{(i)} - \hat{Y}_j\right)^2}{(p+1)S^2}$$

Equation 15.28

With SPSS you can save influence measures and display them with the List Cases procedure (see Chapter 18). Influence measures for the data in Figure 15.22 are shown in Figure 15.23. The measures for case 8 (the circled point) are given in the last row. The case has neither a very large Studentized residual (*SRE_1*), nor a very large Studentized deleted residual (*SDR_1*). However, the deleted residual (*DRE_1*), 5.86, is somewhat larger than the ordinary residual *(RES_1)*. The large Mahalanobis distance (*MAH_1*) identifies the case as having an *X* value far from the mean, while the large Cook's *D* (*COO_1*) identifies the case as an influential point.

Figure 15.23   Influence measures

```
CASEID  Y    RES_1      SRE_1      SDR_1      ADJ_1      DRE_1      MAH_1     COO_1

1.00    7    2.93939    1.48192    1.69900    2.90963    4.09037    1.09471    .42996
2.00    4    -.57580    -.27801    -.25543    4.73486    -.73486    .64013     .01067
3.00    6    .90910     .42617     .39506     4.90624    1.09376    .30683     .01845
4.00    3    -2.60609   -1.20001   -1.25657   6.02516    -3.02516   .09469     .11578
5.00    7    .87881     .40164     .37168     5.99502    1.00498    .00379     .01158
6.00    3    -3.63638   -1.66607   -2.07474   7.17913    -4.17913   .03410     .20715
7.00    8    .84852     .39369     .36412     6.99996    1.00004    .18559     .01384
8.00    12   1.24246    1.15294    1.19289    6.14264    5.85736    4.64016    2.46867
```

The regression coefficients with and without case 8 are shown in Figure 15.24 and Figure 15.25. Both $B_0^{(8)}$ and $B_1^{(8)}$ are far removed from B_0 and B_1, since case 8 is an influential point.

Figure 15.24   Regression coefficients from all cases

```
------------------------------- Variables in the Equation ---------------------------

Variable          B         SE B     95% Confdnce Intrvl B      Beta         T     Sig T

X              .515145    .217717   -.017587      1.047877    .694761     2.366   .0558
(Constant)    3.545466   1.410980    .092941      6.997990                2.513   .0457
```

Figure 15.25   Regression coefficients without case 8

```
------------------------------- Variables in the Equation ---------------------------

Variable          B         SE B     95% Confdnce Intrvl B      Beta         T     Sig T

X              .071407    .427380   -1.027192     1.170005    .074513      .167   .8739
(Constant)    5.142941   1.911317    .229818     10.056065                2.691   .0433
```

You can examine the change in the regression coefficients when a case is deleted from the analysis by saving the change in intercept and X values. For case 8 in Figure 15.26, you see that the change in the intercept (*DFB0_1*) is −1.5975 and the change in slope (*DFB1_1*) is 0.4437.

Figure 15.26 Diagnostic statistics for influential observations

```
CASEID   Y      DFB0_1      DFB1_1

 1.00    7     1.30149     -.15051
 2.00    4     -.20042      .02068
 3.00    6      .24859     -.02131
 4.00    3     -.55002      .03274
 5.00    7      .13704     -.00218
 6.00    3     -.37991     -.02714
 7.00    8      .04546      .01515
 8.00   12    -1.59748      .44374
```

When Assumptions Appear to Be Violated

When there is evidence of a violation of assumptions, you can pursue one of two strategies. You can formulate an alternative model, such as weighted least squares, or you can transform the variables so that the current model will be more adequate. For example, taking logs, square roots, or reciprocals can stabilize the variance, achieve normality, or linearize a relationship.

Coaxing a Nonlinear Relationship to Linearity

To try to achieve linearity, you can transform either the dependent or independent variables, or both. If you alter the scale of independent variables, linearity can be achieved without any effect on the distribution of the dependent variable. Thus, if the dependent variable is normally distributed with constant variance for each value of X, it remains normally distributed.

When you transform the dependent variable, its distribution is changed. This new distribution must then satisfy the assumptions of the analysis. For example, if logs of the values of the dependent variable are taken, log Y—not the original Y—must be normally distributed with constant variance.

The choice of transformation depends on several considerations. If the form of the true model governing the relationship is known, it should dictate the choice. For instance, if it is known that $\hat{Y} = AC^X$ is an adequate model, taking logs of both sides of the equation results in

$$\log \hat{Y}_i = \underbrace{(\log A)}_{[B_0]} + \underbrace{(\log C)}_{[B_1]} X_i \qquad \text{Equation 15.29}$$

Thus, log Y is linearly related to X.

If the true model is not known, you should choose the transformation by examining the plotted data. Frequently, a relationship appears nearly linear for part of the data but is curved for the rest (for example, Figure 15.27). Taking the log of the dependent variable results in an improved linear fit (see Figure 15.28).

Figure 15.27   Nonlinear relationship

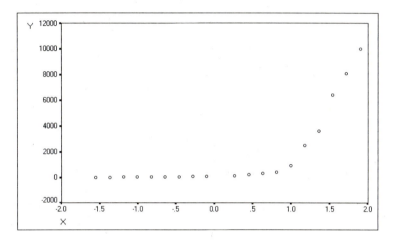

Figure 15.28   Transformed relationship

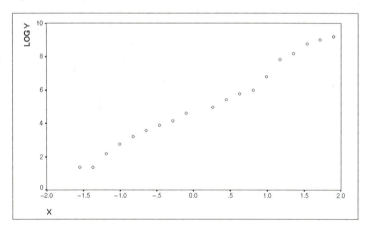

Other transformations that may diminish curvature are $-1/Y$ and the square root of Y. The choice depends, to a certain extent, on the severity of the problem.

Coping with Skewness

When the distribution of residuals is positively skewed, the log transformation of the dependent variable is often helpful. For negatively skewed distributions, the square transformation is common. It should be noted that the F tests used in regression hypothesis testing are usually quite insensitive to moderate departures from normality.

Stabilizing the Variance

If the variance of the residuals is not constant, you can try a variety of remedial measures:

- When the variance is proportional to the mean of Y for a given X, use the square root of Y if all Y_i are positive.
- When the standard deviation is proportional to the mean, try the logarithmic transformation.
- When the standard deviation is proportional to the square of the mean, use the reciprocal of Y.
- When Y is a proportion or rate, the arc sine transformation may stabilize the variance.

Transforming the Salary Data

The assumptions of constant variance and normality appear to be violated with the salary data (see Figure 15.16 and Figure 15.18). A regression equation using logs of beginning salary and current salary was developed to obtain a better fit to the assumptions. Figure 15.29 is a scatterplot of Studentized residuals against predicted values when logs of both variables are used in the regression equation.

Figure 15.29   Scatterplot of transformed salary data

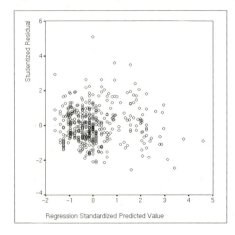

Compare Figure 15.16 and Figure 15.29, and note the improvement in the behavior of the residuals shown in Figure 15.29. The spread no longer increases with increasing salary level. Also compare Figure 15.18 and Figure 15.30, and note that the distribution in Figure 15.30 is nearly normal.

Figure 15.30 Histogram of transformed salary data

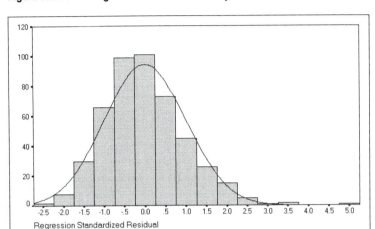

For the transformed data, the multiple R increases slightly to 0.8864, and the outlier plot contains only four cases (compare with Figure 15.6 and Figure 15.20). Thus, the transformation appears to have resulted in a better model. (For more information on transformations, see Chapter 1.)

A Final Comment on Assumptions

Rarely are assumptions not violated one way or another in regression analysis and other statistical procedures. However, this is not a justification for ignoring the assumptions. Cranking out regressions without considering possible violations of the necessary assumptions can lead to results that are difficult to interpret and apply. Significance levels, confidence intervals, and other results are sensitive to certain types of violations and cannot be interpreted in the usual fashion if serious violations exist.

By carefully examining residuals and, if need be, using transformations or other methods of analysis, you are in a much better position to pursue analyses that solve the problems you are investigating. Even if everything isn't perfect, you can at least knowledgeably gauge the potential for difficulties.

Multiple Regression Models

Beginning salary seems to be a good predictor of current salary, given the evidence shown above. Nearly 80% (R^2 = 0.77 from Figure 15.6) of the observed variability in current salaries can be explained by beginning salary levels. But how do variables such as education level, years of experience, race, and sex affect the salary level at which one enters the company?

Predictors of Beginning Salary

Multiple linear regression extends bivariate regression by incorporating multiple independent variables. The model can be expressed as

$$Y_i = \beta_0 + \beta_1 X_{1i} + \beta_2 X_{2i} + \ldots + \beta_p X_{pi} + e_i \qquad \text{Equation 15.30}$$

The notation X_{pi} indicates the value of the *p*th independent variable for case *i*. Again, the β terms are unknown parameters and the e_i terms are independent random variables that are normally distributed with mean 0 and constant variance σ^2. The model assumes that there is a normal distribution of the dependent variable for every combination of the values of the independent variables in the model. For example, if child's height is the dependent variable and age and maternal height are the independent variables, it is assumed that for every combination of age and maternal height there is a normal distribution of children's heights and, though the means of these distributions may differ, all have the same variance.

The Correlation Matrix

One of the first steps in calculating an equation with several independent variables is to calculate a correlation matrix for all variables, as shown in Figure 15.31. The variables are the log of beginning salary, years of education, sex, years of work experience, minority status (race), and age in years. Variables *sex* and *minority* are represented by **indicator variables**, that is, variables coded as 0 or 1. *Sex* is coded 1 for female and 0 for male, and *minority* is coded 1 for nonwhite and 0 for white.

Figure 15.31 The correlation matrix

```
Correlation:
              LOGBEG    EDLEVEL    SEX       WORK      MINORITY   AGE
LOGBEG        1.000      .686     -.548      .040      -.173     -.048
EDLEVEL        .686     1.000     -.356     -.252       .133     -.281
SEX           -.548     -.356     1.000     -.165      -.076      .052
WORK           .040     -.252     -.165     1.000       .145      .804
MINORITY      -.173      .133     -.076      .145      1.000      .111
AGE           -.048     -.281      .052      .804       .111     1.000
```

The matrix shows the correlations between the dependent variable (*logbeg*) and each independent variable, as well as the correlations between the independent variables. Note particularly any large intercorrelations between the independent variables, since such correlations can substantially affect the results of multiple regression analysis.

Correlation Matrices and Missing Data

For a variety of reasons, data files frequently contain incomplete observations. Respondents in surveys scrawl illegible responses or refuse to answer certain questions. Laboratory animals die before experiments are completed. Patients fail to keep scheduled clinic appointments. Thus, before computing the correlation matrix, you must usually decide what to do with cases that have missing values for some of the variables.

Before even considering possible strategies, you should determine whether there is evidence that the missing-value pattern is not random. That is, are there reasons to believe that missing values for a variable are related to the values of that variable or other variables? For example, people with low incomes may be less willing to report their financial status than more affluent people. This may be even more pronounced for people who are poor but highly educated.

One simple method of exploring such possibilities is to subdivide the data into two groups—those with missing values for a variable and those with complete information—and examine the distributions of the other variables in the file across these two groups. SPSS crosstabulation and independent-samples t tests are particularly useful for this. For a discussion of other methods for detecting nonrandomness, see Frane (1976).

If it appears that the data are not missing randomly, use great caution in attempting an analysis. It may be that no satisfactory analysis is possible, especially if there are only a few cases.

If you are satisfied that the missing data are random, several strategies are available. If, for most cases, values are missing for the same few variables, consider excluding those variables from the analysis. Since this luxury is not usually available, you can alternatively keep all variables but eliminate the cases with missing values for any of them. This is termed **listwise** missing-value treatment, since a case is eliminated if it has a missing value for any variable on the list.

If many cases have missing data for some variables, listwise missing-value treatment may eliminate too many cases and leave you with a very small sample. One common technique is to calculate the correlation coefficient between a pair of variables based on all cases with complete information for the two variables, regardless of whether the cases have missing data for any other variable. For example, if a case has values only for variables 1, 3, and 5, it is used only in computations involving variable pairs 1 and 3, 1 and 5, and 3 and 5. This is **pairwise** missing-value treatment.

Several problems can arise with pairwise matrices, one of which is inconsistency. There are some relationships between coefficients that are impossible but may occur when different cases are used to estimate different coefficients. For example, if age and weight, and age and height, have a high positive correlation, it is impossible in the same sample for height and weight to have a high negative correlation. However, if the same cases are not used to estimate all three coefficients, such an anomaly can occur.

Another problem with pairwise matrices is that no single sample size can be obtained, since each coefficient may be based on a different number of cases. In addition, significance levels obtained from analyses based on pairwise matrices must be viewed with caution, since little is known about hypothesis testing in such situations.

Missing-value problems should not be treated lightly. You should always select a missing-value treatment based on careful examination of the data and not leave the choices up to system defaults. In this example, complete information is available for all cases, so missing values are not a problem.

Partial Regression Coefficients

The summary output when all independent variables are included in the multiple regression equation is shown in Figure 15.32. The F test associated with the analysis-of-variance table is a test of the null hypothesis that

$$\beta_1 = \beta_2 = \beta_3 = \beta_4 = \beta_5 = 0$$

Equation 15.31

In other words, it is a test of whether there is a linear relationship between the dependent variable and the entire set of independent variables.

Figure 15.32 Statistics for the equation and analysis-of-variance table

```
Multiple R              .78420
R Square                .61498
Adjusted R Square       .61086
Standard Error          .09559

Analysis of Variance
                    DF      Sum of Squares      Mean Square
Regression           5             6.83039          1.36608
Residual           468             4.27638           .00914

F =      149.50125       Signif F =  .0000
```

The statistics for the independent variables in Figure 15.33 are parallel to those obtained in regression with a single independent variable (see Figure 15.3). In multiple regres-

Figure 15.33 Statistics for variables in the equation

```
------------------ Variables in the Equation ------------------

Variable             B          SE B         Beta         T      Sig T

AGE             .001015     6.6132E-04     .078106     1.535    .1254
SEX            -.103576       .010318    -.336987   -10.038    .0000
MINORITY       -.052366       .010837    -.141573    -4.832    .0000
EDLEVEL         .031443       .001748     .591951    17.988    .0000
WORK            .001608     9.2407E-04    .091428     1.740    .0826
(Constant)     3.385300       .033233                101.866    .0000
```

sion, the coefficients labeled *B* are called **partial regression coefficients**, since the coefficient for a particular variable is adjusted for other independent variables in the equation. The equation that relates the predicted log of beginning salary to the independent variables is

$$\text{logbeg} = 3.3853 + 0.00102(\text{age}) - 0.10358(\text{sex}) \\ - 0.05237(\text{minority}) + 0.03144(\text{edlevel}) \\ + 0.00161(\text{work})$$

Equation 15.32

Since the dependent variable is in log units, the coefficients can be approximately interpreted in percentage terms. For example, the coefficient of -0.104 for *sex* when females are coded as 1 indicates that female salaries are estimated to be about 10% less than male salaries after statistical adjustment for age, education, work history, and minority status.

Determining Important Variables

In multiple regression, you sometimes want to assign relative importance to each independent variable. For example, you might want to know whether education is more important in predicting beginning salary than previous work experience. There are two possible approaches, depending on which of the following questions is asked:

- How important are education and work experience when each one is used alone to predict beginning salary?
- How important are education and work experience when they are used to predict beginning salary along with other independent variables in the regression equation?

The first question is answered by looking at the correlation coefficients between salary and the independent variables. The larger the absolute value of the correlation coefficient, the stronger the linear association. Figure 15.31 shows that education correlates more highly with the log of salary than does previous work experience (0.686 and 0.040, respectively). Thus, you would assign more importance to education as a predictor of salary.

The answer to the second question is considerably more complicated. When the independent variables are correlated among themselves, the unique contribution of each is difficult to assess. Any statement about an independent variable is contingent upon the other variables in the equation. For example, the regression coefficient *(B)* for work experience is 0.0007 when it is the sole independent variable in the equation, compared to 0.00161 when the other four independent variables are also in the equation. The second coefficient is more than twice the size of the first.

Beta Coefficients

It is also inappropriate to interpret the *B*'s as indicators of the relative importance of variables. The actual magnitude of the coefficients depends on the units in which the variables are measured. Only if all independent variables are measured in the same units—years, for example—are their coefficients directly comparable. When variables differ substantially in units of measurement, the sheer magnitude of their coefficients does not reveal anything about relative importance.

One way to make regression coefficients somewhat more comparable is to calculate beta weights, which are the coefficients of the independent variables when all variables are expressed in standardized (Z score) form (see Figure 15.33). The **beta coefficients** can be calculated directly from the regression coefficients using

$$\text{beta}_k = B_k \left(\frac{S_k}{S_Y} \right) \qquad \text{Equation 15.33}$$

where S_k is the standard deviation of the *k*th independent variable.

However, the values of the beta coefficients, like the *B*'s, are contingent on the other independent variables in the equation. They are also affected by the correlations of the independent variables and do not in any absolute sense reflect the importance of the various independent variables.

Part and Partial Coefficients

Another way of assessing the relative importance of independent variables is to consider the increase in R^2 when a variable is entered into an equation that already contains the other independent variables. This increase is

$$R^2_{\text{change}} = R^2 - R^2_{(i)} \qquad \text{Equation 15.34}$$

where $R^2_{(i)}$ is the square of the multiple correlation coefficient when all independent variables except the *i*th are in the equation. A large change in R^2 indicates that a variable provides unique information about the dependent variable that is not available from the other independent variables in the equation. The signed square root of the increase is called the **part correlation coefficient**. It is the correlation between *Y* and X_i when the linear effects of the other independent variables have been removed from X_i. If all independent variables are uncorrelated, the change in R^2 when a variable is entered into the equation is simply the square of the correlation coefficient between that variable and the dependent variable.

The value of *RsqCh* in Figure 15.34 shows that the addition of years of education to an equation that contains the other four independent variables results in a change in R^2 of 0.266. This value tells only how much R^2 increases when a variable is added to the regression equation. It does not indicate what proportion of the unexplained variation this increase constitutes. If most of the variation had been explained by the other variables, a small change in R^2 is all that is possible for the remaining variable.

Figure 15.34 Change in R-squared

```
Block Number 5. Method: Enter EDLEVEL

Step  MultR   Rsq    AdjRsq  F(Eqn)   SigF   RsqCh   FCh      SigCh   Variable       BetaIn   Correl
  5   .7842   .6150   .6109  149.501  .000   .2662   323.554  .000    In: EDLEVEL    .5920    .6857
```

A coefficient that measures the proportional reduction in variation is

$$Pr_i^2 = \frac{R^2 - R^2_{(i)}}{1 - R^2_{(i)}}$$ **Equation 15.35**

The numerator is the square of the part coefficient; the denominator is the proportion of unexplained variation when all but the ith variable are in the equation. The signed square root of Pr_i^2 is the **partial correlation coefficient**. It can be interpreted as the correlation between the ith independent variable and the dependent variable when the linear effects of the other independent variables have been removed from both X_i and Y. Since the denominator of Pr_i^2 is always less than or equal to 1, the part correlation coefficient is never larger in absolute value than the partial correlation coefficient.

Plots of the residuals of Y and X_i, when the linear effects of the other independent variables have been removed, are a useful diagnostic aid. They are discussed in "Checking for Violations of Assumptions" on p. 263.

Building a Model

Our selection of the five variables to predict beginning salary has been arbitrary to some extent. It is unlikely that all relevant variables have been identified and measured. Instead, some relevant variables have no doubt been excluded, while others that were included may not be very important determinants of salary level. This is not unusual; you must try to build a model from available data, as voluminous or scanty as the data may be. Before considering several formal procedures for model building, we will examine some of the consequences of adding and deleting variables from regression equations. The regression statistics for variables not in the equation are also described.

Adding and Deleting Variables

The first step in Figure 15.35 shows the summary statistics when years of education is the sole independent variable and log of beginning salary is the dependent variable. Consider the second step in the same figure, when another variable, *sex*, is added. The value displayed as *RsqCh* in the second step is the change in R^2 when *sex* is added. R^2 for *edlevel* alone is 0.4702, so R^2_{change} is 0.5760 – 0.4702, or 0.1058.

Figure 15.35 Adding a variable to the equation

```
Equation Number 1    Dependent Variable..   LOGBEG
Block Number  1.  Method:  Enter       EDLEVEL
Step    MultR     Rsq   AdjRsq    F(Eqn)  SigF    RsqCh        FCh  SigCh
  1    .6857    .4702   .4691    418.920  .000   .4702      418.920  .000

End Block Number   1   All requested variables entered.

Block Number  2.  Method:  Enter       SEX
Step    MultR     Rsq   AdjRsq    F(Eqn)  SigF    RsqCh        FCh  SigCh
  2    .7589    .5760   .5742    319.896  .000   .1058      117.486  .000

End Block Number   2   All requested variables entered.
```

The null hypothesis that the true population value for the change in R^2 is 0 can be tested using

$$F_{change} = \frac{R^2_{change}(N-p-1)}{q(1-R^2)} = \frac{(0.1058)(474-2-1)}{1(1-0.5760)} = 117.49 \qquad \text{Equation 15.36}$$

where N is the number of cases in the equation, p is the total number of independent variables in the equation, and q is the number of variables entered at this step. This is also referred to as a **partial F test**. Under the hypothesis that the true change is 0, the significance of the value labeled FCh can be obtained from the F distribution with q and $N-p-1$ degrees of freedom.

The hypothesis that the real change in R^2 is 0 can also be formulated in terms of the β parameters. When only the ith variable is added in a step, the hypothesis that the change in R^2 is 0 is equivalent to the hypothesis that $β_i$ is 0. The F value displayed for the change in R^2 is the square of the t value for the test of the coefficient.

When q independent variables are entered in a single step, the test that R^2 is 0 is equivalent to the simultaneous test that the coefficients of all q variables are 0. For example, if sex and age were added in the same step to the regression equation that contains education, the F test for R^2 change would be the same as the F test which tests the hypothesis that $β_{sex} = β_{age} = 0$.

Entering sex into the equation with education has effects in addition to changing R^2. For example, the magnitude of the regression coefficient for education from step 1 to step 2 decreases from 0.0364 to 0.0298. This is attributable to the correlation between sex and level of education.

When highly intercorrelated independent variables are included in a regression equation, results may appear anomalous. The overall regression may be significant, while none of the individual coefficients are significant. The signs of the regression coefficients may be counterintuitive. High correlations between independent variables inflate the variances of the estimates, making individual coefficients quite unreliable without adding much to the overall fit of the model. The problem of linear relationships between independent variables is discussed further in "Measures of Collinearity" on p. 267.

Statistics for Variables Not in the Equation

When you have independent variables that have not been entered into the equation, you can examine what would happen if they were entered at the next step. Statistics describing these variables are shown in Figure 15.36. The column labeled *Beta In* is the standardized regression coefficient that would result if the variable were entered into the equation at the next step. The t test and level of significance are for the hypothesis that the coefficient is 0. (Remember that the t test and the partial F test for the hypothesis that a coefficient is 0 are equivalent.) The partial correlation coefficient with the dependent variable adjusts for the variables already in the equation.

Figure 15.36 Coefficients for variables not in the equation

```
------------ Variables not in the Equation ------------

Variable     Beta In    Partial   Min Toler       T     Sig T

WORK         .144245    .205668    .773818      4.556   .0000
MINORITY    -.129022   -.194642    .847583     -4.302   .0000
AGE          .139419    .205193    .804253      4.545   .0000
```

From statistics calculated for variables not in the equation, you can decide what variable should be entered next. This process is detailed in "Procedures for Selecting Variables" on p. 258.

The "Optimal" Number of Independent Variables

Having seen what happens when sex is added to the equation containing education (Figure 15.35), consider now what happens when the remaining three independent variables are entered one at a time in no particular order. Summary output is shown in Figure 15.37. Step 5 shows the statistics for the equation with all independent variables entered. Step 3 describes the model with education, sex, and work experience as the independent variables.

Figure 15.37 All independent variables in the equation

```
Step   MultR    Rsq   AdjRsq   F(Eqn)   SigF   RsqCh      FCh   SigCh         Variable
  1    .6857   .4702   .4691   418.920   .000   .4702   418.920   .000    In: EDLEVEL

Step   MultR    Rsq   AdjRsq   F(Eqn)   SigF   RsqCh      FCh   SigCh         Variable
  2    .7589   .5760   .5742   319.896   .000   .1058   117.486   .000    In: SEX
Step   MultR    Rsq   AdjRsq   F(Eqn)   SigF   RsqCh      FCh   SigCh         Variable
  3    .7707   .5939   .5913   229.130   .000   .0179    20.759   .000    In: WORK

Step   MultR    Rsq   AdjRsq   F(Eqn)   SigF   RsqCh      FCh   SigCh         Variable
  4    .7719   .5958   .5923   172.805   .000   .0019     2.149   .143    In: AGE

Step   MultR    Rsq   AdjRsq   F(Eqn)   SigF   RsqCh      FCh   SigCh         Variable
  5    .7842   .6150   .6109   149.501   .000   .0192    23.349   .000    In: MINORITY
```

Examination of Figure 15.37 shows that R^2 never decreases as independent variables are added. This is always true in regression analysis. However, this does not necessarily mean that the equation with more variables better fits the population. As the number of parameters estimated from the sample increases, so does the goodness of fit to the sample as measured by R^2. For example, if a sample contains six cases, a regression equation with six parameters fits the sample exactly, even though there may be no true statistical relationship at all between the dependent variable and the independent variables.

As indicated in "The R-squared Coefficient" on p. 229, the sample R^2 in general tends to overestimate the population value of R^2. Adjusted R^2 attempts to correct the optimistic bias of the sample R^2. Adjusted R^2 does not necessarily increase as additional variables are added to an equation and is the preferred measure of goodness of fit because it is not subject to the inflationary bias of unadjusted R^2. This statistic is shown in the column labeled *AdjRsq* in the output.

Although adding independent variables increases R^2, it does not necessarily decrease the standard error of the estimate. Each time a variable is added to the equation, a degree of freedom is lost from the residual sum of squares and one is gained for the regression sum of squares. The standard error may increase when the decrease in the residual sum of squares is very slight and not sufficient to make up for the loss of a degree of freedom for the residual sum of squares. The F value for the test of the overall regression decreases when the regression sum of squares does not increase as fast as the degrees of freedom for the regression.

Including a large number of independent variables in a regression model is never a good strategy, unless there are strong, previous reasons to suggest that they all should be included. The observed increase in R^2 does not necessarily reflect a better fit of the model in the population. Including irrelevant variables increases the standard errors of all estimates without improving prediction. A model with many variables is often difficult to interpret.

On the other hand, it is important not to exclude potentially relevant independent variables. The following sections describe various procedures for selecting variables to be included in a regression model. The goal is to build a concise model that makes good prediction possible.

Procedures for Selecting Variables

You can construct a variety of regression models from the same set of variables. For instance, you can build seven different equations from three independent variables: three with only one independent variable, three with two independent variables, and one with all three. As the number of variables increases, so does the number of potential models (ten independent variables yield 1,023 models).

Although there are procedures for computing all possible regression equations, several other methods do not require as much computation and are more frequently used. Among these procedures are forward selection, backward elimination, and stepwise selection. None of these variable selection procedures are "best" in any absolute sense; they merely identify subsets of variables that, for the sample, are good predictors of the dependent variable.

Forward Selection

In **forward selection**, the first variable considered for entry into the equation is the one with the largest positive or negative correlation with the dependent variable. The F test for the hypothesis that the coefficient of the entered variable is 0 is then calculated. To determine whether this variable (and each succeeding variable) is entered, the F value is compared to an established criterion. You can specify one of two criteria in SPSS. One criterion is the minimum value of the F statistic that a variable must achieve in order to enter, called **F-to-enter** (**FIN**), with a default value of 3.84. The other criterion you can specify is the probability associated with the F statistic, called **probability of F-to-enter** (**PIN**), with a default of 0.05. In this case, a variable enters into the equation only if the probability associated with the F test is less than or equal to the default 0.05 or the value you specify. By default, PIN is the criterion used. (In the output, SPSS generally displays t values and their probabilities. These t probabilities are equivalent to those associated with F. You can obtain F values by squaring t values, since $t^2 = F$.)

The PIN and FIN criteria are not necessarily equivalent. As variables are added to the equation, the degrees of freedom associated with the residual sum of squares decrease while the regression degrees of freedom increase. Thus, a fixed F value has different significance levels depending on the number of variables currently in the equation. For large samples, the differences are negligible.

The actual significance level associated with the F-to-enter statistic is not the one usually obtained from the F distribution, since many variables are being examined and the largest F value is selected. Unfortunately, the true significance level is difficult to compute, since it depends not only on the number of cases and variables but also on the correlations between independent variables.

If the first variable selected for entry meets the criterion for inclusion, forward selection continues. Otherwise, the procedure terminates with no variables in the equation. Once one variable is entered, the statistics for variables not in the equation are used to select the next one. The partial correlations between the dependent variable and each of the independent variables not in the equation, adjusted for the independent variables in the equation, are examined. The variable with the largest partial correlation is the next candidate. Choosing the variable with the largest partial correlation in absolute value is equivalent to selecting the variable with the largest F value.

If the criterion is met, the variable is entered into the equation and the procedure is repeated. The procedure stops when there are no other variables that meet the entry criterion.

Figure 15.38 shows output generated from a forward-selection procedure using the salary data. The default entry criterion is PIN = 0.05. In the first step, education (variable *edlevel*) is entered, since it has the highest correlation with beginning salary. The significance level associated with education is less than 0.0005, so it certainly meets the criterion for entry.

Figure 15.38   Summary statistics for forward selection

```
Step    MultR      Rsq    F(Eqn)    SigF        Variable    BetaIn
  1    .6857     .4702   418.920    .000   In:  EDLEVEL      .6857
  2    .7589     .5760   319.896    .000   In:  SEX         -.3480
  3    .7707     .5939   229.130    .000   In:  WORK         .1442
  4    .7830     .6130   185.750    .000   In:  MINORITY    -.1412
```

To see how the next variable, *sex*, was selected, look at the statistics shown in Figure 15.39 for variables not in the equation when only *edlevel* is in the equation. The variable with the largest partial correlation is *sex*. If entered at the next step, it would have a t value of –10.839. Since the probability associated with the t value is less than 0.05, variable *sex* is entered in the second step.

Figure 15.39   Status of the variables at the first step

```
---------------- Variables in the Equation ------------------

Variable              B         SE B        Beta          T     Sig T

EDLEVEL           .036424    .001780      .685719    20.468    .0000
(Constant)       3.310013    .024551                 134.821    .0000


------------ Variables not in the Equation -------------

Variable     Beta In   Partial   Min Toler        T     Sig T

SEX         -.348017  -.446811    .873274    -10.839    .0000
WORK         .227473   .302405    .936316      6.885    .0000
MINORITY    -.083181  -.113267    .982341     -2.474    .0137
AGE          .157180   .207256    .921128      4.598    .0000
```

Once variable *sex* enters at step 2, the statistics for variables not in the equation must be examined (see Figure 15.36). The variable with the largest absolute value for the partial correlation coefficient is now years of work experience. Its t value is 4.556 with a probability less than 0.05, so variable *work* is entered in the next step. The same process takes place with variable *minority*, leaving *age* as the only variable out of the equation. However, as shown in Figure 15.40, the significance level associated with the *age* coefficient t value is 0.1254, which is too large for entry. Thus, forward selection yields the summary table for the four steps shown in Figure 15.38.

Figure 15.40   Forward selection at the last step

```
------------ Variables not in the Equation -------------

Variable     Beta In   Partial   Min Toler        T     Sig T

AGE          .078106   .070796    .297843      1.535    .1254
```

Backward Elimination

While forward selection starts with no independent variables in the equation and sequentially enters them, **backward elimination** starts with all variables in the equation and sequentially removes them. Instead of entry criteria, removal criteria are used.

Two removal criteria are available in SPSS. The first is the minimum F value that a variable must have in order to remain in the equation. Variables with F values less than this **F-to-remove (FOUT)** are eligible for removal. The second criterion available is the maximum **probability of F-to-remove (POUT)** that a variable can have. The default FOUT value is 2.71 and the default POUT value is 0.10. The default criterion is probability of F-to-remove.

Look at the salary example again, this time constructing the model with backward elimination. The output in Figure 15.41 is from the first step, in which all variables are entered into the equation. The variable with the smallest partial correlation coefficient, *age*, is examined first. Since the probability of its t (0.1254) is greater than the default POUT criterion value of 0.10, variable *age* is removed. (Recall that the t test and the partial F test for the hypothesis that a coefficient is 0 are equivalent.)

Figure 15.41   Backward elimination at the first step

```
------------------ Variables in the Equation ------------------

Variable              B          SE B         Beta            T      Sig T

AGE             .001015   6.6132E-04       .078106        1.535     .1254
SEX            -.103576      .010318      -.336987      -10.038     .0000
MINORITY       -.052366      .010837      -.141573       -4.832     .0000
EDLEVEL         .031443      .001748       .591951       17.988     .0000
WORK            .001608   9.2407E-04       .091428        1.740     .0826
(Constant)     3.385300      .033233                    101.866     .0000
```

The equation is then recalculated without *age*, producing the statistics shown in Figure 15.42. The variable with the smallest partial correlation is *minority*. However, its significance is less than the 0.10 criterion, so backward elimination stops. The equation resulting from backward elimination is the same as the one from forward selection. This is not always the case, however. Forward-selection and backward-elimination procedures can give different results, even with comparable entry and removal criteria.

Figure 15.42   Backward elimination at the last step

```
------------------ Variables in the Equation ------------------

Variable              B          SE B         Beta            T      Sig T

SEX            -.099042      .009901      -.322234      -10.003     .0000
MINORITY       -.052245      .010853      -.141248       -4.814     .0000
EDLEVEL         .031433      .001751       .591755       17.956     .0000
WORK            .002753   5.4582E-04       .156592        5.044     .0000
(Constant)     3.411953      .028380                    120.225     .0000


------------ Variables not in the Equation ------------

Variable    Beta In    Partial    Min Toler         T     Sig T

AGE          .078106    .070796      .297843     1.535    .1254
```

Stepwise Selection

Stepwise selection of independent variables is really a combination of backward and forward procedures and is probably the most commonly used method. The first variable is selected in the same manner as in forward selection. If the variable fails to meet entry requirements (either FIN or PIN), the procedure terminates with no independent variables in the equation. If it passes the criterion, the second variable is selected based on the highest partial correlation. If it passes entry criteria, it also enters the equation.

After the first variable is entered, stepwise selection differs from forward selection: the first variable is examined to see whether it should be removed according to the removal criterion (FOUT or POUT) as in backward elimination. In the next step, variables not in the equation are examined for entry. After each step, variables already in the equation are examined for removal. Variables are removed until none remain that meet the removal criterion. To prevent the same variable from being repeatedly entered and removed, the PIN must be less than the POUT (or FIN greater than FOUT). Variable selection terminates when no more variables meet entry and removal criteria.

In the salary example, stepwise selection with the default criteria results in the same equation produced by both forward selection and backward elimination (see Figure 15.43).

Figure 15.43   Stepwise output at the last step

```
Multiple R              .78297
R Square                .61304
Adjusted R Square       .60974
Standard Error          .09573

F =        185.74958       Signif F =   .0000


------------------ Variables in the Equation ------------------

Variable              B          SE B        Beta           T     Sig T

EDLEVEL         .031433       .001751      .591755      17.956   .0000
SEX            -.099042       .009901     -.322234     -10.003   .0000
WORK            .002753    5.4582E-04      .156592       5.044   .0000
MINORITY       -.052245       .010853     -.141248      -4.814   .0000
(Constant)     3.411953       .028380                  120.225   .0000


Equation Number 1    Dependent Variable..   LOGBEG

------------- Variables not in the Equation -------------

Variable      Beta In   Partial   Min Toler        T    Sig T

AGE           .078106   .070796     .297843    1.535    .1254
```

The three procedures do not always result in the same equation, though you should be encouraged when they do. The model selected by any method should be carefully studied for violations of the assumptions. It is often a good idea to develop several acceptable models and then choose among them based on interpretability, ease of variable acquisition, parsimony, and so forth.

Checking for Violations of Assumptions

The procedures for checking for violations of assumptions in bivariate regression (see "Searching for Violations of Assumptions" on p. 236) apply in multiple regression as well. Residuals should be plotted against predicted values as well as against each independent variable. The distribution of residuals should be examined for normality.

Several additional residual plots may be useful for multiple regression models. One of these is the **partial regression plot**. For the jth independent variable, it is obtained by calculating the residuals for the dependent variable when it is predicted from all the independent variables excluding the jth and by calculating the residuals for the jth independent variable when it is predicted from all of the other independent variables. This removes the linear effect of the other independent variables from both variables. For each case, these two residuals are plotted against each other.

A partial regression plot for educational level for the regression equation that contains work experience, minority, sex, and educational level as the independent variables is shown in Figure 15.44. (Summary statistics for the regression equation with all independent variables are displayed in the last step of Figure 15.43.) The partial regression plot (created by saving residuals in the Linear Regression procedure and then using the Scatter option on the Graphs menu) shows residuals for *logbeg* on the y axis and residual values for *edlevel* on the x axis.

Figure 15.44   Partial regression plot

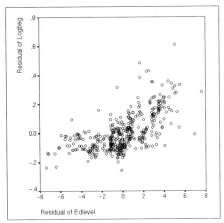

Several characteristics of the partial regression plot make it a particularly valuable diagnostic tool. The slope of the regression line for the two residual variables (0.03143) is equal to the coefficient for the *edlevel* variable in the multiple regression equation after the last step (step 4 in Figure 15.43). Thus, by examining the bivariate plot, you can conveniently identify points that are influential in the determination of the particular regression coefficient. The correlation coefficient between the two residuals, 0.638, is the partial correlation coefficient discussed in "Part and Partial Coefficients" on p. 254. The residuals from the least-squares line in Figure 15.44 are equal to the residuals from the final multiple regression equation, which includes all the independent variables.

The partial regression plot also helps you assess the inadequacies of the selected model and violations of the underlying assumptions. For example, the partial regression plot of educational level does not appear to be linear, suggesting that an additional term, such as years of education squared, might also be included in the model. This violation is much easier to spot using the partial regression plot than the plot of the independent variable against the residual from the equation with all independent variables. Figure 15.45 shows the residual scatterplot created with the Graph procedure and Figure 15.46 shows the partial regression plot produced by the Regression procedure. Note that the nonlinearity is much more apparent in the partial regression plot.

Figure 15.45   Residual plot

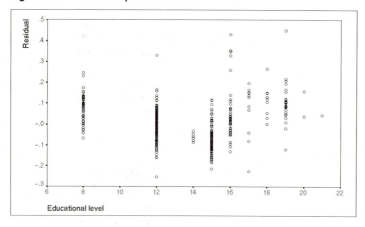

Figure 15.46   Partial regression plot

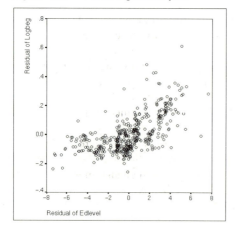

Figure 15.47 contains the summary statistics generated when the number of years of education squared is included in the multiple regression equation. The multiple R^2 increases from 0.61 (step 4 in Figure 15.43) to 0.71, a significant improvement.

Figure 15.47 Regression equation with education squared

```
Multiple R              .84302
R Square                .71068
Adjusted R Square       .70759
Standard Error          .08286

Analysis of Variance
                DF      Sum of Squares      Mean Square
Regression       5             7.89331          1.57866
Residual       468             3.21345           .00687

F =     229.91286       Signif F =    .0000
```

Looking for Influential Points

As discussed earlier, when building a regression model it is important to identify cases that are influential, or that have a disproportionately large effect on the estimated model. (See "Locating Outliers" on p. 242.) We can look for cases that change the values of the regression coefficients and of predicted values, cases that increase the variances of the coefficients, and cases that are poorly fitted by the model.

Among the important influence measures is the **leverage** of a case. The predicted values of the dependent variable can be expressed as

$$\hat{Y} = HY \qquad \text{Equation 15.37}$$

The diagonal elements of the H matrix (commonly called the hat matrix) are called **leverages**. The leverage for a case describes the impact of the observed value of the dependent variable on the prediction of the fitted value. Leverages are important in their own right and as fundamental building blocks for other diagnostic measures. For example, the Mahalanobis distance for a point is obtained by multiplying the leverage value by $N-1$.

SPSS computes centered leverages. They range from 0 to $(N-1)/N$, where N is the number of observations. The mean value for the centered leverage is p/N, where p is the number of independent variables in the equation. A leverage of 0 identifies a point with no influence on the fit, while a point with a leverage of $(N-1)/N$ indicates that a degree of freedom has been devoted to fitting the data point. Ideally, you would like each observation to exert a roughly equal influence. That is, you want all of the leverages to be near p/N. It is a good idea to examine points with leverage values that exceed $2p/N$.

To see the effect of a case on the estimation of the regression coefficients, you can look at the change in each of the regression coefficients when the case is removed from the analysis. SPSS can display or save the actual change in each of the coefficients, including the intercept and the standardized change.

Figure 15.48 is a plot of standardized change values for the *minority* variable on the vertical axis against a case ID number on the horizontal axis. Note that as expected, most of the points cluster in a horizontal band around 0. However, there are a few points far removed from the rest. Belsley et al. (1980) recommend examining standardized change values that are larger than $(2/\sqrt{N})$.

Figure 15.48   Plot of standardized change values for minority status

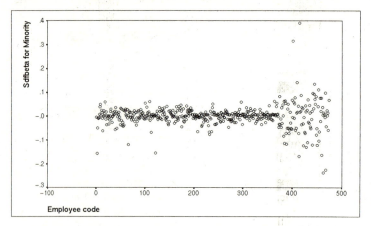

In addition to looking at the change in the regression coefficients when a case is deleted from an analysis, we can look at the change in the predicted value or at the standardized change. Cases with large values far removed from the rest should be examined. As a rule of thumb, you may want to look at standardized values larger than $2/\sqrt{p/N}$.

Another type of influential observation is one that influences the variance of the estimated regression coefficients. A measure of the impact of an observation on the variance-covariance matrix of the parameter estimates is called the **covariance ratio**. It is computed as the ratio of the determinant of the variance-covariance matrix computed without the case to the determinant of the variance-covariance matrix computed with all cases. If this ratio is close to 1, the case leaves the variance-covariance matrix relatively unchanged. Belsley et al. (1980) recommend examining points for which the absolute value of the ratio minus 1 is greater than $3p/N$.

You can save covariance ratios with the Linear Regression procedure and plot them using the Scatter option on the Graphs menu. Figure 15.49 is a plot of covariance ratios for the salary example. Note the circled point, which has a covariance ratio substantially smaller than the rest.

Figure 15.49 Plot of the covariance ratio

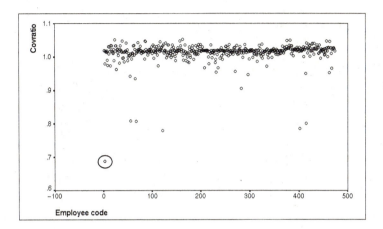

Measures of Collinearity

Collinearity refers to the situation in which there is a high multiple correlation when one of the independent variables is regressed on the others (that is, when there is a high correlation between independent variables). The problem with collinear variables is that they provide very similar information, and it is difficult to separate out the effects of the individual variables. Diagnostics are available which allow you to detect the presence of collinear data and to assess the extent to which the collinearity has degraded the estimated parameters.

The **tolerance** of a variable is a commonly used measure of collinearity. The tolerance of variable i is defined as $1 - R_i^2$, where R_i is the multiple correlation coefficient when the ith independent variable is predicted from the other independent variables. If the tolerance of a variable is small, it is almost a linear combination of the other independent variables.

The **variance inflation factor** (**VIF**) is closely related to the tolerance. In fact, it is defined as the reciprocal of the tolerance. That is, for the ith variable,

$$\text{VIF}_i = \frac{1}{\left(1 - R_i^2\right)} \qquad \text{Equation 15.38}$$

This quantity is called the variance inflation factor, since the term is involved in the calculation of the variance of the ith regression coefficient. As the variance inflation factor increases, so does the variance of the regression coefficient.

Figure 15.50 shows the tolerances and VIF's for the variables in the final model. Note the low tolerances and high VIF's for *edlevel* and *ed2* (the square of *edlevel*). This is to be expected, since there is a relationship between these two variables.

Figure 15.50 Measures of collinearity—tolerance and VIF

```
--------------------------- Variables in the Equation ---------------------------

Variable              B         SE B       Beta    Tolerance     VIF        T     Sig T

WORK              .001794   4.7859E-04    .102038    .834367    1.199     3.749   .0002
MINORITY         -.038225     .009460    -.103342    .945107    1.058    -4.041   .0001
SEX              -.082503     .008671    -.268426    .776799    1.287    -9.515   .0000
EDLEVEL          -.089624     .009751   -1.687260    .018345   54.511    -9.191   .0000
ED2               .004562   3.6303E-04   2.312237    .018263   54.756    12.567   .0000
(Constant)       4.173910     .065417                                    63.804   .0000
```

Two useful tools for examining the collinearity of a data matrix are the eigenvalues of the scaled, uncentered cross-products matrix and the decomposition of regression variance corresponding to the eigenvalues.

Eigenvalues and Condition Indexes

We can compare the eigenvalues of the scaled, uncentered cross-products matrix to see if some are much larger than others. If this is the case, the data matrix is said to be **ill-conditioned**. If a matrix is ill-conditioned, small changes in the values of the independent or dependent variables may lead to large changes in the solution. The condition index is defined as

$$\text{condition index} = \sqrt{\frac{\text{eigenvalue}_{max}}{\text{eigenvalue}_i}}$$

Equation 15.39

There are as many near-dependencies among the variables as there are large condition indexes.

Figure 15.51 shows the eigenvalues and condition indexes for the salary example. You can see that the last two eigenvalues are much smaller than the rest. Their condition indexes are 10.29 and 88.22.

Figure 15.51 Measures of collinearity—eigenvalues and condition indexes

```
Collinearity Diagnostics

Number  Eigenval    Cond    Variance Proportions
                    Index   Constant    SEX    MINORITY   EDLEVEL    ED2      WORK
   1     4.08812    1.000    .00019   .01223   .01375    .00004    .00013   .01466
   2      .79928    2.262    .00005   .08212   .65350    .00002    .00009   .04351
   3      .59282    2.626    .00001   .37219   .22139    .00003    .00022   .17437
   4      .48061    2.917    .00005   .14964   .05421    .00012    .00091   .51370
   5      .03864   10.286    .05223   .37811   .04876    .00004    .02337   .20721
   6      .00053   88.221    .94746   .00571   .00839    .99975    .97527   .04655
```

Variance Proportions

The variances of each of the regression coefficients, including the constant, can be decomposed into a sum of components associated with each of the eigenvalues. If a high proportion of the variance of two or more coefficients is associated with the same eigenvalue, there is evidence for a near-dependency.

Consider Figure 15.51 again. Each of the columns following the condition index tells you the proportion of the variance of each of the coefficients associated with each of the eigenvalues. Consider the column for the *sex* coefficient. You see that 1.22% of the variance of the coefficient is attributable to the first eigenvalue, 8.2% to the second, and 0.57% to the sixth (the proportions in each column sum to 1).

In this table you're looking for variables with high proportions for the same eigenvalue. For example, looking at the last eigenvalue, you see that it accounts for 95% of the variance of the constant, almost 100% of the variance of *edlevel*, and 98% of the variance of *ed2*. This tells you that these three variables are highly dependent. Since the other independent variables have small variance proportions for the sixth eigenvalue, it does not appear that the observed dependencies are affecting their coefficients. (See Belsley et al., 1980, for an extensive discussion of these diagnostics.)

Interpreting the Equation

The multiple regression equation estimated above suggests several findings. Education appears to be the best predictor of beginning salary, at least among the variables included in this study (Figure 15.41). The sex of the employee also appears to be important. Women are paid less than men, since the sign of the regression coefficient is negative (men are coded 0 and women are coded 1). Years of prior work experience and race are also related to salary, but when education and sex are included in the equation, the effect of experience and race is less striking.

Do these results indicate that there is sex discrimination at the bank? Not necessarily. It is well recognized that all education is not equally profitable. Master's degrees in business administration and in political science are viewed quite differently in the marketplace. Thus, a possible explanation of the observed results is that women enter areas that just don't pay very well. Although this may suggest inequities in societal evaluation of skills, it does not necessarily imply discrimination at the bank. Further, many other potential job-related skills or qualifications are not included in the model. As well, some of the existing variables, such as age, may make nonlinear as well as linear contributions to the fit. Such contributions can often be approximated by including new variables that are simple functions of the existing one. For example, the age values squared may improve the fit.

How to Obtain a Linear Regression Analysis

The Linear Regression procedure provides five equation-building methods: forward selection, backward elimination, stepwise selection, forced entry, and forced removal. It can produce residual analyses to help detect influential data points, outliers, and violations of regression model assumptions. You can also save predicted values, residuals, and related measures.

The minimum specifications are:
- One numeric dependent variable.
- One or more numeric independent variables.

To obtain a linear regression analysis, from the menus choose:

Statistics
  Regression ▶
    Linear...

This opens the Linear Regression dialog box, as shown in Figure 15.52.

Figure 15.52 Linear Regression dialog box

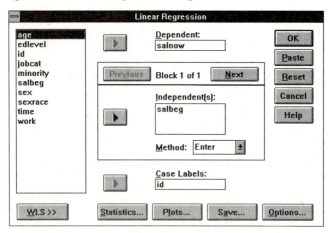

The numeric variables in your data file appear on the source list. Select a dependent variable and a block of one or more independent variables and click on **OK** to get the default analysis using the forced-entry method. By default, cases with missing values for any variable are excluded from the analysis.

⬇ **Method.** Method selection determines the method used in developing the regression model. You can choose one of the following alternatives:

Enter. Forced entry. This is the default method. Variables in the block are entered in a single step.

Stepwise. Stepwise variable entry and removal. Variables in the block are examined at each step for entry or removal.

Remove. Forced removal. Variables in the block are removed in a single step.

Backward. Backward variable elimination. Variables in the block are entered one at a time and then removed one at a time based on removal criteria.

Forward. Forward variable selection. Variables in the block are entered one at a time based on entry criteria.

All variables must pass the tolerance criterion to be entered in the equation, regardless of the entry method specified. The default tolerance level is 0.0001. A variable also is not entered if it would cause the tolerance of another variable already in the model to drop below the tolerance criterion.

For the stepwise method, the maximum number of steps is twice the number of independent variables. For the forward and backward methods, the maximum number of steps equals the number of variables meeting entry and removal criteria. The maximum number of steps for the total model equals the sum of the maximum number of steps for each method in the model.

All independent variables selected are added to a single regression model. However, you can specify different entry methods for different subsets of variables. For example, you can enter one block of variables into the regression model using forward selection and a second block of variables using stepwise selection. To add a second block of variables to the regression model, click on **Next**. Select an alternate selection method if you do not want the default (forced entry). To move back and forth between blocks of independent variables, use **Previous** and **Next**. You can specify up to nine different blocks.

Case Labels. You can designate a variable for labeling cases in scatterplots created by the Linear Regression procedure. For each point in the scatterplot, you can use the Point Selection tool to display the value of the case label variable. You can also display the case number (in the working data file at the time the chart was created) of each point in the scatterplot. For more information about point selection, see the *SPSS Base System User's Guide, Part 1*.

WLS. Optionally, you can obtain a weighted least-squares model. Click on WLS and select a variable containing the weights. An independent or dependent variable cannot be used as a weighting variable. If the value of the weighting variable is zero, negative, or missing, the case is excluded from the analysis.

Linear Regression Statistics

To control the display of statistical output, click on Statistics... in the Linear Regression dialog box. This opens the Linear Regression Statistics dialog box, as shown in Figure 15.53.

Figure 15.53   Linear Regression Statistics dialog box

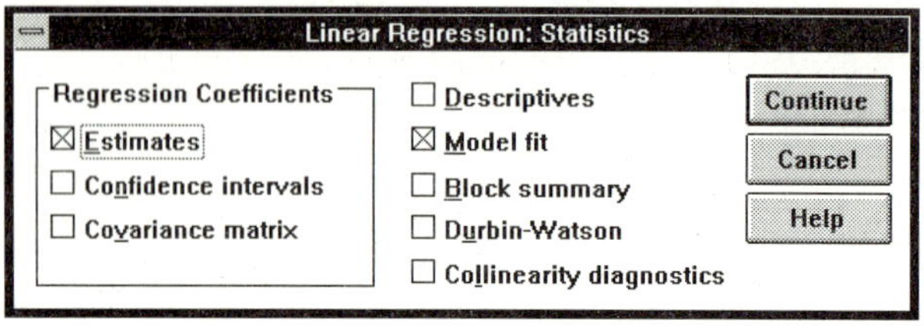

Regression Coefficients. You can choose one or more of the following:

- **Estimates.** Displays regression coefficients and related measures. These statistics are displayed by default. For variables in the equation, statistics displayed are regression coefficient B, standard error of B, standardized coefficient beta, t value for B, and two-tailed significance level of t.

  For independent variables not in the equation, statistics displayed are beta if the variable was entered, t value for beta, t probability, partial correlation with the dependent variable controlling for variables in the equation, and minimum tolerance.

- **Confidence intervals.** Displays the 95% confidence interval for each unstandardized regression coefficient.

- **Covariance matrix.** Variance-covariance matrix of unstandardized regression coefficients. Displays a matrix with covariances below the diagonal, correlations above the diagonal, and variances on the diagonal.

You can also choose one or more of the following statistics:

- **Descriptives.** Variable means, standard deviations, and a correlation matrix with one-tailed probabilities.
- **Model fit.** R, R^2, adjusted R^2, and the standard error. Also, an ANOVA table displays degrees of freedom, sums of squares, mean squares, F value, and the observed probability of F. Model fit statistics are shown by default.
- **Block summary.** Summary statistics for each step (backward, forward, or stepwise method) or block (forced entry or removal method).
- **Durbin-Watson.** Durbin-Watson test statistic. Also displays summary statistics for standardized and unstandardized residuals and predicted values.

❏ **Collinearity diagnostics**. Variance inflation factor (VIF), eigenvalues of the scaled and uncentered cross-products matrix, condition indices, and variance-decomposition proportions (Belsley et al., 1980). Also displays tolerance for variables in the equation; for variables not in the equation, displays the tolerance a variable would have if it were the only variable entered next.

Linear Regression Plots

To obtain scatterplots for variables in the equation, click on Plots... in the Linear Regression dialog box. This opens the Linear Regression Plots dialog box, as shown in Figure 15.54.

Figure 15.54 Linear Regression Plots dialog box

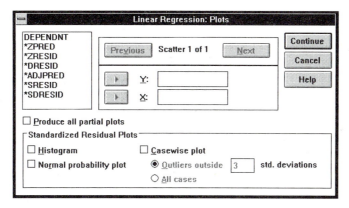

Your dependent variable and the following predicted and residual variables appear on the source list:

- *ZPRED*. Standardized predicted values.
- *ZRESID*. Standardized residuals.
- *DRESID*. Deleted residuals.
- *ADJPRED*. Adjusted predicted values.
- *SRESID*. Studentized residuals.
- *SDRESID*. Studentized deleted residuals.

Select one variable for the vertical (*y*) axis and one variable for the horizontal (*x*) axis. To request additional plots, click on Next and repeat this process. You can specify up to nine scatterplots. All plots are standardized.

Standardized Residual Plots. You can choose one or more of the following:

- **Histogram.** Histogram of standardized residuals. A normal curve is superimposed.
- **Normal probability plot.** Normal probability $(P - P)$ plot of standardized residuals.
- **Casewise plot.** Casewise plot of standardized residuals accompanied by a listing of the values of the dependent and unstandardized predicted (*PRED*) and residual (*RESID*) values. For casewise plots, you can choose one of the following:
  - **Outliers outside n std. deviations.** Limits casewise plot to cases with an absolute standardized residual value greater than a specified value. The default value is 3. To override this value, enter a positive standard deviation value. For example, to display cases with residual values of more than 2 standard deviations above or below the mean, enter 2. A plot is not displayed if no case has an absolute standardized residual value greater than the specified value.
  - **All cases.** Includes all cases in the casewise plot.

If any plots are requested, summary statistics are displayed for unstandardized predicted and residual values (*PRED* and *RESID*, respectively) and for standardized predicted and residual values (*ZPRED* and *ZRESID*).

The following option is also available:

- **Produce all partial plots.** A partial residual plot is a scatterplot of residuals of the dependent variable and an independent variable when both variables are regressed separately on the rest of the independent variables. Plots are displayed for each independent variable in the equation in descending order of standard errors of regression coefficients. All plots are standardized. At least two independent variables must be in the equation for a partial plot to be produced.

Linear Regression Save New Variables

To save residuals, predicted values, or related measures as new variables, click on Save... in the Linear Regression dialog box. This opens the Linear Regression Save New Variables dialog box, as shown in Figure 15.55.

Figure 15.55   Linear Regression Save New Variables dialog box

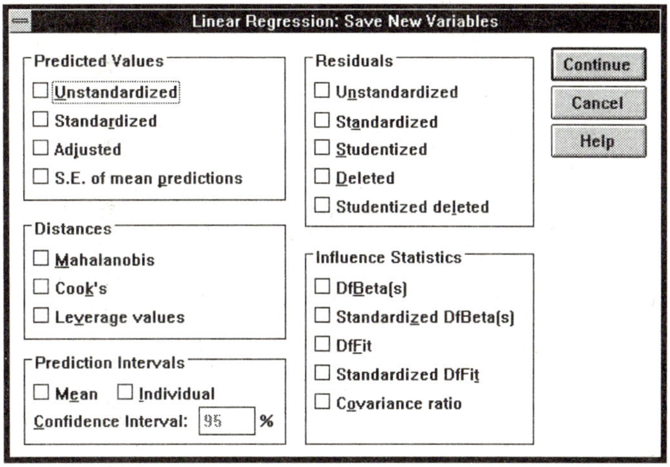

SPSS automatically assigns new variable names for any measures you save as new variables. A table in the output shows the name of each new variable and its contents.

Predicted Values. You can choose one or more of the following:

❑ **Unstandardized.** Unstandardized predicted values.

❑ **Standardized.** Standardized predicted values.

❑ **Adjusted.** Adjusted predicted values.

❑ **S. E. of mean predictions.** Standard errors of the predicted values.

Distances. You can choose one or more of the following:

❑ **Mahalanobis.** Mahalanobis distance.

❑ **Cook's.** Cook's distance.

❑ **Leverage values.** Centered leverage values. (See Velleman & Welsch, 1981.)

Prediction Intervals. You can choose one or both of the following:

❑ **Mean.** Lower and upper bounds for the prediction interval of the mean predicted response. (See Dillon & Goldstein, 1984.)

❏ **Individual.** Lower and upper bounds for the prediction interval for a single observation. (See Dillon & Goldstein, 1984.)

Confidence Interval. For mean and individual confidence intervals, the default is 95%. To override this value, enter a value greater than 0 and less than 100. For example, if you want 99% confidence intervals, enter 99.

Residuals. You can choose one or more of the following:

❏ **Unstandardized.** Unstandardized residuals.

❏ **Standardized.** Standardized residuals.

❏ **Studentized.** Studentized residuals.

❏ **Deleted.** Deleted residuals.

❏ **Studentized deleted.** Studentized deleted residuals. (See Hoaglin & Welsch, 1978.)

Influence Statistics. You can choose one or more of the following:

❏ **DfBeta(s).** The change in the regression coefficient that results from the exclusion of a particular case. A value is computed for each term in the model, including the constant.

❏ **Standardized DfBeta(s)**. Standardized DfBeta values. A value is computed for each term in the model, including the constant.

❏ **DfFit.** The change in the predicted value when a particular case is excluded.

❏ **Standardized DfFit**. Standardized DfFit value.

❏ **Covariance ratio.** The ratio of the determinant of the covariance matrix with a particular case excluded to the determinant of the covariance matrix with all cases included.

If you request one or more new variables, summary statistics are displayed for the following measures:

- *ZPRED*. Standardized predicted values.
- *PRED*. Unstandardized predicted values.
- *SEPRED*. Standard errors of the mean predicted values.
- *ADJPRED*. Adjusted predicted values.
- *ZRESID*. Standardized residuals.
- *RESID*. Unstandardized residuals.
- *SRESID*. Studentized residuals.
- *DRESID*. Deleted residuals.
- *SDRESID*. Studentized deleted residuals.

- *MAHAL*. Mahalanobis distances.
- *COOK D*. Cook's distances.
- *LEVER*. Leverages.

Linear Regression Options

To control the criteria by which variables are chosen for entry or removal from the regression model, to suppress the constant term, or to control the handling of cases with missing values, click on Options... in the Linear Regression dialog box. This opens the Linear Regression Options dialog box, as shown in Figure 15.56.

Figure 15.56　Linear Regression Options dialog box

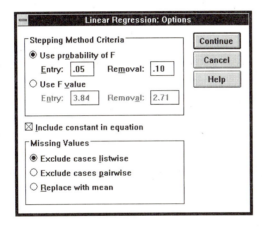

Stepping Method Criteria. The stepping method criteria apply to the forward, backward, and stepwise methods. You can choose one of the following:

○ **Use probability of F.** Use probability of F-to-enter (PIN) and probability of F-to-remove (POUT) as entry and removal criteria. This is the default. The default entry value is 0.05. The default removal value is 0.10. To override these settings, enter new values. Both values must be greater than 0 and less than or equal to 1, and the entry value must be less than the removal value.

○ **Use F value.** Use F values as entry and removal criteria. The default entry value (FIN) is 3.84. The default removal value (FOUT) is 2.71. To override these settings, enter new values. Both values must be greater than 0, and the entry value must be greater than the removal value.

Missing Values. You can choose one of the following:

- **Exclude cases listwise.** Only cases with valid values for all variables are included in the analyses. This is the default.
- **Exclude cases pairwise.** Cases with complete data for the pair of variables being correlated are used to compute the correlation coefficient on which the regression analysis is based. Degrees of freedom are based on the minimum pairwise N.
- **Replace with mean.** Replace missing values with the variable mean. All cases are used for computations, with the mean of a variable substituted for missing observations.

The following option is also available:

- **Include constant in equation.** Regression model contains a constant term. This is the default. To suppress this term and obtain regression through the origin, deselect this item.

Additional Features Available with Command Syntax

You can customize your regression analysis if you paste your selections to a syntax window and edit the resulting REGRESSION command syntax. (For information on syntax windows, see the *SPSS Base System User's Guide, Part 1*.) Additional features include:

- Matrix facility for writing a correlation matrix or for reading a matrix in place of raw data to obtain your regression analysis (with the MATRIX subcommand).
- User-specified tolerance levels (with the CRITERIA subcommand).
- Multiple models for the same or different dependent variables (with the METHOD and DEPENDENT subcommands).
- Additional statistics (with the DESCRIPTIVES and STATISTICS subcommands).

See the *SPSS Base System Syntax Reference Guide* for complete REGRESSION command syntax.

16 Curve Estimation

In many situations when you have two related variables, you want to be able to predict the values of one variable from the other. There are many statistical techniques that allow you to model the relationship between the two variables. They range from the very simple—drawing a straight line—to intricate time-series models. In this chapter, you'll see how the Curve Estimation procedure can be used to fit a variety of simple two-variable models. If you are modeling time-series data, you can specify *time* as the independent variable.

Selecting a Model

Whenever you want to summarize the relationship between two variables, the first step should be to plot them. If the plot resembles a mathematical function that you recognize, you can fit it to the data. For example, if your data points cluster around a straight line, a simple linear regression model may be all that is needed. When the data points don't cluster around a straight line, you can try to apply a transformation, such as taking logs of the independent variable, to try to coax the data to linearity. If this doesn't work, you may have to fit a more complicated model.

The Curve Estimation procedure has 11 regression models that you can fit to your data. The equations for these models, as well as the transformed linear models actually used by the procedure, are given in Table 16.1 on p. 286.

If you aren't sure which of these models fits your data best, you can fit several potential models and then select among them. Consider an example.

The Health Care Composite Index

Figure 16.1 is a plot of the values of Standard and Poor's Health Care Composite Index from January 1987 to January 1993. The Health Care Composite Index tracks the values of 26 stocks. From the plot, you see that, overall, the values of the index increased with time, but the points do not cluster around a straight line. Instead, they seem to follow some type of curve. Although the linear model may not be a particularly good choice, we'll fit linear, quadratic, and cubic models to these data to see how the models compare.

Figure 16.1 Plot of Health Care Composite Index over time

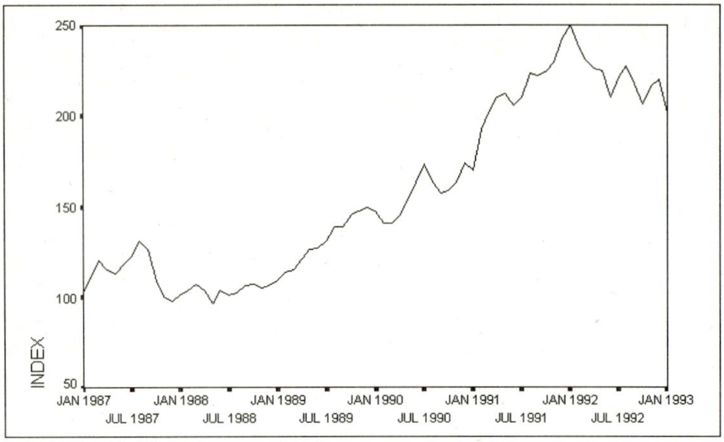

Figure 16.2 contains summary statistics for the three models. The column labeled *Rsq* contains the R^2 for each model. The models are identified in the column labeled *Mth* (for method). The residual degrees of freedom are in the column labeled *d.f.* Since each model estimates a different number of coefficients, the residual degrees of freedom are different for each. The *F* statistic for testing the null hypothesis that all the coefficients in the model are 0 is displayed next, together with its observed significance level (*Sigf*). The coefficients for the models are in the columns labeled *b0*, *b1*, *b2*, and *b3*.

Figure 16.2 Summary statistics for curve estimation models

```
Independent:  Time

Dependent Mth   Rsq   d.f.        F  Sigf         b0        b1      b2       b3
   INDEX  LIN  .847     71   392.02  .000    80.1320   2.0972
   INDEX  QUA  .875     70   245.27  .000    99.0087    .5870   .0204
   INDEX  CUB  .948     69   418.33  .000   136.221  -5.2498   .2163  -.0018
```

More detailed output for the cubic model is shown in Figure 16.3. Here you see both the coefficients and their standard errors, as well as observed significance levels and a complete analysis of variance table. See Chapter 15 for further discussion of this output.

Figure 16.3 Detailed statistics and ANOVA table

```
Dependent variable.. INDEX          Method.. CUBIC

Listwise Deletion of Missing Data

Multiple R            .97359
R Square              .94788
Adjusted R Square     .94562
Standard Error      11.27687

          Analysis of Variance:
          DF     SUM OF SQUARES      MEAN SQUARE
REGRESSION  3         159592.64       53197.546
RESIDUALS  69           8774.59         127.168

F =    418.32527     Signif F =  .0000

------------------- Variables in the Equation -------------------

Variable              B         SE B       Beta        T      Sig T

Time           -5.249826     .646586   -2.303398    -8.119    .0000
Time**2          .216262     .020229    7.245640    10.691    .0000
Time**3         -.001764     .000180   -4.137587    -9.815    .0000
(Constant)    136.221223    5.562684                24.488    .0000
```

The linear model has the smallest R^2. This will always be the case when you compare a linear model to the quadratic and cubic models, since the only difference between them is the additional coefficients. The more coefficients you estimate, the better your model will fit the sample data. However, as mentioned in Chapter 15, you don't want a model with unnecessary coefficients. You want to select the cubic model only if it offers significant advantages over the linear or quadratic models. In this example, there is a reasonable increase in R^2 when the cubic term is added to the quadratic model and the cubic coefficient is significantly different from 0, so the cubic model may be the model of choice.

Predicted Values and Residuals

The Curve Estimation procedure allows you to save four new variables for each model you fit. For each case, these variables contain the predicted value, the residual, and the upper and lower 95% confidence limits for the predicted value.

Figure 16.4 shows the new variables created for this example. You see that *fit_1* is the predicted value for the first model, the linear model; *fit_2* is the predicted value for the quadratic model; and *fit_3* is the predicted value for the cubic model. Figure 16.5 is a plot of the observed values and the three fitted models.

Figure 16.4 New variables created for values of fitted models

```
The following new variables are being created:
   Name        Label
   FIT_1       Fit for INDEX from CURVEFIT, MOD_1 LINEAR
   ERR_1       Error for INDEX from CURVEFIT, MOD_1 LINEAR
   LCL_1       95% LCL for INDEX from CURVEFIT, MOD_1 LINEAR
   UCL_1       95% UCL for INDEX from CURVEFIT, MOD_1 LINEAR
   FIT_2       Fit for INDEX from CURVEFIT, MOD_1 QUADRATIC
   ERR_2       Error for INDEX from CURVEFIT, MOD_1 QUADRATIC
   LCL_2       95% LCL for INDEX from CURVEFIT, MOD_1 QUADRATIC
   UCL_2       95% UCL for INDEX from CURVEFIT, MOD_1 QUADRATIC
   FIT_3       Fit for INDEX from CURVEFIT, MOD_1 CUBIC
   ERR_3       Error for INDEX from CURVEFIT, MOD_1 CUBIC
   LCL_3       95% LCL for INDEX from CURVEFIT, MOD_1 CUBIC
   UCL_3       95% UCL for INDEX from CURVEFIT, MOD_1 CUBIC
```

Figure 16.5 Plot of observed values and three fitted models

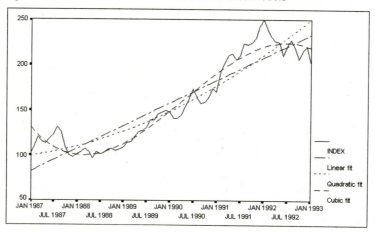

The magnitude of R^2 is only one criterion that is used to see how well a model fits the data. (In fact, you shouldn't use R^2 to compare models if the dependent variable is not in the same units for all of the models.) Examination of the residuals provides very important information about the adequacy of the model.

Consider Figure 16.6, which is a plot of the residuals for the cubic model against time, the independent variable. You see that the residuals do not appear to be randomly distributed about the 0 line. Instead, you see "clumps" of positive and negative residuals. The autocorrelations of the errors are shown in Figure 16.7. You see that the first-order autocorrelation is quite large. This indicates that the cubic model does not fit the data well, since for certain time intervals it always underestimates, while for other intervals it consistently overestimates. In a good model, the residuals don't show any pattern.

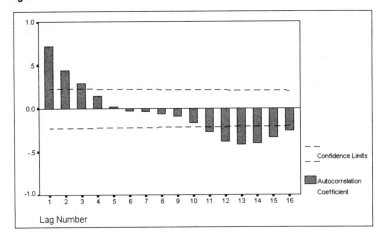

Figure 16.6 Residuals for cubic model

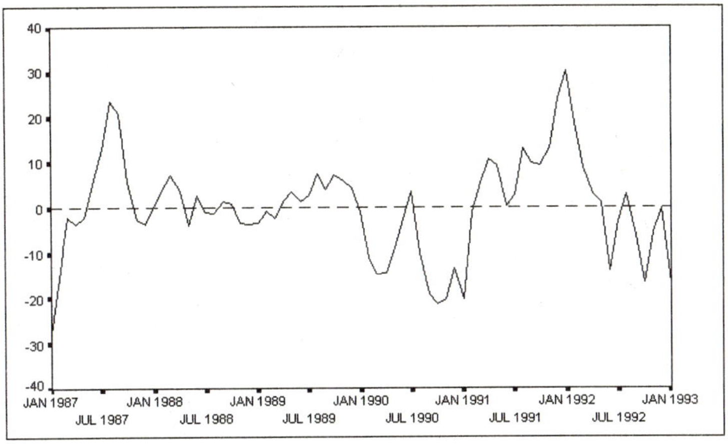

Figure 16.7 Autocorrelations for cubic model residuals

Testing for Normality

You also want to examine the residuals to see if their distribution is normal. You can perform a visual check using the normal probability plot shown in Figure 16.8. If the errors are normally distributed, the values should fall more or less on a straight line. In this example, you see a slight curvature in the plot, suggesting that the distribution is not quite normal.

Figure 16.8 Normal probability plot of cubic residuals

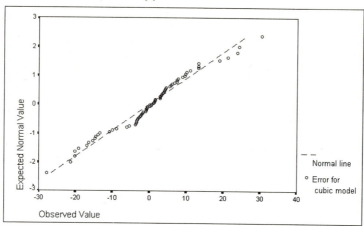

Note that the residuals computed by the Curve Estimation procedure are always in the same units as the original dependent variable. If you fit one of the models in Table 16.1 on p. 286 that transforms the dependent variable, you must examine the residuals for the transformed model, since they must satisfy the regression assumptions. For the Compound, Power, S, Growth, and Exponential models, you can obtain the residuals in the transformed metric by taking the natural log of the observed value minus the natural log of the predicted value. For the Logistic model, calculate the difference between the natural log of the reciprocal of the observed value and the natural log of the reciprocal of the predicted value.

How to Obtain Curve Estimation

The Curve Estimation procedure produces curve estimation regression statistics and related plots for 11 different curve estimation regression models. You can also save predicted values, residuals, and prediction intervals as new variables.

The minimum specifications are:

- One or more dependent variables
- An independent variable that can be either a variable in the working data file or *time*.

To obtain curve estimation regression analysis and related plots, from the menus choose:

Statistics
  Regression ▶
    Curve Estimation...

This opens the Curve Estimation dialog box, as shown in Figure 16.9.

Figure 16.9 Curve Estimation dialog box

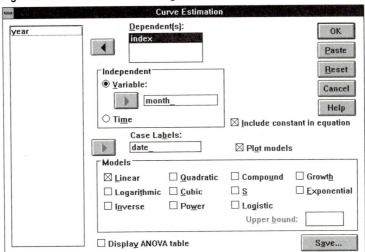

The numeric variables in the working data file are displayed on the source variable list. Select one or more dependent variables and an independent variable and click on **OK** to obtain the default analysis for the linear model.

If you select **Time** instead of a variable from the working data file as the independent variable, the dependent variable should be a **time-series** measure. Time-series analysis requires a data file structure in which each case (row) represents a set of observations at a different time and the length of time between cases is uniform.

Case Labels. You can designate a variable for labeling cases in scatterplots created by the Curve Estimation procedure. For each point in the scatterplot, you can use the Point Selection tool to display the value of the case label variable. You can also display the case number (in the working data file at the time the chart was created) of each point in the scatterplot. In order to use the Point Selection tool, markers should be displayed. For more information about point selection, see the *SPSS Base System User's Guide, Part 1*.

Models. You can choose one or more curve estimation regression models. At least one model must be selected. The available models and corresponding equations are listed in Table 16.1.

Table 16.1 Curve Estimation regression models

Model	Equation	Linear Equation
Linear	$Y = b_0 + b_1 t$	
Logarithmic	$Y = b_0 + b_1 \ln(t)$	
Inverse	$Y = b_0 + (b_1/t)$	
Quadratic	$Y = b_0 + b_1 t + b_2 t^2$	
Cubic	$Y = b_0 + b_1 t + b_2 t^2 + b_3 t^3$	
Compound	$Y = b_0 (b_1)^t$	$\ln(Y) = \ln(b_0) + [\ln(b_1)] t$
Power	$Y = b_0 (t^{b_1})$	$\ln(Y) = \ln(b_0) + b_1 \ln(t)$
S	$Y = e^{(b_0 + b_1/t)}$	$\ln(Y) = b_0 + b_1/t$
Growth	$Y = e^{(b_0 + b_1 t)}$	$\ln(Y) = b_0 + b_1 t$
Exponential	$Y = b_0 (e^{b_1 t})$	$\ln(Y) = \ln(b_0) + b_1 t$
Logistic	$Y = 1/\left(1/u + b_0 \left(b_1^t\right)\right)$	$\ln(1/Y - 1/u) = \ln(b_0) + [\ln(b_1)] t$

where:
b_0 = a constant
b_n = regression coefficient
t = a time value or the value of an independent variable
$\ln$ = natural log (base e)
e = the natural log base
u = upperbound value for the logistic model

Upper bound. For the Logistic model, you can specify the upper boundary value to use in the regression equation. The value must be a positive number, greater than the largest dependent variable value. If you leave the text box blank, infinity is used as the upper boundary, so that $1/u = 0$ and is dropped from the equation. This is the default.

The following options are also available:

- **Include constant in equation**. Estimates a constant term in the regression equation. The constant is included by default. Deselect this item to remove the constant term.
- **Plot models**. Plots the values of the dependent variable and each selected model against the independent variable. A separate chart is produced for each dependent variable. Selected by default. Deselect this item to suppress the charts.
- **Display ANOVA table**. Displays a summary analysis-of-variance table for each selected model.

Saving Predicted Values and Residuals

To save predicted values, residuals, and prediction intervals as new variables, click on Save... in the Curve Estimation dialog box. This opens the Curve Estimation Save dialog box, similar to the one shown in Figure 16.10.

Figure 16.10 Curve Estimation Save dialog box

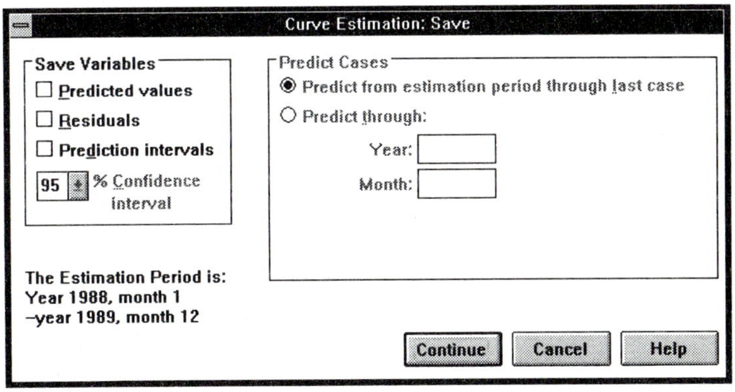

Save Variables. You can choose one or more of the following:

- **Predicted values**. Saves the predicted values for each selected model.
- **Residuals**. Saves the residuals (actual value of the dependent variable minus the model predicted value) for each selected model.
- **Prediction intervals**. Saves the upper and lower bounds (two variables) for the prediction interval of each case for each selected model.
  - **Confidence interval**. Confidence interval for the prediction intervals. You can select 90, 95, or 99% from the drop-down list. The default is 95%.

The new variable names and descriptive labels are displayed in a table in the output window.

Predict Cases. If you select Time instead of a variable in the working data file as the independent variable, you can specify a forecast period beyond the end of the time series. You can choose one of the following alternatives:

○ **Predict from estimation period through last case**. Predicts values for all cases in the file, based on the cases in the estimation period. The estimation period, displayed at the bottom of the dialog box, is defined with the Range subdialog box of the Select Cases option on the Data menu (see Chapter 1). If no estimation period has been defined, all cases are used to predict values. This is the default.

○ **Predict through**. Predicts values through the specified date, time, or observation number, based on the cases in the estimation period. This can be used to forecast values beyond the last case in the time series. The available text boxes for specifying the end of the prediction period are dependent on the currently defined date variables. If there are no defined date variables, you can specify the ending observation (case) number.

Use the Define Dates option on the Data menu to create date variables. See Chapter 1 for more information, including valid ranges for each date variable.

17 Distribution-Free or Nonparametric Tests

Broccoli and Brussels sprouts have recently joined coffee, carrots, red meat, oat bran, saccharin, tobacco, and alcohol on the ever-expanding list of substances thought to contribute to the development or prevention of cancer. This list is necessarily tentative and complicated. The two major sources of evidence—experiments on animals and examination of the histories of people with cancer—are problematic. It is difficult to predict, based on the results of giving large doses of suspect substances to small animals, the consequences for humans of consuming small amounts over a long time span.

In studies of people, lifestyle components are difficult to isolate, and it is challenging—if not impossible—to unravel the contribution of a single factor. For example, what conclusions may be drawn about the role of caffeine, based on a sample of overweight, sedentary, coffee- and alcohol-drinking, cigarette-smoking urban dwellers?

In addition to certain lifestyle factors, dietary fat is thought to play an important role in the development and progression of cancer. Wynder (1976) showed that the per capita consumption of dietary fats is positively correlated with the incidence of breast and colon cancer in humans. In another study, King et al. (1979) examined the relationship between diet and tumor growth in rats. Three groups of animals of the same age, species, and physical condition were injected with tumor cells. The rats were divided into three groups and fed diets of either low, saturated, or unsaturated fat.

One hypothesis of interest is whether the length of time it takes for tumors to develop differs in two of the groups—rats fed saturated fats and rats fed unsaturated fats. If we assume a normal distribution of the tumor-free time, the independent-samples t test (described in Chapter 10) can be used to test the hypothesis that the population means are equal. However, if the distribution of times does not appear to be normal, and especially if the sample sizes are small, we should consider statistical procedures that do not require assumptions about the shape of the underlying distribution.

The Mann-Whitney Test

The **Mann-Whitney test**, also known as the Wilcoxon test, does not require assumptions about the shape of the underlying distributions. It tests the hypothesis that two independent samples come from populations having the same distribution. The form of the distribution need not be specified. The test does not require that the variable be measured on an interval scale; an ordinal scale is sufficient.

Ranking the Data

To compute the test, the observations from both samples are first combined and ranked from smallest to largest value. Consider Table 17.1, which shows a sample of the King data reported by Lee (1992). Case 4 has the shortest elapsed time to development of a tumor: 68 days. It is assigned a rank of 1. Case 3 has the next shortest time (81), so it is assigned a rank of 2. Cases 5 and 6 both exhibited tumors after 112 days. They are both assigned a rank of 3.5, the average of the ranks (3 and 4) for which they are tied. Case 2, with the next longest elapsed time (126 days), is given a rank of 5, and case 1, with the longest elapsed time (199 days), is given a rank of 6.

Table 17.1 Ranking the data

Saturated			Unsaturated		
Case	Time	Rank	Case	Time	Rank
1	199	6	4	68	1
2	126	5	5	112	3.5
3	81	2	6	112	3.5

Calculating the Test

The statistic for testing the hypothesis that the two distributions are equal is the sum of the ranks for each of the two groups. If the groups have the same distribution, their sample distributions of ranks should be similar. If one of the groups has more than its share of small or large ranks, there is reason to suspect that the two underlying distributions are different.

Figure 17.1 shows the output from the Mann-Whitney test for the complete King data. For each group, the mean rank and number of cases is given. (The mean rank is the sum of the ranks divided by the number of cases.) Note that the saturated-fats group has only 29 cases, since one rat died of causes unrelated to the experiment. The number (963) displayed under W is the sum of the ranks for the group with the smaller number of observations. If both groups have the same number of observations, W is the rank sum for the group named first in the Two-Independent-Samples Define Groups dialog box (see Figure 17.23). In this example, the value of W is 963, the sum of the ranks for the saturated-fats group.

Figure 17.1 Mann-Whitney output

```
- - - - - Mann-Whitney U - Wilcoxon Rank Sum W Test

      TUMOR
   by DIET

   Mean Rank    Cases
      26.90       30    DIET = 0    UNSATURATED
      33.21       29    DIET = 1    SATURATED
                  --
                  59    Total

                                  Corrected for ties
         U            W              Z        2-Tailed P
       342.0        963.0         -1.4112       .1582
```

The number (342) identified in the output as U represents the number of times a value in the unsaturated-fats group precedes a value in the saturated-fats group. To understand what this means, consider again the data in Table 17.1. All three cases in the unsaturated-fats group have smaller ranks than the first case in the saturated-fats group, so they all precede case 1 in the rankings. Similarly, all three cases in the unsaturated-fats group precede case 2. Only one unsaturated-fats case (case 4) is smaller in value than case 3. Thus, the number of times the value for an unsaturated-fats case precedes the value for a saturated-fats case is $3 + 3 + 1 = 7$. The number of times the value of a saturated-fats case precedes the value of an unsaturated-fats case is 2, since case 3 has a smaller rank than both cases 5 and 6. The smaller of these two numbers is displayed in the output as U. If the two distributions are equal, values from one group should not consistently precede values in the other.

The significance levels associated with U and W are the same. They can be obtained by transforming the score to a standard normal deviate (Z). If the total sample size is less than 30, an exact probability level based on the distribution of the score is also displayed. From Figure 17.1, the observed significance level for this example is 0.158. Since the significance level is large, the hypothesis that tumor-free time has the same distribution for the two diet groups is not rejected.

Which Diet?

You should not conclude from these findings that it doesn't matter—as far as tumors are concerned—what kind of fat you (or rats) eat. King et al. found that rats fed the unsaturated diet had a total of 96 tumors at the end of the experiment, while rats fed the saturated diet had only 55 tumors. They also found that large tumors were more common in the unsaturated-diet group than in the saturated-diet group. Thus, unsaturated fats may be more hazardous than saturated fats.

Assumptions

The Mann-Whitney test requires only that the sample be random and that values can be ordered. These assumptions—especially randomness—should not be made lightly, but they are less restrictive than those for the two-sample t test for means. The t test requires further that the observations be selected from approximately normally distributed populations with equal variances.

Since the Mann-Whitney test can always be calculated instead of the t test, what determines which should be used? If the assumptions needed for the t test are met, the t test is more powerful than the Mann-Whitney test. That is, the t test will detect true differences between the two populations more often than the Mann-Whitney test, since the t test uses more information from the data. Substituting ranks for the actual values eliminates potentially useful information. On the other hand, using the t test when its assumptions are substantially violated may result in an erroneous observed significance level.

In general, if the assumptions of the t test appear to be reasonable, it should be used. When the data are ordinal—or interval but from a markedly non-normal distribution—the Mann-Whitney test is the procedure of choice.

Nonparametric Tests

Like the Mann-Whitney test, many statistical procedures require limited distributional assumptions about the data. Collectively, these procedures are termed **distribution-free tests** or **nonparametric tests**. Like the Mann-Whitney test, distribution-free tests are generally less powerful than their parametric counterparts. They are most useful in situations where parametric procedures are not appropriate—for example, when the data are nominal or ordinal, or when interval data are from markedly non-normal distributions. Significance levels for certain nonparametric tests can be determined regardless of the shape of the population distribution, since they are based on ranks.

In the following sections, various nonparametric tests will be used to analyze some of the data described in previous chapters. Since the data were chosen to illustrate parametric procedures, they satisfy assumptions that are more restrictive than those required for nonparametric procedures. However, using the same data provides an opportunity to learn new procedures easily and to compare results obtained from different types of analyses.

One-Sample Tests

Various one-sample nonparametric procedures are available for testing hypotheses about the parameters of a population. These include procedures for examining differences in paired samples.

The Sign Test

In Chapter 13, the paired t test for means is used to test the hypothesis that mean buying scores for husbands and wives are equal. Remember that this test requires the assumption that differences are normally distributed.

The **sign test** is a nonparametric procedure used with two related samples to test the hypothesis that the distributions of two variables are the same. This test makes no assumptions about the shape of these distributions.

To compute the sign test, the difference between the buying scores of husbands and wives is calculated for each case. Next, the numbers of positive and negative differences are obtained. If the distributions of the two variables are the same, the numbers of positive and negative differences should be similar.

The output in Figure 17.2 shows that the number of negative differences is 56, while the number of positive differences is 39. The total number of cases is 98, including three with no differences. The observed significance level is 0.1007. Since this value is large, the hypothesis that the distributions are the same is not rejected.

Figure 17.2 Sign test

```
- - - - - Sign Test

     HSSCALE    HUSBAND SELF SCALE
with WSSCALE    WIFE SELF SCALE

     Cases
        56  - Diffs (WSSCALE LT HSSCALE)          Z =        1.6416
        39  + Diffs (WSSCALE GT HSSCALE)
         3    Ties                           2-Tailed P =      .1007
        ---
        98    Total
```

The Wilcoxon Signed-Rank Test

The sign test uses only the direction of the differences between the pairs and ignores the magnitude. A discrepancy of 15 between husbands' and wives' buying scores is treated in the same way as a discrepancy of 1. The **Wilcoxon signed-rank test** incorporates information about the magnitude of the differences and is therefore more powerful than the sign test.

To compute the Wilcoxon signed-rank test, the differences are ranked without considering the signs. In the case of ties, average ranks are assigned. The sums of the ranks for positive and negative differences are then calculated.

As shown in Figure 17.3, the average rank of the 56 negative differences is 45.25. The average positive rank is 51.95. In the row labeled *Ties*, there are three cases with the same value for both variables. The observed significance level associated with the test is large (0.3458), and once again the hypothesis of no difference is not rejected.

Figure 17.3 Wilcoxon signed-rank test

```
- - - - - Wilcoxon Matched-Pairs Signed-Ranks Test

     HSSCALE     HUSBAND SELF SCALE
with WSSCALE     WIFE SELF SCALE

   Mean Rank    Cases
       45.25       56    - Ranks  (WSSCALE LT HSSCALE)
       51.95       39    + Ranks  (WSSCALE GT HSSCALE)
                    3      Ties   (WSSCALE EQ HSSCALE)
                  ---
                   98      Total

       Z =    -.9428              2-Tailed P =   .3458
```

The Wald-Wolfowitz Runs Test

The runs test is a test of randomness. That is, given a sequence of observations, the runs test examines whether the value of one observation influences the values for later observations. If there is no influence (the observations are independent), the sequence is considered random.

A **run** is any sequence of like observations. For example, if a coin is tossed 15 times and the outcomes recorded, the following sequence might result:

HHHTHHHHTTTTTTT

There are four runs in this sequence: HHH, T, HHHH, and TTTTTTT. The total number of runs is a measure of randomness, since too many runs, or too few, suggest dependence between observations. The **Wald-Wolfowitz runs test** converts the total number of runs into a Z statistic having approximately a normal distribution. The only requirement for this test is that the variable tested be dichotomous (have only two possible values).

Suppose, for example, that a weather forecaster records whether it snows for 20 days in February and obtains the following sequence (1=snow, 0=no snow):

01111111010111111100

To test the hypothesis that the occurrence or nonoccurrence of snow on one day has no effect on whether it snows on later days, the runs test is performed, resulting in the output shown in Figure 17.4.

Figure 17.4 Runs test

```
- - - - -  Runs Test

    SNOW

        Runs:    7         Test Value =   1
        Cases:   5    Lt 1
                15    Ge 1                Z =  -.6243
                --
                20    Total 2-tailed P =    .5324
```

Since the observed significance level is quite large (0.5324), the hypothesis of randomness is not rejected. It does not appear, from these data, that snowy (or nonsnowy) days affect the later occurrence of snow.

The Binomial Test

With data that are binomially distributed, the hypothesis that the probability p of a particular outcome is equal to some number is often of interest. For example, you might want to find out if a tossed coin was unbiased. To check this, you could test to see whether the probability of heads was equal to 1/2. The **binomial test** compares the observed frequencies in each category of a binomial distribution to the frequencies expected under a binomial distribution with the probability parameter p.

For example, a nickel is tossed 20 times, with the following results (1=heads, 0=tails):

10011111101111011011

The output in Figure 17.5 shows a binomial test of the hypothesis that the probability of heads equals 1/2 for these data.

Figure 17.5 Binomial test

```
- - - - -  Binomial Test

    HEADS

    Cases
                              Test Prop. =  .5000
         5   = 0              Obs. Prop. =  .2500
        15   = 1
        --                    Exact Binomial
        20   Total            2-tailed P =   .0414
```

The test proportion of cases for the first value (0) is 0.5000 and the observed proportion is 0.2500; that is, 1/4 of the actual tosses were tails. The small (0.0414) observed significance level indicates that it is not likely that p equals 1/2 and it appears that the coin is biased.

The Kolmogorov-Smirnov One-Sample Test

The **Kolmogorov-Smirnov test** is used to determine how well a random sample of data fits a particular distribution (uniform, normal, or Poisson). It is based on comparison of the sample cumulative distribution function to the hypothetical cumulative distribution function.

Suppose we are analyzing the data from an evaluation of 35 beers. The beers were rated on overall quality and a variety of other attributes, such as price, calories, sodium, and alcohol content. We can use the Kolmogorov-Smirnov one-sample test to see whether it is reasonable to assume that the *alcohol* variable is normally distributed. The Kolmogorov-Smirnov output in Figure 17.6 shows an observed significance level of 0.05, small enough to cast doubt on the assumption of normality.

Figure 17.6 Kolmogorov-Smirnov test

```
- - - - - Kolmogorov - Smirnov Goodness of Fit Test
   ALCOHOL    ALCOHOL BY VOLUME (IN %)

   Test Distribution - Normal            Mean:   4.577
                                  Standard Deviation:  .603
        Cases:  35

           Most Extreme Differences
     Absolute       Positive       Negative       K-S Z      2-tailed P
     0.22940        0.15585        -0.22940       1.357        0.050
```

The One-Sample Chi-Square Test

In Chapter 3, frequencies of deaths for the days of the week are examined. The output suggests that all days of the week are equally hazardous in regard to death. To test this conclusion, the one-sample chi-square test can be used. This nonparametric test requires only that the data be a random sample.

To calculate the one-sample chi-square statistic, the data are first classified into mutually exclusive categories of interest—days of the week in this example—and then expected frequencies for these categories are computed. Expected frequencies are the frequencies that would be expected if the null hypothesis is true. For the death data, the hypothesis to be tested is that the probability of death is the same for each day of the week. The day of death is known for 110 subjects. The hypothesis implies that the expected frequency of deaths for each weekday is 110/7, or 15.71. Once the expected frequencies are obtained, the chi-square statistic is computed as

$$\chi^2 = \sum_{i=1}^{k} \frac{(O_i - E_i)^2}{E_i}$$

Equation 17.1

where O_i is the observed frequency for the ith category, E_i is the expected frequency for the ith category, and k is the number of categories.

If the null hypothesis is true, the chi-square statistic has approximately a chi-square distribution with $k - 1$ degrees of freedom. This statistic will be large if the observed and expected frequencies are substantially different. Figure 17.7 shows the output from the one-sample chi-square test for the death data. The observed chi-square value is 3.4, and the associated significance level is 0.757. Since the observed significance level is large, the hypothesis that deaths are evenly distributed over days of the week is not rejected.

Figure 17.7 One-sample chi-square test

```
- - - - - Chi-square Test

    DAYOFWK    DAY OF DEATH

                              Cases
                   Category  Observed   Expected   Residual
    SUNDAY            1         19       15.71       3.29
    MONDAY            2         11       15.71      -4.71
    TUESDAY           3         19       15.71       3.29
    WEDNESDAY         4         17       15.71       1.29
    THURSDAY          5         15       15.71       -.71
    FRIDAY            6         13       15.71      -2.71
    SATURDAY          7         16       15.71        .29
                                ---
                     Total      110

        Chi-Square           D.F.         Significance
          3.400                6              .757
```

The Friedman Test

The **Friedman test** is used to compare two or more related samples. (This is an extension of the tests for paired data.) The k variables to be compared are ranked from 1 to k for each case, and the mean ranks for the variables are calculated and compared, resulting in a test statistic with approximately a chi-square distribution.

The Friedman test can be used to analyze data from a psychology experiment concerned with memory. In this experiment, subjects were asked to memorize first a two-digit number, then a three-digit number, and finally a four-digit number. After each number was memorized, they were shown a single digit and asked if that digit was present in the number memorized. The times taken to reach a decision for the two-, three-, and four-digit numbers are the three related variables of interest.

Figure 17.8 shows the results of the Friedman test, examining the hypothesis that the number of digits memorized has no effect on the time taken to reach a decision. The observed significance level is extremely small, so it appears that the number of digits does affect decision time.

Figure 17.8 Friedman test

```
- - - - - Friedman Two-way ANOVA

    Mean Rank    Variable
        1.21     P2DIGIT
        2.13     P3DIGIT
        2.67     P4DIGIT

        Cases        Chi-Square        D.F.     Significance
         24            26.0833           2           .0000
```

Tests for Two or More Independent Samples

A variety of nonparametric tests involve comparisons between two or more independent samples. (The Mann-Whitney test is one such test.) In this respect, these tests resemble the *t* tests and one-way analyses of variance described in Chapter 10 and Chapter 11.

The Two-Sample Median Test

The **two-sample median test** is used to determine whether two populations have the same median. The two samples are combined and the median for the total distribution is calculated. The number of observations above this median, as well as the number of observations less than or equal to this median, is counted for each sample. The test statistic is based on these counts.

This test can be used to determine whether median sodium levels are the same for the highest-rated and lowest-rated beers in the beer data described earlier. The output in Figure 17.9 shows the largest possible *p* value, 1. Therefore, there is no reason to suspect different medians.

Figure 17.9 Median test of sodium by rating

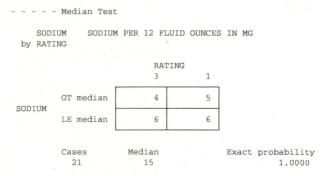

The Two-Sample Wald-Wolfowitz Runs Test

A runs test can be used to test the hypothesis that two samples come from populations with the same distributions. To perform this test, the two samples are combined and the values are sorted. A run in this combined and sorted sample consists of a sequence of values belonging to the first sample or a sequence of values belonging to the second sample. If there are too few runs, it suggests that the two populations have different distributions.

The Wald-Wolfowitz test can be used with the beer data to compare calories for the highest-ranked and lowest-ranked beers. The output in Figure 17.10 shows an observed significance level of 0.0119. Since this is small, the distribution of calories for the highest-ranked beers appears to differ from the distribution of calories for the lowest-ranked beers.

Figure 17.10 Wald-Wolfowitz runs test

```
- - - - - Wald-Wolfowitz Runs Test

     CALORIES   CALORIES PER 12 FLUID OUNCES
 by RATING


       Cases

         10   RATING = 3   FAIR
         11   RATING = 1   VERY GOOD
         --
         21   Total
                                           Exact
                        Runs        Z     1-tailed P
 Minimum Possible:        6      -2.2335     .0119
 Maximum Possible:        6      -2.2335     .0119

 WARNING -- There are   1 Inter-group Ties involving    5 cases.
```

The Two-Sample Kolmogorov-Smirnov Test

The Kolmogorov-Smirnov test for two samples provides another method for testing whether two samples come from populations with the same distributions. It is based on a comparison of the distribution functions for the two samples.

This test can be used with the beer data to compare the alcohol content of the highest-ranked and lowest-ranked beers. Since the observed significance level in Figure 17.11 is small, the alcohol distributions do not appear to be the same. The approximation used to obtain the observed significance level may be inadequate in this case, however, because of the small sample size.

Figure 17.11 Kolmogorov-Smirnov two-sample test

```
- - - - - Kolmogorov - Smirnov 2-Sample Test

    ALCOHOL    ALCOHOL BY VOLUME (IN %)
  by RATING


       Cases

       10   RATING = 3   FAIR
       11   RATING = 1   VERY GOOD
       --
       21   Total

WARNING - Due to small sample size, probability tables should be consulted.
            Most Extreme Differences
     Absolute        Positive        Negative         K-S Z      2-tailed P
     0.60000           0.0           -0.60000         1.373         0.046
```

The K-Sample Median Test

An extension of the two-sample median test, the **k-sample median test** compares the medians of three or more independent samples. Figure 17.12 shows a k-sample median test comparing median prices for the highest-, middle-, and lowest-quality beers. The observed significance level is fairly large (0.091), indicating no real difference in the median price of the three types of beer.

Figure 17.12 K-sample median test

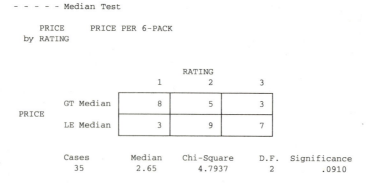

The Kruskal-Wallis Test

The experiment described at the beginning of this chapter investigates the effects of three diets on tumor development. The Mann-Whitney test was calculated to examine possible differences between saturated and unsaturated diets. To test for differences among all three diets, an extension of the Mann-Whitney test can be used. This test is known as the **Kruskal-Wallis one-way analysis of variance**.

The procedure for computing the Kruskal-Wallis test is similar to the procedure used in the Mann-Whitney test. All cases from the three groups are combined and ranked. Average ranks are assigned in the case of ties. For each group, the ranks are summed, and the Kruskal-Wallis H statistic is computed from these sums. The H statistic has approximately a chi-square distribution under the hypothesis that the three groups have the same distribution.

The output in Figure 17.13 shows that the third group, the low-fat-diet group, has the largest average rank. The value of the Kruskal-Wallis statistic is 11.1257. When the statistic is adjusted for the presence of ties, the value changes to 11.2608. The small observed significance level suggests that the time interval until development of a tumor is not the same for all three groups.

Figure 17.13 Kruskal-Wallis one-way analysis of variance output

```
- - - - - Kruskal-Wallis 1-way ANOVA
       TUMOR
   by  DIET

    Mean Rank     Cases
        34.12       30     DIET = 0     UNSATURATED
        43.50       29     DIET = 1     SATURATED
        56.24       29     DIET = 2     LOW-FAT
                    --
                    88     Total

                                            Corrected for Ties
       CASES      Chi-Square  Significance    Chi-Square  Significance
          88        11.1257        0.0038       11.2608        0.0036
```

How to Obtain the Chi-Square Test

The Chi-Square Test procedure tabulates a variable into categories and computes a chi-square statistic based on the differences between observed and expected frequencies.

The minimum specification is one or more numeric variables.

To obtain the chi-square test, from the menus choose:

Statistics
  Nonparametric Tests ▶
    Chi-Square...

This opens the Chi-Square Test dialog box, as shown in Figure 17.14.

Figure 17.14 Chi-Square Test dialog box

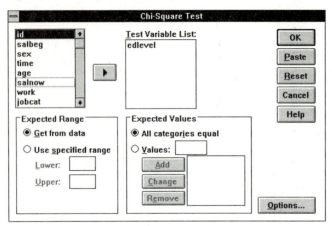

The numeric variables in your data file appear on the source variable list. Select one or more test variables, and click on **OK** to obtain the default chi-square test using equal expected frequencies for each observed category of your variable(s). (See Figure 17.7.) Each variable produces a separate test. To obtain chi-square tests of the relationship between two or more variables, use the Crosstabs procedure (see Chapter 6).

Expected Range. You can choose one of the following alternatives:

- **Get from data.** Each distinct value encountered is defined as a category. This is the default.
- **Use specified range.** Enter integer values for lower and upper bounds. Categories are established for each value within the inclusive range, and cases with values outside the bounds are excluded. For example, if you specify a lowerbound value of 1 and an upperbound value of 4, only the integer values of 1 through 4 are used for the chi-square test. The lowerbound value must be less than the upperbound value, and both values must be specified.

Expected Values. You can choose one of the following alternatives:

- **All categories equal.** All categories have equal expected values. This is the default.
- **Values.** Categories have user-specified expected proportions. Enter a value greater than 0 for each category of the test variable, and click on **Add**. Each time you add a value, it appears at the bottom of the value list. The sequential order of the values is important, since it corresponds to the ascending order of the category values of the

test variable. The first value on the list corresponds to the lowest group value of the test variable, and the last value corresponds to the highest value. Elements of the value list are summed, and then each value is divided by this sum to calculate the proportion of cases expected in the corresponding category. For example, a value list of 3, 4, 5, 4 specifies expected proportions of $3/16$, $4/16$, $5/16$, and $4/16$ for categories 1, 2, 3, and 4, respectively. To remove a value, highlight it on the list and click on **Remove**. To change a value, highlight it, enter a new value, and click on **Change**.

Chi-Square Test Options

To obtain optional summary statistics or to modify the treatment of cases with missing values, click on Options... in the Chi-Square Test dialog box. This opens the Chi-Square Test Options dialog box, as shown in Figure 17.15.

Figure 17.15 Chi-Square Test Options dialog box

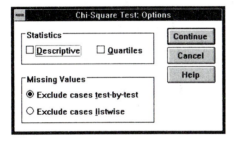

Statistics. You can choose one or both of the following summary statistics:

❏ **Descriptive.** Displays the mean, minimum, maximum, standard deviation, and the number of nonmissing cases.

❏ **Quartiles.** Displays values corresponding to the 25th, 50th, and 75th percentiles.

Missing Values. You can choose one of the following alternatives:

❍ **Exclude cases test-by-test.** When several tests are specified, each test is evaluated separately for missing values. This is the default.

❍ **Exclude cases listwise.** Cases with missing values for any variable are excluded from all analyses.

Additional Features Available with Command Syntax

You can customize your one-sample chi-square test if you paste your selections into a syntax window and edit the resulting NPAR TESTS command syntax. (For information on syntax windows, see the *SPSS Base System User's Guide, Part 1*.) Additional features include:

- Specification of different minimum and maximum values or expected frequencies for different variables (with the CHISQUARE subcommand).
- Tests of the same variable against different expected frequencies or using different ranges (with the EXPECTED subcommand).

See the *SPSS Base System Syntax Reference Guide* for complete NPAR TESTS command syntax.

How to Obtain the Binomial Test

The Binomial Test procedure compares the observed frequency in each category of a dichotomous variable with expected frequencies from the binomial distribution.

The minimum specification is one or more numeric variables.

To obtain the binomial test, from the menus choose:

Statistics
  Nonparametric Tests ▶
    Binomial...

This opens the Binomial Test dialog box, as shown in Figure 17.16.

Figure 17.16 Binomial Test dialog box

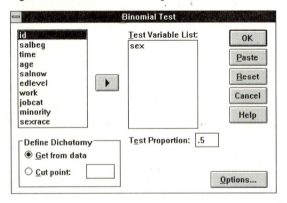

The numeric variables in your data file appear on the source variable list. Select one or more test variables to use in the binomial test. If your variables are dichotomous, you can click on OK to obtain the default binomial test using equal probabilities for each group. Otherwise, you must specify a cut point.

Define Dichotomy. You can choose one of the following alternatives:

- **Get from data.** Assigns cases with the lower category of a dichotomous variable to one group and cases with the higher category to the other group. This is the default.
- **Cut point.** User-specified cut point. Assigns cases with values less than the cut point to one group and cases with values equal to or greater than the cut point to the other group.

Test Proportion. The default null hypothesis is that the data are from a binomial distribution with a probability of 0.5 for both groups. To change the probabilities, enter a test proportion for the first group. For example, specifying .25 tests the null hypothesis that the data are from a binomial distribution with a probability of 0.25 for the first value and 0.75 for the second value. The value you specify must be between .001 and .999 and cannot include leading zeros.

Binomial Test Options

To get optional summary statistics or to modify the treatment of cases with missing values, click on Options... in the Binomial Test dialog box. This opens the Binomial Test Options dialog box, as shown in Figure 17.17.

Figure 17.17 Binomial Test Options dialog box

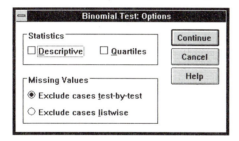

Statistics. You can choose one or both of the following summary statistics:

- **Descriptive.** Displays the mean, minimum, maximum, standard deviation, and the number of nonmissing cases.
- **Quartiles.** Displays values corresponding to the 25th, 50th, and 75th percentiles.

Missing Values. You can choose one of the following alternatives:

- **Exclude cases test-by-test.** When several tests are specified, each test is evaluated separately for missing values. This is the default.

○ **Exclude cases listwise.** Cases with missing values for any variable are excluded from all analyses.

Additional Features Available with Command Syntax

You can customize your binomial test if you paste your selections into a syntax window and edit the resulting NPAR TESTS command syntax. (For information on syntax windows, see the *SPSS Base System User's Guide, Part 1*.) Additional features include:

- Selection of specific groups (and exclusion of others) when a variable has more than two categories (with the BINOMIAL subcommand).
- Different cut points or probabilities for different variables (with the BINOMIAL subcommand).
- Tests of the same variable against different cut points or probabilities (with the EXPECTED subcommand).

See the *SPSS Base System Syntax Reference Guide* for complete NPAR TESTS command syntax.

How to Obtain the Runs Test

The Runs Test procedure tests whether the order of occurrence of two values of a variable is random. A **run** is defined as a sequence of one of the values that is preceded and followed by the other data value (or the end of the series). For example, the sequence

1 1 | 0 0 0 | 1 | 0 0 0 0 | 1 | 0 | 1 |

contains seven runs (vertical bars separate the runs). For a sample of a given size, very many or very few runs suggest that the sample is not random. The Z statistic, which has an approximately normal distribution, is computed.

The minimum specification is one or more numeric variables.

To obtain the runs test, from the menus choose:

Statistics
  Nonparametric Tests ▶
    Runs...

This opens the Runs Test dialog box, as shown in Figure 17.18.

Figure 17.18 Runs Test dialog box

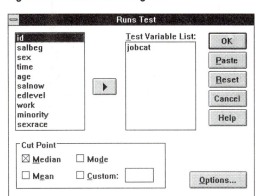

The numeric variables in your data file appear on the source variable list. Select one or more test variables, and click on OK to obtain the default runs test using the median to dichotomize your variable(s).

Cut Point. Assigns cases with values less than the cut point to one group and cases with values equal to or greater than the cut point to the other group. You must select at least one cut point, and one test is performed for each cut point chosen.

You can choose one or more of the following:

- **Median.** The observed median is the cut point. This is the default.
- **Mean.** The observed mean is the cut point.
- **Mode.** The observed mode is the cut point.
- **Custom.** User-specified cut point. For example, if the variable has values of 0 and 1, enter 1 as the cut point.

Runs Test Options

To get optional summary statistics or to modify the treatment of cases with missing values, click on Options... in the Runs Test dialog box. This opens the Runs Test Options dialog box, as shown in Figure 17.19.

Figure 17.19 Runs Test Options dialog box

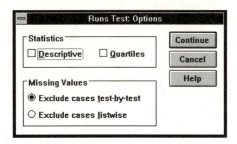

Statistics. You can choose one or both of the following summary statistics:

- **Descriptive.** Displays the mean, minimum, maximum, standard deviation, and the number of nonmissing cases.
- **Quartiles.** Displays values corresponding to the 25th, 50th, and 75th percentiles.

Missing Values. You can choose one of the following alternatives:

- **Exclude cases test-by-test.** When several tests are specified, each test is evaluated separately for missing values. This is the default.
- **Exclude cases listwise.** Cases with missing values for any variable are excluded from all analyses.

Additional Features Available with Command Syntax

You can customize your runs test if you paste your selections into a syntax window and edit the resulting NPAR TESTS command syntax. (For information on syntax windows, see the *SPSS Base System User's Guide, Part 1*.) Additional features include:

- Different cut points for different variables (with the RUNS subcommand).
- Tests of the same variable against different custom cut points (with the RUNS subcommand).

See the *SPSS Base System Syntax Reference Guide* for complete NPAR TESTS command syntax.

How to Obtain the One-Sample Kolmogorov-Smirnov Test

The One-Sample Kolmogorov-Smirnov Test procedure compares the observed cumulative distribution function for a variable with a specified theoretical distribution, which may be normal, uniform, or Poisson. The Kolmogorov-Smirnov Z is computed from the largest difference (in absolute value) between the observed and theoretical distribution functions.

The minimum specification is one or more numeric variables.

To obtain the one-sample Kolmogorov-Smirnov test, from the menus choose:

Statistics
 Nonparametric Tests ▶
  1-Sample K-S...

This opens the One-Sample Kolmogorov-Smirnov Test dialog box, as shown in Figure 17.20.

Figure 17.20 One-Sample Kolmogorov-Smirnov Test dialog box

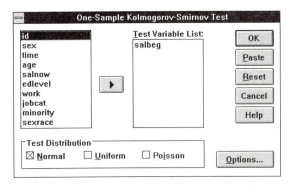

The numeric variables in your data file appear on the source variable list. Select at least one test variable, and click on **OK** to obtain the default (Kolmogorov-Smirnov) test using the normal distribution. Each variable produces a separate test.

Test Distribution. At least one test distribution must be selected. You can choose one or more of the following:

❑ **Normal.** The observed mean and standard deviation are the parameters. This is the default.

❑ **Uniform.** The observed minimum and maximum values define the range of the distribution.

❑ **Poisson.** The observed mean is the parameter.

Tests produced by Kolmogorov-Smirnov assume that the parameters of the test distribution are specified *in advance*. When the parameters of the test distribution are estimated from the sample, the distribution of the test statistic changes. Tests for normality that make this correction are available using the Explore procedure (see Chapter 5). See also "Additional Features Available with Command Syntax," below.

One-Sample Kolmogorov-Smirnov Options

To obtain optional summary statistics or to modify the treatment of cases with missing values, click on Options... in the One-Sample Kolmogorov-Smirnov Test dialog box. This opens the One-Sample K-S Options dialog box, as shown in Figure 17.21.

Figure 17.21 One-Sample K-S Options dialog box

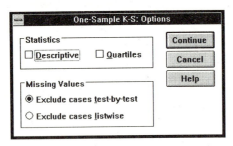

Statistics. You can choose one or both of the following summary statistics:

- **Descriptive.** Displays the mean, minimum, maximum, standard deviation, and the number of nonmissing cases.
- **Quartiles.** Displays values corresponding to the 25th, 50th, and 75th percentiles.

Missing Values. You can choose one of the following alternatives:

- **Exclude cases test-by-test.** When several tests are specified, each test is evaluated separately for missing values. This is the default.
- **Exclude cases listwise.** Cases with missing values for any variable are excluded from all analyses.

Additional Features Available with Command Syntax

You can customize your Kolmogorov-Smirnov test if you paste your selections into a syntax window and edit the resulting NPAR TESTS command syntax. (For information on syntax windows, see the *SPSS Base System User's Guide, Part 1*.) As an additional feature, you can specify the parameters of the test distribution (with the K-S subcommand). See the *SPSS Base System Syntax Reference Guide* for complete NPAR TESTS command syntax.

How to Obtain Two-Independent-Samples Tests

The Two-Independent-Samples Tests procedure compares two groups of cases on one variable (see "The Mann-Whitney Test" on p. 289).

The minimum specifications are:
- One or more numeric test variables.
- One numeric grouping variable.
- Group values for the grouping variable.

To obtain two-independent-samples tests, from the menus choose:

Statistics
  Nonparametric Tests ▶
    2 Independent Samples...

This opens the Two-Independent-Samples Tests dialog box, as shown in Figure 17.22.

Figure 17.22 Two-Independent-Samples Tests dialog box

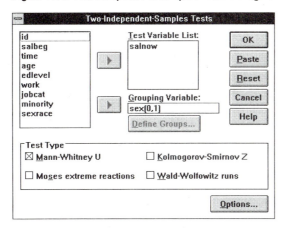

The numeric variables in your data file appear on the source variable list. Select one or more test variables and a grouping variable that splits the file into two groups or samples. After defining values of the grouping variable, click on OK to obtain the default (Mann-Whitney U) two-independent-samples test.

Test Type. At least one test type must be selected. You can choose one or more of the following:

❏ **Mann-Whitney U.** All cases are ranked in order of increasing size, and U (the number of times a score from group 1 precedes a score from group 2) is computed. This is the default test. If the samples are from the same population, the distribution of scores from the two groups on the ranked list should be similar; an extreme value of U indicates a nonrandom pattern. For samples with fewer than 30 cases, the exact significance level for U is computed using the Dineen and Blakesly (1973) algorithm. For larger samples, U is transformed into a normally distributed Z statistic.

- **Moses extreme reactions.** Arranges the scores from the groups in a single ascending sequence. The span of the control group is computed as the number of cases in the sequence containing the lowest and highest control score. The exact significance level can be computed for the span. The control group is defined by the group 1 value in the Two-Independent-Samples Define Groups dialog box (see Figure 17.23). Because chance outliers can easily distort the range of the span, 5% of the cases are trimmed automatically from each end. No adjustments are made for tied observations.

- **Kolmogorov-Smirnov Z.** Computes the observed cumulative distributions for both groups and the maximum positive, negative, and absolute differences. The Kolmogorov-Smirnov Z is then computed along with the two-tailed probability level based on the Smirnov (1948) formula.

- **Wald-Wolfowitz runs.** Combines observations from both groups and ranks them from lowest to highest. If the samples are from the same population, the two groups should be randomly scattered throughout the ranking. A runs test is performed using group membership as the criterion. If there are ties involving observations from both groups, both the minimum and maximum number of runs possible are calculated. If the total sample size is 30 or fewer cases, the exact one-tailed significance level is calculated. Otherwise, the normal approximation is used.

Two-Independent-Samples Define Groups

To define groups based on the values of the grouping variable, highlight the grouping variable and click on Define Groups... to open the Two-Independent-Samples Define Groups dialog box, as shown in Figure 17.23.

Figure 17.23 Two-Independent-Samples Define Groups dialog box

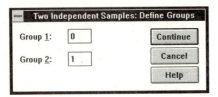

Enter integer values for group 1 and group 2. Cases with other values are excluded.

Two-Independent-Samples Options

To obtain optional summary statistics or to modify the treatment of cases with missing values, click on Options... in the Two-Independent-Samples Tests dialog box. This opens the Two-Independent-Samples Options dialog box, as shown in Figure 17.24.

Figure 17.24 Two-Independent-Samples Options dialog box

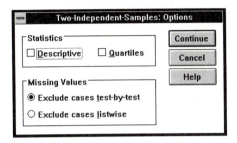

Statistics. You can choose one or both of the following summary statistics:

- ❑ **Descriptive.** Displays the mean, minimum, maximum, standard deviation, and the number of nonmissing cases.
- ❑ **Quartiles.** Displays values corresponding to the 25th, 50th, and 75th percentiles.

Missing Values. You can choose one of the following alternatives:

- ❍ **Exclude cases test-by-test.** When several tests are specified, each test is evaluated separately for missing values. This is the default.
- ❍ **Exclude cases listwise.** Cases with missing values for any variable are excluded from all analyses.

Additional Features Available with Command Syntax

You can customize your two-independent-samples tests if you paste your selections into a syntax window and edit the resulting NPAR TESTS command syntax. (For information on syntax windows, see the *SPSS Base System User's Guide, Part 1*.) As an additional feature, you can specify the number of cases to be trimmed for the Moses test (with the MOSES subcommand). See the *SPSS Base System Syntax Reference Guide* for complete NPAR TESTS command syntax.

How to Obtain Tests for Several Independent Samples

The Tests for Several Independent Samples procedure compares two or more groups of cases on one variable.

The minimum specifications are:
- One or more numeric test variables.
- One numeric grouping variable.
- Minimum and maximum values for the grouping variable.

To obtain tests for several independent samples, from the menus choose:

Statistics
  Nonparametric Tests ▶
    K Independent Samples...

This opens the Tests for Several Independent Samples dialog box, as shown in Figure 17.25.

Figure 17.25 Tests for Several Independent Samples dialog box

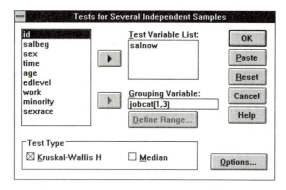

The numeric variables in your data file appear on the source variable list. Select one or more test variables and a grouping variable that splits the file into two or more groups. After defining the range of the grouping variable, click on **OK** to obtain the default (Kruskal-Wallis H) test.

Test Type. At least one test type must be selected. You can choose one or both of the following:

❑ **Kruskal-Wallis H.** Ranks all cases from the specified range in a single series, computes the rank sum for each group, and computes the Kruskal-Wallis H statistic, which has approximately a chi-square distribution. This is the default.

❏ **Median.** Produces a contingency table that indicates, for each group, the number of cases with values greater than the observed median and less than or equal to the median. A chi-square statistic for the table is computed.

Several Independent Samples Define Range

To define ranges based on the values of the grouping variable, highlight the grouping variable and click on **Define Range...** in the Tests for Several Independent Samples dialog box to open the Several Independent Samples Define Range dialog box, as shown in Figure 17.26.

Figure 17.26 Several Independent Samples Define Range dialog box

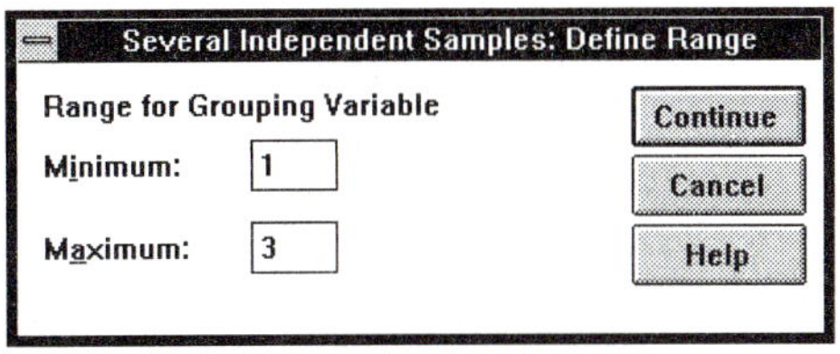

Enter values for minimum and maximum that correspond to the lowest and highest categories of the grouping variable. Both values must be integers, and cases with values outside the bounds are excluded. For example, if you specify a minimum value of 1 and a maximum value of 4, only the integer values of 1 through 4 are used. The minimum value must be less than the maximum value, and both values must be specified.

Several Independent Samples Options

To obtain optional summary statistics or to modify the treatment of cases with missing values, click on **Options...** in the Tests for Several Independent Samples dialog box. This opens the Several Independent Samples Options dialog box, as shown in Figure 17.27.

Figure 17.27 Several Independent Samples Options dialog box

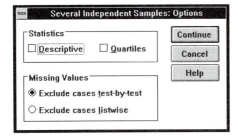

Statistics. You can choose one or both of the following summary statistics:

- **Descriptive.** Displays the mean, minimum, maximum, standard deviation, and the number of nonmissing cases.
- **Quartiles.** Displays values corresponding to the 25th, 50th, and 75th percentiles.

Missing Values. You can choose one of the following alternatives:

- **Exclude cases test-by-test.** When several tests are specified, each test is evaluated separately for cases with missing values. This is the default.
- **Exclude cases listwise.** Cases with missing values for any variable are excluded from all analyses.

Additional Features Available with Command Syntax

You can customize your test for several independent samples if you paste your selections into a syntax window and edit the resulting NPAR TESTS command syntax. (For information on syntax windows, see the *SPSS Base System User's Guide, Part 1*.) As an additional feature, you can specify a value other than the observed median for the median test (with the MEDIAN subcommand). See the *SPSS Base System Syntax Reference Guide* for complete NPAR TESTS command syntax.

How to Obtain Two-Related-Samples Tests

The Two-Related-Samples Tests procedure compares the distributions of two variables (see "The Sign Test" on p. 293).

The minimum specification is one or more pairs of numeric variables.

To obtain two-related-samples tests, from the menus choose:

Statistics
  Nonparametric Tests ▶
    2 Related Samples...

This opens the Two-Related-Samples Tests dialog box, as shown in Figure 17.28.

Figure 17.28 Two-Related-Samples Tests dialog box

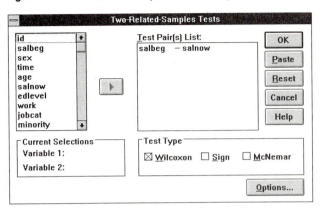

The numeric variables in your data file appear on the source list. Select one or more pairs of variables to use in the two-related-samples tests. To select a pair:

1. Click on one of the variables. It appears as the first variable under Current Selections.

2. Click on another variable. It appears as the second variable. To remove a variable from Current Selections, click on it again.

3. Click on ▶ to move the pair to the Test Pair(s) list.

Repeat this process if you have more than one pair of variables. To obtain the default (Wilcoxon signed-rank) test for two related samples, click on OK.

Macintosh: Use ⌘-click to select pairs of variables.

Test Type. At least one test type must be selected. You can choose one or more of the following:

❑ **Wilcoxon.** Computes differences between pairs of variables, ranks the absolute differences, sums ranks for the positive and negative differences, and computes the test statistic Z from the positive and negative rank sums. This is the default. Under the null hypothesis, the distribution for Z is approximately normal, with a mean of 0 and a variance of 1 for large sample sizes.

❑ **Sign.** Analyzes the signs of the differences between two paired values. Counts the positive and negative differences between each pair of variables and ignores 0 differences. Under the null hypothesis for large sample sizes, the distribution for the test statistic Z is approximately normal, with a mean of 0 and a variance of 1. The binomial distribution is used to compute an exact significance level if 25 or fewer differences are observed.

❑ **McNemar.** Examines the cases with different values for two dichotomous variables. Tests the hypothesis that both combinations of different values are equally likely. McNemar produces a 2×2 table for each pair of variables. Pairs of variables being tested must be coded with the same two values. If your variables are not dichotomous, or if they have different values, recode them (see Chapter 1). A chi-square statistic is computed for cases with different values for the two variables. If fewer than 25 cases have different values for the two variables, the binomial distribution is used to compute the significance level.

Two-Related-Samples Options

To get optional summary statistics or to modify the treatment of cases with missing values, click on Options... in the Two-Related-Samples Tests dialog box. This opens the Two-Related-Samples Options dialog box, as shown in Figure 17.29.

Figure 17.29 Two-Related-Samples Options dialog box

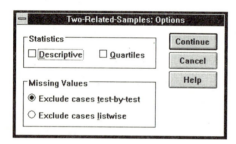

Statistics. You can choose one or both of the following summary statistics:

❑ **Descriptive.** Displays the mean, minimum, maximum, standard deviation, and the number of nonmissing cases.

❑ **Quartiles.** Displays values corresponding to the 25th, 50th, and 75th percentiles.

Missing Values. You can choose one of the following alternatives:

○ **Exclude cases test-by-test.** When several tests are specified, each test is evaluated separately for missing values. This is the default.

○ **Exclude cases listwise.** Cases with missing values for any variable are excluded from all analyses.

Additional Features Available with Command Syntax

You can customize your two-related-samples test if you paste your selections into a syntax window and edit the resulting NPAR TESTS command syntax. (For information on syntax windows, see the *SPSS Base System User's Guide, Part 1*.) As an additional feature, you can test a variable with each variable on a list. See the *SPSS Base System Syntax Reference Guide* for complete NPAR TESTS command syntax.

How to Obtain Tests for Several Related Samples

The Tests for Several Related Samples procedure compares the distributions of two or more variables.

The minimum specification is two or more numeric variables.

To obtain tests for several related samples, from the menus choose:

Statistics
  Nonparametric Tests ▶
    K Related Samples...

This opens the Tests for Several Related Samples dialog box, as shown in Figure 17.30.

Figure 17.30 Tests for Several Related Samples dialog box

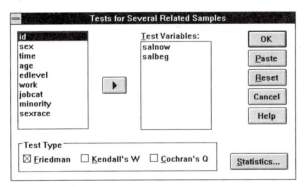

The numeric variables in your data file appear on the source variable list. Select two or more test variables, and click on OK to obtain the default (Friedman) test for several related samples. Cases with missing values for any of the variables are excluded.

Test Type. At least one test type must be selected. You can choose one or more of the following:

❑ **Friedman.** Ranks each variable from 1 to k for each case (where k is the number of variables), calculates the mean rank for each variable over all cases, and then calculates a test statistic with approximately a chi-square distribution. This is the default.

- **Kendall's W.** Ranks k variables from 1 to k for each case, calculates the mean rank for each variable over all cases, and then calculates Kendall's W and a corresponding chi-square statistic, correcting for ties. W ranges between 0 and 1, with 0 signifying no agreement and 1 signifying complete agreement. This test assumes that each case is a judge or rater. If you want to perform this test with variables as judges and cases as entities, you must first transpose your data matrix (see Chapter 2).
- **Cochran's Q.** Tests the null hypothesis that the proportion of cases in a particular category is the same for several dichotomous variables. Produces a $k \times 2$ contingency table (variable versus category) and computes the proportions for each variable. If your variables are not dichotomous or if they have different values, recode them (see Chapter 1). Cochran's Q statistic has approximately a chi-square distribution.

Several Related Samples Statistics

To obtain optional summary statistics, click on Statistics... in the Tests for Several Related Samples dialog box. This opens the Several Related Samples Statistics dialog box, as shown in Figure 17.31.

Figure 17.31 Several Related Samples Statistics dialog box

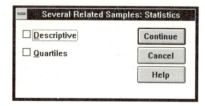

You can choose one or both of the following summary statistics:

- **Descriptive.** Displays the mean, maximum, minimum, standard deviation, and the number of nonmissing cases.
- **Quartiles.** Displays values corresponding to the 25th, 50th, and 75th percentiles.

18 Listing Cases

It is sometimes necessary or useful to review the actual contents of your data file. You may want to make sure data created in another application are being read correctly by SPSS, or you may want to verify the results of transformations or examine cases you suspect contain coding errors. You can review and print the contents of the data file using the Data Editor or the List Cases procedure.

How to Obtain Case Listings

The List Cases procedure produces case listings of selected variables for all cases or a subset of cases.

The minimum specification is one variable.

To obtain case listings with the List Cases procedure, from the menus choose:

Statistics
  Summarize ▶
    List Cases...

This opens the List Cases dialog box, as shown in Figure 18.1.

Figure 18.1 List Cases dialog box

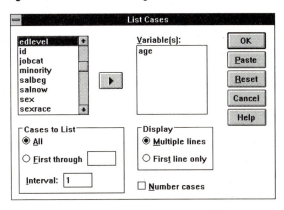

The variables in your data file are displayed on the source list. Select one or more variables for which you want case listings. To obtain the default listing of all cases in the file, click on OK.

Cases to List. You can choose one of the following:

○ **All**. Lists all cases in the data file. This is the default.

○ **First through n**. Lists cases from the first case to the specified number. The number represents the sequential number in the current file order, regardless of the value of any case ID variable that may exist in the file.

The following option is also available for cases to list:

Interval. Increment used to choose cases for listing. For example, if you want to see only every fifth case, enter a value of 5. The default value is 1.

Display. You can choose one of the following:

○ **Multiple lines**. This is the default. SPSS automatically determines the format of the case listing. If all the variables can fit on one line, the variable names are used as column heads (see Figure 18.2). If it can display all variables on one line by displaying some variable names vertically, it does so (see Figure 18.3). If there is not enough room on one line to display all the requested variables, multiple lines are used for each case. SPSS generates a table indicating which variables appear on each line, and the name of the first variable on each line is displayed in the case listings (see Figure 18.4).

○ **First line only**. If there is not enough room for all the variables on a single line, the listing is truncated to include only those variables that fit on a single line per case. Since the multiple line format can be difficult to read, you may want to use this alternative.

The following display option is also available:

❏ **Number cases**. Displays the sequential case number in the current file order. This is the value of the system variable *$casenum*, which reflects the current order of cases in the file.

Figure 18.2   Single-line case listing with variable names displayed horizontally

NAME	ID	SALBEG	SEX	TIME	AGE	SALNOW	EDLEVEL	WORK	JOBCAT
Delbert McManus	926	3600	0	91	53.50	12300	12	26.17	3
Karen Nigida	921	3600	1	97	60.67	6780	12	10.33	1
Kendall Newton	1010	3600	1	97	51.58	8460	15	14.25	1
Christine Martin	1096	3600	1	96	60.50	7680	15	1.92	1
Dakota Becking	741	3900	1	98	27.25	8760	12	.00	1
Kay Lewis	754	3900	1	92	55.50	6480	8	.00	1
Donna Paul	945	3900	1	86	52.00	8760	12	13.00	1
Harriet Smith	995	3900	1	86	62.00	7260	12	6.00	1
Laurie Stolarz	1107	3900	1	88	62.50	6660	8	34.33	1
Lowell George	1077	3900	0	94	29.17	9000	8	3.00	2

Listing Cases

Figure 18.3 Single-line case listing with some variable names displayed vertically

```
                         S                S           J
                         A                A           O
                         L    T           L           B
                      B  S    I           N           C
                      E  E    M           O           A
NAME            ID    G  X    E    AGE    W  EDLEVEL  WORK    T
Delbert McManus  926 3600 0  91  53.50 12300    12    26.17  3
Karen Nigida     921 3600 1  97  60.67  6780    12    10.33  1
Kendall Newton  1010 3600 1  97  51.58  8460    15    14.25  1
Christine Martin 1096 3600 1  96  60.50  7680    15     1.92  1
Dakota Becking   741 3900 1  98  27.25  8760    12      .00  1
Kay Lewis        754 3900 1  92  55.50  6480     8      .00  1
Donna Paul       945 3900 1  86  52.00  8760    12    13.00  1
Harriet Smith    995 3900 1  86  62.00  7260    12     6.00  1
Laurie Stolarz  1107 3900 1  88  62.50  6660     8    34.33  1
Lowell George   1077 3900 0  94  29.17  9000     8     3.00  2
```

Figure 18.4 Case listing with multiple lines

```
THE VARIABLES ARE LISTED IN THE FOLLOWING ORDER:
LINE   1: NAME ID SALBEG SEX TIME AGE SALNOW EDLEVEL WORK
LINE   2: JOBCAT MINORITY SEXRACE

    NAME:  Delbert McManus     926     3600 0 91  53.50     12300 12        26
    JOBCAT:         3 1       2.00

    NAME:  Karen Nigida        921     3600 1 97  60.67      6780 12        10
    JOBCAT:         1 1       4.00

    NAME:  Kendall Newton     1010     3600 1 97  51.58      8460 15        14
    JOBCAT:         1 1       4.00

    NAME:  Christine Martin   1096     3600 1 96  60.50      7680 15         2
    JOBCAT:         1 1       4.00

    NAME:  Dakota Becking      741     3900 1 98  27.25      8760 12         0
    JOBCAT:         1 0       3.00

    NAME:  Kay Lewis           754     3900 1 92  55.50      6480  8         0
    JOBCAT:         1 0       3.00

    NAME:  Donna Paul          945     3900 1 86  52.00      8760 12        13
    JOBCAT:         1 0       3.00

    NAME:  Harriet Smith       995     3900 1 86  62.00      7260 12         6
    JOBCAT:         1 0       3.00

    NAME:  Laurie Stolarz     1107     3900 1 88  62.50      6660  8        34
    JOBCAT:         1 0       3.00

    NAME:  Lowell George      1077     3900 0 94  29.17      9000  8         3
    JOBCAT:         2 1       2.00
```

Additional Features Available with Command Syntax

You can customize your descriptive statistics if you paste your selections to a syntax window and edit the resulting LIST command syntax. (For information on syntax windows, see the *SPSS Base System User's Guide, Part 1*.) An additional feature is the ability to list cases beginning with any case you specify. See the *SPSS Base System Syntax Reference Guide* for complete LIST command syntax.

19 Reporting Results

Case listings and descriptive statistics are basic tools for studying and presenting data. You can obtain case listings with the Data Editor or the List Cases procedure, frequency counts and descriptive statistics with the Frequencies procedure, and subpopulation statistics with the Means procedure. Each of these uses a format designed to make information clear. If you want to display the information in a different format, the Report procedure gives you the control you need over data presentation.

Basic Report Concepts

Reports can contain summary statistics for groups of cases, listings of individual cases, or a combination of both statistics and listings. The number of columns in a report is determined by the number of report variables and break variables. Each report variable selected is displayed in a separate column. If the summaries are in columns, you can select a variable more than once.

Report variables are the variables for which you want case listings or summary statistics. These are displayed in **data columns**. Optional **break variables** divide the data into groups. These are displayed in **break columns**, which appear on the left side of the report.

Summary Reports

Summary reports display summary statistics but do not display case listings. The summary information consists of the statistics you request for the report variables. You can report summary statistics in rows or in columns. Using break variables, you can report summary statistics for various subgroups of cases. Figure 19.1 is an example of a summary report with summary statistics reported in rows, while Figure 19.2 is an example of a report with summary statistics in columns.

Figure 19.1 Summary report (summaries in rows)

Report variables in data columns

Break variable in break column

Subgroup summary statistics in rows

Division	Age	Tenure in Company	Tenure in Grade	Salary--Annual
Carpeting				
Mean	30.75	4.04	3.31	$11,754
Minimum	22.00	2.67	2.17	$9,200
Maximum	44.00	6.00	5.33	$19,500
Appliances				
Mean	31.11	3.81	3.54	$12,508
Minimum	21.00	2.67	2.08	$7,500
Maximum	42.00	6.50	6.50	$28,300
Furniture				
Mean	36.87	4.79	4.08	$13,255
Minimum	25.00	3.17	3.17	$8,975
Maximum	43.00	6.83	6.25	$17,050

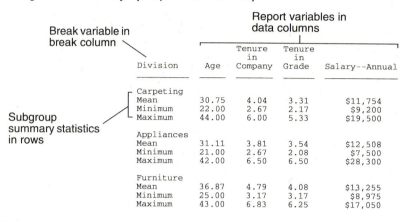

In the summary report shown in Figure 19.1:

- Age, tenure in company, tenure in grade, and salary are the report variables presented in data columns.
- Division is the break variable presented in the break column.
- Mean, minimum value, and maximum value are the summary statistics reported on summary lines for each division.

Figure 19.2 Summary report (summaries in columns)

Summaries of variables in data columns

Break variable in break column

Division	Mean Age	Mean Annual Salary	Minimum Annual Salary	Maximum Annual Salary
Carpeting	30.75	$11,754	$9,200	$19,500
Appliances	31.11	$12,508	$7,500	$28,300
Furniture	36.87	$13,255	$8,975	$17,050
Hardware	36.20	$17,580	$7,450	$22,500

In the summary report shown in Figure 19.2:

- Age and salary are the report variables. Salary is presented in several columns, each column having a different summary statistic.
- Division is the break variable presented in the break column.
- The age column shows the mean age for each division.
- The salary columns show the mean salary, minimum salary, and maximum salary for each division.

Listing Reports

Listing reports list individual cases. The case listings can display the actual data values or the defined value labels recorded for each of the report variables. As with summary reports, you divide a listing report into subgroups using break variables, as in Figure 19.3. Listing reports are available only for summaries in rows.

Figure 19.3 Listing report (summaries in rows)

Division	Age	Tenure in Company	Tenure in Grade	Salary--Annual
Carpeting	27.00	3.67	2.17	$9,200
	22.00	3.92	3.08	$10,900
	23.00	3.92	3.08	$10,900
	24.00	4.00	3.25	$10,000
	30.00	4.08	3.08	$10,000
	27.00	4.33	3.17	$10,000
	33.00	2.67	2.67	$9,335
	33.00	3.75	3.25	$10,000
	44.00	4.83	4.33	$15,690
	36.00	3.83	3.25	$10,000
	35.00	3.50	3.00	$15,520
	35.00	6.00	5.33	$19,500
Appliances	21.00	2.67	2.67	$8,700
	26.00	2.92	2.08	$8,000
	32.00	2.92	2.92	$8,900
	33.00	3.42	2.92	$8,900
	34.00	5.08	4.50	$15,300
	24.00	3.17	3.17	$8,975
	42.00	6.50	6.50	$18,000
	30.00	2.67	2.67	$7,500
	38.00	5.00	4.42	$28,300

Combined Reports

You can combine individual case listings and summary statistics in a single report (only for summaries in rows), as in Figure 19.4. Combined case listing and summary reports are available only with summaries in rows.

Figure 19.4 Combined report with case listings and summary statistics (summaries in rows)

Division	Age	Tenure in Company	Tenure in Grade	Salary--Annual
Carpeting	27.00	3.67	2.17	$9,200
	22.00	3.92	3.08	$10,900
	23.00	3.92	3.08	$10,900
	24.00	4.00	3.25	$10,000
	30.00	4.08	3.08	$10,000
	27.00	4.33	3.17	$10,000
	33.00	2.67	2.67	$9,335
	33.00	3.75	3.25	$10,000
	44.00	4.83	4.33	$15,690
	36.00	3.83	3.25	$10,000
	35.00	3.50	3.00	$15,520
	35.00	6.00	5.33	$19,500
Mean	30.75	4.04	3.31	$11,754
Appliances	21.00	2.67	2.67	$8,700
	26.00	2.92	2.08	$8,000
	32.00	2.92	2.92	$8,900
	33.00	3.42	2.92	$8,900
	34.00	5.08	4.50	$15,300
	24.00	3.17	3.17	$8,975
	42.00	6.50	6.50	$18,000
	30.00	2.67	2.67	$7,500
	38.00	5.00	4.42	$28,300
Mean	31.11	3.81	3.54	$12,508

Multiple Break Variables

You can use more than one break variable to divide your report into groups, and you can display different summary statistics for each break variable division. In Figure 19.5, for example, each division is further divided by store location. For each store location, the minimum and maximum values are displayed and for each division, the mean and standard deviation are presented.

Figure 19.5 Multiple break variables in a summary report (summaries in rows)

Division	Branch Store	Age	Tenure in Company	Tenure in Grade	Salary--Annual
Carpeting	Suburban				
	Minimum	22.00	3.67	2.17	$9,200
	Maximum	35.00	6.00	5.33	$19,500
	Downtown				
	Minimum	24.00	2.67	2.67	$9,335
	Maximum	44.00	4.83	4.33	$15,690
Mean		30.75	4.04	3.31	$11,754
StdDev		6.47	.80	.81	$3,288
Appliances	Suburban				
	Minimum	21.00	2.67	2.08	$8,000
	Maximum	42.00	6.50	6.50	$28,300
	Downtown				
	Minimum	30.00	2.67	2.67	$7,500
	Maximum	34.00	5.08	4.50	$15,300
Mean		31.11	3.81	3.54	$12,508
StdDev		6.70	1.37	1.37	$6,944

Statistics for first break variable — Mean, StdDev (after Carpeting section)

Statistics for second break variable — Mean, StdDev (after Appliances section)

Summary Columns

When the report shows summaries in columns, you can combine two or more data columns in an additional column called a **total column**. In Figure 19.6, the next-to-last column presents the ratio of the two previous columns. The total column can be positioned next to any other data column. The summary function specified for the total column can be a sum, mean, minimum, maximum, difference, ratio, percentage, or product of other data columns.

Figure 19.6 A report with a column that summarizes other columns (summaries in columns)

Total column using the ratio summary function

Division	Branch Store	Average Tenure in Job	Average Tenure in Company	Ratio of Tenure in Job to Tenure in Company	Average Salary
Carpeting	Suburban	3.42	4.38	.78	$12,625
	Downtown	3.25	3.88	.84	$11,318
Appliances	Suburban	3.77	4.05	.93	$14,395
	Downtown	3.25	3.52	.92	$10,150
Furniture	Suburban	4.32	4.71	.92	$12,975
	Downtown	3.86	4.86	.79	$13,500
Hardware	Suburban	4.33	4.33	1.00	$22,500
	Downtown	4.63	4.67	.99	$16,350

Grand Total Summary Statistics

In addition to reporting summary statistics for subgroups based on break variables, you can also include summary statistics for all cases in the report, as in Figure 19.7 and Figure 19.8. Overall report summary statistics are referred to as **grand totals.**

Figure 19.7 Summary report with grand totals (summaries in rows)

```
                  Branch              Tenure    Tenure
                                        in        in
         Division Store       Age    Company    Grade    Salary--Annual

         Furniture  Suburban
                    Minimum   25.00   3.17      3.17      $8,975
                    Maximum   42.00   6.25      6.25      $17,050

                    Downtown
                    Minimum   32.00   4.42      3.50      $12,000
                    Maximum   43.00   6.83      5.33      $14,400
         Mean                 36.87   4.79      4.08      $13,255
         StdDev                5.71    .89       .89       $2,126

         Hardware   Suburban
                    Minimum   32.00   4.33      4.33      $22,500
                    Maximum   32.00   4.33      4.33      $22,500

                    Downtown
                    Minimum   26.00   2.67      2.50      $7,450
                    Maximum   44.00   6.00      6.00      $22,000
         Mean                 36.20   4.60      4.57      $17,580
         StdDev                7.16   1.28      1.35       $6,103

         Grand Total
         Mean                 33.73   4.34      3.79      $13,179
         N                       41     41        41          41
         StdDev                6.76   1.08      1.10       $4,589
```

Grand total rows → Grand Total / Mean / N / StdDev

Figure 19.8 Summary report with grand totals (summaries in columns)

Division	Branch Store	Average Age	Average Tenure in Job	Average Tenure in Company	Average Annual Salary
Carpeting	Suburban	26.75	3.42	4.38	$12,625
	Downtown	32.75	3.25	3.88	$11,318
Appliances	Suburban	30.20	3.77	4.05	$14,395
	Downtown	32.25	3.25	3.52	$10,150
Furniture	Suburban	35.29	4.32	4.71	$12,975
	Downtown	38.25	3.86	4.86	$13,500
Hardware	Suburban	32.00	4.33	4.33	$22,500
	Downtown	37.25	4.63	4.67	$16,350
All divisions		33.73	3.79	4.34	$13,179

Grand total row → All divisions

Formatting Reports

The Report procedure offers a great deal of control over the appearance of your report. You can add titles and footnotes, change the column headings, adjust column width and alignment, and control the display of values or value labels.

Titles and Footnotes

You can add titles and footnotes to reports. You can also include the values of variables in titles and footnotes, including special variables for page number and current date, as shown in Figure 19.9.

Figure 19.9 Titles and footnotes

```
07 Apr 92    Monthly Summary Report  --  Carpeting Division

                                    Tenure     Tenure
                         Branch       in         in
             Division    Store       Age      Company    Grade     Salary--Annual
             _____    _____      ___      _____    _____     _____

             Carpeting   Suburban
                         Minimum    22.00      3.67      2.17         $9,200
                         Maximum    35.00      6.00      5.33        $19,500

                         Downtown
                         Minimum    24.00      2.67      2.67         $9,335
                         Maximum    44.00      4.83      4.33        $15,690

             Mean                   30.75      4.04      3.31        $11,754
             StdDev                  6.47       .80       .81         $3,288




                                      1
```

- Special variable for current date → 07 Apr 92
- Value label for current value of break variable → Carpeting Division
- Special variable for page number → 1

Column Headings

Each column in a report has a heading. By default, the variable label is used for the heading if summaries are in rows. For summaries in columns, the statistic plus the variable label is used. In either type of report, if there is no label, the variable name is used. You can also create headings of your own and control their alignment, as shown in Figure 19.10.

Figure 19.10 User-specified column headings

```
07 Apr 92    Monthly Summary Report  --  Appliances Division

                         Store      Employee   Company     Job      Annual
             Division    Location     Age      Tenure    Tenure     Salary
             _____    _____   _____   _____   _____    _____

             Appliances  Suburban
                         Minimum     21.00      2.67      2.08       $8,000
                         Maximum     42.00      6.50      6.50      $28,300

                         Downtown
                         Minimum     30.00      2.67      2.67       $7,500
                         Maximum     34.00      5.08      4.50      $15,300

             Mean                    31.11      3.81      3.54      $12,508
             StdDev                   6.70      1.37      1.37       $6,944
```

Displaying Value Labels

For break variables, value labels are displayed by default. For report variables in listing reports, data values are displayed by default. You can display actual data values for break variables and/or value labels for report variables in listing reports. For example, if you want to produce a personnel report that includes employee's gender, you might want to display the value labels *Male* and *Female* instead of the numeric values 1 and 2, as in Figure 19.11.

Figure 19.11 Displaying value labels in a listing report

```
                            Annual
Last Name       Gender      Salary      Job Grade           Shift
                                                            
Ford            Female      $9,200      Support Staff       First
Cochran         Female      $10,900     Sales Staff         First
Hoawinski       Female      $10,900     Sales Staff         First
Tygielski       Male        $19,500     Supervisory Staff   Weekend
Gates           Female      $10,000     Sales Staff         Second
Mulvihill       Male        $10,000     Sales Staff         First
Lavelle         Female      $10,000     Sales Staff         Weekend
Mahr            Female      $9,335      Sales Staff         First
Katz            Male        $10,000     Sales Staff         Weekend
Jones           Female      $15,690     Sales Staff         First
Dan             Male        $10,000     Sales Staff         Weekend
McAndrews       Female      $15,520     Supervisory Staff   First
Powell          Female      $8,700      Support Staff       Weekend
Martin          Female      $8,000      Sales Staff         First
Parris          Female      $8,975      Sales Staff         First
Johnson         Female      $18,000     Sales Staff         Second
Sanders         Male        $28,300     Managerial Staff    First
Shavilje        Male        $8,900      Sales Staff         First
Provenza        Female      $8,900      Sales Staff         First
Snolik          Male        $15,300     Sales Staff         First
Sedowski        Male        $7,500      Sales Staff         Weekend
```

How to Obtain Listing Reports and Reports with Summaries in Rows

The minimum specifications for a listing report or a report with summaries in rows are:
- One or more report variables on the Data Columns list.
- One or more summary statistics or selection of the **Display cases** check box.

To obtain and modify row summary reports and case listing reports, from the menus choose:

Statistics
  Summarize ▶
    Report Summaries in Rows...

This opens the Report Summaries in Rows dialog box, as shown in Figure 19.12.

Figure 19.12 Report Summaries in Rows dialog box

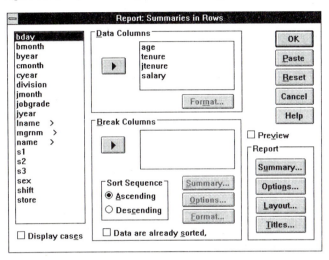

Data Columns. The report variables for which you want case listings or summary statistics. You must select at least one variable for the Data Columns list.

Break Columns. Optional break variables that divide the report into groups. Each successive break variable divides the report into subgroups within groups of the previous break variable. For example, if you select *division* and then *store* as break variables, there will be a separate group for each category of store within each category of division, as shown in Figure 19.5.

Sort Sequence. Sort order for categories of the break variables. Sort order is based on data values, not value labels. String variables are sorted alphabetically, and uppercase letters precede lowercase letters in sort order. For each break variable, you can choose one of the following alternatives for sort sequence:

- **Ascending**. Sorts break variable values by ascending order from low to high. This is the default.
- **Descending**. Sorts break variable values by descending order from high to low.

The following option saves processing time.

- **Data are already sorted**. Data are already sorted by values of the break variables. The Report procedure creates a new break category each time the value of a break variable changes in the data file. Therefore, meaningful summary reports require that the data file be sorted by values of the break variables. By default, the file is automatically sorted before the report is generated. If the data file is already sorted in the proper order, you can save processing time by selecting this option. This option is particularly useful once you have run a report and want to refine the format.

Report. The items in the Report group control the display of grand total summary statistics, treatment of missing values, page layout and numbering, and report titles and footers.

The following display options are also available:

- **Preview.** Displays only the first page of the report. This option is useful for previewing the format of your report without processing the whole report.
- **Display cases**. Displays individual case listings. Select this option to produce listing reports, as shown in Figure 19.3.

Data Column Format

To modify data column headings, column width, and alignment of headings and data, and to control the display of value labels, select a report variable on the Data Columns list and click on Format... in the Report Summaries in Rows dialog box. This opens the Report Data Column Format dialog box, as shown in Figure 19.13.

Figure 19.13 Report Data Column Format dialog box

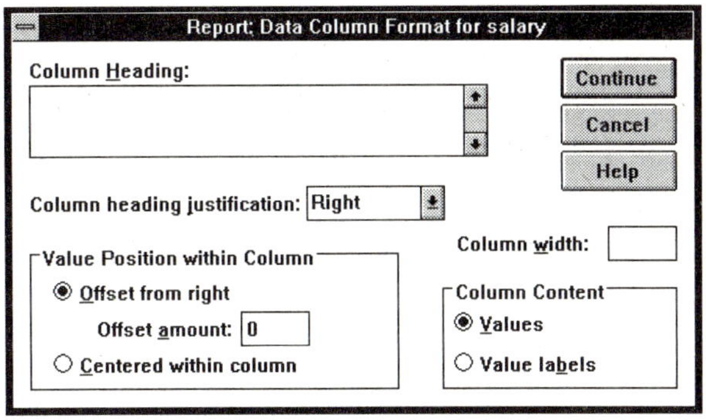

Column Heading. The heading that appears at the top of the column for the selected report variable. If you don't specify a heading, the variable label is used by default. If there is no variable label, the variable name is used. Default column headings are automatically wrapped onto multiple lines to fit in the column width. User-specified column headings are wrapped unless you specify line breaks in the heading. To specify line breaks, press ⏎Enter at the end of each line.

- Column heading justification. Alignment of the column heading. Alignment of the column heading does not affect alignment of the data displayed in the column. You can choose one of the following alternatives:

    Left. Column headings are left-justified. This is the default for string variables.

    Center. Column headings are centered based on column width.

    Right. Column headings are right-justified. This is the default for numeric variables.

Value Position within Column. Alignment of data values or value labels within the column. Alignment of values or labels does not affect alignment of column headings. You can choose one of the following alternatives:

- ○ **Offset from right/Offset from left**. Enter a number of characters for the offset amount. The default is zero. If numeric values are displayed, the offset is from the right side of the column. If alphanumeric values are displayed, the offset is from the left side of the column. The offset value cannot exceed the defined column width.
- ○ **Centered within column**. Data values or value labels are centered in the column.

Column width. Column width expressed as a number of characters. If you don't specify a value, a default column width is determined based on the largest of the following:
- If you specify a column heading, the length of the longest word in the heading. You can string more than one word together by joining them with underscores. The underscores are displayed as spaces in the output.
- If you don't specify a column heading, the length of the longest word in the variable label.
- If value labels are displayed, the length of the longest value label for the variable.
- If values are displayed, the variable format width.

If you specify a value for column width that is shorter than the display format of the variable, numeric values that don't fit in the specified width are converted to scientific notation. If the specified width is less than six characters, asterisks are displayed for numeric values that don't fit. String values and value labels are wrapped onto multiple lines to fit in the column width.

Column Content. You can choose one of the following alternatives:
- **Values**. Data values are displayed. This is the default for data column variables.
- **Value labels**. Value labels are displayed. This is the default for break column variables. If a value doesn't have a defined label, the data value is displayed.

Break Category Summary Statistics

To specify summary statistics for data column variables within categories of a break variable, select a break variable on the Break Columns list and click on **Summary...** in the Report Summaries in Rows dialog box. This opens the Report Summary Lines dialog box, as shown in Figure 19.14.

Figure 19.14 Report Summary Lines dialog box (summaries in rows)

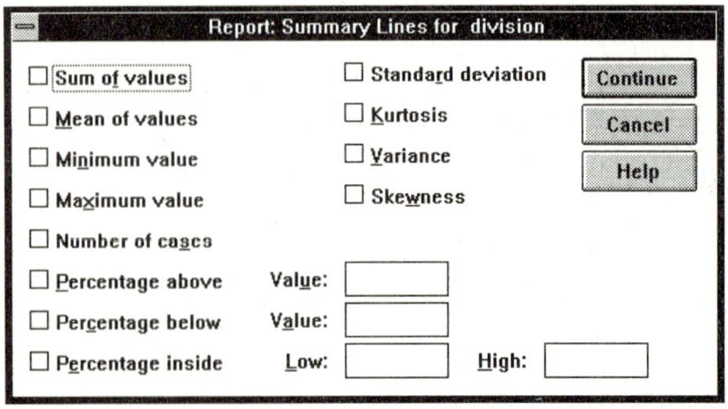

Each summary statistic selected is calculated for all data column variables within each category of the break variable. If you choose more than one summary statistic, each statistic is displayed on a separate row in the report. You can select different summary statistics for each break variable. You can choose one or more of the following summary statistics:

- **Sum of values**. The sum of data values in the break category.
- **Mean of values**. The arithmetic average of data values in the break category.
- **Minimum value**. The smallest data value in the break category.
- **Maximum value**. The largest data value in the break category.
- **Number of cases**. Number of cases in the break category.
- **Percentage above**. Percentage of cases in the break category above a user-specified value. If you select this item, you must enter a value in the text box before you can continue.
- **Percentage below**. Percentage of cases in the break category below a user-specified value. If you select this item, you must enter a value in the text box before you can continue.
- **Percentage inside**. Percentage of cases in the break category inside a user-specified range. If you select this item, you must enter a Low and High value before you can continue.
- **Standard deviation**. A measure of how much observations vary from the mean of values in the break category, expressed in the same units as the data.
- **Kurtosis**. A measure of the extent to which data values in the break category cluster around a central point, given their standard deviation.
- **Variance**. A measure of how much values vary from the mean of values in the break category, equal to the square of the standard deviation. The units are the square of those of the variable itself.
- **Skewness**. An index of the degree to which the distribution of data values in the break category is not symmetric.

Break Spacing and Page Options for Summaries in Rows

To change the line spacing between break categories or between break headings and summary statistics, or to display each break category on a separate page, select a break variable on the Break Columns list and click on **Options...** in the Report Summaries in Rows dialog box. This opens the Report Break Options dialog box, as shown in Figure 19.15.

Figure 19.15 Report Break Options dialog box (summaries in rows)

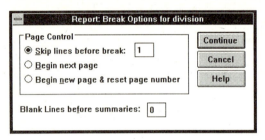

Page Control. You can select one of the following alternatives for spacing between break categories:

- **Skip lines before break**. The number of blank lines between break categories. The default is 1. You can specify 0 to 20 blank lines between break categories.
- **Begin next page**. Starts each break category on a new page.
- **Begin new page & reset page number**. Starts each break category on a separate page and numbers pages for each break category separately.

Blank lines before summaries. The number of blank lines between the break category heading and the summary statistics. The default is 0. You can specify up to 20 blank lines between the break category heading and the rows of summary statistics.

Break Column Format

To modify break column headings, column width, and alignment of headings and data, and to control the display of value labels, select a break variable on the Break Columns list and click on **Format...** in the Report Summaries in Rows dialog box. This opens the Report Break Column Format dialog box, which offers selections identical to those in the Report Data Column Format dialog box, shown in Figure 19.13. See "Data Column Format" on p. 336 for information on the selections available in this dialog box and defaults.

Report Total Summary Statistics

To specify grand total summary statistics for the entire report, click on Summary... in the Report group of selections in the main dialog box. This opens the Report Final Summary Lines dialog box, which offers selections identical to those in the Report Summary Lines dialog box shown in Figure 19.14. For more information on the available summary statistics, see "Break Category Summary Statistics" on p. 338.

Report Options for Summaries in Rows

To change the treatment and display of missing values, save processing time for presorted data, and control the report page numbering, click on Options... in the Report group of selections in the Report Summaries in Rows dialog box. This opens the Report Options dialog box, as shown in Figure 19.16.

Figure 19.16 Report Options dialog box (summaries in rows)

The following options are available:

❏ **Exclude cases with missing values listwise.** Excludes cases that have missing data for any variable in the report. By default, cases with missing data are included in the report if they have valid values for any report variable.

Missing Values Appear as. The character used to indicate both system- and user-missing data. By default, a period (.) is used. You can use any single character.

Number Pages from. The starting page number of the report. By default, pages are numbered from 1. The starting page number can be any integer from 0 to 99999.

Report Layout for Summaries in Rows

To change the width and length of each report page, control the placement of the report on the page, and control the insertion of blank lines and labels, click on **Layout...** in the Report Summaries in Rows dialog box. This opens the Report Layout dialog box, as shown in Figure 19.17.

Figure 19.17 Report Layout dialog box (summaries in rows)

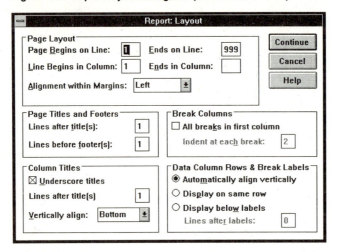

Page Layout. The following options control the placement of the report on the page:

Page begins on line/Ends on line. By default, each report page begins on the first line of the page and ends on the last line of the page as defined by the page length in the Preferences dialog box (see the *SPSS Base System User's Guide, Part 1*). The number of the beginning line must be less than the number of the ending line.

If you specify beginning and ending line values that do not provide the minimum number of lines per page required for the report, the ending line value will be overridden, and a message at the end of the report will indicate this.

Line begins in column/Ends in column. The left and right margins of the report are expressed as the number of characters (columns) across the page. By default, the report begins in column 1 and ends in the column that corresponds to the page width value defined in the Preferences dialog box (see the *SPSS Base System User's Guide, Part 1*). You can specify a value up to 255.

If you specify beginning and ending column values that do not provide a wide enough space for the report, the report will not be generated. If you don't specify an ending column value, the Report procedure will override the default if necessary to display reports that are too wide for the default width. The maximum width of a report is 255 characters.

▼ **Alignment within margins.** The report can be left-aligned, centered, or right-aligned within the left and right page margins. The default is left alignment. If you don't specify beginning and ending column positions for the left and right margins, center and right alignment have no effect.

Page Titles and Footers. The following options control the number of blank lines near the top and bottom of a page:

Lines after title(s)/Lines before footer(s). Indicates the number of blank lines between the report title(s) and the first line of the report, and the number of lines between the bottom of the report and any footers; by default, there is one blank line between the title and the report and one blank line between the bottom of the report and any footers.

Break Columns. If multiple break variables are specified, they can be in separate columns or in the first column. The default is a separate column for each break variable.

❑ **All breaks in first column.** Selecting this item causes the values of all break variables to be listed in the first column.

Indent at each break. If all break categories are in the first column, each break level is indented by the number of spaces specified. The default indentation is two spaces.

Column Titles. The following options apply to columns titles.

❑ **Underscore titles.** Displays a horizontal line underneath each column title. This item is selected by default.

Lines after titles. Indicates the number of blank lines between the column titles and the first line of values.

Vertically align: Indicates whether the tops or bottoms of column titles will be aligned. Bottom alignment of column titles is the default.

Data Column Rows & Break Labels. The following options are for reports with summaries in rows only.

○ **Automatically align vertically.** In a summary report, places the first summary on the next line after the break value. In a listing report, places the first case listing on the same line as the break value.

○ **Display on same row.** In a summary report, places the first summary statistic on the same line as the break value and suppresses the first summary title. In a listing report, places the first case listing on the same line as the break value.

○ **Display below labels.** Places the number of blank lines specified between a break value and the next summary row or case listing.

Lines after labels. Specifies the number of lines to display below labels.

Titles and Footers

To add titles and footers to a report, click on Titles... in the Report Summaries in Rows or the Report Summaries in Columns dialog box. This opens the Report Titles dialog box, as shown in Figure 19.18.

Figure 19.18 Report Titles dialog box

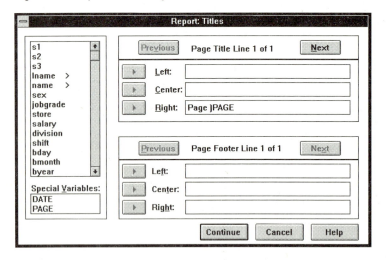

Page Titles. Titles and other text that appears above the report on each page. You can specify any combination of left, center, and right titles. To specify multiple-line titles, click on Next after each title line to specify the next line. You can have up to 10 title lines. By default, the current page number is used as the right title.

Page Footers. Text, such as footnotes, that appears below the report on each page. You can specify any combination of left, center, and right footers. To specify multiple-line footers, click on Next after each footer to specify the next footer line. You can have up to 10 footer lines.

If the combined width of the left, center, and right titles or footers exceeds the defined width of the page, the titles or footers are truncated in the report. Left and right titles and footers are truncated before center ones.

Positioning Titles and Footers

The position of titles and footers is based on the report width unless you explicitly specify left and right report margins (see "Report Layout for Summaries in Rows" on p. 342). If you specify report margins, the position of titles and footers is based on alignment within those margins. For example, if you specify a right margin of 90 but the report is only 70 characters wide, center titles will not be aligned over the center of the report. You can adjust the position of titles and footers by changing the left and right margins.

Using Variables in Titles and Footers

To use a variable in a title or footer, position the cursor in the line where you want the variable to appear and click on the corresponding ▶ pushbutton. The variable name appears in the line, preceded by a right parenthesis. Two special variables, *DATE* and *PAGE*, are also available to display the current date and page number.

In titles, the value label corresponding to the value of the variable at the beginning of the page is displayed (see Figure 19.9). In footers, the value label corresponding to the value of the variable at the end of the page is displayed. If there is no value label, the actual value is displayed.

How to Obtain a Report with Summaries in Columns

The minimum specification for a report with summaries in columns is one or more report variables on the Data Columns list.

To obtain and modify column summary reports, from the menus choose:

Statistics
  Summarize ▶
    Report Summaries in Columns...

This opens the Report Summaries in Columns dialog box, as shown in Figure 19.19.

Figure 19.19 Report Summaries in Columns dialog box

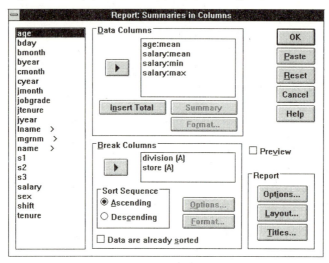

Data Columns. The report variables for which you want summary statistics. You can select a variable more than once and then specify a different summary statistic for each instance of the variable. You must select at least one variable for the Data Columns list.

The default summary statistic for each variable is sum. To specify a different summary statistic for a variable, select the variable and click on **Summary**.

> **Insert Total**. Inserts a column that summarizes other columns, after the currently selected column. You must click on **Summary** and then specify which other columns are summarized and the type of summary.

Break Columns. Optional break variables that divide the report into groups. Each successive break variable divides the report into subgroups within groups of the previous break variable. For example, if you select *division* and then *store* as break variables, there will be a separate group for each category of *store* within each category of *division*, as shown in Figure 19.6.

> **Sort Sequence**. Sort order for categories of the break variables. Sort order is based on data values, not value labels. String variables are sorted alphabetically, and uppercase letters precede lowercase letters in sort order. For each break variable, you can choose one of the following alternatives for sort sequence:
>
> ○ **Ascending**. Sorts break variable values by ascending order from low to high. This is the default.
>
> ○ **Descending**. Sorts break variable values by descending order from high to low.

The following option saves processing time.

❏ **Data are already sorted**. Data are already sorted by values of the break variables. The Report procedure creates a new break category each time the value of a break variable changes in the data file. Therefore, meaningful summary reports require that the data file be sorted by values of the break variables. By default, the file is automatically sorted before the report is generated. If the data file is already sorted in the proper order, you can save processing time by selecting this option. This option is particularly useful once you have run a report and want to refine the format.

Report. The items in the Report group control the display of grand total summary statistics, treatment of missing values, page layout and numbering, and report titles and footers.

The following display option is also available:

❏ **Preview.** Displays only the first page of the report. This option is useful for previewing the format of your report.

Data Column Summary Statistic for a Variable

To specify a statistic for a data column variable, select a variable on the Data Columns list and click on Summary... in the Report Summaries in Columns dialog box. This opens the Report Summary Lines dialog box, as shown in Figure 19.20.

Figure 19.20 Report Summary Lines dialog box (summaries in columns)

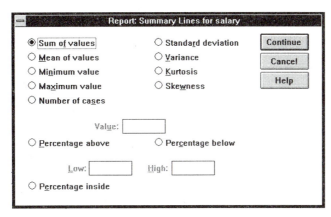

You can select only one summary statistic for a variable column. To add another column with a different summary of the same variable, move the variable again to the Data Columns list in the Report Summaries in Columns dialog box. You can choose one of the following summary statistics for each variable column:

- **Sum of values**. The sum of data values in the break category.
- **Mean of values**. The arithmetic average of data values in the break category.
- **Minimum value**. The smallest data value in the break category.
- **Maximum value**. The largest data value in the break category.
- **Number of cases**. Number of cases in the break category.
- **Percentage above**. Percentage of cases in the break category above a user-specified value. If you select this item, you must enter a value in the text box before you can continue.
- **Percentage below**. Percentage of cases in the break category below a user-specified value. If you select this item, you must enter a value in the text box before you can continue.
- **Percentage inside**. Percentage of cases in the break category inside a user-specified range. If you select this item, you must enter a Low value and a High value before you can continue.
- **Standard deviation**. A measure of how much observations vary from the mean of values in the break category, expressed in the same units as the data.
- **Variance**. A measure of how much values vary from the mean of values in the break category, equal to the square of the standard deviation. The units are the square of those of the variable itself.
- **Kurtosis**. A measure of the extent to which data values in the break category cluster around a central point, given their standard deviation.
- **Skewness**. An index of the degree to which the distribution of data values in the break category is not symmetric.

Composite Summary (Total) Columns

To specify a composite summary for an inserted Total column, select the Total column on the Data Columns list and click on **Summary...** in the Report Summaries in Columns dialog box. This opens the Report Summary Column dialog box, as shown in Figure 19.21.

Figure 19.21 Report Summary Column dialog box

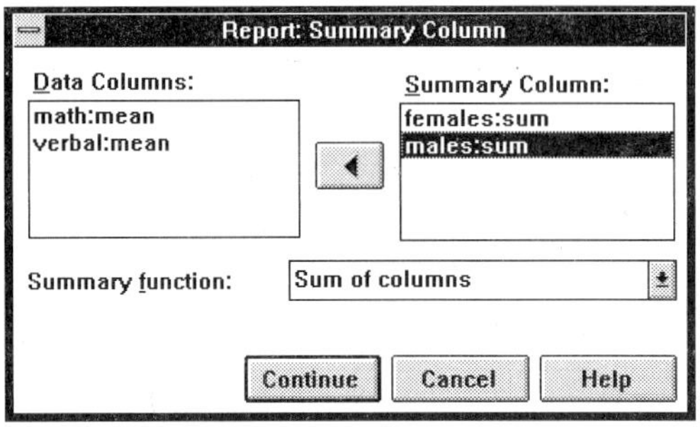

Move the variables you want in the composite summary from the Data Columns list to the Summary Column list. Then, select the function from the Summary function drop-down list.

- **Summary function.** You can choose one of the following functions for the summary function:

    Sum of columns. Add the values in the columns on the Summary Column list.

    Mean of columns. Display the mean of the values in the columns on the Summary Column list.

    Minimum of columns. Display the minimum value in the columns on the Summary Column list.

    Maximum of columns. Display the maximum value in the columns on the Summary Column list.

    1st column - 2nd column. Subtract the value in the second column from the value in the first column and display the difference. Only two columns are allowed on the Summary Column list.

    1st column / 2nd column. Divide the value in the first column by the value in the second column and display the quotient. Only two columns are allowed on the Summary Column list.

    % 1st column / 2nd column. Divide the value in the first column by the value in the second column, multiply by 100, and display the result. Only two columns are allowed on the Summary Column list.

    Product of columns. Multiply the values in the columns on the Summary Column list.

Data Column Format

To modify data column headings, column width, and alignment of headings and data, and to control the display of value labels, select a report variable or a Total column on the Data Columns list and click on Format... in the Report Summaries in Columns dialog box. This opens the Report Data Column Format dialog box, as shown in Figure 19.13. For information on this dialog box, see "Data Column Format" on p. 336.

Break Options for Summaries in Columns

To change the line spacing between break categories or between break headings and summary statistics, or to display each break category on a separate page, select a break variable on the Break Columns list and click on Options... in the Report Summaries in Columns dialog box. This opens the Report Break Options dialog box, as shown in Figure 19.22.

Figure 19.22 Report Break Options dialog box (summaries in columns)

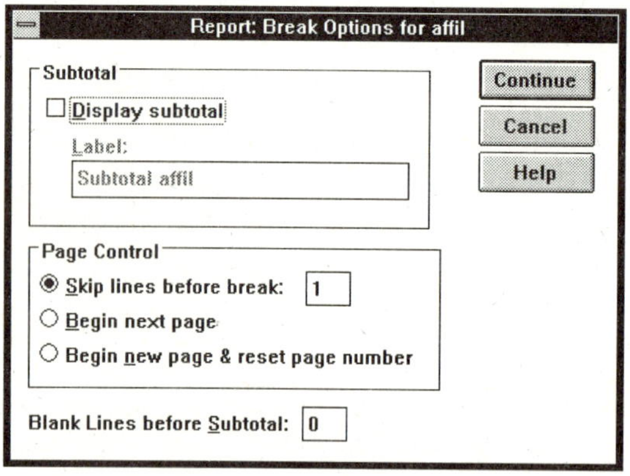

Break options are ignored for the last variable on the Break Columns list.

Subtotal. You can control whether or not to display subtotals.

❏ **Display subtotal.** Displays a subtotal for each break group category.

  Label. You can edit the default label for the break group subtotal. This label is available only if Display subtotal is selected.

Page Control. You can select one of the following alternatives for spacing between break categories:

- **Skip lines before break**. The number of blank lines between break categories. The default is 1. You can specify 0 to 20 blank lines between break categories.
- **Begin next page**. Starts each break category on a new page.
- **Begin new page & reset page number**. Starts each break category on a separate page and numbers pages for each break category separately.

Blank Lines before Subtotal. The number of blank lines before the subtotal. The default is 0. You can specify up to 20 blank lines between the break category heading and the break column subtotal.

Break Column Format

To modify break column headings, column width, and alignment of headings and data, and to control the display of value labels, select a break variable on the Break Columns list and click on Format... in the Report Summaries in Columns dialog box. This opens the Report Break Column Format dialog box, which offers selections identical to those in the Report Data Column Format dialog box, shown in Figure 19.13. See "Data Column Format" on p. 336 for information on the selections available in this dialog box.

Report Options for Summaries in Columns

To display a grand total summary statistic for each column, change the treatment and display of missing values, and control the report page numbering, click on Options... in the Report group of selections in the Report Summaries in Columns dialog box. This opens the Report Options dialog box, as shown in Figure 19.23.

Figure 19.23 Report Options dialog box (summaries in columns)

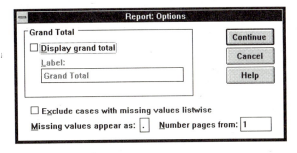

Grand Total. You can display a summary statistic at the bottom of each column and specify a label for the row.

- **Display grand total.** Displays at the bottom of each column a statistic summarizing all cases. The statistic is the one specified previously for the column.

  Label. Text appearing in the break column that identifies the grand total summary row. The default label is *Grand Total*.

- **Exclude cases with missing values listwise.** Excludes cases that have missing data for any variable in the report. By default, cases with missing data are excluded in the report summaries but included in case listings.

Missing values appear as. The character used to indicate both system- and user-missing data. By default, a period (.) is used. You can use any single character.

Number pages from. The starting page number of the report. By default, pages are numbered from 1. The starting page number can be any integer from 0 to 99999.

Report Layout for Summaries in Columns

To change the width and length of each report page, or control the placement of the report on the page, extra blank lines, alignment of break columns, and layout of column titles, click on Layout... in the Report Summaries in Rows dialog box. This opens the Report Layout dialog box, as shown in Figure 19.24.

Figure 19.24 Report Layout dialog box (summaries in columns)

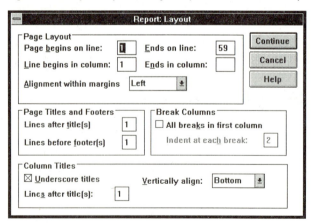

Except for the Data Column Rows & Break Labels group, which is not available here, this dialog box offers selections identical to those in the Report Layout dialog box for Summaries in Rows, shown in Figure 19.17. See "Report Layout for Summaries in Rows" on p. 342 for information on the selections available in this dialog box.

Titles and Footers

To add titles and footers to a report, click on Titles... in the Report Summaries in Columns dialog box. This opens the Report Titles dialog box, as shown in Figure 19.18. For information on this dialog box, see "Titles and Footers" on p. 344.

Additional Features Available with Command Syntax

You can customize your report if you paste your selections into a syntax window and edit the resulting REPORT command syntax. (For information on syntax windows, see the *SPSS Base System User's Guide, Part 1*.) Additional features include:

- Control of spacing between cases in listing reports (with the FORMAT subcommand).
- Stacking of multiple report variables in a single column in listing reports (with the VARIABLES subcommand).
- Summary statistics calculated for specific data column variables instead of all data column variables (with the SUMMARY subcommand).
- Control of descriptive headings for summary statistics (with the SUMMARY subcommand).

See the *SPSS Base System Syntax Reference Guide* for complete REPORT command syntax.

20

Bar, Line, Area, and Pie Charts

Are American cities more violent today than they were several years ago? At what time of the year do major crimes occur? Do different types of crime show similar or different patterns of increase or decrease? These are the kinds of questions that are important to police departments across the United States. And these are the kinds of questions that are often most effectively answered in categorical charts, such as bar, line, area, and pie charts.

Chicago Uniform Crime Reports Data

The Uniform Crime Reports required by the FBI show reported incidents of murder, rape, aggravated assault, armed robbery, burglary, theft, and auto theft on a month-by-month basis. The crimes for which reports are required are called **index crimes**. Each crime is recorded as a separate variable. Each case indicates the number of crimes that occurred that month. A case is identified by two variables, *month* and *year*. Two other variables, *violent* and *property*, record the total number of violent crimes (murder, rape, aggravated assault, and armed robbery) and the total number of property crimes (burglary, theft, and auto theft), respectively. Figure 20.1 shows the first seven cases of the data collected by the Chicago Police Department from 1972 to 1987.

Figure 20.1 Chicago Uniform Crime Reports data

	year	month	murder	rape	assault	robbery	burglary	theft	auto	violent	property
1	'72	Jan	53	174	2061	740	2994	5972	2404	3028	11370
2	'72	Feb	54	110	1671	709	2650	5791	2097	2544	10538
3	'72	Mar	57	78	1541	753	2718	6435	1912	2429	11065
4	'72	Apr	56	139	1728	1018	3069	7010	2578	2941	12657
5	'72	May	51	138	1971	1118	3041	8233	2812	3278	14086
6	'72	Jun	55	122	1770	1051	2935	9030	3083	2998	15048
7	'72	Jul	73	117	2218	1200	3410	9614	3085	3608	16309

Simple Charts

In a bar chart showing the mean monthly incidence of armed robbery each year, it is immediately apparent that the number of robberies stayed fairly constant over the eleven-year period between 1972 and 1982 and then sharply increased.

Figure 20.2 Simple bar chart

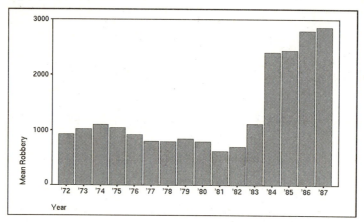

Figure 20.2 is a simple bar chart in which each bar represents the mean monthly incidence of robberies for one year. Often, a long series such as this is best displayed as a simple line chart. Though the data are the same, the chart in Figure 20.3 emphasizes the continuity from one element to the next.

Figure 20.3 Simple line chart

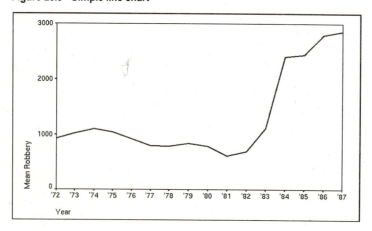

To emphasize the change, the same data might be displayed as a simple area chart, as shown in Figure 20.4. Notice that an area chart is just a line chart with the space underneath the line filled in.

Figure 20.4 Simple area chart

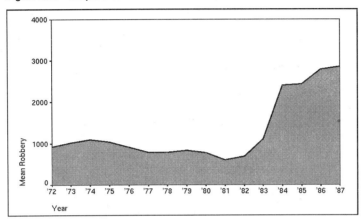

Robbery is only one crime. How does the armed robbery rate compare with that of other crimes? From a chart that shows the mean value of each crime variable as a separate bar, it can be seen that robbery is more common than murder or rape but less common than the other reported crimes (see Figure 20.5).

Figure 20.5 Simple bar chart

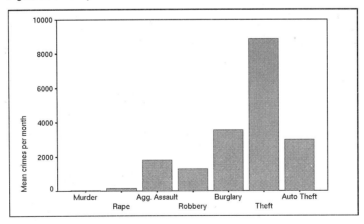

Figure 20.5 clearly shows which is the least and which is the most common index crime. If, however, the intent is to show what proportion of the total index crimes each constitutes, a pie chart is more appropriate, as shown in Figure 20.6. While Figure 20.5 shows the average for one month in each category, Figure 20.6 shows the totals for the entire 16-year period.

Figure 20.6 Simple pie chart

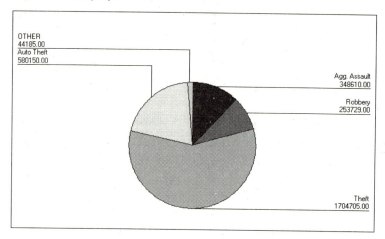

Clustered Bar and Multiple Line Charts

Theft, burglary, and auto theft are collectively known as "property crimes." In a clustered bar chart, as shown in Figure 20.7, we can show the mean monthly incidence of each property crime for each year.

Figure 20.7 Clustered bar chart

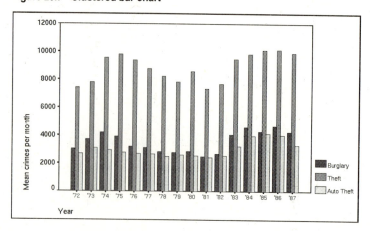

While a bar chart looks good and is fairly clear, we really want to explore patterns. Figure 20.8 shows the data series in Figure 20.7 as a multiple line chart. Here you can see that the three property crimes follow a similar pattern.

Figure 20.8 Multiple line chart

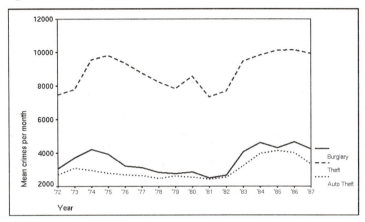

Drop-Line Charts

Sometimes the relationship between two or more changing values is more important than the values themselves. The drop-line chart in Figure 20.9 compares violent crimes in Chicago with violent crimes in Dallas.

Figure 20.9 Drop-line chart

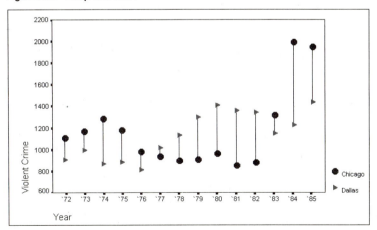

If there are only two values to be compared as in the example above, a difference line chart can also be used. For more information about difference line charts, see Chapter 21.

Stacked Bar and Area Charts

There are three property crimes tracked in the Chicago data. Each crime rate can be thought of as a part of a whole, which is the total recorded number of property crimes. To emphasize that these data are parts of a whole, we can display them in a stacked bar chart, as shown in Figure 20.10. The height of each bar shows the total number of property crimes committed during each year. The colored or patterned segments show the contribution of each individual property crime to that total.

Figure 20.10 Stacked bar chart

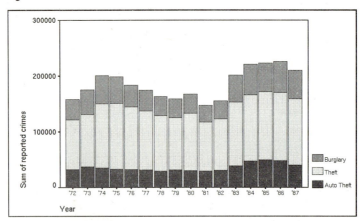

While Figure 20.10 is clear, it returns us to bars, which fail to emphasize the sequential nature of the data. In Figure 20.11, the same data are shown as a stacked area chart.

Figure 20.11 Stacked area chart

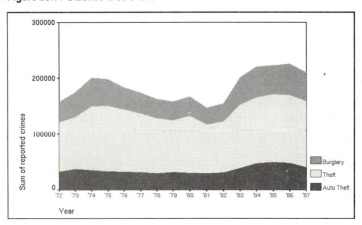

Variations in Bar, Line, and Area Charts

The following chart types require some level of modification from the basic chart types described previously. For a discussion of how to obtain these chart types with the Chart Editor, see the *SPSS Base System User's Guide, Part 1*.

100% Stacked Bar and Area Charts

Stacked bar and area charts show how property crimes as a whole fluctuate and at the same time show how the contribution of each individual crime type changes. In some circumstances, you might just want to show how the percentage contribution of each individual crime type changes, ignoring how property crimes as a whole change. This type of chart is called a 100% stacked chart. A 100% stacked area chart and a 100% stacked bar chart are shown in Figure 20.12.

Figure 20.12 100% stacked area chart and 100% stacked bar chart

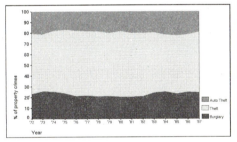
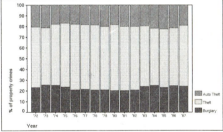

Hanging Bar Charts

A hanging bar chart is often used to show how values fluctuate around a fixed value (the **origin**), as shown in Figure 20.13.

Figure 20.13 Hanging bar chart

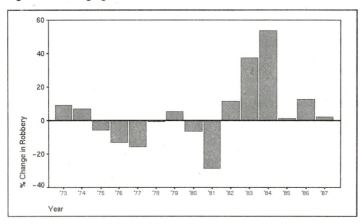

Mixed Charts

A mixed chart overlays one chart type on top of another. This is sometimes a useful way to differentiate between data that are related but somehow qualitatively different. The mixed line and bar chart in Figure 20.14 shows national crime data as a line superimposed over Chicago crime data as bars.

Figure 20.14 Mixed line and bar chart

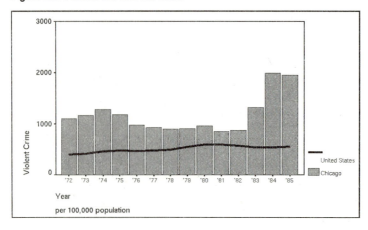

How to Obtain Bar, Line, Area, and Pie Charts

To obtain bar, line, area, or pie charts, choose the appropriate chart type from the Graphs menu, as shown in Figure 20.15.

Figure 20.15 Graphs Menu

This opens a chart dialog box for the selected chart type, as shown in Figure 20.16 (chart dialog boxes for line, area, and pie charts are shown in Figure 20.28, Figure 20.40, and Figure 20.49, respectively).

Figure 20.16 Bar Charts dialog box

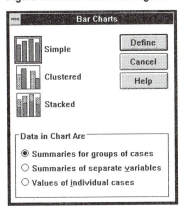

From the chart dialog box, choose the type of chart you want. Your choices depend upon the type of chart you selected on the Graphs menu. For bar charts, the choices are: simple, clustered, or stacked.

Data in Chart Are. Select the choice that describes the structure of your data organization.

364   Chapter   20

- **Summaries for groups of cases.** Cases are counted, or one variable is summarized, in subgroups. The subgroups are determined by one variable for simple charts or by two variables for complex charts.
- **Summaries of separate variables.** More than one variable is summarized. Simple charts summarize each variable over all cases in the file. Complex charts summarize each variable within categories determined by another variable.
- **Values of individual cases.** Individual values of one variable are plotted in simple charts. Values of more than one variable are plotted in complex charts.

Examples of these choices, shown with data organization structures and the charts they produce, are presented in the tables at the beginning of each section.

Bar Charts

To obtain a bar chart, from the menus choose:

Graphs
  Bar...

This opens the Bar Charts dialog box, as shown in Figure 20.16 (chart dialog boxes for line, area, and pie charts are shown in Figure 20.28, Figure 20.40, and Figure 20.49).

Select the type of bar chart you want, and select the choice that describes the structure of your data organization. Click on **Define** to open a dialog box specific to your selections. Examples of these choices, shown with data structures and the charts they produce, are presented in Table 20.1.

Table 20.1 Types of bar charts

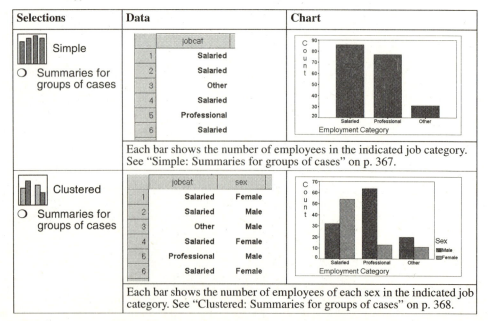

Table 20.1 Types of bar charts (Continued)

Selections	Data	Chart
Stacked ○ Summaries for groups of cases	jobcat / sex: 1 Salaried Female 2 Salaried Male 3 Other Male 4 Salaried Female 5 Professional Male 6 Salaried Female	Stacked bar chart of Count by Employment Category, with Sex (Female/Male) stacked.
	Each bar shows the number of employees of each sex in the indicated job category. See "Stacked: Summaries for groups of cases" on p. 369.	
Simple ○ Summaries of separate variables	burglary auto theft 1 4569 3853 8421 2 4476 3725 8397 3 4661 3712 9045 4 4289 3656 8875 5 4426 3732 9642 6 4369 3593 9594	Simple bar chart showing Mean of Burglary, Auto Theft, Theft.
	The three variables *burglary, auto,* and *theft* are shown in the chart. The first bar indicates the mean of *burglary*, the second indicates the mean of *auto*, and the third indicates the mean of *theft*. See "Simple: Summaries of separate variables" on p. 369.	
Clustered ○ Summaries of separate variables	burglary auto theft year 1 4569 3853 8421 '84 2 4476 3725 8397 '84 3 4661 3712 9045 '84 4 4289 3656 8875 '84 5 4426 3732 9642 '84 6 4369 3593 9594 '84	Clustered bar chart showing Mean of Burglary, Auto Theft, Theft by Year ('84–'87).
	The three variables *burglary, auto,* and *theft* are broken down into categories by values of the variable *year*. Within each category, there are three clustered bars. The first indicates the mean of *burglary*, the second indicates the mean of *auto*, and the third indicates the mean of *theft*. See "Clustered: Summaries of separate variables" on p. 370.	
Stacked ○ Summaries of separate variables	burglary auto theft year 1 4569 3853 8421 '84 2 4476 3725 8397 '84 3 4661 3712 9045 '84 4 4289 3656 8875 '84 5 4426 3732 9642 '84 6 4369 3593 9594 '84	Stacked bar chart showing Sum of Theft, Auto Theft, Burglary by Year ('84–'87).
	The three variables *burglary, auto,* and *theft* are broken down into categories by values of the variable *year*. Within each category, there are three bars stacked one on top of the other. The first indicates the sum of *burglary*, the second indicates the sum of *auto*, and the third indicates the sum of *theft*. See "Stacked: Summaries of separate variables" on p. 371.	

Table 20.1 Types of bar charts (Continued)

Selections	Data	Chart
Simple — Values of individual cases	var00001: 284.00, 114.00, 114.00	(bar chart of individual case values)
Each bar shows the value of a single case. See "Simple: Values of individual cases" on p. 371.		
Clustered — Values of individual cases	var00001: 284.00, 114.00, 114.00; var00002: 135.00, 32.00, 43.00	(clustered bar chart)
Each category shows the values of each variable for the indicated case. See "Clustered: Values of individual cases" on p. 373.		
Stacked — Values of individual cases	var00001: 284.00, 114.00, 114.00; var00002: 135.00, 32.00, 43.00	(stacked bar chart)
Each category shows the values of each variable for the indicated case. See "Stacked: Values of individual cases" on p. 373.		

Defining Bar Charts

Each combination of chart type and data organization structure produces a different definition box. Each is discussed briefly below. The icon and section title indicate the choices that have to be made in the chart dialog box to open that chart definition dialog box. The discussion for each chart type always describes the selections required to enable the OK pushbutton. Optional selections are discussed only with the first chart using each data structure. For a detailed description of optional statistics, see "Summary Functions" on p. 399.

All chart definition dialog boxes have a Titles pushbutton and Template group. These are discussed in the *SPSS Base System User's Guide, Part 1*. Chart definition dialog boxes for summaries for groups of cases and for summaries of separate variables also have an Options... pushbutton. The Options... pushbutton brings up a dialog box that controls missing-value options, discussed in the *SPSS Base System User's Guide, Part 1*.

Simple:
Summaries for groups of cases

Figure 20.17 shows a chart definition dialog box and the resulting simple bar chart with summaries for groups of cases.

Figure 20.17 Simple bar chart with summaries for groups of cases

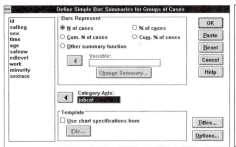 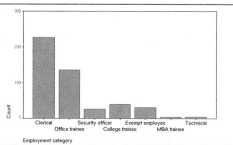

The minimum specification is a category axis variable.

The numeric, short string, and long string variables in your data file are displayed on the source variable list. Select a variable to define the category axis. To get a simple chart showing number of cases for groups of cases in default format, click on OK.

Optionally, you can select a different summary statistic, use a template to control the format of the chart, or add a title, subtitle, or footnote. Optional summary statistics are discussed in "Summary Functions" on p. 399. The other options are discussed in detail in the *SPSS Base System User's Guide, Part 1*.

Category Axis. Select a variable to define the categories shown in the chart. There is one bar for each value of the variable.

If you select Other summary function in the Define Simple Bar Summaries for Groups of Cases dialog box, you must also select a variable to be summarized. Figure 20.18 shows the chart definition dialog box with a variable to be summarized and the resulting simple bar chart with a summarized variable.

Figure 20.18 Simple bar chart with summary of a variable

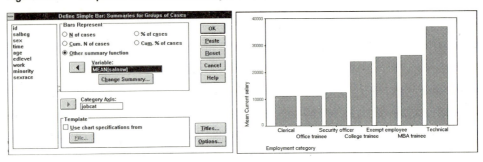

The default chart shows the mean of the selected variable within each category (determined by the category axis variable).

Clustered:
Summaries for groups of cases

Figure 20.19 shows a chart definition dialog box and the resulting clustered bar chart with summaries for groups of cases.

Figure 20.19 Clustered bar chart with summaries for groups of cases

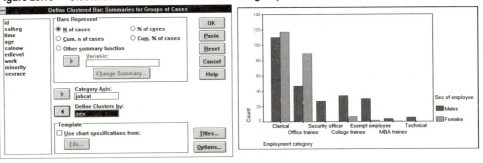

The minimum specifications are:

- A category axis variable.
- A cluster member definition variable.

Category Axis. Select a variable to define the categories shown in the chart. There is one cluster of bars for each value of the variable.

Define Clusters by. Select a variable to define the bars within each cluster. There is one set of differently colored or patterned bars for each value of the variable.

Stacked:
Summaries for groups of cases

Figure 20.20 shows a chart definition dialog box and the resulting stacked bar chart with summaries for groups of cases.

Figure 20.20   Stacked bar chart with summaries for groups of cases

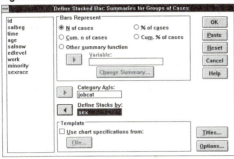
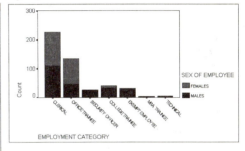

The minimum specifications are:
- A category axis variable.
- A bar segment definition variable.

Category Axis. Select a variable to define the categories shown on the chart. There is one stack of bars for each value of the variable.

Define Stacks by. Select a variable to define the bar segments within each stack. There is one bar segment within each stack for each value of the variable.

 Simple:
Summaries of separate variables

Figure 20.21 shows a chart definition dialog box and the resulting simple bar chart with summaries of separate variables.

Figure 20.21   Simple bar chart with summaries of separate variables

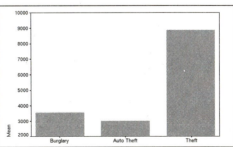

The minimum specifications are two or more bar variables.

The numeric variables in your data file are displayed on the source variable list. Select the variables you want to define the bars. To get a simple bar chart showing the mean value of each variable in default format, click on **OK**.

Optionally, you can select a different summary statistic, use a template to control the format of the chart, or add a title, subtitle, or footnote. Summary statistics are discussed in "Summary Functions" on p. 399. The other options are discussed in detail in the *SPSS Base System User's Guide, Part 1*.

Bars Represent. Select two or more variables to define the categories shown in the chart. There is one bar for each variable. By default, the bar shows the mean of the selected variables.

Clustered:
Summaries of separate variables

Figure 20.22 shows a chart definition dialog box and the resulting clustered bar chart with summaries of separate variables.

Figure 20.22   Clustered bar chart with summaries of separate variables

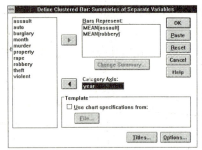 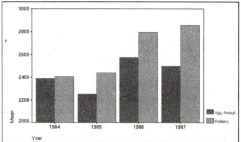

The minimum specifications are:
- Two or more bar variables.
- A category axis variable.

Bars Represent. Select two or more variables. There is one bar within each group for each variable. By default, the bars show the mean of the selected variables.

Category Axis. Select a variable to define the categories shown in the chart. There is one cluster of bars for each value of the variable.

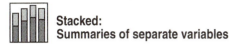
Stacked:
Summaries of separate variables

Figure 20.23 shows a chart definition dialog box and the resulting stacked bar chart with summaries of separate variables.

Figure 20.23   Stacked bar chart with summaries of separate variables

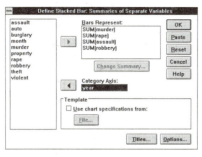
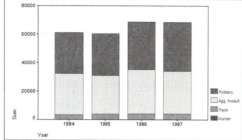

The minimum specifications are:
- Two or more segment variables.
- A category axis variable.

Bars Represent. Select two or more variables. There is one bar within each stack for each variable. By default, the bars show the sum of the selected variables.

Category Axis. Select a variable to define the categories shown in the chart. There is one stack of bars for each value of the variable.

Simple:
Values of individual cases

Figure 20.24 shows a chart definition dialog box and the resulting simple bar chart with values of individual cases.

Figure 20.24   Simple bar chart with values of individual cases

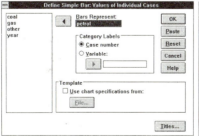
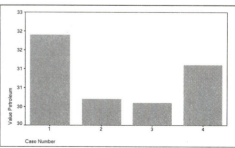

The minimum specification is a bar variable.

The numeric, short string, and long string variables in your data file are displayed on the source variable list. Select the numeric variable you want to define the bars. To get a simple bar chart showing the value of each case in default format, click on OK.

Optionally, you can change the value labels shown in the chart, use a template to control the format of the chart, or add a title, subtitle, or footnote. These options are discussed in detail in the *SPSS Base System User's Guide, Part 1*.

Bars Represent. Select a numeric variable to define the bars. Each case is represented by a separate bar.

Category Labels. Determines how the bars are labeled. You can choose one of the following category label sources:

○ **Case number**. Each category is labeled with the case number. This is the default.

○ **Variable**. Each category is labeled with the current value label of the selected variable.

Figure 20.25 shows a chart definition dialog box with a label variable selected and the resulting bar chart.

Figure 20.25 Bar chart with category labels from the variable year

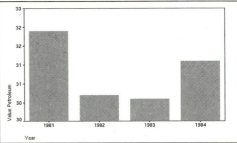

Clustered:
Values of individual cases

Figure 20.26 shows a chart definition dialog box and the resulting clustered bar chart with values of individual cases.

Figure 20.26   Clustered bar chart with bars as values of individual cases

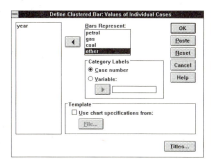
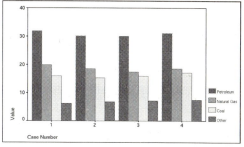

The minimum specification is two or more bar variables.

Bars Represent. Select two or more numeric variables. There is one separately colored or patterned set of bars for each variable. Each case is represented by a separate cluster of bars. The height of each bar represents the value of the variable.

Stacked:
Values of individual cases

Figure 20.27 shows a chart definition dialog box and the resulting stacked bar chart with values of individual cases.

Figure 20.27   Stacked bar chart with values of individual cases

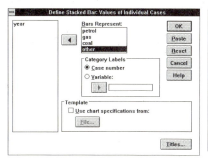
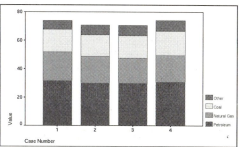

The minimum specifications are two or more segment variables.

Bars Represent. Select two or more numeric variables. Each case is represented by a separate stack. Each variable is represented by a separate bar within each stack.

Line Charts

To obtain a line chart, from the menus choose:

Graphs
  Line...

This opens the Line Charts dialog box, as shown in Figure 20.28.

Figure 20.28 Line Charts dialog box

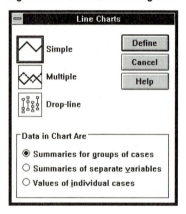

Select the type of line chart you want, and select the choice that describes the structure of your data organization. Click on **Define** to open a dialog box specific to your selections. Examples of these choices, shown with data structures and the charts they produce, are presented in Table 20.2.

Table 20.2 Types of line charts

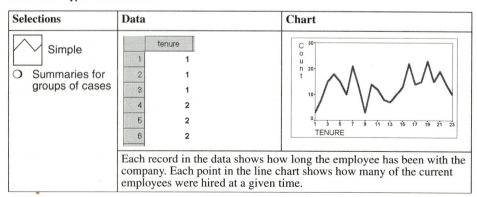

Bar, Line, Area, and Pie Charts 375

Table 20.2 Types of line charts (Continued)

Selections	Data	Chart
Multiple ○ Summaries for groups of cases	tenure / sex: 1: 1 Male 2: 1 Female 3: 1 Female 4: 2 Male 5: 2 Male 6: 2 Female	Count vs TENURE line chart with two lines for Sex of Employee (Male, Female)
	One line shows job seniority for males. The other line shows job seniority for females.	
Drop-line ○ Summaries for groups of cases	tenure / sex: 1: 1 Male 2: 1 Female 3: 1 Female 4: 2 Male 5: 2 Male 6: 2 Female	Drop-line chart of Count vs TENURE with points for Male and Female
	One set of points shows job seniority for males. The other set of points shows job seniority for females.	
Simple ○ Summaries of separate variables	winter / spring / summer / fall: 1: 371 439 443 415 2: 51 106 154 29 3: 427 450 486 426 4: 376 370 402 381 5: 534 512 469 449 6: 728 781 743 755	Mean line chart across Winter, Spring, Summer, Fall
	Each variable represents a different season. Each record represents a different store. The line shows the mean number of sales per store in a given season.	
Multiple ○ Summaries of separate variables	month / cherry / lime / grape: 1: JAN 3.00 9.00 7.00 2: JAN 10.00 16.00 8.00 3: JAN 8.00 11.00 12.00 4: FEB 15.00 18.00 20.00 5: FEB 10.00 7.00 14.00 6: FEB 14.00 14.00 11.00	Mean vs MONTH line chart with three lines: CHERRY, LIME, GRAPE
	The three variables, *cherry*, *lime*, and *grape*, represent the amount of pop sold from each vending machine each month. The variable *month* indicates the month in which the pop was sold. Each point represents the mean number of pop cases sold that month.	

Table 20.2 Types of line charts (Continued)

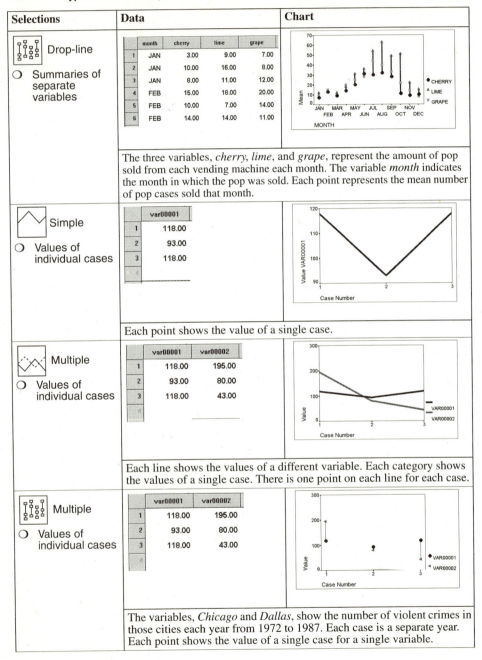

Selections	Data	Chart
Drop-line — Summaries of separate variables	month / cherry / lime / grape: JAN 3.00 9.00 7.00; JAN 10.00 16.00 8.00; JAN 8.00 11.00 12.00; FEB 15.00 18.00 20.00; FEB 10.00 7.00 14.00; FEB 14.00 14.00 11.00	*(drop-line chart by month for cherry, lime, grape)*

The three variables, *cherry*, *lime*, and *grape*, represent the amount of pop sold from each vending machine each month. The variable *month* indicates the month in which the pop was sold. Each point represents the mean number of pop cases sold that month.

Simple — Values of individual cases	var00001: 118.00, 93.00, 118.00	*(simple line chart)*

Each point shows the value of a single case.

Multiple — Values of individual cases	var00001 / var00002: 118.00 / 195.00; 93.00 / 80.00; 118.00 / 43.00	*(multiple line chart)*

Each line shows the values of a different variable. Each category shows the values of a single case. There is one point on each line for each case.

Multiple — Values of individual cases (drop-line)	var00001 / var00002: 118.00 / 195.00; 93.00 / 80.00; 118.00 / 43.00	*(multiple drop-line chart)*

The variables, *Chicago* and *Dallas*, show the number of violent crimes in those cities each year from 1972 to 1987. Each case is a separate year. Each point shows the value of a single case for a single variable.

**Simple:
Summaries for groups of cases**

Figure 20.29 shows a chart definition dialog box and the resulting simple line chart with summaries for groups of cases.

Figure 20.29   Simple line chart with summaries for groups of cases

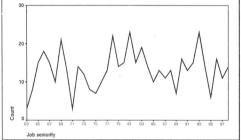

The minimum specification is a category axis variable.

The numeric, short string, and long string variables in your data file are displayed on the source variable list. Select a variable to define the category axis. To get a simple line chart showing the number of cases in each category, click on OK.

Optionally, you can select a different summary statistic, use a template to control the format of the chart, or add a title, subtitle, or footnote. Summary statistics are discussed in "Summary Functions" on p. 399. The other options are discussed in detail in the *SPSS Base System User's Guide, Part 1*.

Category Axis. Select a variable to define the categories shown in the chart. There is one point for each value of the variable.

If you select **Other summary function** in the Define Simple Line Summaries for Groups of Cases dialog box, you must also select a variable to be summarized. Figure 20.30 shows the chart definition dialog box with a variable to be summarized and the resulting chart.

Figure 20.30 Simple line chart with summary of a variable

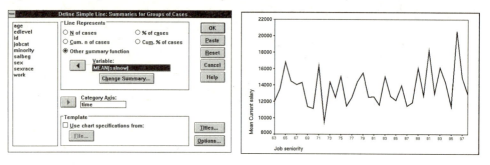

The chart generated by default shows the mean of the selected variable within each category (determined by the category axis variable).

Multiple:
Summaries for groups of cases

Figure 20.31 shows a chart definition dialog box and the resulting multiple line chart with summaries for groups of cases.

Figure 20.31 Multiple line chart with summaries for groups of cases

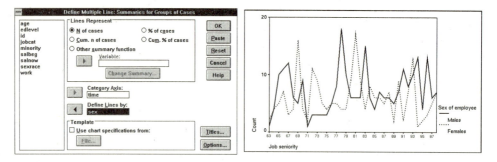

The minimum specifications are:
- A category axis variable.
- A line definition variable.

Category Axis. Select a variable to define the categories shown in the chart. There is one point on each line for each value of the variable.

Define Lines by. Select a variable to define the lines. There is one line for each value of the variable.

Drop-line:
Summaries for groups of cases

Figure 20.32 shows a chart definition dialog box and the resulting drop-line chart with summaries for groups of cases.

Figure 20.32   Drop-line chart with summaries for groups of cases

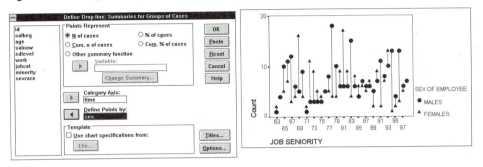

The minimum specifications are:

- A category axis variable.
- A point definition variable.

Category Axis. Select a variable to define the categories shown in the chart. There is one vertical line for each value of the variable.

Define Points by. Select a variable to define the points. There is one sequence of differently colored, patterned, or shaped points for each value of the variable.

Simple:
Summaries of separate variables

Figure 20.33 shows a chart definition dialog box and the resulting simple line chart with summaries of separate variables.

Figure 20.33   Simple line chart with summaries of separate variables

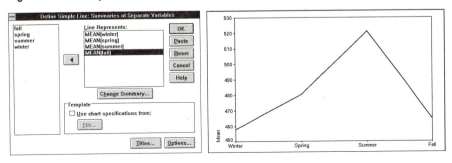

The minimum specifications are two or more point variables.

The numeric variables in your data file are displayed on the source variable list. Select the variables you want the line to represent. To get a simple line chart showing the mean value of each variable in default format, click on OK.

Optionally, you can select a different summary statistic, use a template to control the format of the chart, or add a title, subtitle, or footnote. Summary statistics are discussed in "Summary Functions" on p. 399. The other options are discussed in detail in the *SPSS Base System User's Guide, Part 1*.

Line Represents. Select two or more variables to define the categories shown in the chart. There is one point on the line for each variable. By default, the points show the mean of the selected variables.

**Multiple:
Summaries of separate variables**

Figure 20.34 shows a chart definition dialog box and the resulting multiple line chart with summaries of separate variables.

Figure 20.34 Multiple line chart with summaries of separate variables

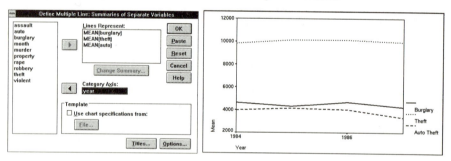

The minimum specifications are:
- Two or more line variables.
- A category axis variable.

Lines Represent. Select two or more variables to define the lines. There is one line for each variable. By default, the lines show the mean of the selected variables.

Category Axis. Select a variable to define the categories shown in the chart. There is one point on each line for each value of the variable.

Drop-line:
Summaries of separate variables

Figure 20.35 shows a chart definition dialog box and the resulting drop-line chart with summaries of separate variables.

Figure 20.35 Drop-line chart with summaries of separate variables

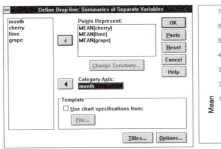
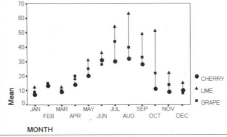

The minimum specifications are:

- Two or more point variables.
- A category axis variable.

Points Represent. Select two or more variables to define the points. There is one sequence of differently colored, patterned, or shaped points for each variable. By default, the points show the mean of the selected variables.

Category Axis. Select a variable to define the categories shown in the chart. There is one vertical line for each value of the variable.

Simple:
Values of individual cases

Figure 20.36 shows a chart definition dialog box and the resulting simple line chart with values of individual cases.

Figure 20.36 Simple line chart with values of individual cases

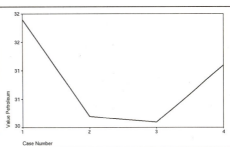

The minimum specification is a line variable.

The numeric, short string, and long string variables in your data file are displayed on the source variable list. Select the numeric variable you want to define the line. To get a simple line chart showing the value of each case in default format, click on OK.

Optionally, you can change the value labels shown in the chart, use a template to control the format of the chart, or add a title, subtitle, or footnote. These options are discussed in detail in the *SPSS Base System User's Guide, Part 1*.

Line Represents. Select a numeric variable to define the line. Each case will be displayed as a point.

Category Labels. Determines how the categories are labeled. You can choose one of the following category label sources:

○ **Case number.** Each category is labeled with the case number. This is the default.

○ **Variable.** Each category is labeled with the current value label of the selected variable.

Figure 20.37 shows a chart definition dialog box with a label variable selected and the resulting simple line chart with category labels.

Figure 20.37 Line chart with category labels from the variable year

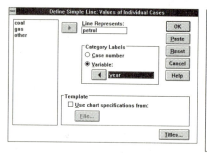 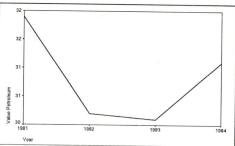

**Multiple:
Values of individual cases**

Figure 20.38 shows a chart definition dialog box and the resulting multiple line chart with values of individual cases.

Figure 20.38 Multiple line chart with values of individual cases

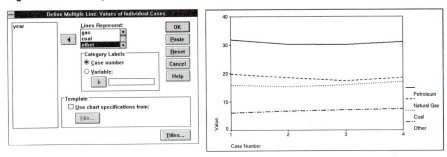

The minimum specification is two or more line variables.

Lines Represent. Select two or more numeric variables to define the lines. There is one line for each variable. There is one point on each line for each case.

Drop-line:
Values of individual cases

Figure 20.39 shows a chart definition dialog box and the resulting drop-line chart with values of individual cases.

Figure 20.39 Drop-line chart with values of individual cases

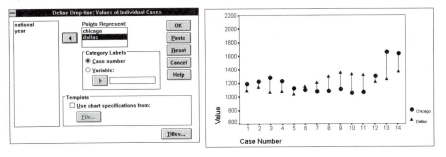

The minimum specification is two or more point variables.

Points Represent. Select two or more numeric variables to define the points. There is one sequence of differently colored, patterned, or shaped points for each variable. There is one vertical line for each case.

Area Charts

To obtain an area chart, from the menus choose:

Graphs
  Area...

This opens the Area Charts dialog box, as shown in Figure 20.40.

Figure 20.40 Area Charts dialog box

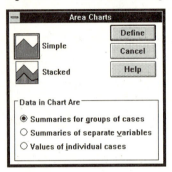

Select the type of area chart you want, and select the choice that describes the structure of your data organization. Click on **Define** to open a dialog box specific to your selections. Examples of these choices, shown with data structures and the charts they produce, are presented in Table 20.3.

Table 20.3 Types of area charts

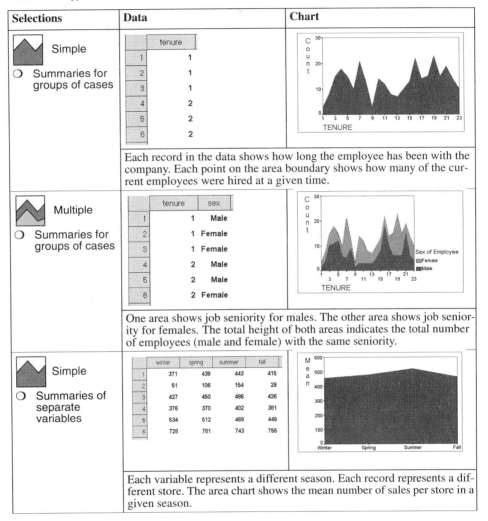

Table 20.3 Types of area charts (Continued)

Selections	Data	Chart
Stacked ○ Summaries of separate variables	month, cherry, lime, grape: 1 JAN 3.00 9.00 7.00 2 JAN 10.00 16.00 8.00 3 JAN 8.00 11.00 12.00 4 FEB 15.00 18.00 20.00 5 FEB 10.00 7.00 14.00 6 FEB 14.00 14.00 11.00	Stacked area chart of Sum by MONTH with GRAPE, LIME, CHERRY series
	The three variables, *cherry*, *lime*, and *grape*, represent the amount of pop sold from each vending machine each month. The variable *month* indicates the month in which the pop was sold. Each point represents the total number of pop cases sold that month.	
Simple ○ Values of individual cases	var00001: 1 284.00 2 114.00 3 114.00	Area chart of VAR00001 by Case Number
	Each point on the boundary of the area shows the value of a single case.	
Stacked ○ Values of individual cases	var00001, var00002: 1 118.00 195.00 2 93.00 80.00 3 118.00 43.00	Stacked area chart of Value by Case Number with VAR00002, VAR00001
	Each area shows the values of a different variable. Each category shows the values of a single case. There is one point on each area for each case.	

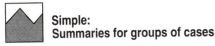

Simple:
Summaries for groups of cases

Figure 20.41 shows a chart definition dialog box and the resulting simple area chart with summaries for groups of cases.

Figure 20.41   Simple area chart with summaries for groups of cases

 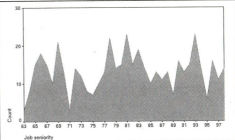

The minimum specification is a category axis variable.

The numeric, short string, and long string variables in your data file are displayed on the source variable list. Select the variable you want to define the category axis. To get a simple area chart showing the number of cases in each category, click on **OK**.

Optionally, you can select a different summary statistic, use a template to control the format of the chart, or add a title, subtitle, or footnote. Summary statistics are discussed in "Summary Functions" on p. 399. The other options are discussed in detail in the *SPSS Base System User's Guide, Part 1*.

Category Axis. Select a variable to define the categories shown in the chart. There is one point on the boundary of the area for each value of the variable.

If you select Other summary function in the chart definition dialog box, you must also select a variable to be summarized. Figure 20.42 shows the dialog box with a variable to be summarized and the resulting chart.

Figure 20.42 Summary of a variable in a simple area chart

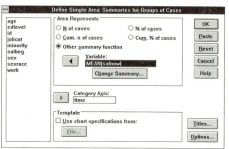
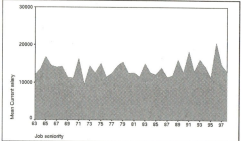

The chart generated by default shows the mean of the selected variable within each category (determined by the category axis variable). For a detailed description of optional statistics, see "Summary Functions" on p. 399.

Stacked:
Summaries for groups of cases

Figure 20.43 shows a chart definition dialog box and the resulting stacked area chart with summaries for groups of cases.

Figure 20.43 Stacked area chart with summaries for groups of cases

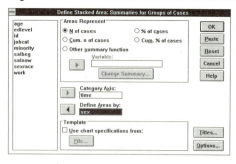
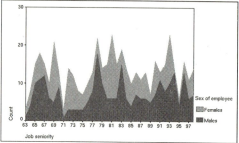

The minimum specifications are:
- A category axis variable.
- An area definition variable.

Category Axis. Select a variable to define the categories shown in the chart. There is one point on the boundary of each area for each value of the variable.

Define Areas by. Select a variable to define the areas. There is one differently colored or patterned area for each value of the variable.

**Simple:
Summaries of separate variables**

Figure 20.44 shows a chart definition dialog box and the resulting simple area chart with summaries of separate variables.

Figure 20.44   Simple area chart with summaries of separate variables

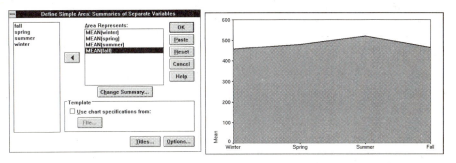

The minimum specifications are two or more point variables.

The numeric variables in your data file are displayed on the source variable list. Select the variables you want to define points on the boundary of the area. To get a simple area chart showing the mean value of each variable in default format, click on **OK**.

Optionally, you can select a different summary statistic, use a template to control the format of the chart, or add a title, subtitle, or footnote. Summary statistics are discussed in "Summary Functions" on p. 399. The other options are discussed in detail in the *SPSS Base System User's Guide, Part 1*.

Area Represents. Select two or more variables to define the categories shown in the chart. There is one point on the boundary of the area for each variable. By default, the points show the mean of the selected variables.

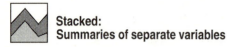

Stacked:
Summaries of separate variables

Figure 20.45 shows a chart definition dialog box and the resulting stacked area chart with summaries of separate variables.

Figure 20.45   Stacked area chart with summaries of separate variables

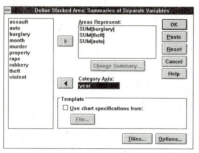 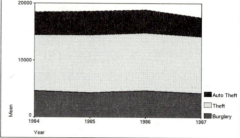

The minimum specifications are:
- Two or more area variables.
- A category axis variable.

Areas Represent. Select two or more variables to define the areas. There is one area for each variable. By default, the value axis shows the sum of the selected variables.

Category Axis. Select a variable to define the categories shown in the chart. There is one point on the boundary of each area for each value of the variable.

Simple:
Values of individual cases

Figure 20.46 shows a chart definition dialog box and the resulting simple area chart with values of individual cases.

Figure 20.46   Simple area chart with values of individual cases

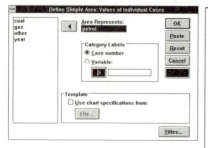 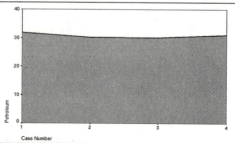

The minimum specification is an area variable.

The numeric, short string, and long string variables in your data file are displayed on the source variable list. Select the numeric variable you want to define the area. To get a simple area chart showing the value of each case in default format, click on OK.

Optionally, you can change the value labels shown in the chart, use a template to control the format of the chart, or add a title, subtitle, or footnote. These options are discussed in detail in the *SPSS Base System User's Guide, Part 1*.

Area Represents. Select a numeric variable to define the area. Each case will be displayed as a category.

Category Labels. Determines how the categories are labeled. You can choose one of the following category label sources:

- ○ **Case number.** Each category is labeled with the case number. This is the default.
- ○ **Variable.** Each category is labeled with the current value label of the selected variable.

Figure 20.47 shows the chart definition dialog box with a label variable selected and the resulting area chart.

Figure 20.47   Area chart with category labels from the variable year

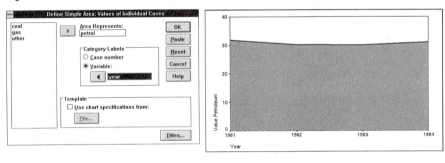

Stacked: Values of individual cases

Figure 20.48 shows the chart definition dialog box and the resulting stacked area chart with values of individual cases.

Figure 20.48 Stacked area chart with values of individual cases

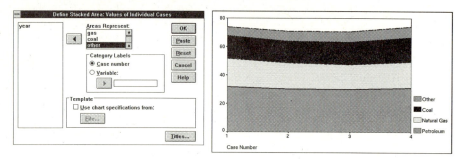

The minimum specifications are two stacked area variables.

Areas Represent. Select two or more numeric variables. There is one area for each variable. There is one point on the boundary of each area for each case.

Pie Charts

To obtain a pie chart, from the menus choose:

Graphs
 Pie...

This open the Pie Charts dialog box, as shown in Figure 20.49.

Figure 20.49 Pie Charts dialog box

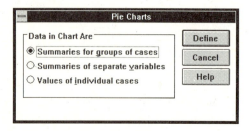

Select the choice that describes the structure of your data organization, and click on Define to open a dialog box specific to your selection (see Table 20.4).

Table 20.4 Types of pie charts

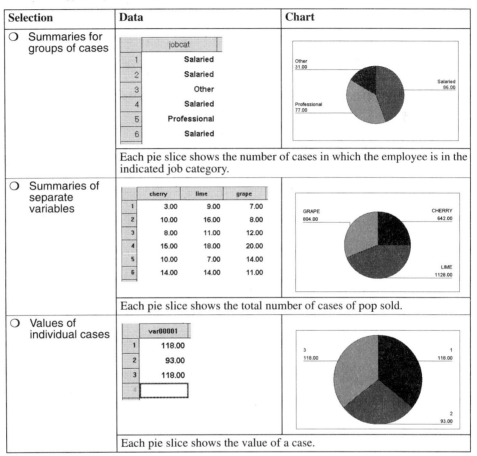

Summaries for Groups of Cases

Figure 20.50 shows a chart definition dialog box and the resulting simple pie chart with summaries for groups of cases.

Figure 20.50 Pie chart with summaries for groups of cases

The minimum specification is a slice definition variable.

The numeric, short string, and long string variables in your data file are displayed on the source variable list. Select the variable you want to define the categories or slices. To get a simple pie chart showing the number of cases in each category, click on **OK**.

Optionally, you can select a different summary statistic, use a template to control the format of the chart, or add a title, subtitle, or footnote. Summary statistics are discussed in "Summary Functions" on p. 399. The other options are discussed in detail in the *SPSS Base System User's Guide, Part 1*.

Define Slices by. Select a variable to define the pie slices shown in the chart. There is one slice for each value of the variable. A slice definition variable must be selected to enable the **OK** pushbutton.

If you select **Other summary function** in the Define Pie Summaries for Groups of Cases dialog box, you must also select a variable to be summarized. Figure 20.51 shows the chart definition dialog box with a variable to be summarized and the resulting simple pie chart.

Figure 20.51   Simple pie chart with summary of a variable

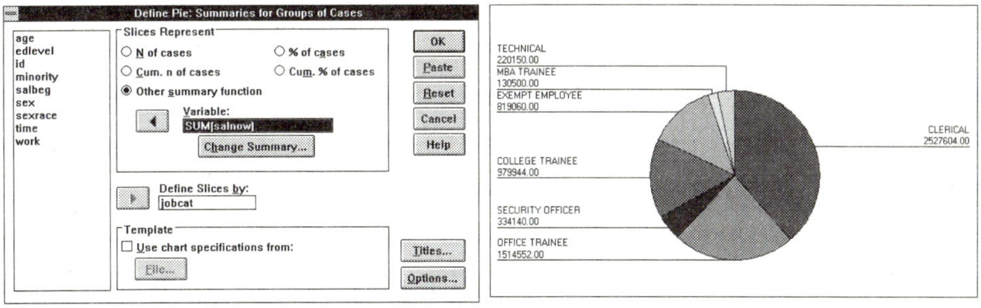

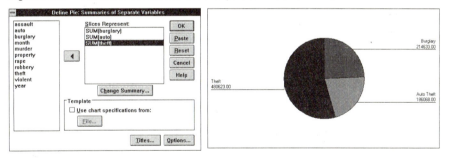

The chart generated by default shows the sum of the selected variable within each category (determined by the slice variable).

Summaries of Separate Variables

Figure 20.52 shows a chart definition dialog box and the resulting simple pie chart with summaries of separate variables.

Figure 20.52   Pie chart with summaries of separate variables

The minimum specifications are two or more slice variables.

The numeric variables in your data file are displayed on the source variable list. Select the variables you want to define the pie slices. To get a simple pie chart showing the sum of each variable in default format, click on OK.

Optionally, you can select a different summary statistic, use a template to control the format of the chart, or add a title, subtitle, or footnote. Summary statistics are discussed in "Summary Functions" on p. 399. The other options are discussed in detail in the *SPSS Base System User's Guide, Part 1*.

Slices Represent. Select two or more variables to define the slices shown in the chart. There is one slice for each variable. By default, the slices show the sum of the selected variables. Two or more slice variables must be selected to enable the **OK** pushbutton.

Values of Individual Cases

Figure 20.53 shows a chart definition dialog box and the resulting simple pie chart with values of individual cases.

Figure 20.53   Pie chart with values of individual cases

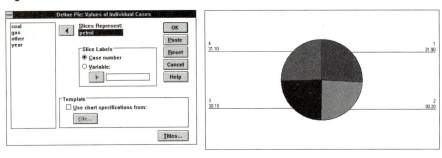

The minimum specification is a slice variable.

The numeric, short string, and long string variables in your data file are displayed on the source variable list. Select the numeric variable you want slices to represent. To get a simple pie chart showing the value of each case in default format, click on **OK**.

Optionally, you can change the value labels shown in the chart, use a template to control the format of the chart, or add a title, subtitle, or footnote. These options are discussed in detail in the *SPSS Base System User's Guide, Part 1*.

Slices Represent. Select a numeric variable to define the slices. Each case will be displayed as a separate pie slice. A variable must be selected to enable the **OK** pushbutton.

Slice Labels. Determines how the slices are labeled. You can choose one of the following sector label sources:

○ **Case number.** Each slice is labeled with the case number. This is the default.

○ **Variable.** Each slice is labeled with the current value label of the selected variable.

Figure 20.54 shows the chart definition dialog box with a label variable selected and the resulting pie chart.

Figure 20.54 Pie chart with category labels from the variable petrol

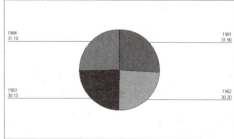

Transposed Charts

Sometimes, especially with inventory or accounting time-series data, the categories you want are defined as separate cases or values while each date is a separate variable. For example, the inventory data in Figure 20.55 are defined this way.

Figure 20.55 Inventory data

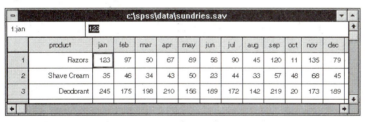

If you draw a line chart of these data, you get the chart in Figure 20.56.

To flip this chart so that each line is a separate product and each month is a separate category, edit the chart. From the menu of the chart window select:

Series
 Transpose Data

This produces the chart shown in Figure 20.57.

Figure 20.56 Chart of inventory data

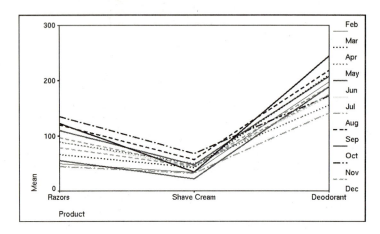

Figure 20.57 Transposed chart

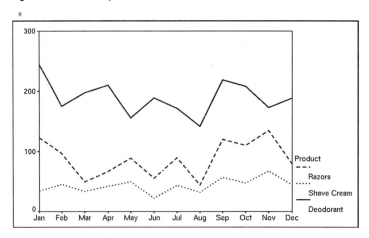

You can transpose other multiple-series categorical charts, such as clustered bar charts (see the *SPSS Base System User's Guide, Part 1*).

Summary Functions

Data can be summarized by counting the number of cases in each category or subcategory, or by calculating a statistic summarizing the values in each category or subcategory.

Count Functions

For simple summaries of groups of cases, the dialog box in Figure 20.58 shows the general layout of the chart definition dialog boxes for bar, line, area, and pie charts. For complex summaries of groups of cases, the summaries in the dialog box are similar, as shown in Figure 20.59.

Figure 20.58 Define simple summaries for groups of cases dialog box

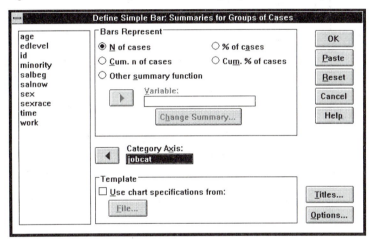

Figure 20.59 Define multi-series summaries for groups of cases dialog box

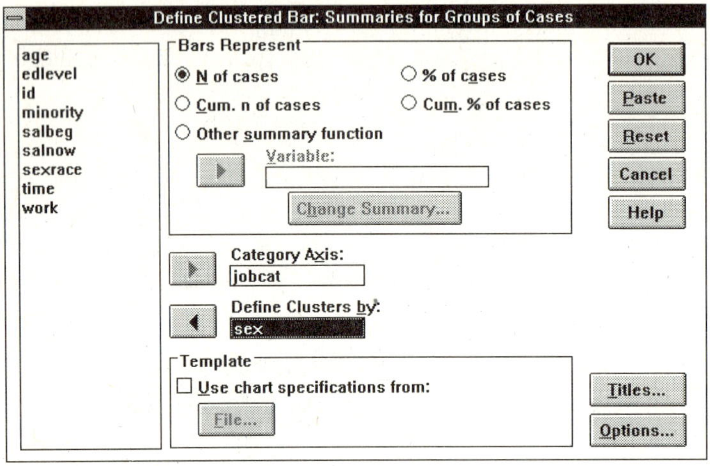

Bars/Lines/Areas/Slices Represent. Determines the summary statistic used to generate the data series illustrated by the chart. You can choose one of the following alternatives:

- **N of cases.** Each bar, point on a line, point on the boundary of an area, or pie slice represents the number of cases in a category. This is the default.

- **% of cases.** Each bar, point on a line, point on the boundary of an area, or pie slice represents the percentage of cases in a category.

- **Cum. n of cases.** Cumulative number of cases. Each bar, point on a line, point on the boundary of an area, or pie slice represents the number of cases in the current category plus all cases in previous categories. This function is not appropriate for some charts; see "Cumulative Functions" on p. 403.

- **Cum. % of cases.** Cumulative percentage of cases. Each bar, point on a line, or point on the boundary of an area represents the cumulative number of cases as a percentage of the total number of cases. This function is not appropriate for some charts; see "Cumulative Functions" on p. 403.

- **Other summary function.** The values in a series are calculated from a summary measure of a variable. In most cases, the mean of the variable is the default. For stacked bar, stacked area, and pie charts, the sum of the variable is the default.

Other Summary Functions

You can request statistical summary functions for any chart where values are summarized. When values are summarized for *groups of cases*, select **Other summary function**;

then select a variable to summarize and click on [▶]. The Variable box indicates the default summary function (mean or sum). If you want a summary function other than the default, click on Change Summary.... This opens the Summary Function dialog box, as shown in Figure 20.60.

When values are summarized for *separate variables*, first move the variables to the box for bars, lines, areas, or slices, as shown in Figure 20.21 and Figure 20.52. The default measure (mean or sum) is indicated for each variable on the list. If you want a summary function other than the default, select a variable on the list and click on Change Summary.... This opens the Summary Function dialog box, as shown in Figure 20.60. If you want the same summary function to apply to more than one variable, you can select several variables by dragging over them and then clicking on Change Summary....

Figure 20.60 Summary Function dialog box

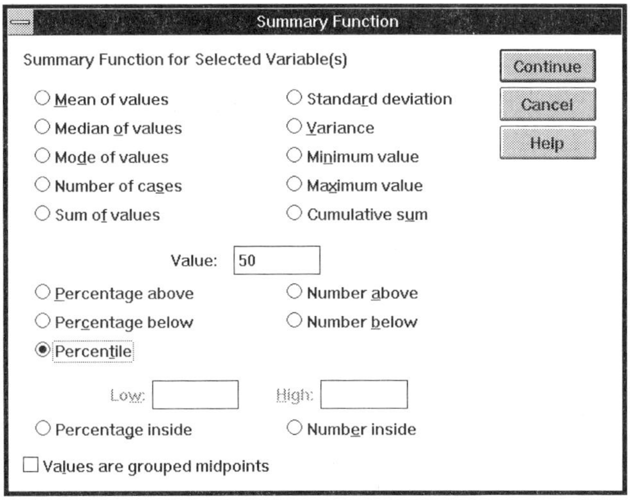

You can choose one of the following summary functions:

- **Mean of values.** The arithmetic average within the category. This is the default in most cases.
- **Median of values.** The value below which half the cases fall. If you select this option, the Values are grouped midpoints check box is enabled.
- **Mode of values.** The most frequently occurring value.
- **Number of cases.** The number of cases having a nonmissing value of the selected variable. If there are no missing values, this is the same as N of cases in the previous dialog box.
- **Sum of values.** The default for stacked bar charts, stacked area charts, or pie charts.

- **Standard deviation.** A measure of how much observations vary from the mean, expressed in the same units as the data.
- **Variance.** A measure of how much observations vary from the mean, expressed in squared units.
- **Minimum value.** The smallest value.
- **Maximum value.** The largest value.
- **Cumulative sum.** The sum of all values in the current category plus all values in previous categories. This function is not appropriate for some charts; see "Cumulative Functions," below.
- **Percentage above.** The percentage of cases above the indicated value.
- **Percentage below.** The percentage of cases below the indicated value.
- **Percentile.** The data value below which the specified percentage of values fall. If you select this option, the Values are grouped midpoints check box is enabled.
- **Number above.** The number of cases above the specified value.
- **Number below.** The number of cases below the specified value.
- **Percentage inside.** The percentage of cases with values between the specified high and low value, including the high and low values. Select this item and then type in the high and low values.
- **Number inside.** The number of cases with values between the specified high and low values, including the high and low values. Select this item and then type in the high and low values.

If you are plotting values that represent midpoints of groups (for example, if all people in their thirties are coded 35), you can plot estimated percentiles or medians for the original ungrouped data, assuming that cases are uniformly distributed in each interval.

❑ **Values are grouped midpoints.** Enabled when Median of values or Percentile is selected. Calculates the percentile or median as if the values were uniformly distributed over the whole interval.

The two charts in Figure 20.61 illustrate the differences when the check box is off or on:
- At the left is a chart of the 50th percentile in each employment category using the age group values. The check box is not selected.
- At the right is a chart of the 50th percentile in each employment category as estimated by assuming that the values are uniformly distributed in each interval. These are the values plotted when Values are grouped midpoints is selected.

Figure 20.61 Charts illustrating the "Values are grouped midpoints" selection

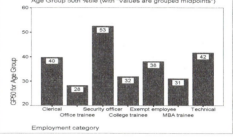

Cumulative Functions

Cum. N of cases, *Cum. % of cases*, and *Cumulative sum* are inappropriate in pie charts. These functions are also inappropriate in stacked bar charts and area charts that have been transposed so that the cumulative function is along the scale axis. Because the Chart Editor does not recalculate summary functions, many Displayed Data operations (from the Series menu) will invalidate cumulative functions, particularly if scaled to 100%.

21 High-Low Charts

Stocks, commodities, currencies, and other market data fluctuate considerably from hour to hour, day to day, or week to week. To graph the long-term changes and still convey a sense of the short-term changes, each category in a chart must show a range of values. High-low charts are designed to graph these kinds of data.

Simple High-Low Charts

Typically, market data have three important values: the highest value during a period of time, the lowest value during the same period, and the closing value, or value at the end of the period. These kinds of data are displayed in a high-low-close chart, as shown in Figure 21.1.

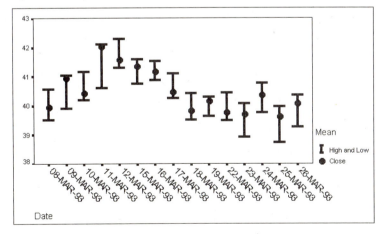

Figure 21.1 Simple high-low-close chart

The chart shows the mean stock values for eight medical companies on the New York Stock Exchange. A bar shows the mean high and low value for each day, and a point on the bar shows the mean closing value for the day.

Often, you have data with high and low values but you don't want to show closing values. You can display the data either as a high-low-close chart without close points or as a range bar chart. The range bar chart shown in Figure 21.2 shows the daily mean high and low for the eight medical stocks.

Figure 21.2 Simple range bar chart

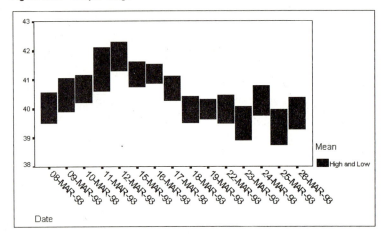

Clustered High-Low Charts

Medical companies can be divided into two groups: those that are exclusively pharmaceutical companies and those that are not. To show the mean high, low, and close values for the two groups, use a clustered high-low-close chart, as shown in Figure 21.3.

Figure 21.3 Clustered high-low-close chart

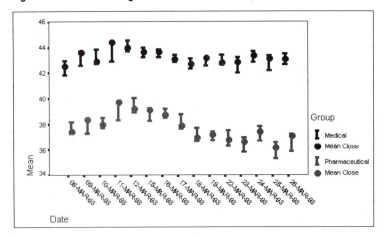

To show just the high and low values, use either a high-low-close chart without close points or a range bar chart, as shown in Figure 21.4.

Figure 21.4 Clustered range bar chart

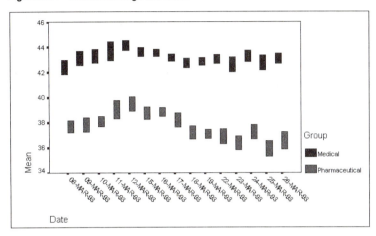

Difference Line Charts

High-low-close charts and range bar charts are useful for showing high and low data where one value is consistently high and the other value is consistently low. What about data where sometimes one value is high and sometimes the other value is high? To show the changing relationship between two such values, use a difference line chart. For example, Figure 21.5 compares the daily closing value of a medical company's stocks with similarly valued stocks from a petroleum company.

Figure 21.5 Difference line chart

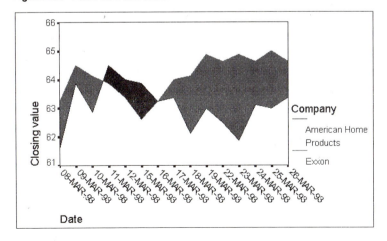

The two types of shaded areas between the lines show where the values of both the medical and petroleum companies' stocks are high. If you want to compare more than two changing values at the same time, use a drop-line chart, as described in Chapter 20.

How to Obtain High-Low Charts

To obtain a high-low chart, from the menus choose:

Graphs
  High-Low...

This opens the High-Low Charts dialog box, as shown in Figure 21.6.

Figure 21.6 High-Low Charts dialog box

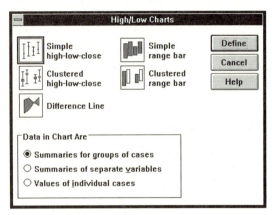

From the High-Low Charts dialog box, choose one of the chart types, and then select the choice that describes the structure of your data organization.

Data in Chart Are. Select the choice that describes the structure of your data organization.

- **Summaries for groups of cases.** There is one bar, point on a line, or cluster of bars for each category of the category axis variable. In simple charts (simple high-low-close, simple range bar, and difference line), a variable with two values defines the high and low points for each category. In a simple high-low-close chart, a variable with three values may be used instead to define high, low, and closing values. In clustered charts, two variables determine the high and low values, and a third variable defines the bars within each cluster. In a clustered high-low-close chart, another variable may also be used to determine a closing value for each bar.

○ **Summaries of separate variables.** More than one variable is summarized. Simple high-low charts summarize each variable over all cases in the file. Clustered high-low charts summarize each variable within categories determined by another variable.

○ **Values of individual cases.** Each case in the data is a separate category in the chart.

Examples of these choices, shown with data structures and the charts they produce, are presented in Table 21.1.

Table 21.1 Types of high-low charts

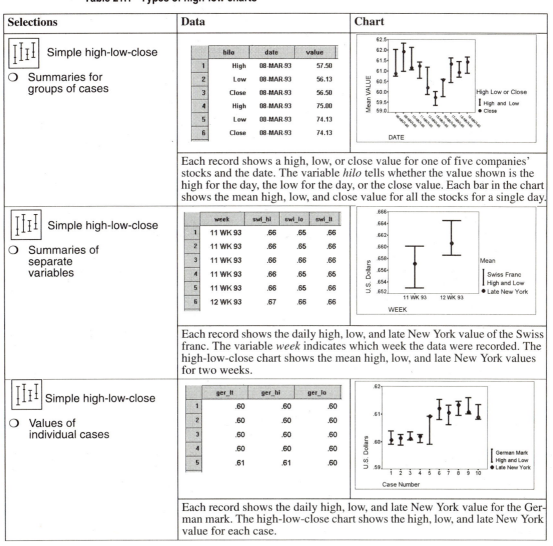

Table 21.1 Types of high-low charts (Continued)

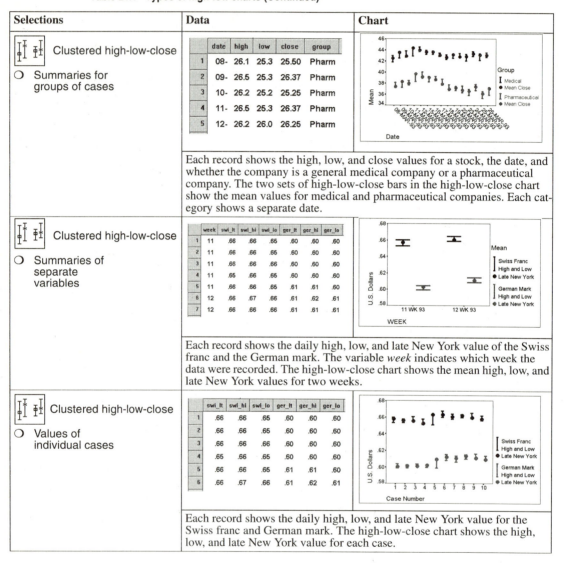

Table 21.1 Types of high-low charts (Continued)

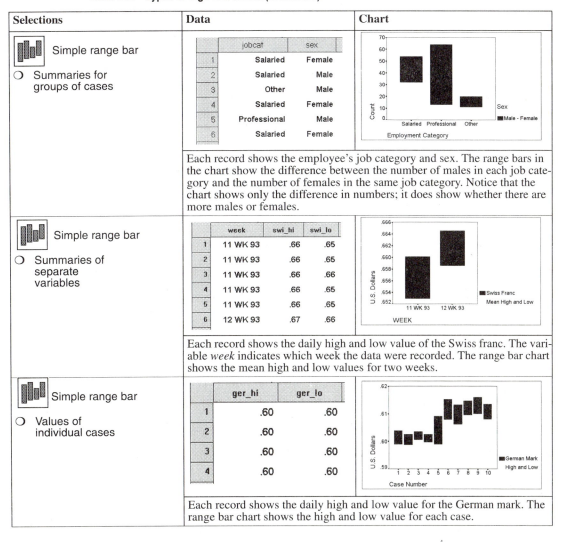

Table 21.1 Types of high-low charts (Continued)

Selections	Data	Chart
Clustered range bar ○ Summaries for groups of cases	date / high / low / group 1 08- 26.1 25.3 Pharm 2 09- 26.5 25.3 Pharm 3 10- 26.2 25.2 Pharm 4 11- 26.5 25.3 Pharm	(range bar chart of Mean vs Date, grouped by Medical / Pharmaceutical)
	Each record shows the high and low values for a stock, the date, and whether the company is a general medical company or a pharmaceutical company. The two sets of range bars in the range bar chart show the mean high and low values for medical and pharmaceutical companies. Each category shows a separate date.	
Clustered range bar ○ Summaries of separate variables	week / swi_hi / swi_lo / ger_hi / ger_lo 1 11 .66 .65 .60 .60 2 11 .66 .65 .60 .60 3 11 .66 .66 .60 .60 4 11 .66 .65 .60 .60 5 11 .66 .65 .61 .60	(range bar chart of U.S. Dollars vs WEEK for Swiss Franc High and Low and German Mark High and Low at 11 WK 93 and 12 WK 93)
	Each record shows the daily high and low value of the Swiss franc and the German mark. The variable *week* indicates which week the data were recorded. The range bar chart shows the mean high and low values for two weeks.	
Multiple ○ Values of individual cases	swi_hi / swi_lo / ger_hi / ger_lo 1 .66 .65 .60 .60 2 .66 .65 .60 .60 3 .66 .66 .60 .60 4 .66 .65 .60 .60 5 .66 .65 .61 .60 6 .67 .66 .62 .61	(range bar chart of U.S. Dollar vs Case Number 1–10 for Swiss Franc High and Low and German Mark High and Low)
	Each record shows the daily high and low value for the Swiss franc and the German mark. The range bar chart shows the high and low value for each case.	

Table 21.1 Types of high-low charts (Continued)

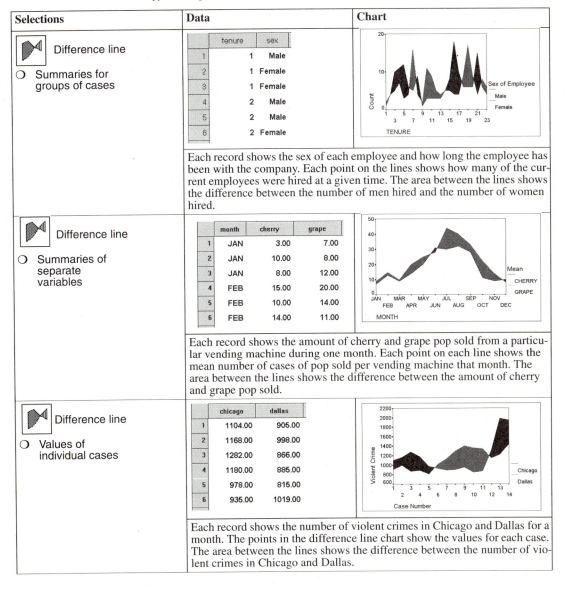

Selections	Data	Chart
Difference line ○ Summaries for groups of cases	tenure / sex 1. 1 Male 2. 1 Female 3. 1 Female 4. 2 Male 5. 2 Male 6. 2 Female	
	Each record shows the sex of each employee and how long the employee has been with the company. Each point on the lines shows how many of the current employees were hired at a given time. The area between the lines shows the difference between the number of men hired and the number of women hired.	
Difference line ○ Summaries of separate variables	month / cherry / grape 1. JAN 3.00 7.00 2. JAN 10.00 8.00 3. JAN 8.00 12.00 4. FEB 15.00 20.00 5. FEB 10.00 14.00 6. FEB 14.00 11.00	
	Each record shows the amount of cherry and grape pop sold from a particular vending machine during one month. Each point on each line shows the mean number of cases of pop sold per vending machine that month. The area between the lines shows the difference between the amount of cherry and grape pop sold.	
Difference line ○ Values of individual cases	chicago / dallas 1. 1104.00 905.00 2. 1168.00 998.00 3. 1282.00 866.00 4. 1180.00 885.00 5. 978.00 815.00 6. 935.00 1019.00	
	Each record shows the number of violent crimes in Chicago and Dallas for a month. The points in the difference line chart show the values for each case. The area between the lines shows the difference between the number of violent crimes in Chicago and Dallas.	

Each combination of chart type and data organization structure produces a different definition box. Each is discussed briefly below. The icon and section title indicate the choices that have to be made in the chart dialog box to open that chart definition dialog box. The discussion for each chart type always describes the selections required to enable the OK pushbutton. Optional selections are discussed only with the first chart using each data structure. For a detailed description of optional statistics, see "Summary Functions" on p. 399 in Chapter 20.

Simple high-low-close:
Summaries for groups of cases

Figure 21.7 shows a chart definition dialog box and the resulting simple high-low-close chart with summaries for groups of cases.

Figure 21.7 Simple high-low-close chart with summaries for groups of cases

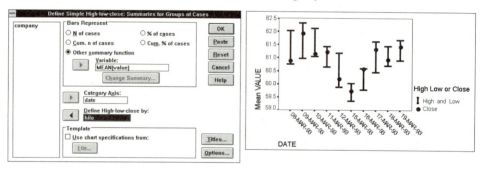

The minimum specifications are:
- A category axis variable.
- A high-low-close variable. This variable must have two or three values.
- If Other summary function is selected, you must specify a variable.

The numeric, short string, and long string variables in your data file are displayed on the source variable list. Select the variable you want to define the category axis and select the variable you want to define the high-low-close bars. The high-low-close variable must have either two or three values. To get a simple high-low-close chart showing high-low-close bars for each category, click on OK.

Optionally, you can select a different summary statistic, use a template to control the format of the chart, or add a title, subtitle, or footnote. Summary statistics are discussed in "Summary Functions" on p. 399 in Chapter 20. The other options are discussed in detail in the *SPSS Base System User's Guide, Part 1*.

High-Low Charts

Bars Represent. If Other summary function in the chart definition dialog box is selected, you must select a variable to be summarized. The chart generated by default shows the mean of the selected variable within each category (determined by the category axis variable). For a detailed description of optional statistics, see "Summary Functions" on p. 399 in Chapter 20.

Category Axis. Select a variable to define the categories shown in the chart. There is one high-low-close bar for each value of the variable.

Define High-Low-Close by. Select a variable with two or three values. If there are two values, they are shown as high-low-close bars without close points. If there are three values, the first and second define the high and low ends of the bars and the third value determines the position of the close points. If your data are coded in the wrong order and all the close points appear above or below the high-low bars, you can edit the displayed series in the chart so that the close points appear between the high and low points. See the *SPSS Base System User's Guide, Part 1* for more information on editing the displayed series. Figure 21.8 shows a high-low-close chart for a variable with two categories.

Figure 21.8 Simple high-low-close chart without close points

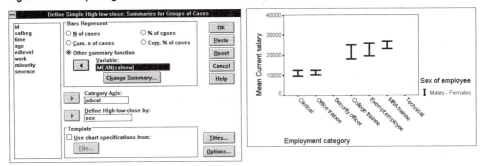

If Other summary function is not selected, you do not need to specify a variable. Figure 21.9 shows a high-low-close chart that shows number of cases.

Figure 21.9 High-low-close chart with number of cases

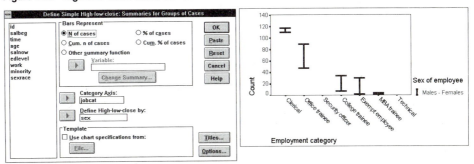

**Simple range bar:
Summaries for groups of cases**

Figure 21.10 shows a chart definition dialog box and the resulting simple range bar chart with summaries for groups of cases.

Figure 21.10 Simple range bar chart with summaries for groups of cases

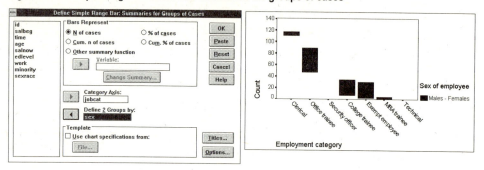

The minimum specifications are:
- A category axis variable.
- A variable that defines two groups (has two values).

Category Axis. Select a variable to define the categories shown in the chart. There is one range bar for each value of the variable.

Define 2 Groups by. Select a variable with two values. The top of each range bar is determined by cases with one value; the bottom of each range bar is determined by cases with the other value.

 **Difference line:
Summaries for groups of cases**

Figure 21.11 shows a chart definition dialog box and the resulting difference line chart with summaries for groups of cases.

Figure 21.11 Difference line chart with summaries for groups of cases

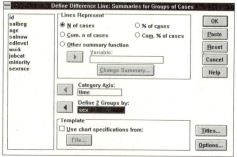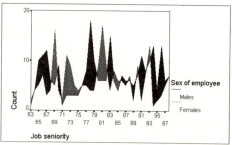

The minimum specifications are:
- A category axis variable.
- A line definition variable. The line definition variable must have exactly two values.

Category Axis. Select a variable to define the categories shown in the chart. There is one point on each line for each value of the variable.

Define 2 Groups by. Select a variable to define the lines. The variable must have two values. There are two differently colored or patterned lines in the chart, one for each value of this variable.

Clustered high-low-close: Summaries for groups of cases

Figure 21.12 shows a chart definition dialog box and the resulting clustered high-low-close chart with summaries for groups of cases.

Figure 21.12 Clustered high-low-close chart with summaries for groups of cases

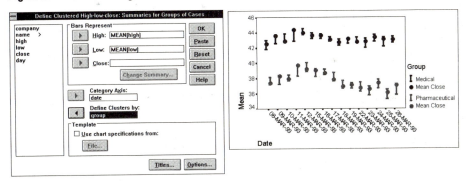

The minimum specifications are:
- A high variable.
- A low variable.
- A category axis variable.
- A cluster definition variable.

High. Select a variable to determine one end of each high-low-close bar. By default, the bars show the mean of the selected value.

Low. Select a variable to determine the other end of each high-low-close bar. By default, the bars show the mean of the selected value.

Close. You may optionally select a variable to determine the position of close points. By default, the close points show the mean of the selected value. Close points are connected by a line.

Category Axis. Select a variable to define the categories shown in the chart. There is one cluster of high-low-close bars for each value of the category axis variable.

Define Clusters by. Select a variable to define the bars within each cluster. There is a differently colored or patterned series of high-low-close bars for each value of the cluster variable.

Clustered range bar:
Summaries for groups of cases

Figure 21.13 shows a chart definition dialog box and the resulting clustered range bar chart with summaries for groups of cases.

Figure 21.13 Clustered range bar chart with summaries for groups of cases

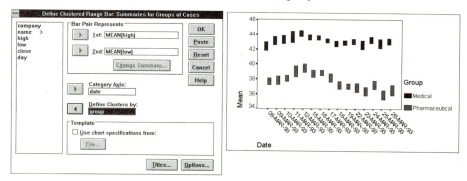

The minimum specifications are:
- A 1st variable.
- A 2nd variable.
- A category axis variable.
- A cluster definition variable.

1st. Select a variable to determine one end of each range bar. By default, each bar shows the mean of the selected value.

2nd. Select a variable to determine the other end of each range bar. By default, each bar shows the mean of the selected value.

Category Axis. Select a variable to define the categories shown in the chart. There is one cluster of range bars for each value of the category axis variable.

Define Clusters by. Select a variable to define the bars within each cluster. There is a differently colored or patterned series of range bars for each value of the cluster variable.

Simple high-low-close: Summaries of separate variables

Figure 21.14 shows a chart definition dialog box and the resulting simple high-low-close chart with summaries for groups of cases.

Figure 21.14 Simple high-low-close chart with summaries of separate variables

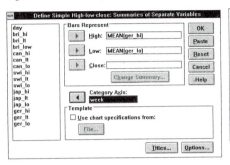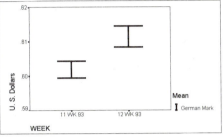

The minimum specifications are:

- A high variable.
- A low variable.
- A category variable.

The numeric, short string, and long string variables in your data file are displayed on the source variable list. Select the variable you want to define the high end of each bar, the variable you want to define the low end of each bar, and a category axis variable. The high and low variables must be numeric. To get a simple high-low-close chart showing means for each category, click on **OK**.

Optionally, you can add close points, select a different summary statistic, use a template to control the format of the chart, or add a title, subtitle, or footnote. Summary statistics are discussed in "Summary Functions" on p. 399 in Chapter 20. The other options are discussed in detail in the *SPSS Base System User's Guide, Part 1*.

High. Select a variable to determine one end of each high-low-close bar. By default, the bars show the mean of the selected variable.

Low. Select a variable to determine the other end of each high-low-close bar. By default, the bars show the mean of the selected variable.

Close. You may optionally select a variable to determine the position of close points. By default, the close points show the mean of the selected variable. Figure 21.15 shows a high-low-close chart with close points.

Figure 21.15 Simple high-low-close chart with close points

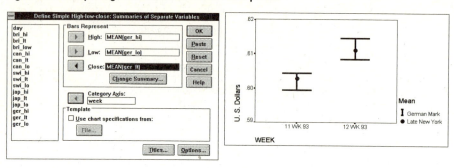

Category Axis. Select a variable to define the categories shown in the chart. There is one high-low-close bar for each value of the variable.

Simple range bar:
Summaries of separate variables

Figure 21.16 shows a chart definition dialog box and the resulting simple range bar chart with summaries of separate variables.

Figure 21.16 Simple range bar chart with summaries of separate variables

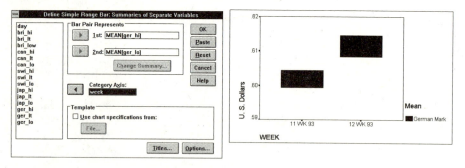

The minimum specifications are:
- Two bar variables.
- A category axis variable.

1st. Select a variable to determine one end of each range bar. By default, each bar shows the mean of the selected variable.

2nd. Select a variable to determine the other end of each range bar. By default, each bar shows the mean of the selected variable.

Category Axis. Select a variable to define the categories shown in the chart. There is one range bar for each value of the variable.

**Difference line:
Summaries of separate variables**

Figure 21.17 shows a chart definition dialog box and the resulting difference line chart with summaries of separate variables.

Figure 21.17 Difference line chart with summaries of separate variables

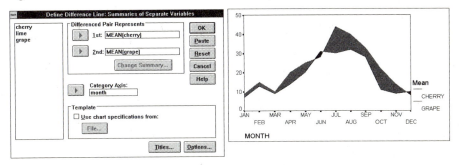

The minimum specifications are:
- Two 1st variables.
- Two 2nd variables.
- A category axis variable.

1st. Select a variable to determine one line in the set. By default, the line shows the mean of the selected value.

2nd. Select a variable to determine the other line in the set. By default, the line shows the mean of the selected value.

Category Axis. Select a variable to define the categories shown in the chart. There is one point on each line for each value of the category axis variable.

Clustered high-low-close: Summaries of separate variables

Figure 21.18 shows a chart definition dialog box and the resulting clustered high-low-close chart with summaries of separate variables.

Figure 21.18 Clustered high-low-close chart with summaries of separate variables

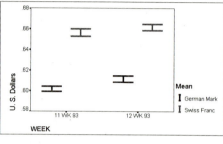

The minimum specifications are:
- Two high variables.
- Two low variables.
- A category axis variable.

High. Select a variable to determine one end of each high-low-close bar in the set. By default, the bars show the mean of the selected variable. To edit a different set of high, low, and close values, press **Previous** or **Next**.

Low. Select a variable to determine the other end of each high-low-close bar in the set. By default, the bars show the mean of the selected variable. To edit a different set of high, low, and close values, press **Previous** or **Next**.

Close. You may optionally select a variable to determine the position of close points in the set. By default, the close points show the mean of the selected variable. To edit a different set of high, low, and close values, press **Previous** or **Next**.

Category Axis. Select a variable to define the categories shown in the chart. There is one cluster of high-low-close bars for each value of the category axis variable.

**Clustered range bar:
Summaries of separate variables**

Figure 21.19 shows a chart definition dialog box and the resulting clustered range bar chart with summaries of separate variables.

Figure 21.19 Clustered range bar chart with summaries of separate variables

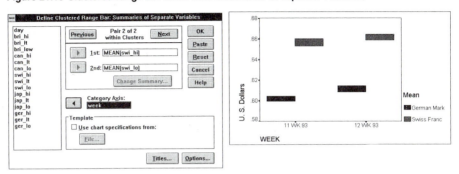

The minimum specifications are:
- Two 1st variables.
- Two 2nd variables.
- A category axis variable.

1st. Select a variable to determine one end of each range bar in the set. By default, the bars show the mean of the selected variable. To edit a different set of 1st and 2nd values, press Previous or Next.

2nd. Select a variable to determine the other end of each range bar in the set. By default, the bars show the mean of the selected variable. To edit a different set of 1st and 2nd values, press Previous or Next.

Category Axis. Select a variable to define the categories shown in the chart. There is one cluster of high-low-close bars for each value of the category axis variable.

Simple high-low-close: Values of individual cases

Figure 21.20 shows a chart definition dialog box and the resulting simple high-low-close chart with values of individual cases.

Figure 21.20 Simple high-low-close chart with values of individual cases

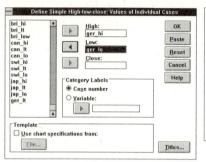
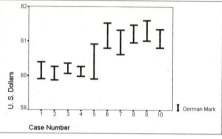

The minimum specifications are:
- A high variable.
- A low variable.

The numeric, short string, and long string variables in your data file are displayed on the source variable list. Select the numeric variable you want to define the high end of each bar and the numeric variable you want to define the low end of each bar. To get a simple high-low-close chart showing the value for each case, click on **OK**.

Optionally, you can add close points, add category labels, use a template to control the format of the chart, or add a title, subtitle, or footnote. Summary statistics are discussed in "Summary Functions" on p. 399 in Chapter 20. The other options are discussed in detail in the *SPSS Base System User's Guide, Part 1*.

High. Select a variable to determine one end of each high-low-close bar. Each case is represented by a separate bar.

Low. Select a variable to determine the other end of each high-low-close bar. Each case is represented by a separate bar.

Close. You may optionally select a variable to determine the position of close points. Figure 21.21 shows a high-low-close chart with close points.

Figure 21.21 Simple high-low-close chart with close points

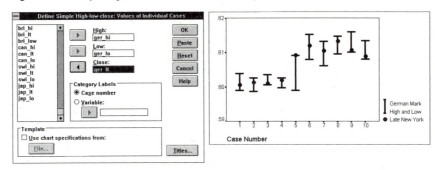

Category Labels. Determines how the bars are labeled. You can choose one of the following category label sources:

○ **Case number.** Each category is labeled with the case number.

○ **Variable.** Each category is labeled with the current value label of the selected variable.

Figure 21.22 shows a chart definition dialog box with a label variable selected and the resulting high-low-close chart.

Figure 21.22 High-low-close chart with category labels from variable day

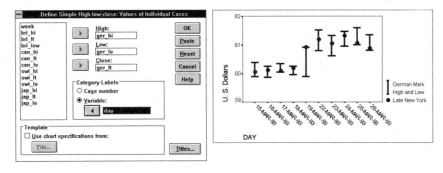

Simple range bar:
Values of individual cases

Figure 21.23 shows a chart definition dialog box and the resulting simple range bar chart with values of individual cases.

Figure 21.23 Simple range bar chart with values of individual cases

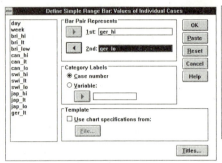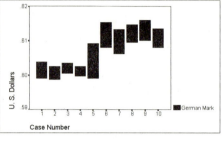

The minimum specifications are:
- Two bar variables.

1st. Select a variable to determine one end of each range bar. Each case is represented by a separate bar.

2nd. Select a variable to determine the other end of each range bar. Each case is represented by a separate bar.

Difference line:
Values of individual cases

Figure 21.24 shows a chart definition dialog box and the resulting difference line chart with values of individual cases.

Figure 21.24 Difference line chart with values of individual cases

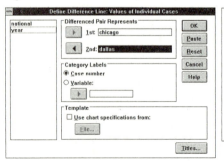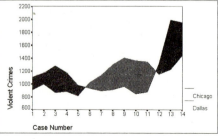

The minimum specifications are:
- A 1st variable.
- A 2nd variable.

1st. Select a variable to determine one line in the set. Each case is represented by a separate point on the line.

2nd. Select a variable to determine the other line in the set. Each case is represented by a separate point on the line.

Clustered high-low-close: Values of individual cases

Figure 21.25 shows a chart definition dialog box and the resulting clustered high-low-close chart with values of individual cases.

Figure 21.25 Clustered high-low-close chart with values of individual cases

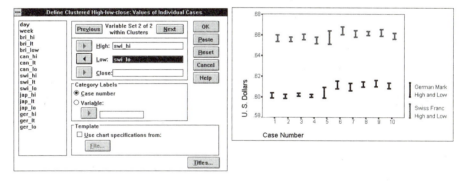

The minimum specifications are:
- Two high variables.
- Two low variables.

High. Select a variable to determine one end of each high-low-close bar in the set. Each case is represented by a separate bar. To edit a different set of high, low, and close values, press **Previous** or **Next**.

Low. Select a variable to determine the other end of each high-low-close bar in the set. Each case is represented by a separate bar. To edit a different set of high, low, and close values, press **Previous** or **Next**.

Close. You may optionally select a variable to determine the position of close points in the set. Each case is represented by a separate close point. Close points are connected by a line. To edit a different set of high, low, and close values, press **Previous** or **Next**.

Clustered range bar:
Values of individual cases

Figure 21.26 shows a chart definition dialog box and the resulting clustered range bar chart with values of individual cases.

Figure 21.26 Clustered range bar chart with values of individual cases

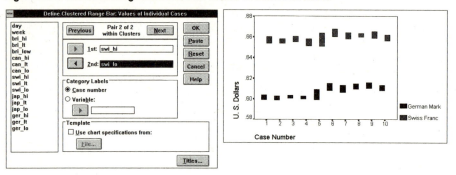

The minimum specifications are:
- Two 1st variables.
- Two 2nd variables.

1st. Select a variable to determine one end of each range bar in the set. Each case is represented by a separate bar. To edit a different set of 1st and 2nd values, press **Previous** or **Next**.

2nd. Select a variable to determine the other end of each range bar in the set. Each case is represented by a separate bar. To edit a different set of 1st and 2nd values, press **Previous** or **Next**.

22 Boxplots and Error Bar Charts

Boxplots and error bar charts help you visualize distributions and dispersion. Boxplots show the actual distribution of the data. Error bar charts show confidence intervals, standard deviations, or standard errors of the mean. You can get simple boxplots from the Explore statistical procedure or the Boxplot graphics procedure. More complex boxplots can be obtained only from the Boxplot procedure. Error bar charts can be obtained from the Error Bar graphics procedure. This chapter describes the Boxplot and Error Bar graphics procedures. For a description of the components of a boxplot, see Chapter 5, which also describes other methods of exploratory analysis.

Boxplots

In Chapter 5, there is an example of a simple boxplot, which is used to compare the distribution of beginning salaries for people employed in several different positions at a bank. If we break the data down further by sex, we can see the distribution of male and female salaries in different positions throughout the company. Figure 22.1 shows a clustered boxplot of beginning salary.

Figure 22.1 Clustered boxplot of beginning salary by job category and sex

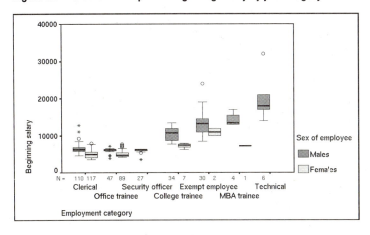

Each cluster shows both sexes. Each category shows the job category of the employees. You can see that women's starting salaries were lower in all job categories, especially the categories with higher pay. You can also see that the men's salaries in the four higher-paid categories have similar distributions, while all the other salaries have much less variability. Also, notice how few women are in the higher-paid categories. In the college trainee, exempt employee, MBA trainee, and technical categories, there are seven, two, one, and zero, respectively.

Both this example and the chart in Chapter 5 show data summarized by groups of cases. Often, we are interested in comparing the distribution of two or more different variables. For example, the starting and current salaries of bank employees are recorded as two separate variables. The simple boxplot of starting salary and current salary is shown in Figure 22.2. Here you can see that starting salary is lower and has a little less variability than current salary.

Figure 22.2 Boxplot of starting and current salaries

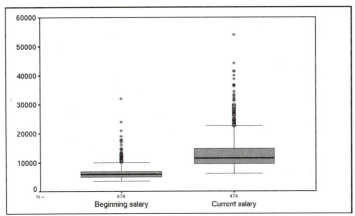

If you want to see beginning salary and current salary by job category, use a clustered boxplot, as shown in Figure 22.3. Here you can see that the spread of current salaries for employees in the technical, exempt, and college trainee categories are larger than for the other categories. Also, as expected, the higher categories generally show a greater difference between starting salary and current salary.

Figure 22.3 Boxplot of starting and current salary by job category

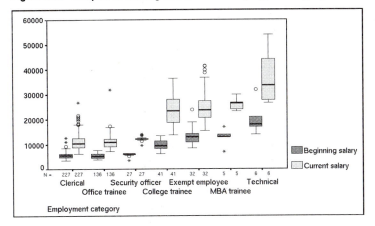

Error Bar Charts

While boxplots show the distribution of your data, error bar charts show the estimated dispersion of the population from which the data were drawn. Like boxplots, error bar charts can be simple or clustered and can show summaries for groups of cases or summaries of separate variables. Unlike boxplots, error bar charts can show one of three different statistics: confidence intervals, standard errors, or standard deviations.

Assume that the bank data are a random sample of bank employees and that the number of employees in the study is the sample size. The sample is used to represent all the employees in the bank, or the population of the study.

Error bars can be used to show confidence intervals for the mean. Figure 22.4 shows the 95% confidence intervals for mean salary by job category.

Figure 22.4 Simple error bar chart showing a 95% confidence interval

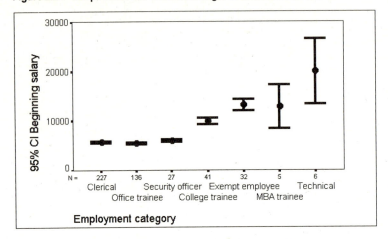

Confidence intervals are one way to specify the estimated dispersion. A 95% confidence interval reaches approximately two standard deviations on either side of the mean. Instead of a confidence interval, you can specify a number of standard deviations, as in Figure 22.5.

Figure 22.5 Simple error bar chart showing three standard deviations

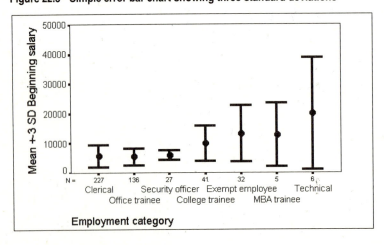

This chart shows the mean values with bars that stretch three standard deviations on either side of the mean.

The mean of a sample will, in general, differ from the mean of another sample. The standard error of the mean is an estimate of how much different samples of the same size vary. An error bar chart can show a specified number of standard errors on either side of the mean, as in Figure 22.6.

Figure 22.6 Simple error bar chart showing two standard errors of the mean

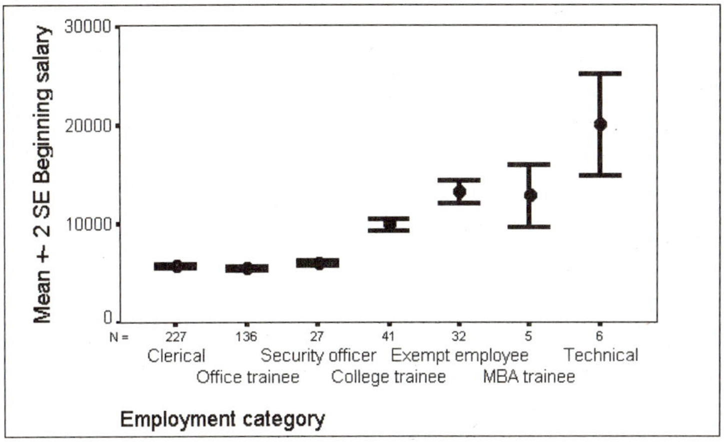

This chart shows the mean salary within each job category with bars that stretch two standard errors on either side of the mean.

How to Obtain a Boxplot

To obtain a boxplot, from the menus choose:

Graphs
  Boxplot...

This opens the Boxplot dialog box, as shown in Figure 22.7.

Figure 22.7   Boxplot dialog box

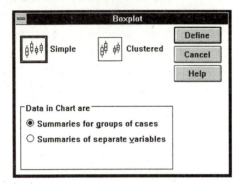

From the Boxplot dialog box, choose either simple or clustered boxplots, and then select the choice that describes the structure of your data organization.

Data in Chart Are. Select the choice that describes the structure of your data organization.

- **Summaries for groups of cases.** One variable is summarized in subgroups. The subgroups are determined by one variable for simple boxplots or two variables for clustered boxplots.

- **Summaries of separate variables.** More than one variable is summarized. Simple boxplots summarize each variable over all cases in the file. Clustered boxplots summarize each variable within categories determined by another variable.

Examples of these choices, shown with data structures and the charts they produce, are presented in Table 22.1.

Table 22.1 Boxplot types and data organization

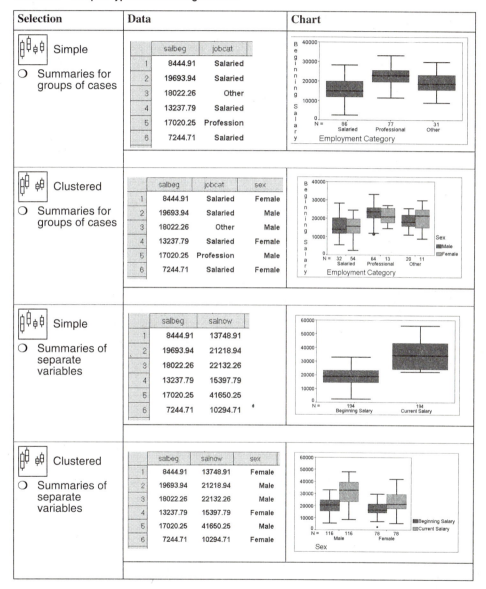

Defining Boxplots

Each combination of boxplot type and data structure produces a different definition dialog box. Each is briefly discussed below. The icon and section title indicate the choices that have to be made in the Boxplot dialog box to open that chart definition dialog box. The discussion for each boxplot type always describes the selection required to enable the **OK** pushbutton. Optional selections are discussed only with the first chart using each data structure.

Simple:
Summaries for groups of cases

Figure 22.8 shows a simple boxplot with summaries for groups of cases. The specifications are on the left and the resulting chart is on the right.

Figure 22.8 Simple boxplot of groups of cases

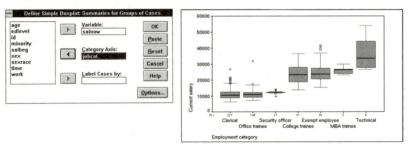

The minimum specifications are:
- A variable to be summarized.
- A category axis variable.

The numeric, short string, and long string variables in your data file are displayed on the source variable list. Select the numeric variable you want summarized and the variable you want to use to define the categories. To get a simple boxplot showing the distribution of cases in each category, click on **OK**.

Variable. Select a numeric variable to be summarized.

Category Axis. Select a variable to define the categories shown in the boxplot. There is one boxplot for each value of the variable.

Label Cases by. Select a variable whose value labels are to be used to label outliers and extremes. For instance, if the boxplot variable is *salnow* and cases are labeled by *sex* and the third case is an outlier, the boxplot will indicate the sex of the person with that outlier salary. If this field is left blank, case numbers are used to label outliers and extremes. If two outliers or extremes have the same value, but different case labels, no label is displayed. In the Chart Editor, you can turn off labels altogether, as was done in Figure 22.8.

Clustered:
Summaries for groups of cases

Figure 22.9 shows a clustered boxplot with summaries for groups of cases. The specifications are on the left and the resulting boxplot is on the right.

Figure 22.9 Clustered boxplot of groups of cases

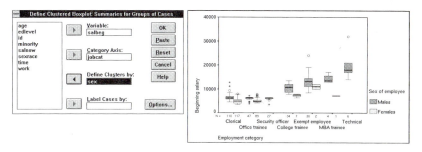

The minimum specifications are:
- A variable to be summarized.
- A category axis variable.
- A cluster variable.

Variable. Select a numeric variable to be summarized.

Category Axis. Select a variable to define the categories shown in the boxplot. There is one boxplot for each value of the variable.

Define Clusters by. Select a variable to define the boxplots within each cluster. In each cluster, there is one boxplot for each value of the variable. A cluster variable must be selected to enable the OK pushbutton.

**Simple:
Summaries of separate variables**

Figure 22.10 shows a simple boxplot with summaries of separate variables. The specifications are on the left and the resulting boxplot is on the right.

Figure 22.10 Simple boxplot of separate variables

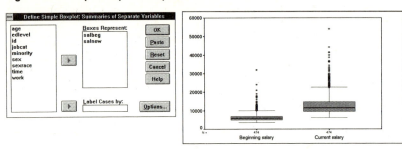

The minimum specification is one or more box variables.

The numeric, short string, and long string variables in your data file are displayed on the source variable list. Select the numeric variables you want to define the boxplots. To get a simple boxplot showing the distribution of each variable in default format, click on OK.

Boxes Represent. Select one or more variables to define the boxplots shown in the chart. There is one boxplot for each variable.

 **Clustered:
Summaries of separate variables**

Figure 22.11 shows a clustered boxplot of separate variables. The specifications are on the left and the resulting boxplot is on the right.

Figure 22.11 Clustered boxplot of separate variables

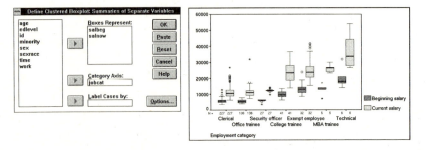

The minimum specification are:
- Two or more box variables.
- A category axis variable.

Boxes Represent. Select two or more variables to define the boxplots shown in the chart. There is one boxplot for each variable. Two or more box variables must be selected to enable the OK pushbutton.

Category Axis. Select a variable to define the categories shown in the boxplot. There is one cluster of boxplots for each value of the variable. A category axis variable must be selected to enable the OK pushbutton.

How to Obtain an Error Bar Chart

To obtain an error bar chart, from the menus choose:

Graphs
  Error Bar...

This opens the Error Bar dialog box, as shown in Figure 22.12.

Figure 22.12 Error Bar dialog box

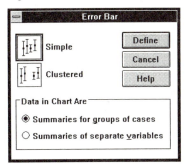

From the Error Bar dialog box, choose either simple or clustered error bars, and then select the choice that describes the structure of your data organization.

Data in Chart Are. Select the choice that describes the structure of your data organization.
- ○ **Summaries for groups of cases.** One variable is summarized in subgroups. The subgroups are determined by one variable for simple error bars or two variables for clustered error bars.
- ○ **Summaries of separate variables.** More than one variable is summarized. Simple error bars summarize each variable over all cases in the file. Clustered error bars summarize each variable within categories determined by another variable.

Examples of these choices, shown with data structures and the charts they produce, are presented in Table 22.2.

Table 22.2 Error bar types and data organization

Selection	Data	Chart
Simple — Summaries for groups of cases	salbeg / jobcat: 8444.91 Salaried; 19693.94 Salaried; 18022.26 Other; 13237.79 Salaried; 17020.25 Profession; 7244.71 Salaried	95% CI Beginning salary vs Employment category (Clerical, Office trainee, Security officer, College trainee, Exempt employee, MBA trainee, Technical)
Clustered — Summaries for groups of cases	salbeg / jobcat / sex: 8444.91 Salaried Female; 19693.94 Salaried Male; 18022.26 Other Male; 13237.79 Salaried Female; 17020.25 Profession Male; 7244.71 Salaried Female	95% CI Beginning salary vs Employment category, clustered by Sex of employee (Males, Females)
Simple — Summaries of separate variables	salbeg / salnow: 8444.91 13748.91; 19693.94 21218.94; 18022.26 22132.26; 13237.79 15397.79; 17020.25 41650.25; 7244.71 10294.71	95% CI for Beginning salary and Current salary (N = 474, 474)
Clustered — Summaries of separate variables	salbeg / salnow / sex: 8444.91 13748.91 Female; 19693.94 21218.94 Male; 18022.26 22132.26 Male; 13237.79 15397.79 Female; 17020.25 41650.25 Male; 7244.71 10294.71 Female	95% CI for Beginning salary and Current salary, clustered by Sex of employee (Males, Females)

Defining Error Bar Charts

Each combination of error bar type and data structure produces a different definition dialog box. Each is briefly discussed below. The icon and section title indicate the choices that have to be made in the Error Bar dialog box to open that chart definition dialog box. The discussion for each error bar type always describes the selection required to enable the OK pushbutton. Optional selections are discussed only with the first chart using each data structure.

Simple:
Summaries for groups of cases

Figure 22.13 shows a simple error bar chart with summaries for groups of cases. The specifications are on the left and the resulting chart is on the right.

Figure 22.13 Simple error bar chart of groups of cases

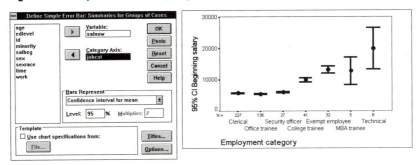

The minimum specifications are:
- A numeric variable to be summarized.
- A category axis variable.

The numeric, short string, and long string variables in your data file are displayed on the source variable list. Select the numeric variable you want summarized and the variable you want to use to define the categories. To get a simple error bar chart showing the 95% confidence interval in each category, click on OK.

Variable. Select a numeric variable to be summarized.

Category Axis. Select a variable to define the categories shown in the error bar chart. There is one error bar for each value of the variable.

Bars Represent. Select the statistic used to determine the length of the error bars.

◆ **Confidence interval for mean.** Bars represent confidence intervals. Enter the confidence level.

Standard error of mean. The multiplier indicates the number of standard errors each bar represents.

Standard deviation. The multiplier indicates the number of standard deviations each bar represents.

Clustered:
Summaries for groups of cases

Figure 22.14 shows a clustered error bar chart with summaries for groups of cases. The specifications are on the left and the resulting error bar chart is on the right.

Figure 22.14 Clustered error bar chart of groups of cases

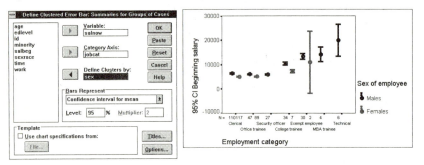

The minimum specifications are:
- A numeric variable to be summarized.
- A category axis variable.
- A cluster variable.

Variable. Select a numeric variable to be summarized.

Category Axis. Select a variable to define the categories shown in the error bar chart. There is one error bar for each value of the variable.

Define Clusters by. Select a variable to define the error bars within each cluster. In each cluster, there is one error bar for each value of the variable. A cluster variable must be selected to enable the OK pushbutton.

Simple:
Summaries of separate variables

Figure 22.15 shows a simple error bar chart with summaries of separate variables. The specifications are on the left and the resulting error bar chart is on the right.

Figure 22.15 Simple error bar chart of separate variables

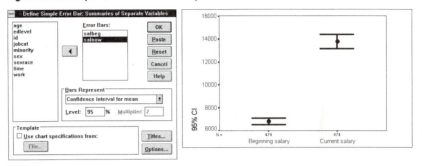

The minimum specification is one or more error bar variables.

The numeric, short string, and long string variables in your data file are displayed on the source variable list. Select the numeric variables you want to define the error bars. To get a simple error bar chart showing the confidence interval of each variable in default format, click on OK.

Error Bars. Select one or more numeric variables to define the error bars shown in the chart. There is one error bar for each variable.

Clustered:
Summaries of separate variables

Figure 22.16 shows a clustered error bar chart of separate variables. The specifications are on the left and the resulting error bar chart is on the right.

Figure 22.16 Clustered error bar of separate variables

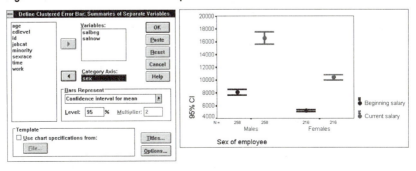

The minimum specifications are:
- Two or more numeric error bar variables.
- A category axis variable.

Variables. Select two or more variables to define the error bars shown in the chart. There is one error bar in each category for each variable. Two or more variables must be selected to enable the **OK** pushbutton.

Category Axis. Select a variable to define the categories shown in the error bar chart. There is one cluster of error bars for each value of the variable. A category axis variable must be selected to enable the **OK** pushbutton.

23 Scatterplots and Histograms

Summaries that describe data are useful, but nothing beats taking a look at the actual values. You wouldn't consider buying a house based solely on an appraiser's report. You know there's much more to a house than square footage and number of rooms. Similarly, you shouldn't draw conclusions about data based only on summary statistics, such as the mean and the correlation coefficient. Your data have a story that only a picture can tell.

In Chapter 3 and Chapter 5 you saw how histograms and stem-and-leaf plots (from the Frequencies and Explore procedures) are used to examine the distribution of the values of single variables. In this chapter you'll see how plotting two or more variables together helps you untangle and identify possible relationships.

Further discussion of how to obtain histograms from the Graphs menu is also included.

A Simple Scatterplot

As American corporations come under increasing scrutiny, the compensation paid to CEO's is often described as excessive and unrelated to corporate performance. Let's look at the relationship between 1989 total yearly compensation (in thousands) and profits (in millions). The data are a sample from those published in *Forbes* (1990).

Figure 23.1 is a scatterplot of total compensation (on the vertical axis) and profits (on the horizontal axis). Total compensation does not appear to be strongly related to profits, though there does appear to be a weak positive relationship.

Figure 23.1 Scatterplot of compensation with profits

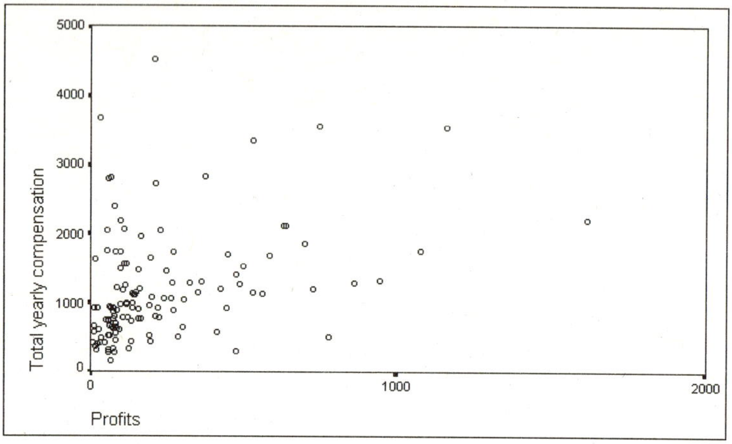

The plot is somewhat difficult to read, since many points overlap in the bottom left corner. Traditionally, in a plotting system which had limited resolution, such overlapping points were represented by a numeral which indicated how many cases each point represented. Such numerals, however, don't easily translate to a visual representation of density. You still tend to "see" only one case at each point on the plot.

Cleveland and McGill (1984) proposed that overlapping or nearly overlapping points be represented by **sunflowers**. The idea is fairly simple. You divide the entire plotting grid into equal-sized regions (cells) and count the number of points that fall into each region, just as for a low-resolution plot. Instead of a numeral, you then use the sunflower symbol to display this count. If a cell contains only one point, it is represented by a small circle. If a cell has more than one point, each point is represented by a short line (a "petal") originating from the circle. Optionally, you can specify an integer larger than 1 for the number of cases represented by each petal. (For more details, see the *SPSS Base System User's Guide, Part 1*.)

The sunflower plot for the CEO compensation data is shown in Figure 23.2.

Figure 23.2 Sunflower scatterplot of compensation with profits

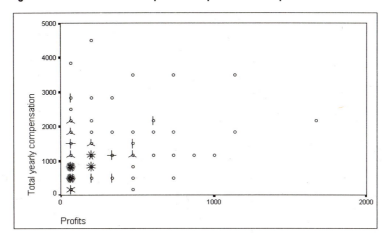

You can see that the overlapping points are now represented by sunflowers. It's easy to see where the cases cluster. The more petals on a sunflower, the more cases there are. But although it's easier to read the plot now, the relationship between CEO compensation and company profits doesn't appear to be straightforward.

Profits, Growth, and Compensation

Profits are, of course, only one indication of the success of a business, albeit an important one. Variables like corporate growth are also indicators of a CEO who performs well. Let's look at the relationship between growth, profits, and CEO compensation. Instead of considering the actual values, we'll look at the ranks assigned to the total compensation, profits, and growth for the selected companies. (*Forbes* ranked approximately 800 companies on these variables. A rank of 1 was assigned to the best performer.)

Figure 23.3 is a scatterplot of the ranks of profit and growth for the selected companies.

Figure 23.3 Scatterplot with summary curve

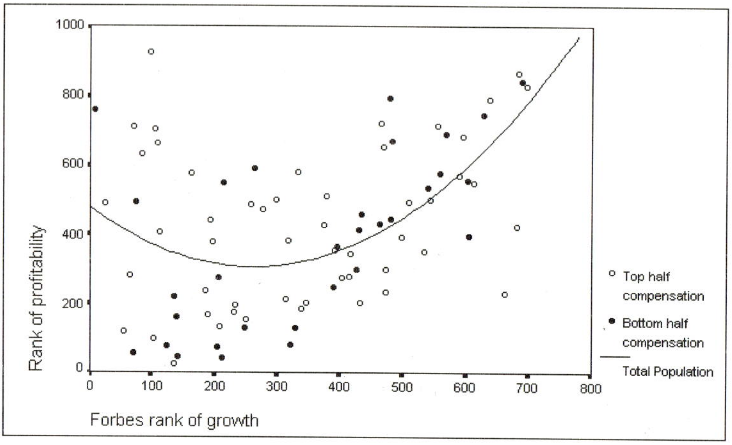

[Figure 23.3: Scatterplot showing Rank of profitability vs Forbes rank of growth with a U-shaped quadratic summary curve. Legend: Top half compensation (open circles), Bottom half compensation (filled circles), Total Population (line).]

In this plot, different markers are used to identify the points in different categories. The squares are for companies with CEO's in the top half of the compensation ratings. The crosses are for companies whose CEO's are in the bottom half of compensation. There is also a summary curve drawn on the plot—a quadratic regression. From Figure 23.3 you see that the relationship between growth and profits is somewhat U-shaped. Once again there's not a clear relationship between compensation and the other two variables.

If you think that the relationship between growth and profit ranks may be different for the two types of CEO's (high pay and "low" pay), you can draw separate summary curves for the two categories and for the total sample. These are shown in Figure 23.4.

Figure 23.4 Scatterplot with subgroup curves

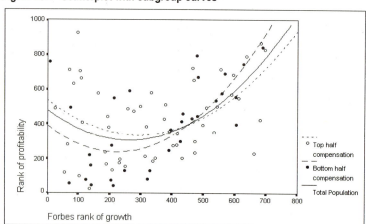

The relationship between ranks of growth and profits appears to be similar for each of the two categories of CEO's.

Scatterplot Matrices

When you want to examine the relationships between several pairs of variables, instead of plotting all pairs separately, you can select a **scatterplot matrix**. Consider Figure 23.5, which is a scatterplot matrix of the ranks of compensation, profits, and growth.

Figure 23.5 Scatterplot matrix with lowess fit lines

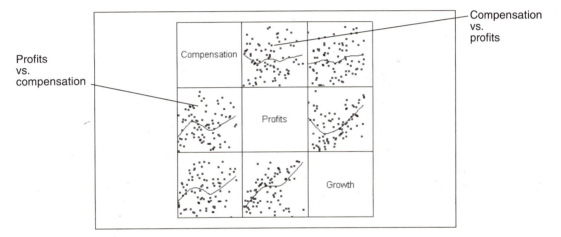

A scatterplot matrix has the same number of rows and columns as there are variables. In this example, the scatterplot matrix contains three rows and three columns. Each cell of the matrix is a plot of a pair of variables. The diagonal cells identify the variables plotted in the other cells. The first diagonal cell contains the label *Compensation*. That tells you that, for all plots in the first row, the rank of total compensation is plotted on the *y* axis (vertical). For all plots in the first column, the rank of compensation is plotted on the *x* axis (horizontal). Similarly, the label *Profits* is in the second diagonal cell, indicating that the rank of profits is plotted on the vertical axis for all plots in the second row and on the horizontal axis for all plots in the second column.

Look at the first plot in the first row. It is the plot of compensation (*y* axis) against profits (*x* axis). The second plot in the first row is the plot of compensation (*y* axis) against growth (*x* axis). The easiest way to read a scatterplot matrix is to scan across an entire row or column. For example, if you read across the first row you see how total compensation relates first to profit and then to growth. The third row tells you how growth relates to compensation and then how growth relates to profitability.

Similarly, the easiest way to identify an individual plot in a scatterplot matrix is to scan up or down to find which variable is on the horizontal axis, and scan right or left to find out which variable is on the vertical axis.

In a scatterplot matrix, all possible pairs of plots are displayed. The plots above the diagonal are the same as the plots below the diagonal. The only difference is that the variables are "flipped." That is, the horizontal and vertical variables are switched. For example, above the diagonal you see a plot of compensation and profits where compensation is on the vertical axis and profits are on the horizontal axis. Below the diagonal you see a plot of profits on the vertical axis and compensation on the horizontal axis.

The scatterplot matrix in Figure 23.5 reinforces our previous conclusions about compensation, profits, and growth. There appears to be little relationship between compensation and either profits or growth. However, there does appear to be a relationship between profits and growth.

Smoothing the Data

The curves added to the plots in the scatterplot matrix help you see possible trends in the data. There are many different lines and curves which can be superimposed on plots. If you know that a linear, quadratic, or cubic regression model fits your data (see Chapter 15), you can plot the appropriate model by choosing **Options**... from the Chart menu (see the *SPSS Base System User's Guide, Part 1*). If you don't know what kind of model fits your data, you can request lowess smoothing (Chambers et al., 1983).

Lowess smoothing doesn't require you to specify a particular model. Instead, for each value of the independent variable, it computes a predicted value using cases that have similar values for the independent variable. Points that are close to the one being predicted are assigned more importance in the computations. Lowess smoothing is robust, meaning that it isn't affected much by extreme values. That's a desirable property. Lowess smoothing requires many computations, especially for large data sets, so it may take a while for your plots to be drawn.

Plotting in Three Dimensions

So far, all of the plots you have seen in this chapter have been two-dimensional. That is, points are plotted only on two axes. You can also create scatterplots in three dimensions. Consider Figure 23.6, which is a three-dimensional plot of the ranks of compensation, growth, and profits.

Figure 23.6 3-D plot

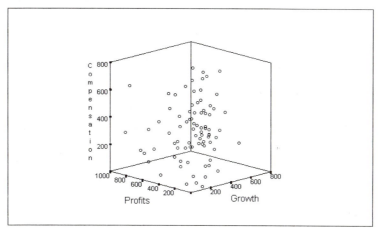

The position of each point is based on its values for all three variables. Unfortunately, since there isn't a strong relationship among the three variables, the plot is not particularly informative.

To see a more interesting three-dimensional plot, consider a hypothetical compensation strategy in which the rank of compensation is simply the average of the ranks of growth and profits. The plot of the hypothetical compensation rank is shown in Figure 23.7 for a sample including approximately a quarter of the cases. The smaller number of cases makes it easier to interpret the plot.

Figure 23.7 3-D plot with hypothetical relationship

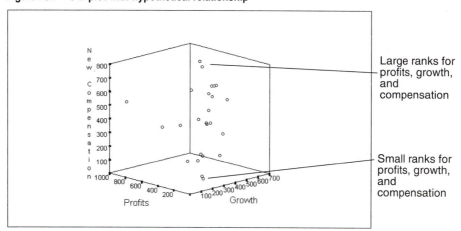

If you examine the plot carefully, you'll see the relationship between the three variables. Cases with low ranks for profits and growth have a low rank for compensation. Similarly, cases with large ranks for profits and growth have large ranks for compensation. Other cases have intermediate values.

It's easier to see the relationship between the three variables if you spin the plot until you notice a pattern. For example, if you spin Figure 23.7, you can obtain Figure 23.8. (See the *SPSS Base System User's Guide, Part 1*.)

Figure 23.8 Previous 3-D plot with spin applied

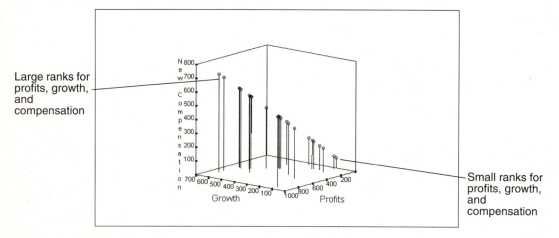

This figure has been further enhanced with **spikes** connecting each point to the floor (the bottom plane of the plot). For information on obtaining spikes, see the *SPSS Base System User's Guide, Part 1*. By looking at the base of a spike, you can see which point on the floor each plotted point is directly above. This strengthens the three-dimensional impression. From this figure, it's easy to see what the relationship is between compensation and the other two variables. Spinning a three-dimensional plot is useful for examining the relationships among the variables, as well as for identifying points which are far removed from the rest.

How to Obtain a Scatterplot

Scatterplots and histograms are graphical ways of looking at the actual values in a data set. In the examples in the remainder of this chapter, a survey of colleges will be used to illustrate most of the scatterplots and histograms you can obtain. Each record in this data set represents a different college. The data show SAT scores of admitted students, tuition, number of students, number of faculty, and other similar statistics. Examples that don't use the colleges data use the bank data.

To obtain a scatterplot, from the menus choose:

Graph
  Scatter...

This opens the Scatterplot dialog box, as shown in Figure 23.9.

Figure 23.9 Scatterplot dialog box

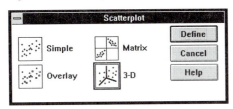

You can choose one of the following scatterplot types:

Simple. Each point represents the values of two variables for each case.

Matrix. Defines a square matrix of simple scatterplots, two for each combination of variables specified.

Overlay. Plots multiple scatterplots in the same frame.

3-D. Each point represents the value of three variables for each case. The points are plotted in a 3-D coordinate system which can be rotated.

Defining Simple Scatterplots

To obtain a simple scatterplot, select the Simple picture button in the Scatterplot dialog box and click on Define. This opens the Simple Scatterplot dialog box, as shown in Figure 23.10. The specifications are on the left and the resulting scatterplot is on the right.

Figure 23.10 Simple Scatterplot dialog box and chart

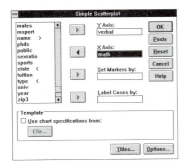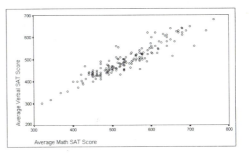

The minimum specifications are:

- An *x* axis variable.
- A *y* axis variable.

The numeric, short string, and long string variables in your data file are displayed on the source variable list. Select the numeric variables you want to define the *x* and *y* axis. To get a simple scatterplot in default format, click on OK.

Optionally, you can divide the scatterplot points into groups, label each point, use a template to control the format of the scatterplot, add a title, subtitle, or footnote, or change the missing value options.

Y Axis. Select the variable that will determine the vertical position of each point.

X Axis. Select the variable that will determine the horizontal position of each point.

Set Markers by. Select a variable to determine the categories that will be shown on the chart. Each value of the variable is a different color or marker symbol on the scatterplot.

Label Cases by. Select a variable to provide labels for each marker. The value label of each case is placed above the point on the scatterplot. If there is no value label, the actual value will be placed above the point. The value label displayed is truncated after the 20th character.

Template. You can use another file to define the format of your charts (see the *SPSS Base System User's Guide, Part 1*).

Titles. You can add titles, subtitles, and footnotes to your charts (see the *SPSS Base System User's Guide, Part 1*).

Options. You can control the display of missing values and case labels. You can exclude cases with missing values listwise or by variable. You can also display groups defined by missing values. For more details, see the *SPSS Base System User's Guide, Part 1*.

Defining Scatterplot Matrices

To obtain a scatterplot matrix, select Matrix in the Scatterplot dialog box and click on Define. This opens the Scatterplot Matrix dialog box, as shown in Figure 23.11. The specifications are on the left and the resulting scatterplot is on the right.

Figure 23.11 Scatterplot Matrix dialog box and chart

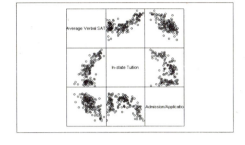

The minimum specification is two or more matrix variables.

The numeric, short string, and long string variables in your data file are displayed on the source variable list. Select two or more numeric variables to define the cells of the matrix. To get a scatterplot matrix in the default format, click on **OK**.

Optionally, you can show different markers for different categories, use a template to control the format of the scatterplot, or add a title, subtitle, or footnote.

Matrix Variables. Select two or more variables to define the cells of the matrix. There is one row and one column for each variable. Each cell contains a simple scatterplot of the row variable and the column variable.

Set Markers by. Select a variable to determine the categories that will be shown on the chart. Each value of the variable is a different marker symbol on the scatterplot matrix.

Label Cases by. Select a variable to provide labels for each marker. The value label of each case is placed above the point on the scatterplot. If there is no value label, the actual value will be placed above the point. The value label displayed is truncated after the 20th character.

Template. You can use another file to define the format of your charts (see the *SPSS Base System User's Guide, Part 1*).

Titles. You can add titles, subtitles, and footnotes to your charts (see the *SPSS Base System User's Guide, Part 1*).

Options. You can control the display of missing values and case labels. You can exclude cases with missing values listwise or by variable. You can also display groups defined by missing values. For more details, see the *SPSS Base System User's Guide, Part 1*.

Defining Overlay Scatterplots

To obtain an overlay scatterplot, select **Overlay** in the Scatterplot dialog box and click on **Define**. This opens the Overlay Scatterplot dialog box, as shown in Figure 23.12. The specifications are on the left and the resulting overlay scatterplot is on the right.

Figure 23.12 Overlay Scatterplot dialog box and chart

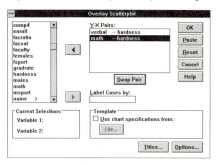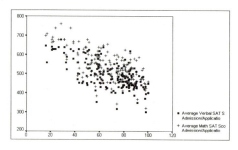

The minimum specification is two or more *y-x* pairs.

The numeric, short string, and long string variables in your data file are displayed on the source variable list. Select two or more numeric *y-x* variable pairs. To get an overlay scatterplot in default format, click on **OK**.

Optionally, you can label the scatterplot points, use a template to control the format of the scatterplot, or add a title, subtitle, or footnote.

Y-X Pairs. Select two or more variable pairs. Each pair of variables is plotted on the same scatterplot with a separate marker symbol. To select a variable pair, highlight two variables on the source variable list by clicking on each one. The selected variables are indicated on the Current Selections list. Click on the ▶ pushbutton. This copies the variables from the Current Selection list to the *y-x* pairs list. The same variable may be selected in multiple variable pairs. To swap the *y* and *x* variables in a *y-x* pair, highlight the pair and click on **Swap Pair**.

Macintosh: Use ⌘-click to select pairs of variables.

Label Cases by. Select a variable to provide labels for each marker. The value label of each case is placed beside the point on the scatterplot. If there is no value label, the actual value will be placed beside the point. The value label displayed is truncated after the 20th character.

Template. You can use another file to define the format of your charts (see the *SPSS Base System User's Guide, Part 1*).

Titles. You can add titles, subtitles, and footnotes to your charts (see the *SPSS Base System User's Guide, Part 1*).

Options. You can exclude cases with missing values listwise or by variable. You can also display groups defined by missing values. For more details, see the *SPSS Base System User's Guide, Part 1*.

Defining 3-D Scatterplots

To obtain a 3-D scatterplot, select **3-D** in the Scatterplot dialog box and click on **Define**. This opens the 3-D Scatterplot dialog box, as shown in Figure 23.13. The specifications are on the left and the resulting 3-D scatterplot is on the right.

Figure 23.13   3-D Scatterplot dialog box and chart

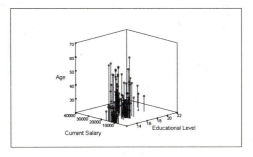

The minimum specifications are:

- A *y* axis variable.
- An *x* axis variable.
- A *z* axis variable.

The numeric, short string, and long string variables in your data file are displayed on the source variable list. Select the numeric variables you want to define the *z*, *y*, and *x* axes. To get a 3-D scatterplot in default format, click on **OK**.

Optionally, you can show different markers for different categories, label each point, use a template to control the format of the scatterplot, and add a title, subtitle, and footnote.

Y Axis. Select the variable that will determine the height of each point.

X Axis. Select the variable that will determine the horizontal position of each point.

Z Axis. Select the variable that will determine the depth of each point.

Set Markers by. Select a variable to determine the categories that will be shown on the chart. Each value of the variable is a different marker symbol on the scatterplot.

Label Cases by. Select a variable to provide labels for each marker. The value label of each case is placed beside the point on the scatterplot. If there is no value label, the actual value will be placed beside the point. The value label displayed is truncated after the 20th character.

Template. You can use another file to define the format of your charts (see the *SPSS Base System User's Guide, Part 1*).

Titles. You can add titles, subtitles, and footnotes to your charts (see the *SPSS Base System User's Guide, Part 1*).

Options. You can control the display of missing values and case labels. You can exclude cases with missing values listwise or by variable. You can also display groups defined by missing values. For more details, see the *SPSS Base System User's Guide, Part 1*.

Displaying Case Labels in Scatterplots

If you have selected a case label variable for your scatterplot, you can display the case labels in several ways:

- To automatically display all case labels when you create the chart: Select **Display chart with case labels** in the Options dialog box (accessed from the main dialog box for the selected scatterplot chart type).
- To turn the display of case labels on and off in a scatterplot: Use the Options dialog box for the scatterplot in the active chart window (Options on the Chart menu).
- To display case labels for selected points in the scatterplot: Use the point selection tool on the toolbar for the scatterplot in the active chart window.

For more information on displaying case labels in scatterplots, see the *SPSS Base System User's Guide, Part 1*.

How to Obtain a Histogram

For a discussion of how to interpret histograms, see Chapter 3. To obtain a histogram, from the menus choose:

Graphs
  Histogram...

This opens the Histogram dialog box, as shown in Figure 23.14.

Figure 23.14 Histogram dialog box and chart

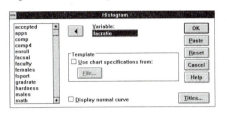 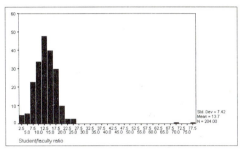

The minimum specification is a variable.

The numeric variables in your data file are displayed on the source variable list. Select the variable for which you want a histogram. To get a histogram in the default format, as shown above, click on **OK**.

Optionally, you can use a template to control the format of the histogram, add a title, subtitle, or footnote, or superimpose a normal curve on the histogram.

Variable. Select the variable for which you want a histogram. By default, you get bars showing the data divided into several evenly spaced intervals. The height of each bar shows the number of cases in each interval. The data series used to create the bar chart contains the individual values of each case. This means you can alter the intervals shown on the bar chart from the chart editor.

Template. You can use another file to define the format of your charts (see the *SPSS Base System User's Guide, Part 1*).

Display normal curve. Select this to superimpose over the histogram a normal curve with the same mean and variance as your data.

Titles. You can add titles, subtitles, and footnotes to your charts (see the *SPSS Base System User's Guide, Part 1*).

24 Pareto and Control Charts

Pareto and control charts are tools used to analyze and improve the quality of an ongoing process. Pareto charts focus attention on the most important category out of a wide variety of possibilities. Control charts help differentiate between random variations in a process and variations that are meaningful. Pareto and control charts can be used in manufacturing processes, where the things being measured are physical and are usually produced on an assembly line. Or, these charts can be used in service processes, where the things being measured, such as opinions, budgetary flows, or the effect of a medical treatment, are more abstract.

Pareto Charts

A **Pareto chart** is a bar chart, sorted in descending order; a line may be added to show the cumulative frequency across categories.

Often managers or researchers are confronted with a wide variety of categories and need a quick, visual way to gauge the relative importance of each. For example, pneumonia can be caused by a wide variety of flora. In most cases, only normal upper respiratory flora can be found with a sputum gram stain test. To see which of the remaining flora are found in the majority of pneumonia patients at a hospital, a Pareto chart can be generated. Figure 24.1 shows a simple Pareto chart based on results of a sputum gram stain test.

Figure 24.1 Simple Pareto chart

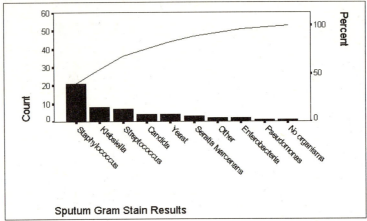

In this chart, you can quickly see that staphylococcus is found in one third of the patients with abnormal flora.

Control Charts

Any process naturally has random variations. A control chart helps differentiate between random variations and variations with an assignable cause. The kind of control chart used depends upon the data. Figure 24.2 shows an example of an X-Bar chart.

Figure 24.2 X-Bar chart

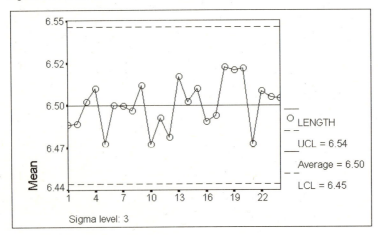

Each point on the fluctuating line represents the mean of a measured value within each subgroup. The center line is the mean of the subgroups and the dotted lines are the upper and lower control limits.

In any control chart, each **subgroup** usually represents a time interval. This can be either an abstract measurement, such as a batch number, or an actual measure of time, such as an hour or a day. The subgroups are sorted in ascending order, so hour 2 is shown to the right of hour 1, and so on. If your subgroups are time intervals, they should be recorded as numeric variables or date variables so that they will be sorted in the expected order. Usually, each subgroup contains multiple units. A **unit** is the thing being measured.

The types of control charts available are:

- **X-Bar and s.** Shows the mean of a measured value within each subgroup in the X-Bar chart and the standard deviation of the value within each subgroup in the s chart. Use this rather than the X-Bar and R charts when the number of values in each subgroup is large (more than 10).
- **X-Bar and R.** Shows the mean of a measured value within each subgroup in the X-Bar chart and the range of values within each subgroup.
- **Individuals and moving range.** Shows each measured value in the individuals chart. The individual values appear in the chart in the same order as the data. The moving range chart shows the range of values within the selected span. That is, if the span is 3, the moving range shows the range of values between the current case, the previous case, and the case before that.
- **p.** Shows the number of nonconforming units as a fraction of the total number of units in each subgroup. Use this rather than an np chart when the number of units varies between subgroups.
- **np.** Shows the number of nonconforming units in each subgroup.
- **u.** Shows the number of nonconformities as a fraction of the total number of units in each subgroup. Use this rather than a p chart when each unit can have multiple nonconformities.
- **c.** Shows the number of nonconformities in each subgroup. Use this rather than an np chart when each unit can have multiple nonconformities.

Table 24.1 shows which chart types to use depending upon the type of data available.

Table 24.1 Choosing the appropriate control chart

The data contain variable measured values, such as length, tensile strength, or age.	The number of units per subgroup is large (greater than 10).		X-Bar and s
	The number of units per subgroup is small.		X-Bar and R
	There is one unit per subgroup.		individual and moving range
The data contain attributes such as the number of nonconformities or the number of nonconforming units.	The data contain the number of nonconforming units.	The number of units per subgroup is constant.	p or np
		The number of units per subgroup varies.	p
	The data contain the number of nonconformities, and each unit can have multiple nonconformities.	The number of units per subgroup is constant.	c or u
		The number of units per subgroup varies.	u

Using the Same Data in Pareto and Control Charts

Pareto charts, p, np, c, and u charts all show attribute data. However, data structured for display in a Pareto chart often need to be modified before they can be displayed in a control chart. Figure 24.3 shows a Pareto chart of types of defects found on circuit boards.

Figure 24.3 Defects on circuit boards

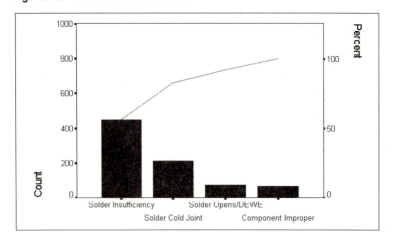

Each record in the data shows defects for a batch of 500 parts. Each type of defect is recorded as a separate variable that counts the number of boards with that type of defect. The variables are: *cmpimp*, which counts the number of boards with improper components, *sldropen*, which counts the number of boards with open solder joints, *sldrcold*, which counts the number of boards with cold solder joints, and *sldrins*, which counts the number of boards with insufficient solder.

To generate a p chart from this data, a new variable showing the total number of defective parts needs to be computed. To open the Compute Variable dialog box, select **Compute** on the **Transform** menu. For Target Variable, enter the name of the new variable—in this case, *totdef*. For Numeric Expression, enter the names of the existing defect variables separated by plus signs. For the circuit board defects, you would enter

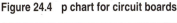

When you click on **OK**, the new variable, *cmpimp*, is generated. Figure 24.4 shows a p chart of defective circuit boards.

Figure 24.4 p chart for circuit boards

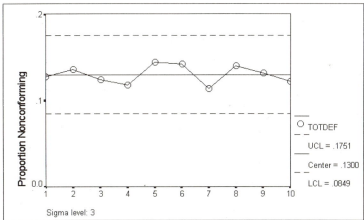

How to Obtain a Pareto Chart

To obtain a Pareto chart, from the menus choose:

Graphs
  Pareto...

This opens the Pareto Charts dialog box, as shown in Figure 24.5.

Figure 24.5 Pareto Charts dialog box

From the Pareto Charts dialog box, choose one of the chart types, and then select the choice that describes the structure of your data organization.

Data in Chart Are. Select the choice that describes the organization of your data.

- **Counts or sums for groups of cases.** One variable is counted or summed in subgroups. The subgroups are determined by one variable for simple Pareto charts or two variables for stacked Pareto charts.
- **Sums of separate variables.** More than one variable is summed. Simple Pareto charts sum each variable over all cases in the file. Stacked Pareto charts sum each variable within categories determined by another variable.
- **Values of individual cases.** Each case in the data is a separate category in the chart.

Examples of these choices, along with data structures and the charts they produce, are shown in Table 24.2.

Table 24.2 Types of Pareto charts

Selections	Data	Chart
Simple ○ Counts or sums for groups of cases With counts selected in the chart definition dialog box		sputres
1	Staphylococcus
2	Staphylococcus
3	Normal up Resp Flora
4	Normal up Resp Flora
5	Staphylococcus		*Pareto chart of Sputum Gram Stain Results*
	Each case shows the sputum gram stain results for a different patient. The results indicate the type of flora present. The chart shows a bar for each type of flora. The bars are sorted in descending order, so the one on the left is highest. A line shows the cumulative sum across types of flora.	
Simple ○ Counts or sums for groups of cases With sums selected in the chart definition dialog box		totalchg	sputres
1	$2,973	Staphyloc
2	$1,925	Staphyloc
3	$4,081	Normal u
4	$7,823	Normal u		*Pareto chart of Sputum Gram Stain Results (Charges in Millions)*
	Each case shows the sputum gram stain results for a different patient and the cost of treatment. The results indicate the type of flora present. The chart shows a bar for each type of flora. The bars are sorted in descending order, so the one on the left is highest. A line shows the cumulative sum across types of flora.	
Stacked ○ Counts or sums for groups of cases With counts selected in the chart definition dialog box		severity	sputres
1	No sig findings	Staphyloco
2	No sig findings	Staphyloco
3	Minimal findings	Normal up
4	Minimal findings	Normal up
5	Minimal findings	Staphyloco		*Stacked Pareto chart of Sputum Gram Stain Results by Severity of Illness (No sig findings, Critical, Minimal findings, Acute and severe, Acute or severe)*
	Each case shows the severity and the sputum gram stain results for a different patient. The chart shows a bar for each type of flora. Each bar is broken down into segments by the severity of the illness.	

Table 24.2 Types of Pareto charts (Continued)

Selections	Data	Chart
Stacked ○ Counts or sums for groups of cases With sums selected in the chart definition dialog box	asg / totalchg / sputres 1 No sig findi $2,973 Staphy 2 No sig findi $1,925 Staphy 3 Minimal fin $4,081 Normal 4 Minimal fin $7,823 Normal 5 Minimal fin $7,454 Staphy	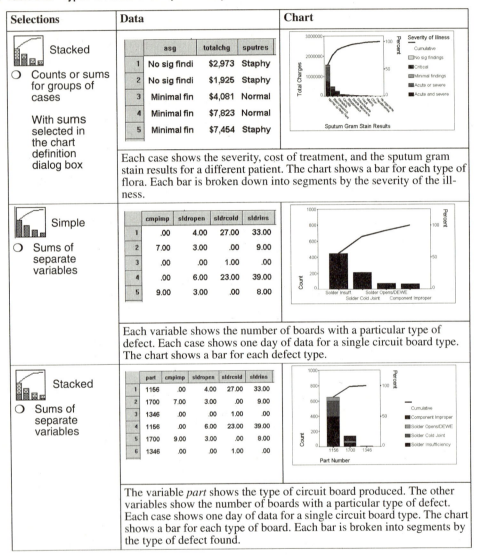
	Each case shows the severity, cost of treatment, and the sputum gram stain results for a different patient. The chart shows a bar for each type of flora. Each bar is broken down into segments by the severity of the illness.	
Simple ○ Sums of separate variables	cmpimp / sldropen / sldrcold / sldrins 1 .00 4.00 27.00 33.00 2 7.00 3.00 .00 9.00 3 .00 .00 1.00 .00 4 .00 6.00 23.00 39.00 5 9.00 3.00 .00 8.00	
	Each variable shows the number of boards with a particular type of defect. Each case shows one day of data for a single circuit board type. The chart shows a bar for each defect type.	
Stacked ○ Sums of separate variables	part / cmpimp / sldropen / sldrcold / sldrins 1 1156 .00 4.00 27.00 33.00 2 1700 7.00 3.00 .00 9.00 3 1346 .00 .00 1.00 .00 4 1156 .00 6.00 23.00 39.00 5 1700 9.00 3.00 .00 8.00 6 1346 .00 .00 1.00 .00	
	The variable *part* shows the type of circuit board produced. The other variables show the number of boards with a particular type of defect. Each case shows one day of data for a single circuit board type. The chart shows a bar for each type of board. Each bar is broken into segments by the type of defect found.	

Table 24.2 Types of Pareto charts (Continued)

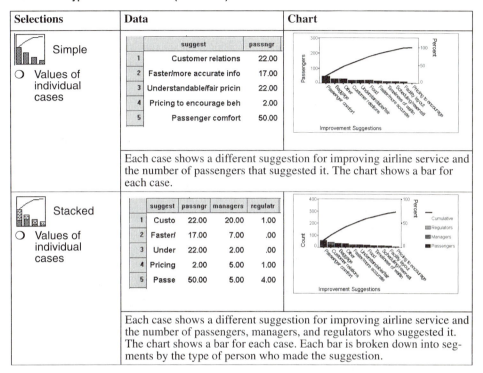

Selections	Data	Chart
Simple — Values of individual cases	suggest / passngr: 1 Customer relations 22.00; 2 Faster/more accurate info 17.00; 3 Understandable/fair pricin 22.00; 4 Pricing to encourage beh 2.00; 5 Passenger comfort 50.00	(chart)
	Each case shows a different suggestion for improving airline service and the number of passengers that suggested it. The chart shows a bar for each case.	
Stacked — Values of individual cases	suggest / passngr / managers / regulatr: 1 Custo 22.00 20.00 1.00; 2 Faster/ 17.00 7.00 .00; 3 Under 22.00 2.00 .00; 4 Pricing 2.00 5.00 1.00; 5 Passe 50.00 5.00 4.00	(chart)
	Each case shows a different suggestion for improving airline service and the number of passengers, managers, and regulators who suggested it. The chart shows a bar for each case. Each bar is broken down into segments by the type of person who made the suggestion.	

Each combination of chart type and data organization structure produces a different definition box. Each is discussed briefly below. The icon and section title indicate the choices that have to be made in the chart dialog box to open that chart definition dialog box. The discussion for each chart type always describes the selections required to enable the OK pushbutton. Optional selections are discussed only with the first chart using each data structure.

**Simple:
Counts or sums for groups of cases**

Figure 24.6 shows a chart definition dialog box and the resulting simple Pareto chart with counts for groups of cases.

Figure 24.6 Simple Pareto chart with counts for groups of cases

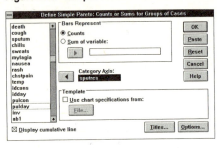 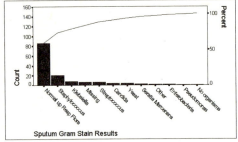

The minimum specification is a category axis variable.

The numeric, short string, and long string variables in your data file are displayed on the source variable list. Select a variable to define the category axis. To get a simple chart showing number of cases for groups of cases in default format, click on **OK**.

Optionally, you can select sums of a variable rather than counts, use a template to control the format of the chart, turn off the cumulative line, or add a title, subtitle, or footnote. Templates, titles, subtitles, and footnotes are discussed in detail in the *SPSS Base System User's Guide, Part 1*.

Bars Represent. Determines what the scale axis of the Pareto chart represents. Choose one of the following:

○ **Counts.** The number of cases in each category determines the height of each bar.

○ **Sum of variable.** The height of each bar is calculated from the sum of the specified variable. If you select Sum of variable, you must specify a numeric variable to be summed. Figure 24.7 shows the chart definition dialog box with a variable to be summed and the resulting simple Pareto chart.

Category Axis. Select a variable to define the categories shown in the chart. There is one bar for each value of the variable. The bars are sorted in descending order.

Display cumulative line. By default, a line will be drawn in the Pareto chart. This line indicates the cumulative sum of the values shown by the bars. Deselect this option to get a Pareto chart without the line.

Figure 24.7 Simple Pareto chart with sums of a variable

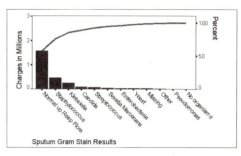

 **Stacked:
Counts or sums for groups of cases**

Figure 24.8 shows a chart definition dialog box and the resulting clustered bar chart with summaries for groups of cases.

Figure 24.8 Stacked Pareto chart with counts for groups of cases

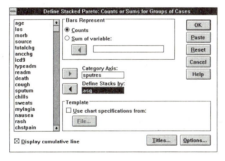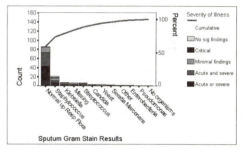

The minimum specifications are:
- A category axis variable.
- A variable that defines segments in each bar.

Category Axis. Select a variable to define the categories shown in the chart. There is one stack of bars for each value of the variable.

Define Stacks by. Select a variable to define the bar segments within each stack. There is one bar segment within each stack for each value of the variable.

Simple:
Sums of separate variables

Figure 24.9 shows a chart definition dialog box and the resulting simple bar chart with sums of separate variables.

Figure 24.9 Simple Pareto chart with sums of separate variables

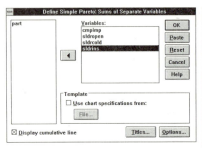
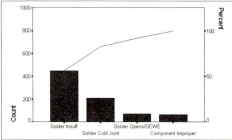

The minimum specification is two or more variables.

The numeric variables in your data file are displayed on the source variable list. Select the variables you want to define the bars. To get a simple Pareto chart showing the sum of each variable in default format, click on **OK**.

Optionally, use a template to control the format of the chart, or add a title, subtitle, or footnote. These options are discussed in detail in the *SPSS Base System User's Guide, Part 1*.

Variables. Select two or more variables to define the categories shown in the chart. There is one bar for each variable. The bars show the sum of each variable and are sorted in descending order.

Stacked:
Sums of separate variables

Figure 24.10 shows a chart definition dialog box and the resulting stacked Pareto chart with sums of separate variables.

Figure 24.10 Stacked Pareto chart with summaries of separate variables

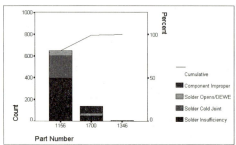

The minimum specifications are:

- Two or more numeric variables which define the segments within each bar.
- A category axis variable.

Variables. Select two or more variables. There is one bar within each stack for each variable. The bars show the sum of the selected variables.

Category Axis. Select a variable to define the categories shown in the chart. There is one stack of bars for each value of the variable.

Simple:
Values of individual cases

Figure 24.11 shows a chart definition dialog box and the resulting simple Pareto chart with values of individual cases.

Figure 24.11 Simple Pareto chart with values of individual cases

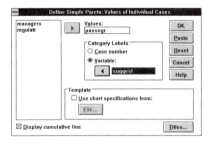
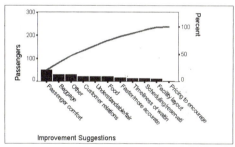

The minimum specifications are:

- A numeric values variable.
- If **Variable** is selected for **Category Labels**, a category label variable.

The numeric, short string, and long string variables in your data file are displayed on the source variable list. Select the numeric variable you want to define the bars. To get a simple Pareto chart showing the value of each case in default format, click on **OK**.

Optionally, you can change the value labels shown in the chart, use a template to control the format of the chart, disable the cumulative line, or add a title, subtitle, or footnote. Templates, titles, subtitles, and footnotes are discussed in detail in the *SPSS Base System User's Guide, Part 1*.

Values. Select a numeric variable to define the bars. Each case will be displayed as a separate bar.

Category Labels. Determines how the bars are labeled. You can choose one of the following category label sources:

❍ **Case number.** Each category is labeled with the case number.

❍ **Variable.** Each category is labeled with the current value of the selected variable.

**Stacked:
Values of individual cases**

Figure 24.12 shows a chart definition dialog box and the resulting stacked Pareto chart with values of individual cases.

Figure 24.12 Stacked Pareto chart with values of individual cases

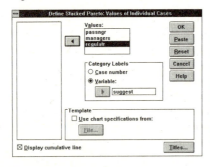
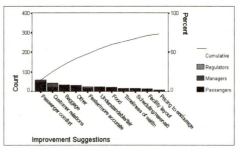

The minimum specifications are:

- Two or more numeric variables that define bar segments.
- A category label variable, if **Variable** is selected under **Category Labels**.

Values. Select two or more numeric variables. There is one bar within each stack for each variable. The bars show the value of each case. If there is a cumulative line, there is one point on the line for each case.

How to Obtain a Control Chart

To obtain a control chart, from the menus choose:

Graphs
  Control...

This opens the Control Charts dialog box, as shown in Figure 24.13.

Figure 24.13 Control Charts dialog box

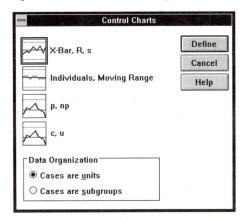

From the Control Charts dialog box, choose one of the chart types, and then select the choice that describes the structure of your data organization.

Data Organization. Select the choice that describes the organization of your data.

○ **Cases are units.** Each unit is a separate case (row of data). One variable identifies the subgroup to which the unit belongs. Another variable records the value being measured. Each point in the control chart shows a different subgroup. The number of units can vary from subgroup to subgroup.

○ **Cases are subgroups.** All units within a subgroup are recorded in a single case. Each unit is a separate variable. Like the previous organization, each point in the control chart shows a different subgroup. The number of samples per subgroup should be the same.

Examples of these choices, along with data structures and the charts they produce, are shown in Table 24.3.

Table 24.3 Types of control charts

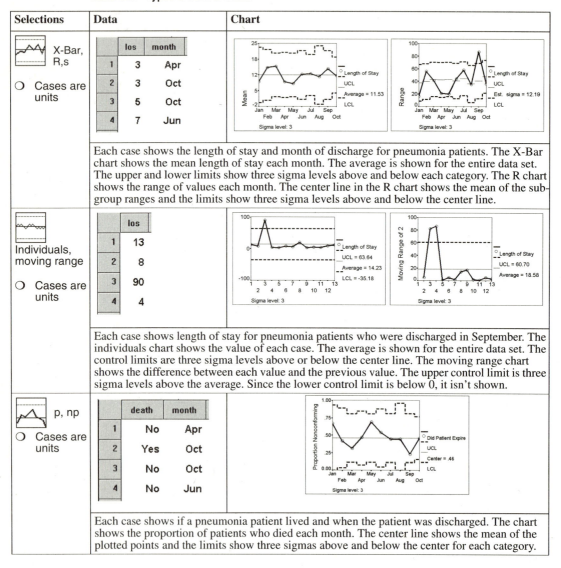

Table 24.3 Types of control charts (Continued)

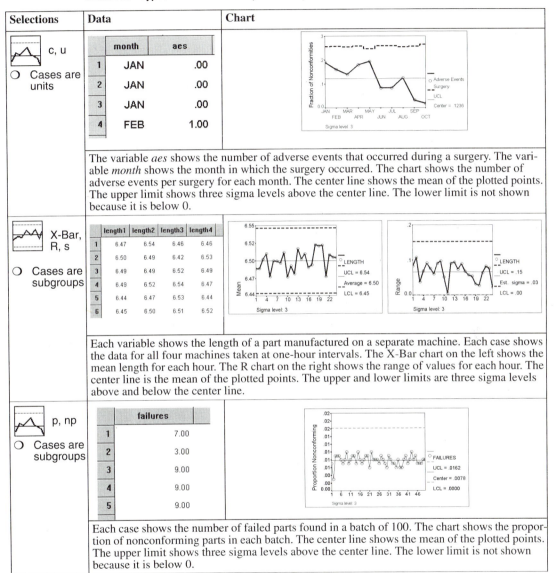

Selections	Data	Chart
c, u ○ Cases are units	month / aes 1 JAN .00 2 JAN .00 3 JAN .00 4 FEB 1.00	(Fraction of Nonconformities chart: Adverse Events, Surgery; UCL; Center = .1236; Sigma level 3)
	The variable *aes* shows the number of adverse events that occurred during a surgery. The variable *month* shows the month in which the surgery occurred. The chart shows the number of adverse events per surgery for each month. The center line shows the mean of the plotted points. The upper limit shows three sigma levels above the center line. The lower limit is not shown because it is below 0.	
X-Bar, R, s ○ Cases are subgroups	length1 length2 length3 length4 1 6.47 6.54 6.46 6.46 2 6.50 6.49 6.42 6.53 3 6.49 6.49 6.52 6.49 4 6.49 6.52 6.54 6.47 5 6.44 6.47 6.53 6.44 6 6.45 6.50 6.51 6.52	(Mean chart: LENGTH; UCL = 6.54; Average = 6.50; LCL = 6.45; Sigma level 3) (Range chart: LENGTH; UCL = .15; Est. sigma = .03; LCL = .00; Sigma level 3)
	Each variable shows the length of a part manufactured on a separate machine. Each case shows the data for all four machines taken at one-hour intervals. The X-Bar chart on the left shows the mean length for each hour. The R chart on the right shows the range of values for each hour. The center line is the mean of the plotted points. The upper and lower limits are three sigma levels above and below the center line.	
p, np ○ Cases are subgroups	failures 1 7.00 2 3.00 3 9.00 4 9.00 5 9.00	(Proportion Nonconforming chart: FAILURES; UCL = .0162; Center = .0078; LCL = .0000; Sigma level 3)
	Each case shows the number of failed parts found in a batch of 100. The chart shows the proportion of nonconforming parts in each batch. The center line shows the mean of the plotted points. The upper limit shows three sigma levels above the center line. The lower limit is not shown because it is below 0.	

478   Chapter 24

Table 24.3 Types of control charts (Continued)

Selections	Data	Chart
c, u ○ Cases are subgroups	errors 1 9.00 2 5.00 3 14.00 4 16.00 5 15.00	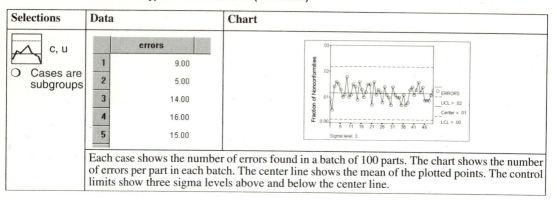
Each case shows the number of errors found in a batch of 100 parts. The chart shows the number of errors per part in each batch. The center line shows the mean of the plotted points. The control limits show three sigma levels above and below the center line.		

Each combination of chart type and data organization structure produces a different definition box. Each is discussed briefly below. The icon and section title indicate the choices that have to be made in the chart dialog box to open that chart definition dialog box.

X-Bar, R, s:
Cases are units

Figure 24.14 shows a chart definition dialog box and the resulting X-bar and R charts with cases as units. To plot this type of chart, your data file must contain one variable (column) that measures the process in question and one variable that breaks the process into subgroups. A subgroup can contain one or more rows from the data file. Each subgroup is plotted as a single point.

Figure 24.14 X-Bar and R charts with cases as units

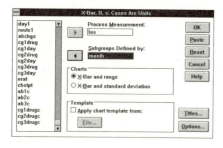
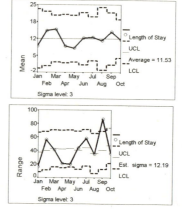

The minimum specifications are:
- A numeric process measurement variable.
- A subgroups variable.

All variables are shown on the source variable list. Select a variable that measures the process of interest and select a variable that breaks the process into subgroups. To get a chart that shows the mean value for each subgroup and a chart that shows the range within each subgroup, click on **OK**.

Optionally, you can select standard deviation rather than range, change the number of sigmas used for control limits, specify an upper or a lower limit, alter the minimum subgroup sample size, display subgroups defined by missing values, use a template to control the format of the chart, or add a title, subtitle, or footnote. Templates, titles, subtitles, and footnotes are discussed in detail in the *SPSS Base System User's Guide, Part 1*. The number of sigmas in the calculated control limits, specified control limits, minimum subgroup sample size, and missing values are described in "Control Chart Options" on p. 491.

If you don't have a subgroup variable but know that cases are sorted by subgroup within the file, it is easy to compute a subgroup variable. For Target Variable in the Compute Variable dialog box (select **Compute** on the Transform menu), type the name of your new subgroup variable. For the Numeric Expression, enter

```
trunc(($CASENUM-1)/n)+1
```

where *n* is the number of cases in each subgroup.

Process Measurement. Select a numeric variable that measures the process of interest. The charts show the mean and range or standard deviation of this variable within each subgroup. (See Figure 24.15.)

Subgroups Defined by. Select a variable that divides the process into subgroups. There is one point on the process line for each value of this variable. Usually the variable represents a unit of time.

Charts. Two charts are produced. The first is an X-Bar chart. The second can be either a range chart (an R chart) or a standard deviation chart (an s chart).

An X-Bar chart shows the mean of the process for each subgroup. The center line is the mean of the process over the entire data set and the control limits are a number of standard deviations above and below the center line for each category. The number of standard deviations is shown as the sigma level.

○ **X-Bar and range.** A range chart shows the range of the process within each subgroup. The center line shows the mean of the subgroup ranges (which is different for subgroups of different size). The upper and lower limits show three sigma levels above and below the center line for each category.

○ **X-Bar and standard deviation.** A standard deviation chart shows the standard deviation of the process within each subgroup. The center line shows the mean of the subgroup standard deviations. The upper and lower limits show three sigma levels above and below the center line for each category.

Figure 24.15 X-Bar and s charts with cases as units

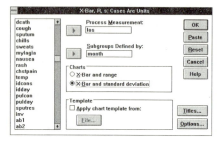
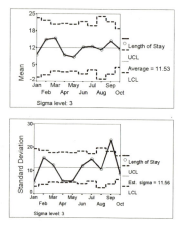

 Individuals, moving range: Cases are units

Figure 24.16 shows a chart definition dialog box and the resulting control charts for individuals with cases as units. To plot this type of chart, your data file must contain a variable (column) that measures the process in question; each row in the data file is plotted as a single point.

Figure 24.16 Control charts for individuals with cases as units

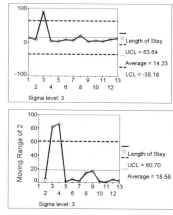

The minimum specification is a numeric process measurement variable.

All variables are shown on the source variable list. Select a numeric variable that measures the process of interest. To obtain control charts that show the value of each case and the moving range in default format, click on **OK**.

Optionally, you can select a subgroup label variable, suppress the moving range chart, select a different span, change the number of sigmas used for control limits, specify an upper or a lower limit, use a template to control the format of the chart, or add a title, subtitle, or footnote. Templates, titles, subtitles, and footnotes are discussed in detail in the *SPSS Base System User's Guide, Part 1*. The number of sigmas in the calculated control limits and specified control limits are described in "Control Chart Options" on p. 491.

Process Measurement. Select a numeric variable that measures the process of interest. The charts show the value of the variable for each case and the moving range.

Subgroups Labeled by. When a subgroup label variable is used, each category is labeled with the current value label of the selected variable. Figure 24.17 shows a control chart for individuals with a subgroup labels variable.

Figure 24.17 Control chart for individuals with category labels from variable

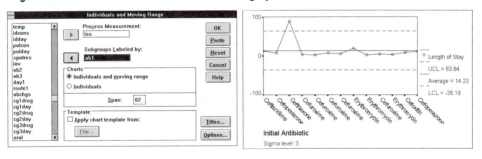

Charts. Determines the types of charts generated. You can choose from the following options:

○ **Individuals and moving range.** Both an individuals and a moving range chart are generated.

○ **Individuals.** Only an individuals chart is generated.

Span. Indicate the number of cases used for calculating the control limits in both charts and for calculating the moving range. For example, if the span is 3, the current case and the previous two cases are used in the calculations.

p, np: Cases are units

Figure 24.18 shows a chart definition dialog box and the resulting p chart with cases as units. To plot this type of chart, your data file must contain a variable (column) that indicates the presence of a nonconforming characteristic and a variable that divides the data into subgroups. A subgroup can contain one or more rows from the data file. Each subgroup is plotted as a single point.

Figure 24.18 p chart with cases as units

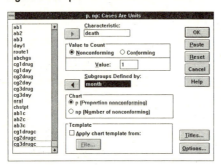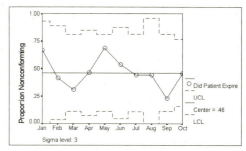

The minimum specifications are:

- A characteristic variable.
- A subgroup variable.

All variables are shown on the source variable list. Select a variable that indicates the presence of the characteristic of interest and a variable that divides the data into subgroups. Then, enter the value to count. To obtain a control chart that shows the proportion of nonconforming cases in default format, click on **OK**.

Optionally, you can change the value to be counted, get an np chart rather than a p chart, change the number of sigmas used for control limits, display subgroups defined by missing values, use a template to control the format of the chart, or add a title, subtitle, or footnote. Templates, titles, subtitles, and footnotes are discussed in detail in the *SPSS Base System User's Guide, Part 1*. The number of sigmas in the calculated control limits and missing values are described in "Control Chart Options" on p. 491.

Characteristic. Select a variable that indicates the presence of the characteristic to be measured.

Value to Count. Either nonconforming or conforming cases can be counted. In both instances, the chart shows the proportion or number of nonconforming cases.

○ **Nonconforming.** The indicated value is a nonconforming value. The chart shows the proportion or number of cases with this value.

○ **Conforming.** The indicated value is a conforming value. The chart shows the proportion or number of cases that do not have this value.

Value. Indicate the value to be counted. The value must be of the same type as the characteristic variable. (For example, if the characteristic variable is numeric, the value must be a number.)

Subgroups Defined by. Select a variable that divides the process into subgroups. There is one point on the process line for each value of this variable. Usually the variable represents a unit of time.

Chart. Determines the type of chart generated. You can choose one of the following chart types:

○ **p (Proportion nonconforming).** The chart shows the proportion of nonconformities within each subgroup. Use this chart type if the number of cases varies between subgroups.

○ **np (Number of nonconforming).** The chart show the number of nonconformities within each subgroup. Use this chart type if all subgroups have the same number of cases. Figure 24.19 shows a chart definition dialog box and the resulting np chart.

Figure 24.19 np chart with cases as units

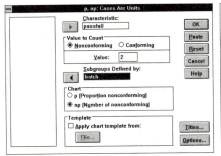
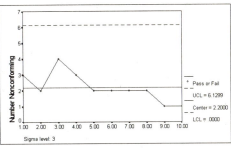

c, u:
Cases are units

Figure 24.20 shows a chart definition dialog box and the resulting u chart with cases as units. To plot this type of chart, your data file must contain one variable (column) that counts the number of nonconformities and one variable that divides the data into subgroups. A subgroup can contain one or more rows from the data file. Each subgroup is plotted as a single point.

Figure 24.20 u chart with cases as units

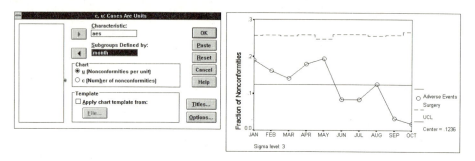

The minimum specifications are:

- A numeric characteristic variable.
- A subgroups variable.

All variables are shown on the source variable list. Select a numeric variable that counts the characteristic of interest and select a variable that divides the data into subgroups. To get a control chart that shows the number of nonconformities per unit for each subgroup in default format, click on OK.

Optionally, you can get a c chart rather than a u chart, change the number of sigmas used for control limits, display subgroups defined by missing values, use a template to control the format of the chart, or add a title, subtitle, or footnote. Templates, titles, subtitles, and footnotes are discussed in detail in the *SPSS Base System User's Guide, Part 1*. The number of sigmas in the calculated control limits and missing values are described in "Control Chart Options" on p. 491.

Characteristic. Select a numeric variable that indicates the number of times the characteristic to be measured is found.

Subgroups Defined by. Select a variable that divides the process into subgroups. There is one point on the process line for each value of this variable. Usually the variable represents a unit of time.

Chart. Determines the type of chart generated. You can choose one of the following chart types:

- **u (Nonconformities per unit).** The chart shows the proportion of nonconformities per case within each subgroup. Use this chart type if each subgroup does not have the same number of items.

- **c (Number of nonconformities).** The chart shows the total number of nonconformities per subgroup. Use this chart type if each subgroup has the same number of items. Figure 24.21 shows a chart definition dialog box and the resulting c chart.

Figure 24.21 c chart with cases as units

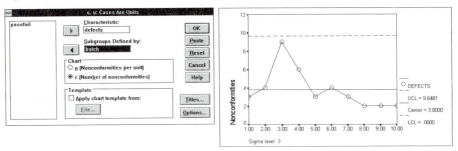

 **X-Bar, R, s:
Cases are subgroups**

Figure 24.22 shows a chart definition dialog box and the resulting X-bar and R charts with cases as subgroups. To plot this type of chart, your data file must contain two or more variables (columns) that measure the process in question; each row in the data file is plotted as a single point.

Figure 24.22 X-Bar and R charts with cases as subgroups

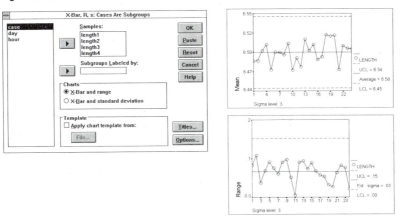

The minimum specification is two or more numeric sample variables.

All variables are shown on the source variable list. Select two or more numeric sample variables. To get a chart that shows the mean value for each subgroup and a chart that shows the range within each subgroup, click on OK.

Optionally, you can show standard deviation rather than the range, specify a variable to be used for subgroup labels, change the number of sigmas used for control limits, specify an upper or a lower limit, alter the minimum subgroup sample size, display subgroups defined by missing values, use a template to control the format of the chart, or add a title, subtitle, or footnote. Templates, titles, subtitles, and footnotes are discussed in detail in the *SPSS Base System User's Guide, Part 1*. The number of sigmas in the calculated control limits, specified control limits, minimum subgroup sample size, and missing values are described in "Control Chart Options" on p. 491.

Samples. Select two or more numeric variables. A single value from each selected variable is incorporated into each point. The charts show the mean and range or standard deviation for each row of data.

Subgroups Labeled by. Select a variable to use for labels. Each subgroup is labeled with the value label from the selected variable. If there is no value label, the actual value is used. Figure 24.23 shows an X-Bar chart using the variable *day* for labels.

Figure 24.23 X-Bar chart using variable day for labels

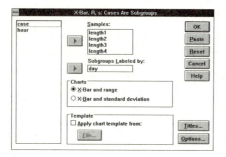
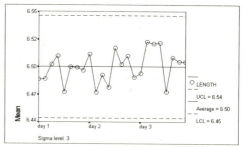

Charts. Two charts are produced. The first is an X-Bar chart. The second can be either a range chart (an R chart) or a standard deviation chart (an s chart).

An X-Bar chart shows the mean of the process for each subgroup. A subgroup contains all the values of the sample variables from a single row of data. The center line is the mean of the process and the control limits are a number of standard deviations above and below the center line for each category. The number of standard deviations is shown as the sigma level.

○ **X-Bar and range.** A range chart shows the range of the process within each subgroup. The center line shows the mean of the subgroup ranges. The upper and lower limits show three sigma levels above and below the center line for each category.

○ **X-Bar and standard deviation.** A standard deviation chart shows the standard deviation of the process for each subgroup. The center line shows the mean of the subgroup standard deviations. The upper and lower limits show three sigma levels above and below the center line for each category. Figure 24.24 shows X-Bar and s charts with cases as subgroups.

Figure 24.24 **X-Bar and s charts with cases as subgroups**

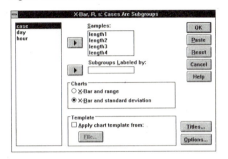
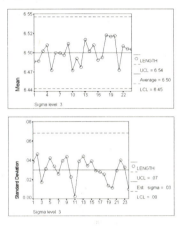

**p, np:
Cases are subgroups**

Figure 24.25 shows a chart definition dialog box and the resulting p chart with cases as subgroups. To plot this type of chart, your data file must contain a variable (column) that counts the number of nonconformities; each row in the data file is plotted as a single point.

Figure 24.25 **p chart with cases as subgroups**

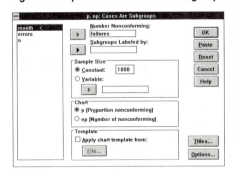
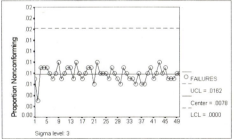

The minimum specifications are:
- A numeric variable containing the number of nonconforming cases.
- A constant or variable defining the sample size.

All variables in your data file are displayed on the source variable list. Select a numeric variable that indicates the number of nonconforming cases in each sample and enter the sample size. To see a control chart that shows the proportion of nonconforming cases in default format, click on **OK**.

Optionally, you can specify a variable sample size, specify the name of a variable to be used for labels, generate an np chart rather than a p chart, change the number of sigmas used for control limits, display subgroups defined by missing values, use a template to control the format of the chart, or add a title, subtitle, or footnote. Templates, titles, subtitles, and footnotes are discussed in detail in the *SPSS Base System User's Guide, Part 1*. The number of sigmas in the calculated control limits and missing values are described in "Control Chart Options" on p. 491.

Number Nonconforming. Select a numeric variable indicating the number of nonconforming units in each sample. The chart shows the number or proportion of nonconforming units for each sample.

Subgroups Labeled by. Select a variable to use for labels. Each subgroup is labeled with the value label from the selected variable (if the variable has not been labeled, the value of the variable will be displayed). Figure 24.26 shows a p chart using the variable *month* for labels.

Figure 24.26 p chart using variable month for labels and sample size

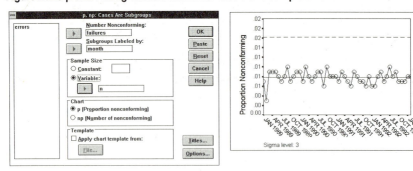

Sample Size. The number of units per sample can be constant or variable.
○ **Constant.** Enter the number of units per sample.
○ **Variable.** Select a variable that indicates the number of units in each sample.

Chart. Determines the type of chart generated. You can choose one of the following chart types:

○ **p (Proportion nonconforming).** The chart shows the proportion of nonconformities out of the total sample. Use this chart type if the sample size varies between cases.

○ **np (Number of nonconforming).** The chart shows the total number of nonconformities for each subgroup. Use this chart type if the sample size is constant. Figure 24.27 shows a chart definition dialog box and the resulting np chart.

Figure 24.27 np chart with cases as subgroups

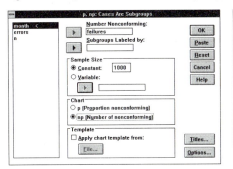
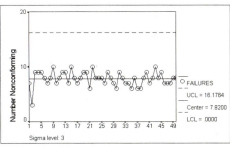

c, u: Cases are subgroups

Figure 24.28 shows a chart definition dialog box and the resulting u chart with cases as subgroups. To plot this type of chart, your data file must contain a variable (column) that counts the number of nonconformities; each row in the data file is plotted as a single point.

Figure 24.28 u chart with cases as subgroups

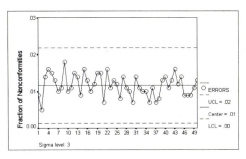

The minimum specifications are:
- A numeric variable specifying the number of nonconformities.
- A constant value or variable defining the sample size.

All variables in the working data file are displayed on the source variable list. Select a numeric variable that specifies the number of nonconformities for each case and enter the sample size. To generate a control chart that shows the number of nonconformities per unit for each subgroup in default format, click on **OK**.

Optionally, you can specify a variable sample size, specify a variable to use for labels, generate a c chart rather than a u chart, change the number of sigmas used for control limits, display subgroups defined by missing values, use a template to control the format of the chart, or add a title, subtitle, or footnote. Templates, titles, subtitles, and footnotes are discussed in detail in the *SPSS Base System User's Guide, Part 1*. The number of sigmas in the calculated control limits and missing values are described in "Control Chart Options" on p. 491.

Number of Nonconformities. Select a variable indicating the number of nonconformities in each sample. The chart shows the number or proportion of nonconformities for each row of data.

Subgroups Labeled by. Select a variable to use for labels. Each subgroup is labeled with the value label from the selected variable. If there is no value label, the value of the variable will be displayed. Figure 24.29 shows a u chart using the variable *month* for labels.

Figure 24.29 u chart using variable month for labels and sample size

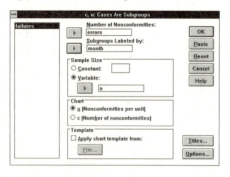
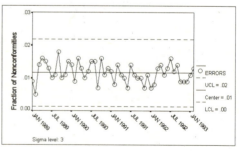

Sample Size. The number of units per sample can be constant or variable.
- **Constant.** Enter the number of units per sample.
- **Variable.** Select a variable that indicates the number of units in each sample.

Chart. Determines the type of chart generated. You can choose one of the following chart types:

- **u (Nonconformities per unit).** The chart shows the proportion of nonconformities per unit within each subgroup. Use this chart type if the sample size differs between cases.
- **c (Number of nonconformities).** The chart shows the total number of nonconformities per subgroup. Use this chart type if the sample size does not vary between cases. Figure 24.30 shows a c chart with cases as subgroups.

Figure 24.30 c chart with cases as subgroups

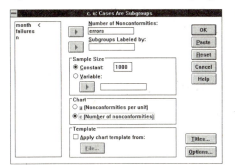
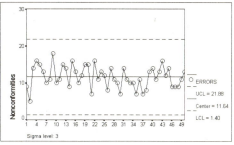

Control Chart Options

Figure 24.31 shows the Options dialog box for X-Bar, R, and s charts, which includes all of the options found in other control chart Options dialog boxes.

Figure 24.31 Options dialog box for X-Bar, R, and s charts

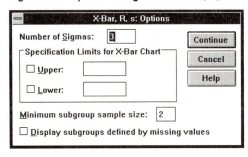

Number of Sigmas. Determines the number of standard deviations above and below the center line for the calculated upper and lower control limits.

Specification Limits for X-Bar Chart. You may specify upper and lower control limits in addition to the calculated limits for X-Bar and individuals charts. This is useful if you want to see if the process falls within predetermined tolerances.

- **Upper.** Displays the specified upper control limit.
- **Lower.** Displays the specified lower control limit.

Minimum subgroup sample size. In X-Bar, R, and s charts, you can change the minimum subgroup sample size. Subgroups with fewer units than the specified size are not shown in the chart.

- **Display subgroups defined by missing values.** In all control charts except individuals and moving range charts, you can display subgroups defined by missing values.

25 Normal Probability Plots

The normal distribution plays an important role in many statistical analyses. That's why you often want to check whether your data appear to be a sample from a normal distribution. Similarly, after you have fit a statistical model to the data, you want to examine the distribution of the residuals, or errors, to see if it is approximately normal. Both visual displays and formal statistical tests, such as the Shapiro-Wilks' test (see Chapter 5), can be used for assessing normality.

Histograms and stem-and-leaf plots are useful displays for visually assessing the distributions of data values. However, it can sometimes be difficult to mentally superimpose a normal distribution on the data values. The normal probability plot is a special type of display for checking for normality. In a normal probability plot, the data points cluster around a straight line if your sample is from a normal distribution.

Consider Figure 25.1, which shows a normal probability plot of 100 values from a normal distribution, with a mean of 0 and a variance of 1. You see that the points fall almost exactly on a straight line. In Figure 25.1, the observed values are plotted against expected values from a normal distribution. That is, each observed value is paired with an "expected" value from the normal distribution. The expected values are based on the rank of the observed value and the number of cases in the sample. Figure 25.1 is called a **Q-Q normal probability plot**.

Figure 25.1 Q-Q normal probability plot of a normally distributed variable

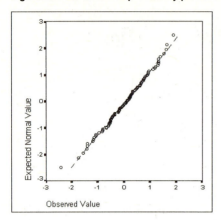

Another type of normal probability plot, the **P-P plot**, is based on the cumulative probability distributions of the observed data and the normal distribution. For a series of points, you plot the observed cumulative proportion against the cumulative proportion that would be expected if the data were a sample from a normal distribution. Again, if the sample is from a normal distribution, the points should cluster around a straight line. Figure 25.2 is the corresponding P-P plot for the data shown in Figure 25.1.

Figure 25.2 P-P normal probability plot

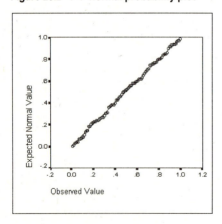

How to Obtain Normal Probability Plots

To obtain P-P or Q-Q normal probability plots and detrended normal probability plots, from the menus choose:

Graphs
  Normal P-P...

or

Graphs
  Normal Q-Q...

The Normal P-P Plots and Normal Q-Q Plots dialog boxes are identical. The Normal P-P Plots dialog box is shown in Figure 25.3.

Figure 25.3 Normal P-P Plots dialog box

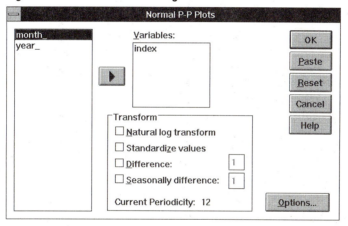

The numeric variables in the working data file are displayed on the source variable list. The minimum specification is one or more variables. A normal probability plot and a detrended normal probability chart are produced for each variable.

Transform. You can produce normal probability plots for transformed values using any combination of the following transformation options:

❏ **Natural log transform.** Transforms the variable using the natural logarithm (base e) of the variable. This is useful for removing varying amplitude over time in time series data. If a variable contains any values that are less than or equal to 0, the normal probability plot for that variable will not be produced because non-positive values cannot be log transformed.

❏ **Standardize values.** Transforms the variable into a sample with a mean of 0 and a standard deviation of 1.

❑ **Difference**. Transforms the variable by calculating the difference between successive values of the variable. Enter a positive integer to specify the degree of differencing (the number of previous values used to calculate the difference). The number of values used in the calculations decreases by 1 for each degree of differencing. Differencing a time series converts a nonstationary series to a stationary one with a constant mean and variance.

❑ **Seasonally difference**. Transforms time series data by calculating the difference between series values a constant span apart. The span is based on the currently defined periodicity. Enter a positive integer to specify the degree of differencing (the number of previous seasonal periods used to calculate the difference). To compute seasonal differences, you must have defined date variables that include a periodic component (such as months of the year).

Current Periodicity. Indicates the currently defined period used to calculate seasonal differences for time series data. If the current periodicity is **None**, seasonal differencing is not available. To create a date variable with a periodic component used to define periodicity, select the Define Dates option on the Data menu (see Chapter 1).

These transformations affect only the normal probability plot and do not alter the values of the variables. For time series data, you can create new time series variables based on transformed values of existing time series with the Create Time Series option on the Transform menu (see Chapter 1).

Options

To change the method used to calculate the expected normal distribution or control the ranking of tied values, click on Options.. in the Normal P-P Plots or Normal Q-Q Plots dialog box. The Normal P-P Plots Options dialog box is shown in Figure 25.4.

Figure 25.4   Normal P-P Plots Options dialog box

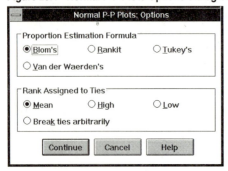

Proportion Estimation Formula. Choose one of the following alternatives:

- **Blom's.** Uses Blom's transformation, defined by the formula

  $(r - (3/8))/(n + (1/4))$

  where n is the number of observations and r is the rank, ranging from 1 to n (Blom, 1958). This is the default.

- **Rankit.** Uses the formula

  $(r - (1/2))/n$

  where n is the number of observations and r is the rank, ranging from 1 to n (Chambers et al., 1983).

- **Tukey's.** Uses Tukey's transformation, defined by the formula

  $(r - (1/3))/(n + (1/3))$

  where n is the number of observations and r is the rank, ranging from 1 to n (Tukey, 1962).

- **Van der Waerden's.** Uses Van der Waerden's transformation, defined by the formula

  $r/(n+1)$

  where n is the number of observations and r is the rank, ranging from 1 to n (Lehmann, 1975).

Rank Assigned to Ties. Choose one of the following alternatives:

- **Mean.** Cases with the same values for a variable are assigned the average (mean) of the ranks for the tied values. This is the default.
- **High.** Highest rank assigned to tied values.
- **Low.** Lowest rank assigned to tied values.
- **Break ties arbitrarily.** Multiple cases with the same value are plotted, and case weights are ignored.

If you want to create a Q-Q normal probability plot and have selected Van der Waerden's and Mean, you will create the same plots as when you select Normality plots with tests in the Explore Plots dialog box available in the Explore procedure.

26 Sequence Charts

For most of the statistical analyses described in this book, the sequence in which you obtain your data values is not important. In fact, for hypothesis tests, you assume that the observations are independent and that the order in which you observe your data values has no effect.

Data for which time, or the sequence in which the values occur, is an essential component are known as **time series** data. In a time series, the values of a variable are recorded at regular intervals over a period of time. Examples of time series are daily stock prices, the annual GNP, the quarterly unemployment rate, and monthly sales data. This chapter contains examples of how time series can be displayed using sequence charts.

Plotting Health Care Stock

As an illustration of time series data, consider Standard and Poor's Health Care Composite Index, which is based on the values of stocks of 26 businesses in the health care industry. The index is a composite measure of how well these stocks perform in the stock market and is used as an indicator of how the health care industry is performing.

Figure 26.1 is a plot of the values of the Health Care Composite Index from January, 1987, to December, 1992. The horizontal axis displays the time points—in this example, the months. The vertical axis displays the values of the index. Looking at the plot, you see that although there have been substantial fluctuations in the index during the five years, the overall impression is that the value of the index is rapidly rising. That is, there is an upward trend.

Figure 26.1 Sequence chart of Health Care Composite Index

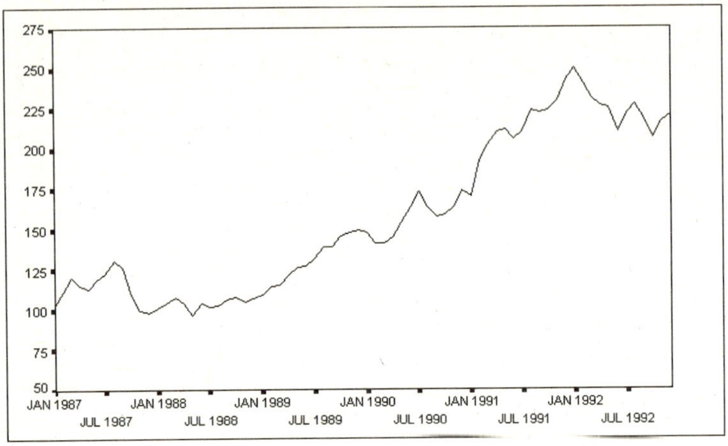

Seasonal Trends

When you examine plots of time series data, you should always check to see if there is any type of repeating, or seasonal, pattern to the values. In the health care index data there doesn't seem to be a particular month or season associated with increases or decreases. The peaks and troughs do not occur at regular intervals. However, in many types of time series data, there is a strong seasonal pattern. For example, consider the plot of college textbook sales shown in Figure 26.2.

Figure 26.2 Sequence chart of college textbook sales

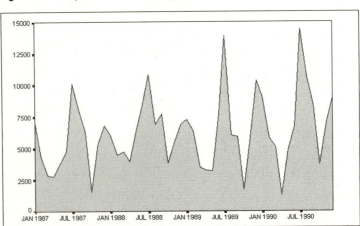

You see that there are spikes associated with certain months. The largest volume of academic book sales is in July, when bookstores place orders for the fall term. There are smaller spikes for each January, when orders for the second semester are placed. The January spike is smaller because the same books are often used throughout the year, and bookstores often have stock remaining from the first semester. When a seasonal pattern exists in time series data, as shown in Figure 26.2, the data are said to show a **seasonal trend**, or component.

Forecasting

Many decisions are dependent on predicting future values of time series data, and there are countless statistical techniques devoted to modeling time series data. If there is a strong relationship between successive values of a time series, you can use moving averages to predict the next value in a series. You can use the prior moving average function in the Create Time Series facility (see Chapter 1) to predict each time point as the average of the values of a specified number of preceding time points. Figure 26.3 is a plot of the Health Care Composite Index and predicted values based on a prior moving average of five points. From the plot, you see that, overall, the predicted values based on the moving average do reasonably well. However, whenever there is a sharp change in the series, the prediction is poor, since the only information the prediction uses are the preceding points.

Figure 26.3 Sequence chart with prior moving average prediction

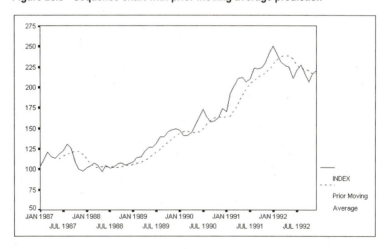

Examining the Errors

Whenever you obtain predictions, you should look at the residuals—that is, the differences between the observed and predicted values. The residuals provide you with much useful information about how well the model fits. Figure 26.4 is a plot of the residuals from the prior moving average model. You see that the errors have a definite pattern. There are clusters of positive and negative values. This is an indication that your prediction model has undesirable properties.

Figure 26.4 Residuals (errors) from prior moving average prediction

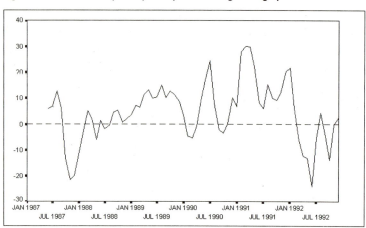

How to Obtain Sequence Charts

To obtain sequence charts, from the menus choose:

Graphs
  Sequence...

This opens the Sequence Charts dialog box, as shown in Figure 26.5.

Figure 26.5 Sequence Charts dialog box

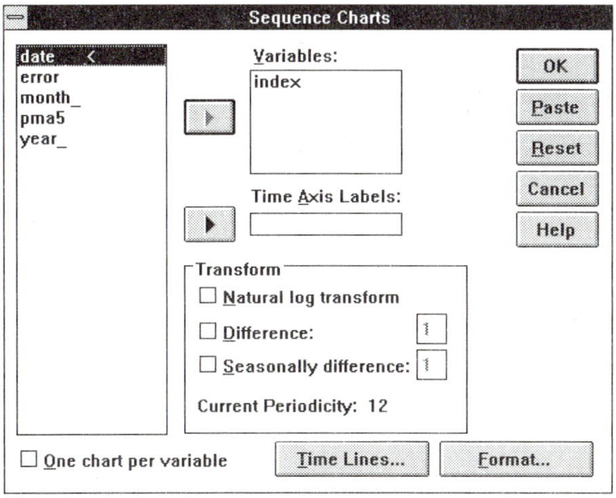

The numeric variables in the working data file are displayed on the source variable list. The minimum specification is one or more numeric sequence or time series variables. Sequence charts require a data file structure in which cases (rows) are sorted in a sequential order or represent observations at regular time intervals.

Time Axis Labels. You can use a numeric or string variable to label the time (sequence) axis of the chart. By default, the time axis is simply labeled 1 to n, or it is labeled with the values of the string variable *date_* if you have defined date variables (see Chapter 1).

Transform. You can plot transformed data values using any combination of the following transformation options:

❏ **Natural log transform.** Transforms data values using the natural logarithm (base e) of the values. This is useful for removing varying amplitude over time. If a variable contains values that are less than or equal to 0, no chart will be created for the variable because non-positive values cannot be log transformed.

❏ **Difference.** Transforms the data values by calculating the difference between successive values of the variable. Enter a positive integer to specify the degree of differencing (the number of previous values used to calculate the difference). The number of values used in the calculations decreases by one for each degree of differencing. Differencing a time series converts a nonstationary series to a stationary one with a constant mean and variance.

❑ **Seasonally difference**. Transforms the data values by calculating the difference between values a constant span apart. The span is based on the currently defined periodicity. Enter a positive integer to specify the degree of differencing (the number of previous seasonal periods used to calculate the difference). To compute seasonal differences, you must have defined date variables that include a periodic component (such as months of the year).

Current Periodicity. Indicates the currently defined period used to calculate seasonal differences. If the current periodicity is **None**, seasonal differencing is not available. To create a date variable with a periodic component used to define periodicity, use the Define Dates option on the Data menu (see Chapter 1).

These transformations affect only the plotted values in the sequence chart and do not alter the values of the actual variables. To create new time series variables based on transformed values of existing time series, use the Create Time Series option on the Transform menu (see Chapter 1).

The following option is also available:

❑ **One chart per variable**. Creates a separate sequence chart for each selected variable. By default, all selected variables are plotted in a single chart.

Time Axis Reference Lines

To display reference lines on the time (sequence) axis at each change in a reference variable or at a specific date or time, click on Time Lines... in the Sequence Charts dialog box. This opens the Time Axis Reference Lines dialog box, similar to the one shown in Figure 26.6.

Figure 26.6 Time Axis Reference Lines dialog box

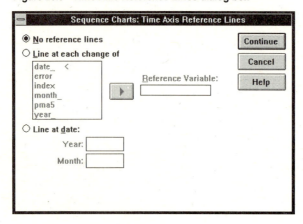

You can choose one of the following alternatives:

- **No reference lines**. This is the default.
- **Line at each change of**. Displays a reference line each time the value of the selected reference variable changes. For example, you could use the date variable *year_* to display a reference line at the beginning of each year. (Do *not* use the date variable *date_*, since that would display a reference line at each case.)
- **Line at date**. You can display a single reference line at the value of a specific date, time or observation number. The available text boxes for specifying the date and/or time are dependent on the currently defined date variables. If there are no defined date variables, you can specify an observation (case) number.

If you enter a value for a lower-order date variable, you must also enter a value for all higher-order date variables above it. For example, in Figure 26.6, you cannot specify a **Month** value without a **Year** value. If you enter a value for a higher-order date variable without entering any values for lower-order date variables, the reference line will be drawn at the first occurrence of the value.

Use the Define Dates option on the Data menu to create date variables. See Chapter 1 for more information, including valid ranges for each date variable.

Formatting Options

To change formatting options, such as switching the axis used as the time (sequence) axis or displaying area charts instead of line charts, click on Format... in the Sequence Charts dialog box. This opens the Sequence Charts Format dialog box, as shown in Figure 26.7.

Figure 26.7 Sequence Charts Format dialog box

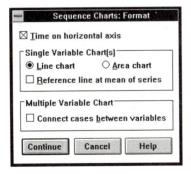

The following formatting options are available:

❏ **Time on horizontal axis**. Uses the horizontal axis as the time (sequence) axis. This is the default. Deselect this item to use the vertical axis as the time axis.

Single Variable Chart(s). If only a single variable is plotted in each chart, you can choose one of the following alternatives:

○ **Line chart**. Displays a line chart for each variable. This is the default.

○ **Area chart**. Displays an area chart for each variable, with the area between the line and the time (sequence) axis filled in with a color or pattern.

The following option is also available for single variable charts:

❏ **Reference line at mean of series**. Displays a reference line on the scale axis at the mean value of the variable.

Multiple Variable Chart. If more than one variable is plotted in a chart, the following formatting option is available:

❏ **Connect cases between variables**. Draws a line at each case between values of the plotted variables.

27 Autocorrelation and Cross-Correlation

In time series, adjacent data values are often highly correlated. **Autocorrelation** coefficients are used to examine the strength of the relationship among the values at different lags. Identifying the pattern of autocorrelation is especially important for selecting parameters for certain types of statistical models used for time series and for evaluating the residuals from a model. In this chapter, you'll see examples of how autocorrelation, partial autocorrelation, and cross-correlation functions can be used to explore time series data.

The Autocorrelation Function

Consider again the Health Care Composite Index, described in Chapter 26. From the time sequence plot of the data values, you saw that successive monthly values are closely related to each other. Another way of demonstrating this is to plot each value of the series with the value that precedes it. (Note that there won't be a value for the first time point, since there is no value that precedes it.) Figure 27.1 is a plot of the series values against the values that precede them, the values lagged by one. You see that there is an almost perfect linear relationship between the two values. The R^2 value (labeled *Rsq* in the chart) is 0.976. The square root of that value, 0.988, is the simple correlation coefficient. This is called the **first-order autocorrelation coefficient**, since it is the correlation coefficient of values within the same series when the values are lagged by one.

Figure 27.1 Scatterplot of first-order autocorrelation

[Scatterplot: LAG1 vs INDEX, Rsq = 0.9761]

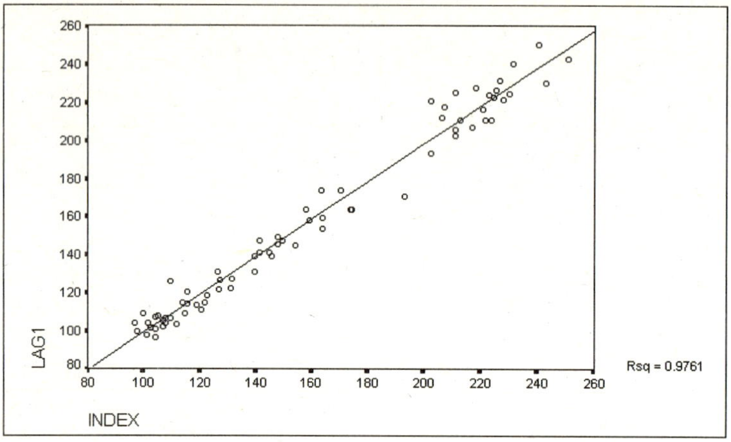

Similarly, if you plotted each value with the value two time points before, the lag 2 values, you would obtain the plot shown in Figure 27.2. Again, you note that there is a strong linear relationship. The correlation coefficient is called the **second-order autocorrelation coefficient**. You can create such plots and compute autocorrelation coefficients for any number of lags.

Figure 27.2 Scatterplot of second-order autocorrelation

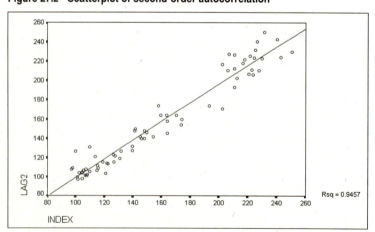

The autocorrelation coefficients at various lags can be displayed in an autocorrelation plot, as shown in Figure 27.3. Each bar corresponds to a particular lag. The 95% confidence limits of the autocorrelations around 0 are also displayed in the chart. If your observed autocorrelation falls within the confidence limits around 0, you don't have enough evidence to reject the null hypothesis that the true value is 0. In this example, all of the observed autocorrelations fall outside the confidence limits.

The autocorrelation coefficients produced by the Autocorrelations procedure will not be identical to simple correlation coefficients produced with the Correlations procedure. That's because the autocorrelation coefficients and simple correlation coefficients are calculated slightly differently. Autocorrelation computations utilize as much of the available information as possible, while the simple correlation coefficient computations exclude cases that have missing values due to lagging.

Figure 27.3 Autocorrelation coefficients

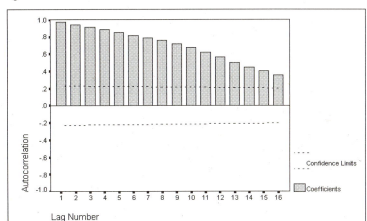

If you are using autocorrelation plots to evaluate residuals from a time series model, your autocorrelation plot should not show anything of interest. The autocorrelations should be small and there should be no patterns or spikes. The **Box-Ljung statistic**, which is displayed in the output window, can be used to test the hypothesis that the series appears to be white noise.

The Partial Autocorrelation Function

From the large value of the autocorrelation coefficient at the first lag, you know that there is a very strong relationship between the values at adjacent time points, the lag 1 values. The large value of the lag 2 autocorrelation tells you that values two time points away are also closely related. The interesting question is whether the autocorrelations of order greater than one are really important or whether they are large only because of the presence of lag 1 autocorrelations. If you were to build a regression model that predicts a current value from previous ones, how many preceding values would you have to include?

You can examine the **partial autocorrelation** function shown in Figure 27.4 to answer this question. In this chart, each correlation coefficient has the effects of lower-order correlation coefficients removed. That is, each coefficient can be thought of as the coefficient for that lag when lower-order lags are already in a regression model. From Figure 27.4, you see that only lag 1 autocorrelation appears to be important. All other partial autocorrelation coefficients fall within the confidence limits of plus and minus two standard errors.

Figure 27.4 Partial autocorrelation coefficients

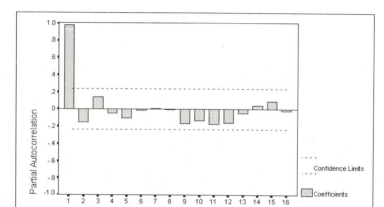

The Cross-Correlation Function

Autocorrelation and partial autocorrelation plots show the relationships between lagged values in the same series. If you want to examine the relationship between two time series, you can compute **cross-correlation** functions. Cross-correlation functions are useful for determining whether one series can be predicted from another and what orders of lags may be most useful. When current values of one series are used to predict future values of a second series, the first series is known as a **leading indicator**. For example, current dollars spent on marketing may be a leading indicator for future sales. Cross-correlation plots are also useful as diagnostics for evaluating the relationships between residuals and other variables in time series models.

Whenever you want to look at the relationship between two series using the cross-correlation function, you must make sure that the two series are **stationary**—that is, that the mean and the variance of each of the series stay about the same during the series. The reason for this is that if you take series which are increasing or decreasing over time, you can always line them up so that they appear to be highly correlated even though the two series are not related. One way to make a series stationary is to **difference** it. When you difference a series, you replace each value of the original series by the differences between adjacent values in the original series. As an example of cross-correlation functions, let's consider the relationship between Standard and Poor's weekly index for computer software and services (variable *softserv*) and the weekly index for computer systems (variable *systems*) during the last 45 weeks of 1992. Both of these series are not stationary, so the cross-correlations are computed not from the original series but from the differenced series.

Figure 27.5 Cross-correlation coefficients

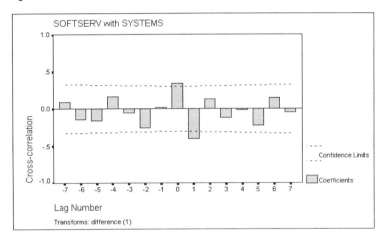

Figure 27.5 is the cross-correlation plot for the differenced computer software and services index and the computer systems index. Notice that both positive and negative lags are shown in the plot. A negative lag indicates that the second series, computer systems in this example, is the leading indicator. That is, it is used as the predictor of system sales. For example, when the lag is −3, the correlation is between the software and service index and the computer system index three weeks prior. A positive lag indicates that the first series, software and services, is the leading indicator, or predictor, of computer systems. A zero lag indicates that the correlation is for the two differenced series when neither one is lagged. Based on the cross-correlation plot, it appears that for the short time period under consideration, the computer systems index is not a good leading indicator for the software and services index. However, the software and services index may be a leading indicator for computer systems.

How to Obtain Autocorrelation and Partial Autocorrelation Charts

To obtain autocorrelation charts, partial autocorrelation charts, and related statistics for time series data, from the menus choose:

Graphs
  Time Series ▶
    Autocorrelations...

This opens the Autocorrelations dialog box, as shown in Figure 27.6.

Figure 27.6 Autocorrelations dialog box

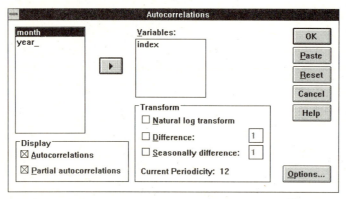

The numeric variables in the working data file are displayed on the source variable list. The minimum specification is one or more time series variables. Time Series analysis requires a data file structure in which each case (row) represents a set of observations at a different time, and the length of time between cases is uniform.

Display. You can choose one or both of the following display options:

❏ **Autocorrelations.** Displays a chart of autocorrelation coefficients and confidence intervals (two standard errors). Autocorrelation coefficient values, standard errors, the Box-Ljung statistic, and probabilities for each lag are displayed in the output window.

❏ **Partial autocorrelations.** Displays a chart of partial autocorrelation coefficients and confidence intervals (two standard errors). Partial autocorrelation coefficient values and standard errors for each lag are displayed in the output window.

Transform. You can calculate autocorrelations for transformed time series values using any combination of the following transformation options:

- **Natural log transform.** Transforms the time series using the natural logarithm (base *e*) of the series. This is useful for removing varying amplitude over time. If a series contains values that are less than or equal to 0, autocorrelations will not be calculated for that series because non-positive values cannot be log transformed.

- **Difference.** Transforms the time series by calculating the difference between successive values in the series. Enter a positive integer to specify the degree of differencing (the number of previous values used to calculate the difference). The number of values used in the calculations decreases by one for each degree of differencing. Differencing the series converts a nonstationary series to a stationary one with a constant mean and variance.

- **Seasonally difference.** Transforms the time series by calculating the difference between series values a constant span apart. The span is based on the currently defined periodicity. Enter a positive integer to specify the degree of differencing (the number of previous seasonal periods used to calculate the difference). To compute seasonal differences, you must have defined date variables that include a periodic component (such as months of the year).

    Current Periodicity. Indicates the currently defined period used to calculate seasonal differences. If the current periodicity is **None**, seasonal differencing is not available. To create a date variable with a periodic component used to define periodicity, use the Define Dates option on the Data menu (see Chapter 1).

These transformations affect only the calculation of the autocorrelations and do not alter the values of the time series variables. To create new time series variables based on transformed values of existing time series, use the Create Time Series option on the Transform menu (see Chapter 1).

Options

To change the maximum number of lags plotted, or change the method used to calculate the standard error, or display autocorrelations of periodic lags, click on **Options...** in the Autocorrelations dialog box. This opens the Autocorrelations Options dialog box, as shown in Figure 27.7.

Figure 27.7 Autocorrelations Options dialog box

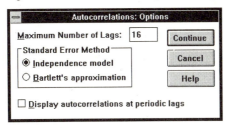

Maximum number of lags. Controls the maximum number of lags plotted. The default is 16.

Standard Error Method. For autocorrelations, you can change the method used to calculate the standard error. (This option is not available for partial autocorrelations.) You can choose one of the following methods:

- **Independence model.** Assumes the underlying process is white noise. This is the default.
- **Bartlett's approximation.** Standard errors grow at increased lags. Appropriate where the order of the moving average process is *k-1*.

The following option is also available for time series data with defined periodicity:

- **Display autocorrelations at periodic lags.** Displays autocorrelations *only* for periodic intervals, based on the currently defined periodicity.

How to Obtain Cross-Correlation Charts

To obtain cross-correlation charts and related statistics, from the menus choose:
Graphs
  Time Series ▶
    Cross-Correlations...

This opens the Cross-Correlations dialog box, as shown in Figure 27.8.

Figure 27.8 Cross-Correlations dialog box

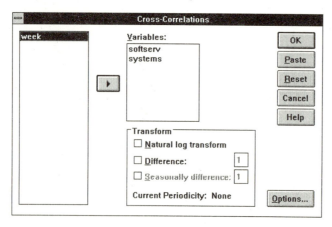

The numeric variables in the working data file are displayed on the source variable list. The minimum specification is two or more time series variables. A separate cross-correlation chart is created for each possible pair of variables. Time Series analysis requires a data file structure in which each case (row) represents a set of observations at a different time, and the length of time between cases is uniform.

Transform. You can calculate cross-correlations for transformed time series values using any combination of the following transformation options:

- **Natural log transform.** Transforms the time series using the natural logarithm (base e) of the series. This is useful for removing varying amplitude over time. If any values in a pair of series are less than or equal to 0, cross-correlations will not be calculated for that pair because non-positive values cannot be log transformed.
- **Difference.** Transforms the time series by calculating the difference between successive values in the series. Enter a positive integer to specify the degree of differencing (the number of previous values used to calculate the difference). The number of values used in the calculations decreases by 1 for each degree of differencing. Differencing the series converts a nonstationary series to a stationary one with a constant mean and variance.
- **Seasonally difference.** Transforms the time series by calculating the difference between series values a constant span apart. The span is based on the currently defined periodicity. Enter a positive integer to specify the degree of differencing (the number of previous seasonal periods used to calculate the difference). To compute seasonal differences, you must have defined date variables that include a periodic component (such as months of the year).

  Current Periodicity. Indicates the currently defined period used to calculate seasonal differences. If the current periodicity is None, seasonal differencing is not available. To create a date variable with a periodic component used to define periodicity, use the Define Dates option on the Data menu (see Chapter 1).

These transformations affect only the calculation of the cross-correlations and do not alter the values of the time series variables. To create new time series variables based on transformed values of existing time series, use the Create Time Series option on the Transform menu (see Chapter 1).

Options

To change the maximum number of lags plotted or display cross-correlations of periodic lags, click on Options... in the Cross-Correlations dialog box. This opens the Cross-Correlations Options dialog box, as shown in Figure 27.9.

Figure 27.9 Cross-Correlations Options dialog box

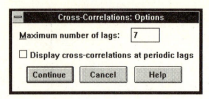

Maximum number of lags. Controls the maximum number of lags plotted. The default is 7.

The following option is also available for time series data with defined periodicity:

- **Display cross-correlations at periodic lags**. Displays cross-correlations *only* for periodic intervals, based on the currently defined periodicity.

Bibliography

Anderson, R., and S. Nida. 1978. Effect of physical attractiveness on opposite and same-sex evaluations. *Journal of Personality*, 46:3, 401–413.

Beard, C. M., V. Fuster, and L. R. Elveback. 1982. Daily and seasonal variation in sudden cardiac death, Rochester, Minnesota, 1950–1975. *Mayo Clinic Proceedings*, 57: 704–706.

Belsley, D. A., E. Kuh, and R. E. Welsch. 1980. *Regression diagnostics: Identifying influential data and sources of collinearity*. New York: John Wiley and Sons.

Benedetti, J. K., and M. B. Brown. 1978. Strategies for the selection of log-linear models. *Biometrics*, 34: 680–686.

Berk, K. N. 1977. Tolerance and condition in regression computation. *Journal of the American Statistical Association*, 72: 863–866.

———. 1978. Comparing subset regression procedures. *Technometrics*, 20: 1–6.

Bishop, Y. M. M., S. E. Fienberg, and P. W. Holland. 1975. *Discrete multivariate analysis: Theory and practice*. Cambridge, Mass.: MIT Press.

Blalock, H. M. 1979. *Social statistics*. New York: McGraw-Hill.

Blom, G. 1958. *Statistical estimates and transformed beta variables*. New York: John Wiley and Sons.

Borgatta, E. F., and G. W. Bohrnstedt. 1980. Level of measurement once over again. *Sociological Methods and Research*, 9:2, 147–160.

Cedercreutz, C. 1978. Hypnotic treatment of 100 cases of migraine. In: *Hypnosis at Its Bicentennial*, F. H. Frankel and H. S. Zamansky, eds. New York: Plenum.

Chambers, J. M., W. S. Cleveland, B. Kleiner, and P. A. Tukey. 1983. *Graphical methods for data analysis*. Belmont, Calif.: Wadsworth, Inc.; Boston: Duxbury Press.

Churchill, G. A., Jr. 1979. *Marketing research: Methodological foundations*. Hinsdale, Ill.: Dryden Press.

Cleveland, W. S. 1979. Robust locally weighted regression and smoothing scatterplots. *Journal of the American Statistical Association,* 74: 829–836.

Cleveland, W. S., and R. McGill. 1984. The many faces of a scatterplot. *Journal of the American Statistical Association*, 79: 807–822.

Cohen, J. 1960. A coefficient of agreement for nominal scales. *Educational and Psychological Measurement*, 20: 37–46.

Conover, W. J. 1974. Some reasons for not using the Yates continuity correction on 2×2 contingency tables. *Journal of the American Statistical Association*, 69: 374–376.

———. 1980. *Practical nonparametric statistics*. 2nd ed. New York: John Wiley and Sons.

Cook, R. D. 1977. Detection of influential observations in linear regression. *Technometrics*, 19: 15–18.

Daniel, C., and F. Wood. 1980. *Fitting Equations to Data*. Rev. ed. New York: John Wiley and Sons.

Davis, H., and E. Ragsdale. 1983. Unpublished working paper. Graduate School of Business, University of Chicago.

Davis, J. A. and T. W. Smith. 1993. *General social surveys, 1972–1993: Cumulative codebook*. Chicago: National Opinion Research Center.

Dillon, W. R., and M. Goldstein. 1984. *Multivariate analysis: Methods and applications.* New York: John Wiley and Sons.

Dineen, L. C., and B. C. Blakesley. 1973. Algorithm AS 62: A generator for the sampling distribution of the Mann-Whitney U statistic. *Applied Statistics,* 22: 269–273.

Draper, N. R., and H. Smith. 1981. *Applied regression analysis.* New York: John Wiley and Sons.

Duncan, O. D. 1966. Path analysis: Sociological examples. *American Journal of Sociology,* 72: 1–16.

Everitt, B. S. 1977. *The analysis of contingency tables.* London: Chapman and Hall.

Fienberg, S. E. 1977. *The analysis of cross-classified categorical data.* Cambridge, Mass.: MIT Press.

Fox, J. 1984. *Linear statistical models and related methods.* New York: John Wiley and Sons.

Frane, J. W. 1976. Some simple procedures for handling missing data in multivariate analysis. *Psychometrika,* 41: 409–415.

———. 1977. A note on checking tolerance in matrix inversion and regression. *Technometrics,* 19: 513–514.

Goodman, L. A., and W. H. Kruskal. 1954. Measures of association for cross-classification. *Journal of the American Statistical Association,* 49: 732–764.

Haberman, S. J. 1978. *Analysis of qualitative data.* Vol. 1. New York: Academic Press.

Hoaglin, D. C., and R. E. Welsch. 1978. The hat matrix in regression and ANOVA. *American Statistician,* 32: 17–22.

Hoaglin, D. C., F. Mosteller, and J. W. Tukey. 1983. *Understanding robust and exploratory data analysis.* New York: John Wiley and Sons.

Hocking, R. R. 1976. The analysis and selection of variables in linear regression. *Biometrics,* 32: 1–49.

Hogg, R. V. 1979. An introduction to robust estimation. *Robustness in Statistics,* 1–18.

Judge, G. G., W. E. Griffiths, R. C. Hill, H. Lutkepohl, and T. C. Lee. 1985. *The theory and practice of econometrics.* 2nd ed. New York: John Wiley and Sons.

Kendall, M. G., and A. Stuart. 1973. *The advanced theory of statistics.* Vol. 2. New York: Hafner Press.

King, M. M., et al. 1979. Incidence and growth of mammary tumors induced by 7,12-dimethylbenz(a) anthracene as related to the dietary content of fat and antioxidant. *Journal of the National Cancer Institute,* 63:3, 657–663.

Kleinbaum, D. G., and L. L. Kupper. 1978. *Applied regression analysis and other multivariable methods.* Boston, Mass.: Duxbury Press.

Kleinbaum, D. G., L. L. Kupper, and H. Morgenstern. 1982. *Epidemiological research: Principles and quantitative methods.* Belmont, Calif.: Wadsworth, Inc.

Kraemer, H. C. 1982. Kappa coefficient. In: *Encyclopedia of Statistical Sciences,* S. Kotz and N. L. Johnson, eds. New York: John Wiley and Sons.

Lee, E. T. 1992. *Statistical methods for survival data analysis.* New York: John Wiley and Sons.

Lehmann, E. L. 1975. *Nonparametrics: Statistical methods based on ranks.* San Francisco: Holden-Day.

Loether, H. J., and D. G. McTavish. 1976. *Descriptive and inferential statistics: An introduction.* Boston: Allyn and Bacon.

Lord, F. M., and M. R. Novick. 1968. *Statistical theories of mental test scores.* Reading, Mass.: Addison-Wesley.

Mantel, N. 1974. Comment and a suggestion on the Yates continuity correction. *Journal of the American Statistical Association,* 69: 378–380.

Mantel, N., and W. Haenszel. 1959. Statistical aspects of the analysis of data from retrospective studies of disease. *Journal of the National Cancer Institute*, 22: 719–748.

Meyer, L. S., and M. S. Younger. 1976. Estimation of standardized coefficients. *Journal of the American Statistical Association*, 71: 154–157.

Montgomery, D.C. 1991 *Introduction to statistical quality control.* New York: John Wiley & Sons

Neter, J., W. Wasserman, and R. Kutner. 1985. *Applied linear statistical models.* 2nd ed. Homewood, Ill.: Richard D. Irwin, Inc.

Nunnally, J. 1978. *Psychometric theory.* 2nd ed. New York: McGraw-Hill.

Olson, C. L. 1976. On choosing a test statistic in multivariate analysis of variance. *Psychological Bulletin*, 83: 579–586.

Overall, J. E., and C. Klett. 1972. *Applied multivariate analysis.* New York: McGraw-Hill.

Paul, O., et al. 1963. A longitudinal study of coronary heart disease. *Circulation*, 28: 20–31.

Rabkin, S. W., F. A. Mathewson, and R. B. Tate. 1980. Chronobiology of cardiac sudden death in men. *Journal of the American Medical Association*, 244:12, 1357–1358.

Roberts, H. V. 1979. An analysis of employee compensation. *Report 7946*, October. Center for Mathematical Studies in Business and Economics, University of Chicago.

_____. 1980. Statistical bases in the measurement of employment discrimination. In: *Comparable Worth: Issues and Alternatives*, E. Robert Livernash, ed. Washington, D.C.: Equal Employment Advisory Council, 173–195.

Siegel, S. 1956. *Nonparametric statistics for the behavioral sciences.* New York: McGraw-Hill.

Sigall, H., and N. Ostrove. 1975. Beautiful but dangerous: Effects of offender attractiveness and nature of the crime on juridic judgment. *Journal of Personality and Social Psychology*, 31: 410–414.

Smirnov, N. V. 1948. Table for estimating the goodness of fit of empirical distributions. *Annals of Mathematical Statistics*, 19: 279–281.

Snedecor, G. W., and W. G. Cochran. 1967. *Statistical methods.* Ames: Iowa State University Press.

Somers, R. H. 1962. A new symmetric measure of association for ordinal variables. *American Sociological Review*, 27: 799–811.

Speed, M. F. 1976. Response curves in the one way classification with unequal numbers of observations per cell. *Proceedings of the Statistical Computing Section*, American Statistical Association.

SPSS Inc. 1991. *SPSS statistical algorithms.* 2nd ed. Chicago: SPSS Inc.

Stevens, S. S. 1946. On the theory of scales of measurement. *Science*, 103: 677–680.

Tatsuoka, M. M. 1971. *Multivariate analysis.* New York: John Wiley and Sons.

Theil, H. 1967. *Economics and information theory.* Chicago: Rand McNally.

Tukey, J. W. 1962. The future of data analysis. *Annals of Mathematical Statistics*, 33: 22.

Velleman, P. F., and R. E. Welsch. 1981. Efficient computing of regression diagnostics. *American Statistician*, 35: 234–242.

Winer, B. J., D. R. Brown, and K. M. Michels. 1991. *Statistical principles in experimental design.* 3rd ed. New York: McGraw-Hill.

Wright, S. 1960. Path coefficients and path regressions: Alternative or complementary concepts? *Biometrics*, 16: 189–202.

Wynder, E. L. 1976. Nutrition and cancer. *Federal Proceedings*, 35: 1309–1315.

Wyner, G. A. 1980. Response errors in self-reported number of arrests. *Sociological Methods and Research*, 9:2, 161–177.

Index

R= Base System Syntax Reference Guide

absolute value function, 3
active system file, R23, R24
Add Cases procedure, 33–37, R83–R89
   case source variable, 34, R88–R89
   dictionary information, 37, R85
   key variables, R87
   limitations, R85
   removing variables, 36, R87–R88
   renaming variables, 36–37, R86–R87
   selecting variables, 35, R87–R88
   unpaired variables, 34, R85
   variables in the new file, 34, R89
Add Variables procedure, 37–42, R454–R461
   case source variable, 39, R460
   dictionary information, R456
   duplicate cases, R458
   excluded variables, 38, R459–R460
   file sort order, 38, 39, R456, R457
   key variables, 39–40, R457–R458
   keyed tables, 39, R458
   limitations, R456
   renaming variables, 41–42, R459
   variables in the new file, 39, R461
adjusted predicted values, 244
adjusted R^2, 230
aggregating data, 43–47, R93–R102
   aggregate functions, 45–46, R98–R100
   aggregate variables, 44, R99–R100
   break variables, 44, R93, R96–R97
   saving files, 47, R96
   variable labels, 47, R98
   variable names, 47, R97–R98
agreement measures, 117–118
Akaike information criterion
   in Linear Regression procedure, R628
Ameniya's prediction criterion
   in Linear Regression procedure, R628
analysis of variance, 181, 193–202, R103–R111, R541–R550

degrees of freedom, 195
explained sum of squares, 195
   in Curve Estimation procedure, 287, R188
   in Linear Regression procedure, 272, R628
   in Means procedure, 136, R490
   in regression, 230
interaction effects, 196–197
main effects, 195
nonorthogonal designs, 197
observed significance level, 196
sums of squares, 195
See also one-way analysis of variance, One-Way ANOVA procedure, Simple Factorial ANOVA procedure
ANOVA. *See* analysis of variance, Simple Factorial ANOVA procedure
arcsine function, 4, R47
arctangent function, 4, R47
area charts, 384–392
   100% stacked, 361
   category labels, 391
   means for groups of cases, 388
   sequence, 506, R130, R787
   simple, 387, 389, 390
   stacked, 388, 390, 392
   summaries for groups of cases, 387–389
   summaries of separate variables, 389–390
   time series, 506
   values of individual cases, 390–392
arguments
   complex, R46
   defined, R46
arithmetic functions, 3–4, R151
arithmetic operators, 2, R45, R150
arrays. *See* vectors
ASCII text data files
   See also raw data files
assignment expression
   computing values, R148

522 Index

association measures, 111–121
asymptotic standard error, 118
autocorrelation, 507–510, 512–514, R76–R82
    charts, 507–510, 512–514
    first-order, 507
    partial, 509–510, 512–514, R551–R556
    second-order, 508
Autocorrelations procedure, 512–516, R76–R82, R551–R556
    lags, 513–514
    partial autocorrelation, R81, R551–R556
    periodic lags, 514, R80, R554
    specifying periodicity, R79, R553
    standard error method, 514, R81
    transforming values, 512–513, R78–R80, R553
    using a previously defined model, R81, R555

backward elimination, 261
    in Linear Regression procedure, 271, R626
bar charts, 59, 364–374, R384
    100% stacked, 361
    category labels, 372
    clustered, 368, 370, 373
    in Frequencies procedure, 65, R330–R331, R332
    interval width, R330–R331
    means for groups of cases, 367
    scale, R330–R331
    simple, 367, 369, 371
    stacked, 369, 371, 373
    summaries for groups of cases, 367–369
    summaries of separate variables, 369–371
    values of individual cases, 371–374
Bartlett's approximation
    in Autocorrelations procedure, 514, R81
Bernoulli distribution function, R50
beta coefficients, 254
    in Linear Regression procedure, 272
beta distribution function, R48
between-groups mean square, 183
between-groups variability, 183
binomial distribution function, R50
binomial test
    in Binomial Test procedure, R516–R517
Binomial Test procedure, 304–306, R516–R517
    dichotomies, 305
    expected proportions, R517
    missing values, 305
    observed proportions, R516–R517
    statistics, 305
Bivariate Correlation procedure, 210–213, R155–R160, R508–R513, R557–R564
    case count, R510
    control variables, R559
    correlation coefficients, 211, R155
    format, R158, R508, R511, R561
    limitations, R156, R509, R558
    matrix input, R562–R564
    matrix output, R158–R160, R508, R512–R513, R562–R564
    missing values, 212, R158, R511, R561, R563
    order values, R559
    random sampling, R508, R511
    rank-order coefficients, R508–R513
    significance levels, 211, R157, R508, R510–R511, R560
    statistics, 212, R157–R158, R510–R511, R560
blank
    delimiter, R17
blank data fields
    treatment of, R731
blank lines
    displaying, R594–R595
    See also printing cases
Blom's transformation, 21, R602
    in normal probability plots, 497, R533
BMDP files
    conversion to SPSS, R341–R342, R619–R620
    format specification, R619
    numeric variables, R619
    reading, R340–R345
    string variables, R619
Bonferroni test, 185
    in One-Way ANOVA procedure, 190
box-and-whiskers plots. *See* boxplots
Box-Ljung statistic, 509
    in Autocorrelations procedure, 512, R77
boxplots, 87–89, 429–439
    comparing factor levels, 100, R277
    comparing variables, 100, R277
    extreme values, 87
    identifying outliers, R278
    in Explore procedure, 100, R280
    outliers, 87
    scale, R277–R278

simple, 436, 438, 443
stacked, 437, 438, 443
summaries for groups of cases, 436–437
summaries of separate variables, 438, 443
break variables, 325

c charts, 483–485, 489–491, R758–R760
data organization, 478, R759
nonconforming values, 485, 491
sample size, 490
sigma, 491, R760
subgroup identifier, 484, 490, R759
calculator pad, 2–3
case identification variable, R615–R616
case selection, 49–54, R505–R506
See also subsets of cases
case-control studies
estimating risk, 122–123
cases
limiting, R505–R506
listing, 321–324, R441–R444
sampling, 52, R704–R706
selecting, 49–54, R505–R506, R723–R727
sorting, 31–32, R746–R747
weighting, 54–55, R819–R821
casewise plots, 235
in Linear Regression procedure, 274
categorical charts, 355–402
Cauchy distribution function, R48
cell frequency, 104
cells, 103
centered moving average function, 27, R168
centered running median function, R169
central tendency measures, 74–75
character sets, R847–R853
charts, R379–R409
area, 384–392
autocorrelation, 507–510, 512–514
bar, 364–374, R384
boxplot, 429–439
case labels, 285
categorical, 355–402
control, R748–R761
count functions, R381
cross-correlation, 510–511, 514–516

difference line, R390
drop-line, 379, 381, 383, R390
error bar, 431–433, 439–444, R400
high-low, 405–428, R397
histograms, 458–459, R404
line, 374–383, R390
mixed, 362
normal probability, 493–497, R531–R538
Pareto, R405
partial autocorrelation, 509–510, 512–514
pie, 392–397, R396
P-P normal probability, 493–497, R534
Q-Q normal probability, 493–497, R534
range bar, R385
resolution, R740
scatterplots, 445–458, R401
sequence, 499–506, R124–R134, R781–R790
simple, 356–358
summaries for groups of cases, 356–357
summaries of separate variables, 357–360
summary functions, 399–402, R381
templates, R407
transposing data, 397
chi-square, 108–111, 169
degrees of freedom, 110
Fisher's exact test, 111
in Chi-Square Test procedure, R517–R518
in Crosstabs procedure, 125, R178
likelihood ratio, 110
Mantel-Haenszel, 118
nonparametric tests, 296–297
observed significance level, 110
Pearson, 110
Yates' correction, 111
chi-square distribution function, R48
Chi-Square Test procedure, 301–303, R517–R518
expected proportions, R518
missing values, 303
observed proportions, R518
statistics, 303
chi-square-based measures, 103, 112–113
Cochran's Q
in Tests for Several Related Samples procedure, 320, R518–R519
coefficient of contingency, 112
coefficient of determination, 229
coefficient of variance function, 4
coefficient of variation, R47

Cohen's kappa. *See* kappa
cohort studies
    estimating risk, 121–122
collinearity, 267–269
    in Linear Regression procedure, 273
column headings, R588–R590
    See also page ejection
column percentages, 104–105
    in Crosstabs procedure, 126, R177
column variable, 104
column-style format specifications, R203
combined reports, 328
comma
    delimiter, R17
command
    order, R17–R19
    syntax, R13–R15
command files, R20, R423–R424
command order, R837–R845
command terminator
    specifying, R738–R739
commands
    processed through your operating system, R14–R15
    run within SPSS, R13–R14
    that read data, R18–R19
    that take effect immediately, R18–R19
comments
    in commands, R142
complex data files, R610–R618
    case identification variable, R615–R616
    defining, R610–R618
    duplicate records, R617
    grouped files, R610
    missing records, R616–R617
    mixed files, R610
    nested files, R610
    repeating groups, R610
    skipping records, R614–R615
    spreading values across cases, R617–R618
    undefined records, R613–R614
complex files
    defining, R253–R254, R264–R267, R267–R268
complex raw data files, R855–R868
    defining, R295–R309
    grouped, R301
    mixed, R300

nested, R301
compound model
    in Curve Estimation procedure, 286, R185, R186
computing values, 1–9, R143–R154
    arithmetic functions, 3–4, R151
    arithmetic operators, 2, R150
    assignment expression, R148
    calculator pad, 2–3
    conditional expressions, 7–8, R247–R249, R413–R415
    cross-case functions, R152
    date and time functions, R153
    distribution functions, 5
    formats of new variables, R149–R150
    functions, 3–6, R143–R147
    if case satisfies condition, 7–8, R246–R254, R413–R418
    logical expressions, R247–R249, R413–R415
    logical functions, 5, R152
    logical operators, 3, R246, R413
    loop structures, R445–R453
    missing values, 6, R149–R150
    missing-value functions, R151–R152
    nested functions, 6
    new variables, 8–9
    random-number functions, 5, R153
    relational operators, 3, R246, R413
    statistical functions, 4, R151
    string data, 9, R148, R150
    string functions, R154
    subsets of cases, 7–8
    syntax rules, 9, R148–R149
    target variable, 2, R148
concordant pairs, 118
condition index
    in Linear Regression procedure, R628
conditional expressions, 7–8
    See also logical expressions
conditional transformations, 7–8, R246–R254, R413–R418
    conditional expressions, 7–8, R247–R249, R413–R415
    formats of new variables, R248, R415
    logical expressions, 7–8, R247–R249, R413–R415
    logical operators, 8, R246, R413
    missing values, R249, R415
    nested, R253
    relational operators, 8, R246, R413
    string data, R247, R248, R414, R415

confidence intervals
    in Curve Estimation procedure, 287, R188
    in error bar charts, 442
    in Explore procedure, R282
    in Linear Regression procedure, 272, R629, R631, R641
    in One-Sample T Test procedure, 159
    in one-sample *t* tests, 156
    in One-Way ANOVA procedure, 191
    in regression, 229
    one-way analysis of variance, 180
    saving in Linear Regression procedure, 276
    time series settings, R777
conforming values
    in control charts, 483
consecutive integers
    converting numeric data, 22–23, R116–R120
    converting string data, 22–23, R116–R120
constants, R45–R46
contingency coefficient, 112
    in Crosstabs procedure, 125, R178
contour plots, R568
contrasts
    analysis of variance, R543–R544
    in One-Way ANOVA procedure, 189
control charts, 462–465, 474–492, R748–R761
    c charts, 483–485, 489–491, R758–R760
    conforming values, 483
    control limits, 491
    data organization, 475
    individuals charts, 480–481, R754–R755
    missing values, R761
    moving range charts, 480–481, R754–R755
    nonconforming values, 482–485, 487–491
    np charts, 482–483, 487–489, R756–R758
    p charts, 482–483, 487–489, R756–R758
    R charts, 478–480, 485–487, R751–R754
    s charts, 478–480, 485–487, R751–R754
    sigma, 491, R760
    u charts, 483–485, 489–491, R758–R760
    X-bar charts, 478–480, 485–487, R751–R754
control variables, 105–107
    in Crosstabs procedure, 124, R176
    in Partial Correlations procedure, 220
convergence criteria
    time series settings, R777
converting data files. *See* data files
Cook's distance, 243–246
    in Linear Regression procedure, 275, R641

correlation, R155–R160
    bivariate, 203–213
    crosstabulation, 118
    in Linear Regression procedure, R629, R634
    in multiple regression, 250–252
    nonparametric measures, 207, 209
    partial, 215–222
    scatterplots, 203–205
    zero-order, 216
    See also Bivariate Correlation procedure
cosine function, 4
counting occurrences, 10–12, R161–R162
    defining values, 11–12, R161
    if case satisfies condition, 12
    missing values, R162
    subsets of cases, 12
counts
    in Report Summaries in Rows procedure, R685
covariance
    in Linear Regression procedure, 272, R628, R634
covariance ratio, 266
    in Linear Regression procedure, 276, R641
Cp. *See* Mallow's *Cp*
Cramér's *V*, 113
    in Crosstabs procedure, 125, R178
cross-case functions, R152
cross-correlation, 510–511, 514–516, R135–R140
    charts, 510–511, 514–516
Cross-correlations procedure, R135–R140
    lags, 515–516
    periodic lags, 516, R139
    specifiying periodicity, R138
    transforming values, 515, R137–R139
    using a previously defined model, R140
cross-product deviation
    in Linear Regression procedure, R634
Crosstabs procedure, 123–128, R172–R182
    boxes around cells, 127, R180
    column percentages, 126, R177
    control variables, 124, R176
    expected count, 126, R178
    general mode, R176
    index of tables, 127, R180
    integer mode, R177
    labels, 127, R180
    layers, 124, R176
    missing values, R179
    observed count, 126, R177

reproducing tables, R182
residuals, 126–127, R178
row order, 127, R180
row percentages, 126, R177
statistics, 125–126, R178–R179
suppressing tables, 124, R180
table format, 127, R179–R180
total percentage, 126, R178
writing tables, R180–R182
crosstabulation, 103–123, R172–R182
agreement measures, 117–118
association measures, 111–121
case-control studies, 122–123
cell frequency, 104
cells, 103
chi-square, 108–111
chi-square-based measures, 103, 112–113
cohort studies, 121–122
column percentages, 104–105
column variable, 104
control variables, 105–107
correlation, 118
data screening, 107–108
degrees of freedom, 110
dependent variable, 105
expected count, 108
graphical representation, 107
in Means procedure, R488–R489
independent variable, 105
interval data measures, 121
marginals, 104
multiple response, 140–141, 146–149, R500–R502
nominal measures, 112–118
observed count, 108
ordinal measures, 118–120
percentages, 104–105
proportional reduction in error, 113–116
residuals, 109
row percentages, 104–105
row variable, 104
statistics, 108–123
table percentage, 104
writing to a file, R596–R597
See also Crosstabs procedure
cubic model
in Curve Estimation procedure, 286, R185, R186
cumulative distribution functions, 5
cumulative percentage, 58
cumulative sum function, 27, R165

curve estimation, 279–288, R183–R189
predicted values, 281–282
residuals, 281–282
selecting a model, 279–281
Curve Estimation procedure, 284–288, R183–R189
analysis of variance, 287, R188
confidence intervals, 287, R188
forecasting, 288, R184, R185, R577–R580
including constant, 287, R187
models, 286–287, R186–R187
saving predicted values, 287, R188
saving prediction intervals, 287, R188
saving residuals, 287, R188
time series analysis, 285
using a previously defined model, R189
curve fitting. *See* curve estimation
custom currency formats
creating, R735–R736

d. *See* Somers' *d*, R179
data
inline, R121–R122, R192, R193
invalid, R731
data compression
scratch files, R737
data files
aggregating, 43–47, R93–R102
applying data dictionary, 42–43, R112–R115
BMDP, R340–R345, R619–R620
complex, R264–R267, R295–R309, R610–R618, R855–R868
converting, R716–R722
dBASE, R373, R716–R722
default file extension, R738
direct access, R433–R438
documents, R244–R245, R260
Excel, R371–R372, R716–R722
file information, R241–R243, R769
grouped, R610
keyed, R433–R438, R573–R576
labels, R294
Lotus 1-2-3, R371–R372, R716–R722
master files, R796–R802
merging, 33–42, R83–R89, R454–R461
mixed, R610
Multiplan, R371–R372
nested, R610

opening, R336–R339
OSIRIS, R352–R357
raw, R190–R207
reading, R191, R336–R378, R419–R422, R433–R438
repeating data groups, R610
SAS, R358–R362
saving, R707–R712, R830–R835
SCSS, R366–R369, R713–R715
split-file processing, 47–49, R762–R764
spreadsheet, R371–R372, R717–R718
SPSS, R336
SPSS portable, R286–R291, R419
SPSS/PC+, R419
subsets of cases, 49–54, R310–R311, R723–R727, R803–R805
SYLK, R371–R372, R716–R722
tab-delimited, R373–R374, R718–R719
time series, 23
transaction files, R796–R802
transformations, 31–55
updating, R796–R802
weighting cases, 54–55
data formats. *See* data types; display formats; input formats; output formats
Data menu. *See* Data Editor, file transformations
data records
　defining, R196–R197, R610–R618
data transformations, 1–30
　arithmetic functions, 3–4, R151
　arithmetic operators, 2, R150
　calculator pad, 2–3
　clearing, R141
　computing values, 1–9, R143–R154
　conditional, 7–8, R246–R254, R413–R418
　conditional expressions, 7–8, R247–R249, R413–R415
　consecutive integers, 22–23, R116–R120
　controlling calculation, 30
　converting strings to numeric, 22–23, R116–R120, R608–R609
　counting occurrences, 10–12, R161–R162
　counting the same value across variables, 10–12, R161
　cross-case functions, R152
　date and time functions, R153
　functions, 3–6, R143–R147
　if case satisfies condition, 7–8, R246–R254, R413–R418
　logical expressions, 7–8, R247–R249, R413–R415

logical functions, 5, R152
logical operators, 3, R246, R413
loop structures, R445–R453
missing-value functions, R151–R152
nested functions, 6
new variables, 8–9
pending, 30
random-number functions, 5, R153
random-number seed, 10
ranking data, 18–22
recoding values, 12–18, R116–R120, R604–R609
relational operators, 3, R246, R413
repeating, R255–R259
statistical functions, 4, R151
string functions, R154
subsets of cases, 7–8
syntax rules, 9
time series, 23–30, R163–R171, R208–R215, R700–R703
data types, R190–R191
　custom currency, R735–R736
database files, R718
date and time functions, R153
date functions, R62–R75
date variables
　creating, 24–25, R208–R215
　current status, R817–R818
dates, R62–R75
dBASE files
　reading, R370–R378
　saving, R719–R720
decimal indicator
　specifying, R736
decimal places
　implied, R204–R206
Define Multiple Response Sets procedure, 143–144, R497–R498
　categories, 144, R497–R498
　dichotomies, 144, R497–R498
　set labels, 144, R497–R498
　set names, 144, R497–R498
degrees of freedom
　analysis of variance, 195
deleted residuals, 243–246
　in Linear Regression procedure, 276
delimiter, R17
　blank, R17
　comma, R17

special, R17
dependent variable, 105
descriptive statistics, 69–82, R234–R240
    for residuals, R314–R317
    in Explore procedure, R281
    See also Descriptives procedure
Descriptives procedure, 79–82, R234–R240
    display order, 82, R239–R240
    format options, 80, R237–R238
    index of variables, 81, R238
    limitations, R235
    missing values, R240
    output width, R237–R238
    saving Z scores, 80, R236–R237
    statistics, 81–82, R238–R239
detrended normal plots, 91, R535
    in Explore procedure, 101, R280–R281
dfBeta
    in Linear Regression procedure, 276, R641
dfFit
    in Linear Regression procedure, 276, R641
difference
    in cross-correlation, 511
difference function, 26, R165
difference line charts, 407, R390
    simple, 416
    summaries for groups of cases, 416
    summaries of separate variables, 421
    values of individual cases, 426
difference transformation
    in Autocorrelations procedure, 513, R78, R553
    in Cross-correlations procedure, 515, R137
    in normal probability plots, 496, R535
    in sequence charts, 503, R128, R784
direct-access files
    reading, R433–R438
discordant pairs, 118
dispersion measures, 75–76
display file, R24
display formats, R322–R325, R591–R593
distribution functions, 5, R47–R51
    Bernoulli, R50
    beta, R48
    binomial, R50
    Cauchy, R48
    chi-square, R48
    exponential, R49
    F, R49
    gamma, R49
    geometric, R51
    hypergeometric, R51
    Laplace, R49
    logisitic, R49
    lognormal, R49
    negative binomial, R51
    normal, R49
    Pareto, R50
    Poisson, R51
    t, R50
    uniform, R50
    Weibull, R50
documentation
    online, R425–R428
documents
    dropping, R260
    for SPSS data files, R244–R245
    retaining in aggregated files, R97
domain errors
    defined, R52
    numeric expressions, R52–R60
drop-line charts, 359, 379, 381, 383, R390
Duncan's multiple range test
    in One-Way ANOVA procedure, 190
Durbin-Watson statistic
    in Linear Regression procedure, 272, R643

EBCDIC data, R293
eigenvalues, 268
    in Linear Regression procedure, 273, R628
elementary variables, 138
end-of-file control
    in input programs, R197–R199
equality of variance
    in regression, 226, 239
erasing files, R273
error bar charts, 431–433, 439–444, R400
    clustered, 442, 443
    confidence intervals, 442
    simple, 441, 443
    standard deviation, 442
    standard error, 442
    summaries for groups of cases, 439, 441, 442
    summaries of separate variables, 439, 443

errors
  displaying, R732–R733
  maximum number, R731–R732
eta, 121
  in Crosstabs procedure, 125, R179
  in Means procedure, 136, R490
evaluating assumptions, 89–93
exact-size sample, R704
examining data, 83–101, R274–R284
  See also Explore procedure, exploring data
Excel files
  read range, R376
  read variable names, R375
  reading, R370–R378
  saving, R719
expected count, 108
  in Crosstabs procedure, 126, R178
expected normal distribution
  in normal probability plots, 496, R533
expected value, 163
Explore procedure, 97–101, R274–R284
  factor variable, 98, R276
  frequency tables, 99, R278–R279
  grouped frequency table, 99
  limitations, R275
  missing values, 101, R283–R284
  plots, 99–101, R280–R281
  scaling plots, R277–R278
  statistics, 98–99, R279–R280, R281–R283
exploring data, 83–101, R274–R284
  boxplots, 87–89
  detrended normal plots, 91
  displaying data, 84–89
  evaluating assumptions, 89–93
  extreme values, 86
  histograms, 84
  normal probability plots, 91
  normality tests, 91–93
  outliers, 87
  robust measures, 93–97
  spread-and-level plots, 90–91
  stem-and-leaf plots, 85–87
  See also Explore procedure, 83
exponent function, 4
exponential distribution function, R49
exponential model
  in Curve Estimation procedure, 286, R185, R186

extreme values, 86
  boxplots, 87
  in Explore procedure, 99, R281

F distribution function, R49
F ratio
  analysis of variance, 195
  in Linear Regression procedure, R628, R629
  in Means procedure, 136, R490
  one-way analysis of variance, 184
F test
  in Linear Regression procedure, 272
  partial, 256
file, R20
file definition, R20
file handle, R292
file information
  SPSS data files, R769
  working data file, R241–R243
file specifications, R292
file transformations, 31–55, R796–R802
  aggregating, 43–47, R93–R102
  applying data dictionary, 42–43, R112–R115
  merging files, 33–42, R83–R89, R454–R461
  sorting cases, 31–32
  subsets of cases, R723–R727
  transposing cases and variables, 32–33
  weighting cases, 54–55
filter variable, 50
filtering cases, 50
Fisher's exact test, 111
  in Crosstabs procedure, 125, R178
fixed format, R192, R192–R193, R194–R195, R200–R202
forced entry
  in Linear Regression procedure, 271, R626
forced removal
  in Linear Regression procedure, 271, R627
forecasting, 501, R577–R580
  current forecast period, R817–R818
  in Curve Estimation procedure, 288, R184, R185, R577–R580
foreign files
  input files, R22
formats, R33–R44

of new variables, R149–R150, R248, R415
See also data types; display formats; input formats; output formats
FORTRAN-like format specifications, R203–R204
forward entry
    in Linear Regression procedure, R626
forward selection, 259–260
    in Linear Regression procedure, 271
Fourier transformation function, R166
    inverse, R166
freefield format, R192, R193, R194–R195, R202
Frequencies procedure, 62–67, R326–R335
    charts, 65–66, R330–R332
    condensed format, 66, R329
    display order, 66, R329
    general mode, R327–R328
    index of tables, 67, R330
    integer mode, R327–R328
    limitations, R328
    missing values, R335
    page format, 66–67, R329
    statistics, 63–65, R334–R335
    suppressing tables, 67, R330
    value labels, 67, R329
    writing tables, R330
frequency tables, 57–67, R327–R330
    format, R329–R330
    in Explore procedure, 99, R278–R279
    increment, R278–R279
    percentages, 58
    screening data, 62
    starting value, R278–R279
    values, 57
    writing to a file, R596–R597
    See also Frequencies procedure
Friedman test
    in Tests for Several Related Samples procedure, 319, R519–R520
F-to-enter, 259
    in Linear Regression procedure, 277, R630
F-to-remove, 261
    in Linear Regression procedure, 277, R630
functions, 3–6, R143–R147
    absolute value, 3
    arcsine, 4
    arctangent, 4
    arithmetic, 3–4
    coefficient of variance, 4

cosine, 4
count, in charts, 399
distribution, 5, R47–R51
examples, R150–R154
exponent, 4
logarithm, 4
logical, 5
maximum, 4
mean, 4
mean, in charts, 367, 377, 388
minimum, 4
missing values in, 6, 7, R149–R150
nested, 6
numeric variables, R46–R60
random-normal, 5
random-number, 5
random-number seed, 10
random-uniform, 5
range, 5
remainder, 3
round, 3
sine, 4
square root, 4
standard deviation, 4
statistical, 4
string variables, R52–R55
sum, 4
sum, in charts, 394
summary, in charts, 400
syntax rules, 9
time series, 26–28, R165–R171
truncate, 3
variance, 4

gamma, 119
    in Crosstabs procedure, 125, R179
gamma distribution function, R49
general mode
    Crosstabs procedure, R176
    Frequencies procedure, R327–R328
    Means procedure, R484, R485, R488
geometric distribution function, R51
Goodman and Kruskal's gamma. *See* gamma
Goodman and Kruskal's lambda. *See* lambda
Goodman and Kruskal's tau, 115–116
    in Crosstabs procedure, 125, R178
goodness of fit, R314–R317

in regression, 229–232
grand totals, 332
grouped files, R301, R610
growth model
    in Curve Estimation procedure, 286, R185, R186

H. See Kruskal-Wallis H
hanging bar charts, 362
harmonic average
    in One-Way ANOVA procedure, 190
harmonic means
    in analysis of variance, R546
help, R410–R411
hidden relationships, 218
hierarchical files. See nested file
high-low charts, 405–428
    clustered, 406
    simple, 405
    summaries for groups of cases, 408
    summaries of separate variables, 409
    values of individual cases, 409
    See also difference line charts, high-low-close charts, range bar charts
high-low-close charts
    clustered, 417, 422, 427, R398
    simple, 414–415, 419, 424, R397
    summaries for groups of cases, 414–415, 417
    summaries of separate variables, 419, 422
    values of individual cases, 424, 427
histograms, 60–61, 84, 458–459, R404
    in Explore procedure, 100, R280
    in Frequencies procedure, 65, R331–R332
    in Linear Regression procedure, 274, R643
    interval width, R331
    scale, R277–R278, R331
    with normal curve, R332
homogeneity-of-variance
    in One-Way ANOVA procedure, 191
hypergeometric distribution function, R51
hypothesis testing, 161–172
    assumptions, 172
    chi-square, 169
    correlation, 207–208
    in analysis of variance, 181
    in regression, 228–229

preparing for, 84

ill-conditioned matrix, 268
implied decimal format, R204–R206
independence
    in regression, 227
independence model
    in Autocorrelations procedure, 514, R81
independence of error, 239–240
independent variable, 105
Independent-Samples T Test procedure, 172–175, R791–R795
    defining groups, 173–174
    dependent variables, R793
    grouping variables, 173, R793
    limitations, R792
    missing values, 175, R794–R795
    string variables, 174
    variable labels, R794
independent-samples t test. See t test
indexing clause
    in loop structures, R447–R452
indexing strings, R55
indicator variables, 34, 250
individuals charts, 480–481, R754–R755
    control limits, 491, R761
    data organization, 476
    sigma, 491, R760
    span, R760
    subgroup labels, 481, R755
initialization
    scratch variables, R33
    suppressing, R439–R440
initializing variables, R539–R540, R765–R766
    formats, R539, R540, R765–R766
    numeric variables, R539–R540
    scratch variables, R539
    string variables, R765–R766
inline data, R121–R122, R192, R193
input data, R21
    file, R21
input formats, R190–R191, R203–R207
    column-style specifications, R203
    FORTRAN-like specifications, R203–R204
    numeric, R204–R206

string, R206–R207
input programs, R429–R432
    end-case control, R263–R270
    end-of-file control, R197–R199, R271–R272
    examples, R198–R199, R254, R257, R264–R270, R272, R431–R432, R449–R451, R452, R453, R540, R574–R575, R814–R815
input state, R430
integer mode
    Crosstabs procedure, R177
    Frequencies procedure, R327–R328
    Means procedure, R484, R485, R488
interaction effects
    analysis of variance, 196–197, R106
interval measurement, 72
invalid data
    treatment of, R731
inverse cumulative distribution functions, 5
inverse Fourier transformation function, R166
inverse model
    in Curve Estimation procedure, 286, R186

journal file, R20, R21, R739

kappa, 117
    asymptotic standard error, 118
    in Crosstabs procedure, 125, R179
Kendall's tau-a, 119
Kendall's tau-b, 119, 207
    in Bivariate Correlation procedure, 211, R510
    in Crosstabs procedure, 125, R178
Kendall's tau-c, 119
    in Crosstabs procedure, 125, R178
Kendall's W
    in Tests for Several Related Samples procedure, 320, R522–R523
key variables, 39, R796–R802
keyed data files, R573–R576
    defining, R573–R576
    file handle, R575
    file key, R573, R574–R575, R575–R576
keyed files
    reading, R433–R438

keyed tables, 39, R458
keywords
    reserved, R31
    syntax, R16
Kolmogorov-Smirnov Z
    in One-Sample Kolmogorov-Smirnov Test procedure, 308, R520–R521
    in Two-Independent-Samples Tests procedure, 312, R521
Kruskal-Wallis H, 301
    in Tests for Several Independent Samples procedure, 314, R522
kurtosis, 78
    in Descriptives procedure, 82, R239
    in Explore procedure, 98, R281
    in Frequencies procedure, 65, R334
    in Report Summaries in Columns procedure, 348
    in Report Summaries in Rows procedure, 339, R685

lag function, 27, R167
lags
    in autocorrelation, 507–509
    in Autocorrelations procedure, 513–514
    in Cross-correlations procedure, 515–516
lambda, 115
    in Crosstabs procedure, 125, R178
Laplace distribution function, R49
lead function, 28, R167
leading indicator, 510
least squares, 225
least-significant difference
    in One-Way ANOVA procedure, 190
leptokurtic distribution, 78
level of measurement, 71–72
Levene test, 89, 182
    in Explore procedure, 100, R280
    in One-Way ANOVA procedure, 191
leverage values, 265
    in Linear Regression procedure, 275, R641
likelihood-ratio chi-square, 110
    in Crosstabs procedure, 125, R178
Lilliefors test, 92
    in Explore procedure, 101, R280–R281
limitations. See individual procedures

line charts, 374–383, R390
  category labels, 382
  difference line, 407
  means for groups of cases, 377
  multiple, 378, 379, 380, 381, 382, 383
  sequence, 506, R130, R787
  simple, 377, 379, 381
  summaries for groups of cases, 377–378
  summaries of separate variables, 379–381
  time series, 506
  values of individual cases, 381–383
linear association, 203–213
  scatterplots, 203–205
linear model
  in Curve Estimation procedure, 286, R186
linear regression, R621–R638
  See also Linear Regression procedure
Linear Regression procedure, 270–278, R621–R638, R639–R647
  blocks, 270
  case selection, R634–R635
  casewise plots, R644
  constant term, R631–R632
  dependent variables, R625
  format, R637–R638
  histograms, R643
  matrix input, R635–R637
  matrix output, R635–R637
  missing values, 278, R636–R637
  model criteria, R629–R631
  normal probability plots, R643
  partial residual plots, R645–R646
  plots, 273–274
  residuals, 273–277, R639–R647
  saving new variables, 275–277, R646–R647
  scatterplots, R644–R645
  statistics, 272–273, R627–R629, R633–R634
  tolerance, 271, R629, R630, R631
  variable selection methods, 270–271, R626–R627
  weights, 271, R632–R633
linear regression. See regression
linearity
  in regression, 227, 237–238
linearity test
  in Means procedure, 136, R490
List Cases procedure, 321–324, R441–R444
listing cases, 321–324, R441–R444
listing reports, 327

local documentation, R425, R427
logarithm function, 4
logarithmic model
  in Curve Estimation procedure, 286, R186
logical expressions, 7–8, R52, R55–R61, R247–R249, R413–R415
  defined, R55–R56
  in END LOOP, R56
  in LOOP, R56
  in loop structures, R447
  in SELECT IF, R56
  missing values, R59, R60
  order of evaluation, R59
  selecting cases, R723
  string variables, R52
  See also conditional transformations

logical functions, 5, R56, R152
logical operators, 3, R58, R246, R413, R723
  defined, R58
  in conditional expressions, 8
  missing values, R59, R249, R415
logical variables
  defined, R55
logistic distribution function, R49
logistic model
  in Curve Estimation procedure, 286, R186
lognormal distribution function, R49
long string variables, R41
loop structures, R445–R453
  increment value, R451–R452
  indexing variable, R447–R452
  initial value, R448
  logical expression, R447
  macro facility, R231–R233
  terminal value, R448
looping structures
  terminating, R123
loops
  maximum number, R732
Lotus 1-2-3 files, R719
  read range, R376
  read variable names, R375
  reading, R370–R378
lower case
  specifying, R734–R735

macro facility, R216–R233
   assigning defaults, R226–R227
   conditional processing, R231
   display macro commands, R739–R740
   examples, R869–R883
   keyword arguments, R221–R222
   loop structures, R231–R233
   macro call, R218
   macro definition, R217–R218
   macro expansion, R739–R740
   positional arguments, R222–R223
   SET command, R229–R230
   string functions, R227–R229
   tokens, R223–R226
Mahalanobis distance, 243
   in Linear Regression procedure, 275, R641
Mallow's C_p
   in Linear Regression procedure, R628
Mann-Whitney test, 289
Mann-Whitney U
   in Two-Independent-Samples Tests procedure, 311, R523–R524
Mantel-Haenszel chi-square, 118
   in Crosstabs procedure, 125, R178
marginals, 104
master files, R796–R802
matrices
   correlation, 208, R155–R160, R508–R513, R557–R564
   covariance, R158
   split-file processing, R763
matrix data files
   converting correlation to covariance, R481–R483
   converting covariance to correlation, R481–R483
   raw, R462–R480
   See also raw matrix data files
matrix system files, R25, R28
   format, R28
   matrix input, R25
maximum, 75
   in Descriptives procedure, 82, R239
   in Explore procedure, 98, R281
   in Frequencies procedure, 64, R335
   in Report Summaries in Columns procedure, 348
   in Report Summaries in Rows procedure, 339, R685

maximum function, 4
MCA. *See* multiple classification analysis
McNemar test
   in Two-Related-Samples Tests procedure, 318, R524
mean, 75
   comparing, 129–134, 161–172
   in Descriptives procedure, 81, R239
   in Explore procedure, 98, R281
   in Frequencies procedure, 64, R334
   in Linear Regression procedure, R633
   in Means procedure, 135, R489
   in One-Way ANOVA procedure, 191
   in Report Summaries in Columns procedure, 348
   in Report Summaries in Rows procedure, 339, R685
   subgroup, 129–134
   testing differences, 161–172
   trimmed, 94
mean function, 4
mean substitution
   in Linear Regression procedure, R637
Means procedure, 134–136, R484–R491
   crosstabulation, R488–R489
   general vs. integer mode, R484, R485, R488
   labels, 136, R490–R491
   layers, 135, R488
   missing values, R490
   statistics, 135–136, R489–R490
measurement level, 71–72
measures of association, 111–121
median, 74
   in Explore procedure, 98, R281
   in Frequencies procedure, 64, R334
   in Report Summaries in Rows procedure, R685
median test
   in Tests for Several Independent Samples procedure, 315, R525
merging data files, 33–42
   files with different cases, 33–37, R83–R89
   files with different variables, 37–42, R454–R461
   raw data files, R86, R457
   See also Add Cases Procedure, Add Variables procedure
M-estimators, 94–97
   in Explore procedure, 99, R282–R283
minimum, 75
   in Descriptives procedure, 81, R239

in Explore procedure, 98, R281
in Frequencies procedure, 64, R335
in Report Summaries in Columns procedure, 348
in Report Summaries in Rows procedure, 339, R685
minimum function, 4
missing values
   and aggregated data, R100–R102
   and logical operators, R249, R415
   counting occurrences, 12, R162
   defining, R492–R494
   functions, R59, R60
   in Binomial Test procedure, 305
   in Bivariate Correlation procedure, 212
   in Chi-Square Test procedure, 303
   in control charts, R761
   in correlation matrices, 208–209, 251–252
   in Explore procedure, 101
   in functions, 6, 7, R149–R150
   in Independent-Samples T Test procedure, 175
   in Linear Regression procedure, 278
   in logical expressions, R59, R60
   in loop structures, R452–R453
   in Multiple Response Crosstabs procedure, 149, R502–R503
   in Multiple Response Frequencies procedure, 145, R502–R503
   in numeric expressions, R51
   in One-Sample Kolmogorov-Smirnov Test procedure, 310
   in One-Way ANOVA procedure, 191
   in Paired-Samples T Test procedure, 176
   in Partial Correlations procedure, 221
   in Report Summaries in Columns procedure, 352
   in Report Summaries in Rows procedure, 341
   in Runs Test procedure, 308
   in Tests for Several Independent Samples procedure, 316
   in time series functions, 28
   in transposed data files, 33
   in Two-Independent-Samples Tests procedure, 313
   in Two-Related-Samples Tests procedure, 318
   listwise deletion, 208, 251
   MISSING function, R59–R60
   NMISS function, R60
   pairwise deletion, 208, 251
   recoding, 14, 17–18
   replacing, 28–30, R700–R703
   SYSMIS function, R60
   system-missing, R492

   time series settings, R777
   user-missing, R492–R494
   VALUE function, R60
   with logical operators, R59
   See also individual procedures
missing-value functions, R151–R152
mistakes
   identifying, 83
mixed files, R300, R610
mode, 74
   in Frequencies procedure, 64, R334
   in Report Summaries in Rows procedure, R685
Moses test
   in Two-Independent-Samples Tests procedure, 312, R526
moving averages, R168–R169
   See also centered moving average function, prior moving average function
moving range charts, 480–481, R754–R755
   control limits, R761
   data organization, 476
   sigma, 491, R760
   span, R760
   subgroup labels, 481, R755
Multiplan files
   read range, R376
   read variable names, R375
   reading, R370–R378
   saving, R719
multiple classification analysis
   analysis of variance, R111
   in Simple Factorial ANOVA procedure, 201
multiple comparisons, 185–187
   analysis of variance, R544–R546
   in One-Way ANOVA procedure, 190–191
multiple R, 249
   in Linear Regression procedure, R628
multiple regression, 250–269, R621–R638
   backward elimination, 261
   beta coefficients, 254
   building a model, 255–258
   collinearity, 267–269
   correlation matrix, 250–252
   determining important variables, 253–255
   forward selection, 259–260
   indicator variables, 250
   influential points, 265–266
   part correlation, 254–255

partial correlation, 254–255
partial *F* test, 256
partial regression coefficients, 252
selecting independent variables, 257–262
stepwise selection, 262
variables not in equation, 257
violations of assumptions, 263–265
See also Linear Regression procedure
multiple response analysis, 137–149, R495–R504
counted values, 138
crosstabulation, 140–141, 146–149
defining sets, 143–144, R495–R496
elementary variables, 138
frequency tables, 144–146
multiple category, 138, R495–R496
multiple dichotomy, 137, 138, R495–R496
See also Define Multiple Response Sets procedure, Multiple Response Crosstabs procedure, Multiple Response Frequencies procedure
Multiple Response Crosstabs procedure, 146–149, R500–R502
cell percentages, 148, R501–R502
defining value ranges, 147, R498–R499
matching variables across response sets, 149, R501
missing values, 149, R502–R503
percents based on cases, 149, R502
percents based on responses, 149, R502
value labels, R503
Multiple Response Frequencies procedure, 144–146, R499
missing values, 145, R502–R503
table format, R503–R504
value labels, R503
multipunch data, R293

natural log transformation
in Autocorrelations procedure, 513, R79, R554
in Cross-correlations procedure, 515, R138
in normal probability plots, 495, R537
in sequence charts, 503, R129, R785
negative binomial distribution function, R51
nested conditions, R253
nested files, R301, R610
nested functions, 6
nominal measurement, 71
nominal measures, 112–118

nonconforming values
in control charts, 482–485, 487–491
noninteger weights, R820
nonparametric tests, 289–320
normal distribution, 76–79
normal distribution function, R49
normal probability plots, 91, 493–497, R531–R538
detrended, R535
expected normal method, 496, R533
in Explore procedure, 101, R280–R281
in Linear Regression procedure, 274, R643
rank assigned to ties, 497
specifying periodicity, R536
transforming values, 495–496, R535–R537
using a previously defined model, R537
normality
in regression, 226, 240–241
normality tests, 91–93
in Explore procedure, 101
np charts, 482–483, 487–489, R756–R758
conforming values, 483, R760
data organization, 476, 477, R756
nonconforming values, 482, 489, R760
sample size, 488
sigma, 491, R760
subgroup identifier, 483, 488, R758
null hypothesis, 171
numeric data
input formats, R190–R191, R204–R206
output formats, R322–R325, R591–R593, R827–R829
numeric expressions, R45–R52
missing values, R51

observed count, 108
in Crosstabs procedure, 126, R177
in Linear Regression procedure, R634
observed significance level, 110, 166, 167, 196
odds ratio, 122
One-Sample Kolmogorov-Smirnov Test procedure, 308–310, R520–R521
missing values, 310
statistics, 310
test distribution, 309, R520
One-Sample T Test procedure, 158–159

one-sample *t* test. *See t* test
one-sample test
    chi-square, 296–297
    t test, 151–159
one-tailed test, 168
one-way analysis of variance, 179–192
    assumptions, 182
    between groups variability, 183
    hypothesis testing, 181
    multiple comparisons, 184–187
    within groups variability, 183–184
One-Way ANOVA procedure, 187–192, R541–R550
    contrasts, 189, R543–R544
    defining factor ranges, 188, R542, R543
    display labels, R546
    factor variables, 187, R542, R543
    harmonic means, R546
    limitations, R542
    matrix input, R547–R550
    matrix output, R547–R550
    missing values, 191, R547, R549
    multiple comparisons, 190–191, R544–R546
    orthogonal polynomials, R543
    polynomial contrasts, 188–189
    sample size estimates, 190–191
    statistics, 191, R546
online documentation, R425–R428
online help, R410–R411
opening files
    data files, R336–R339
options
    displaying, R742–R745
order of commands, R17–R19
order of operations
    numeric expressions, R45–R46
ordinal measurement, 72
ordinal measures, 118–120
orthogonal polynomials
    analysis of variance, R543
OSIRIS files
    conversion to SPSS, R353–R354
    reading, R352–R357
outliers
    boxplots, 87
    identifying, 87, R278
    in Explore procedure, 99
    in Linear Regression procedure, 274, R643, R644
    in regression, 242–246
    scatterplots, 224
output files
    borders for tables, R741
    chart characters, R740–R741
    destination of, R732–R733
    display command syntax, R732–R733
    display output page titles, R735
    letter case, R734–R735
    page size, R734
output formats, R192, R591–R593, R827–R829
    custom currency, R322, R591, R827
    displaying, R592, R828
    format specification, R591, R827
    print (display), R322–R325
    string data, R322
    write, R322–R325, R827–R829
overlay plots, R568

p charts, 482–483, 487–489, R756–R758
    conforming values, 483, R760
    data organization, 476, 477, R756
    nonconforming values, 482, 489, R760
    sigma, 491, R760
    subgroup identifier, 483, 488, R758
padding strings, R55, R56
page ejection, R588–R590
    missing values, R589
    variable list, R589
page size, R734
paired samples, 170–171
Paired-Samples T Test procedure, 175–177, R791–R795
    limitations, R792
    missing values, 176, R794–R795
    selecting paired variables, 176
    variable labels, R794
    variable list, R793
paired-samples *t* test. *See t* test
Pareto charts, R405
    simple, R405
    stacked, R405
pareto charts, 461–462, 465–474
    counts or sums for groups of cases, 470, 471
    cumulative line, 470
    simple, 470, 472, 473

stacked, 471, 472, 474
   sums of separate variables, 472
   values of individual cases, 473, 474
Pareto distribution function, R50
part correlation, 254–255
   in Linear Regression procedure, R629
partial autocorrelation, 509–510, 512–514, R551–R556
   charts, 509–510, 512–514
   See also Autocorrelations procedure
partial correlation, 215–222, 254–255, R557–R564
   hidden relationships, 218
   in Linear Regression procedure, 272, R629
   significance test, 216
   spurious correlations, 216
   See also Bivariate Correlation procedure
Partial Correlations procedure, 219–222
   control variables, 220
   missing values, 221
   statistics, 221
   zero-order correlations, 221
partial regression coefficients, 252
Pearson chi-square, 110
   in Crosstabs procedure, 125, R178
Pearson correlation coefficient, 121, 204–206
   hypothesis testing, 207–208
   in Bivariate Correlation procedure, 211, R155
   in Crosstabs procedure, 125, R179
   linear association, 205
Pearson's *r*. *See* Pearson correlation coefficient
percentages, 58
   cummulative, 58
   in Crosstabs procedure, 126, R177–R178
   in Report Summaries in Columns procedure, 348
   in Report Summaries in Rows procedure, 339, R685
   valid, 58
percentiles, 61–62
   break points, R279–R280
   estimating from grouped data, 65, R332–R333
   in Explore procedure, 99, R279–R280
   in Frequencies procedure, 64, R333–R334
   methods, R279–R280
periodic lags
   in Autocorrelations procedure, 514, R554
   in Cross-correlations procedure, 516
periodicity, 24
   in Autocorrelations procedure, 513, R79, R553

   in Cross-correlations procedure, 515, R138
   in normal probability plots, 496, R536
   in sequence charts, 504, R128, R785
   time series settings, R779
phi, 112
   in Crosstabs procedure, 125, R178
pie charts, 58, 392–397, R396
   summaries for groups of cases, 394
   summaries of separate variables, 395
   values of individual cases, 396
platykurtic distribution, 78
Poisson distribution function, R51
polynomial contrasts
   in One-Way ANOVA procedure, 188–189
pooled-variance *t* test. *See* *t* test
population, 162
   estimate, 162
   parameter, 162
portable files. *See* SPSS portable files
post hoc multiple comparisons. *See* multiple comparisons
post-hoc tests. *See* multiple comparisons
power model
   in Curve Estimation procedure, 286, R185, R186
P-P normal probability plots, 493–497, R534
predicted values
   adjusted, 244, R641
   in curve estimation, 281–282
   in regression, 232–236
   saving in Curve Estimation procedure, 287, R188
   saving in Linear Regression procedure, 275
   standard errors, R641
   standardized, R641
   unstandardized, R640
prediction intervals
   saving in Curve Estimation procedure, 287, R188
   saving in Linear Regression procedure, 275
preferences
   blank data fields, R731
   borders for tables, R741
   charts, R740
   command terminator, R738–R739
   custom currency formats, R735–R736
   data compression, R737
   decimal indicator, R736
   default file extension, R738
   default variable format, R734

display errors, R732–R733
display macro commands, R739–R740
display resource messages, R732–R733
display statistical results, R732–R733
display warnings, R732–R733
displaying, R742–R745
errors, R731–R732
graphics, R740, R741
invalid data, R731
journal file, R739
letter case, R734–R735
macro expansion, R739–R740
maximum loops, R732
output, R732–R733, R735
output page size, R734
preserving, R581, R699
random number seed, R736–R737
restoring, R581, R699
sort program, R737
thousands separator, R736
time series, R775–R779
warnings, R731–R732
print formats. *See* output formats
printing cases, R582–R587, R594–R595
    column headings, R588–R590
    displaying blank lines, R594–R595
    formats, R582, R584, R824
    missing values, R583
    number of records, R586
    output file, R582, R586–R587, R594
    page ejection, R588–R590
    strings, R582, R585
    summary table, R582, R587
prior moving average function, 27, R169
probability of F-to enter
    in Linear Regression procedure, 277
probability of F-to-enter
    in Linear Regression procedure, R630
probability of F-to-remove
    in Linear Regression procedure, 277, R630
procedure output
    output file, R596–R597
    writing to a file, R596–R597
procedures
    update documentation, R427
program states, R837–R845
proportional reduction in error, 113–116
proportional sample, R704

prospective studies, 121

Q. *See* Cochran's *Q*
Q-Q normal probability plots, 493–497, R534
quadratic model
    in Curve Estimation procedure, 286, R185, R186
quartiles, 61
    in Frequencies procedure, 64

R
    in Linear Regression procedure, 272
    in Means procedure, 136, R490
r, 121, 204–206
    See also Pearson correlation coefficient
R charts, 478–480, 485–487, R751–R754
    control limits, R761
    data organization, 476, 477, R752
    minimum sample size, 492, R760
    sigma, 491, R760
    subgroup identifier, 479, 486, R753
R^2, 229–232
    adjusted, 230
    explained variance, 232
    in Linear Regression procedure, 272, R628
random number generator distribution functions, 5
random sample, 162
    in nonparametric tests, R530
    selecting from data file, 52
random-number functions, 5, R153
random-number seed, 10, R736–R737
range, 75
    in Descriptives procedure, 81, R239
    in Explore procedure, R281
    in Frequencies procedure, 64, R335
range bar charts, R385
    clustered, 418, 423, 428
    simple, 416, 420, 426
    summaries for groups of cases, 416, 418
    summaries of separate variables, 420, 423
    values of individual cases, 426, 428
range charts. *See* R charts
range function, 5
rank correlation coefficient. *See* Spearman correlation coefficient

ranking data, 18–22, R598–R603
    fractional rank, 20
    method, 19–20, R600–R601
    missing values, R603
    new variable names, 19, R601
    normal scores, 20–21
    ntiles, 20
    order, 19, R599
    proportion estimate method, 20–21
    proportion estimates, 20–21, R602–R603
    Savage scores, 20
    sum of case weights, 20
    tied values, 21–22, R602
    within subgroups, 19, R599
Rankit method, 21
    in normal probability plots, 497, R533
rank-order correlation coefficients
    in Bivariate Correlation procedure, R508
raw data files
    blanks, R192–R193
    data types, R190–R191
    fixed format, R192, R192–R193, R194–R195, R200–R202
    freefield format, R192, R193, R194–R195, R202
    reading, R190–R207
    variable definition, R199–R207, R610–R618
raw matrix data files, R462–R480
    factors, R474–R476, R478–R479
    format, R462–R463, R465–R473
    N, R480
    record types, R476–R480
    split files, R473–R474
    within-cells records, R476, R478–R479
recoding values, 12–18, R604–R609
    conditional, 15
    converting strings to numeric, 17, R116–R120, R608–R609
    defining values to recode, 13–15, 16–18
    if case satisfies condition, 15, 18
    into different variable, 15–18
    into same variable, 13–15
    limitations, R606
    missing values, 14, 17–18, R605–R606
    numeric variables, R605–R609
    string variables, R606–R609
    subsets of cases, 15, 18
    target variable, R607–R608
records
    defining, R196–R197, R610–R618
    duplicate, R617
    missing, R616–R617
    skipping, R614–R615
    types, R610–R618
reference lines
    in sequence charts, 504–505, 506, R130, R787, R789
regression, 223–278
    adjusted predicted values, 244
    analysis of variance, 230
    casewise plots, 235
    confidence intervals, 229
    curve estimation, 279–288
    equality of variance, 226, 239
    explained variance, 232
    goodness of fit, 229–232
    hypothesis testing, 228–229
    independence, 227
    independence of error, 239–240
    least squares, 225
    linear transformations, 246–247
    linearity, 227, 237–238
    multiple, 250–269
    normality, 226, 240–241
    outliers, 224, 242–246
    population parameters, 227–228
    predicted values, 232–236
    regression line, 224–225
    residuals, 230, 236–237, 243–246
    scatterplots, 223
    standard error, 233
    standardized regression coefficient, 226
    sums of squares, 231
    violations of assumptions, 236–241
    See also Linear Regression procedure, multiple regression
regression coefficients
    in Linear Regression procedure, 272, R628
regression line, 224–225
regression plots, R569
    in Linear Regression procedure, 273
relational operators, 3, R57, R246, R413, R723
    defined, R57
    in conditional expressions, 8
relative risk ratio, 121
    in Crosstabs procedure, 125, R179
remainder function, 3
repeating data, R650–R663

case identification, R662–R663
defining variables, R658
input file, R658–R659
repeating groups, R657–R659
starting column, R656–R657
summary table, R663
repeating data groups, R610
repeating fields. *See* repeating data
replacing missing values, 28–30, R700–R703
linear interpolation, 30, R701
linear trend, 30, R703
mean of nearby points, 29, R702
median of nearby points, 30, R702
series mean, 29, R703
Report Summaries in Columns procedure, 345–353
break column format, 351
composite summary columns, 348
data column format, 350
defining subgroups, 346
footnotes, 344–345, 353
grand totals, 351
margins, 352
missing values, 352
page control, 350
pre-sorted data, 347
preview, 347
report layout, 352
sorting data, 347
subtotals, 350
summary statistic for a variable, 347–348
titles, 344–345, 353
total column format, 350
total columns, 348
Report Summaries in Rows procedure, 335–353, R664–R692
break column format, 340
break columns, 343
break spacing, 340
column contents, R677, R680–R681
column heading alignment, 337
column headings, 337, R665, R677–R678, R681
column spacing, R666
column titles, 343
column width, 338, R666, R666, R678, R682
data value alignment, 337
defining subgroups, 335, R680–R683
footnotes, 344–345, R691–R692
format, R671–R673
grand totals, 341

limitations, R669–R670
listing reports, 336
margins, 342
missing values, 341, R668, R692
output file, R668, R676
page control, 340
page layout, R673–R676
pre-sorted data, 336
preview, 336
print formats, R689–R691
report alignment, 342
report layout, 341–343
report types, R668
sorting data, 336
string variables, R678–R680
summary statistics, 338–339, R668, R683–R691
summary titles, R688
titles, 344–345, R691–R692
value labels, 338
variable list, R676–R678
variables in titles, 345
vertical alignment, 343
reports, 325–353, R664–R692
break columns, 325
break variables, 325
column headings, 333
combined reports, 328
data columns, 325
footnotes, 333
formatting, 333–334
grand totals, 331
listing reports, 327
multiple break variables, 328
report variables, 325
summary columns, 329
summary reports, 325
titles, 333
total columns, 329
value labels, 334
See also Report Summaries in Columns procedure, Report Summaries in Rows procedure
re-reading records, R693–R698
input file, R696–R697
starting column, R697–R698
residual sum of squares, 231
residuals, 109
degrees of freedom, R316
deleted, 243–246, R641
descriptive statistics, R314–R317

goodness of fit, R314–R317
  in Crosstabs procedure, 126–127, R178
  in curve estimation, 281–282
  in regression, 230, 236–237
  in time series analysis, 502
  saving in Curve Estimation procedure, 287, R188
  saving in Linear Regression procedure, 276, R646
  standardized, 237, R641
  Studentized, 237, R641
  Studentized deleted, 244, R641
  unstandardized, R641
resistant measures, 93
robust estimators, 93–97
round function, 3
row percentages, 104–105
  in Crosstabs procedure, 126, R177
row variable, 104
Run Pending Transforms, 30
running commands
  batch mode, R14–R15
  interactive mode, R13–R14
running median function, 27, R169
runs test
  in Runs Test procedure, R526–R527
Runs Test procedure, 306–308, R526–R527
  cut points, 307
  cutting point, R527
  missing values, 308
  statistics, 308

s charts, 478–480, 485–487, R751–R754
  control limits, R761
  data organization, 476, 477, R752
  minimum sample size, 492, R760
  sigma, 491, R760
  subgroup identifier, 479, 486, R753
sample, 162
  exact-size, 52, R704
  proportional, 52, R704
sample size estimates
  in One-Way ANOVA procedure, 190–191
sampling cases, 52, R704–R706
  See also subsets of cases
sampling distribution, 162–166
  expected value, 163

  of mean, 164–166
  standard error, 163
SAS files
  conversion to SPSS, R360–R362
  reading, R358–R362
Savage scores, 20
saving files
  aggregated data files, 47, R96
  data compression, R711–R712, R834–R835
  data files, R707–R712, R830–R835
  dBASE format, R716–R722
  dropping variables, R710–R711, R832–R833
  Excel format, R716–R722
  keeping variables, R710–R711, R832–R833
  Lotus 1-2-3, R716–R722
  renaming variables, R710–R711, R833–R834
  SCSS format, R713–R715
  spreadsheet format, R716–R722
  SPSS portable files, R286–R291
  SYLK format, R716–R722
  tab-delimited data files, R716–R722
  variable map, R834
saving SCSS data files, R713–R715
  dropping variables, R714–R715
  keeping variables, R714–R715
  missing values, R714
  numeric precision, R714
  output file, R714
  renaming variables, R715
  string variables, R714
scatterplots, 445–458, R401, R565–R572
  3-D, 450–452, 457–458
  bivariate, 445
  contour plots, R568
  control variables, R567–R568
  cutpoints, R569–R570
  horizontal axis, R567, R571–R572
  limitations, R567
  lowess fit, 450
  marker categories, 454, 455, 457
  marker labels, 454, 455, 456, 458
  matrix, 449–450, 454–455
  missing values, R572
  overlay, 456–457
  overlay plots, R568
  plot resolution, R566
  plot scaling, R571–R572
  plot types, R566
  regression curves, 448

regression plots, R569
simple, 445–449, 453–454
spikes, 452
sunflowers, 446
symbols, R569–R570
titles, R572
vertical axis, R567, R571–R572
Scheffé test
in One-Way ANOVA procedure, 190
Schwarz Bayesian criterion
in Linear Regression procedure, R628
scratch variables
defined, R33
screening data, 62
SCSS files
conversion to SPSS, R366–R367
reading, R366–R369
saving data files as, R713–R715
seasonal difference function, 27, R170
seasonal difference transformation
in Autocorrelations procedure, 513, R79, R553
in Cross-correlations procedure, 515, R137
in normal probability plots, 496, R536
in sequence charts, 504, R128
seasonal trends, 500–501
seed. *See* random-number seed
selecting cases, 49–54, R803–R805
See also subsets of cases
semi-partial correlation. *See* part correlation
sequence charts, 499–506, R124–R134, R781–R790
area charts, R130, R787
changing axes, 506
connecting cases between variables, 506, R131, R788
line charts, 506, R130, R787
multiple variables, 504, R131, R788
plotting highest and lowest values, R131, R788
scale axis reference line, 506, R130, R787
specifying periodicity, R128, R785
split-file scaling, R133, R789
time axis labels, 503
time axis reference lines, 504–505, R132, R789
transforming values, 503–504, R128–R129, R784–R786
using previously defined specifications, R133, R790
settings
displaying, R742–R745

Shapiro-Wilks' test, 92
in Explore procedure, 101, R280–R281
short string variable, R41
sigma
in control charts, 491
sign test, 293
in Two-Related-Samples Tests procedure, 317, R527–R528
signed-ranks test, 293
significance level
in Linear Regression procedure, R634
t test, 167–168
Simple Factorial ANOVA procedure, 198–202
covariates, 199, 201, R106, R106
defining factor ranges, 199, R105–R106
display labels, 202, R111
factor variables, 199, R105–R106
full factorial model, 199
interaction effects, 201–202, R106
limitations, R104–R105
methods, 200, R106–R108
missing values, R111
multiple classification analysis, 201, R111
statistics, 201, R110–R111
sums of squares, R106–R108, R109
treatment effects, R111
sine function, 4
skewness, 77
in Descriptives procedure, 82, R239
in Explore procedure, 98, R281
in Frequencies procedure, 65, R334
in Report Summaries in Columns procedure, 348
in Report Summaries in Rows procedure, 339, R685
smoothing function, 28, R171
Somers' *d*, 120
in Crosstabs procedure, 125, R179
sorting cases, 31–32, R746–R747
sort keys, R746
sort order, 32, R746
specifying sort program, R737
Spearman correlation coefficient, 118, 207, 209
in Bivariate Correlation procedure, 211, R510
in Crosstabs procedure, 125, R179
split-file processing, 47–49, R762–R764
break variables, R762
matrices, R763
scratch variables, R762

system variables, R762
  temporary, R770–R771
  with matrix system files, R28
spread-and-level plots, 90–91
  determining transformation, 90–91
  in Explore procedure, 100, R280
spreadsheet files
  read ranges, R376
  read variable names, R375
  reading, R370–R378
  saving, R716–R722
SPSS data files
  documents, R244–R245, R260
  reading, R336–R339
SPSS portable files, R22
  reading, R419–R422
  saving, R286–R291
SPSS/PC+ files
  reading, R419–R422
spurious correlations, 216
square root function, 4, R46–R47
stacked area charts, 388, 390, 392
stacked bar charts, 369, 371, 373
standard deviation, 76
  in Descriptives procedure, 81, R239
  in error bar charts, 442
  in Explore procedure, 98, R281
  in Frequencies procedure, 64, R334
  in Linear Regression procedure, R634
  in Means procedure, 135, R489
  in Report Summaries in Columns procedure, 348
  in Report Summaries in Rows procedure, 339, R685
standard deviation charts. *See* s charts
standard deviation function, 4, R47
standard error, 163
  in Descriptives procedure, 82
  in error bar charts, 442
  in Explore procedure, 98, R281
  in Frequencies procedure, 64
  in Linear Regression procedure, R628, R629
  in regression, 233
standard error of the estimate, 228, 235
standard error of the mean, 153
  in Descriptives procedure, R239
  in Frequencies procedure, R334
standard scores, 78–79

standardized regression coefficient, 226
standardized residuals, 237
  in Linear Regression procedure, 274, 276
standardized values
  in normal probability plots, 495, R535
stand-in variable, R255–R256
stationary series, 511
statistical functions, 4, R151
stem-and-leaf plots, 85–87
  in Explore procedure, 100, R280
  scale, R277–R278
stepwise selection, 262
  in Linear Regression procedure, 271, R626
string data
  computing values, R148, R150, R154
  conditional transformations, R247, R248, R414, R415
  converting to numeric, 17, 22–23, R116–R120
  input formats, R190–R191, R206–R207
  missing values, R492–R493
  output formats, R322, R591–R592, R827–R828
  value labels, R91–R92, R806
string expressions
  defined, R52
string functions, R52–R55, R154
  macro facility, R227–R229
string variables
  in logical expressions, R52
Studentized residuals, 237
  in Linear Regression procedure, 276
Student-Newman-Keuls test
  in One-Way ANOVA procedure, 190
subcommand
  syntax, R16
subgroup means, 129–134
subgroups
  splitting data files into, R762–R764
subpopulation, 129–134
subsets of cases
  based on dates and times, 50, 52, R803–R805
  conditional expressions, 51–52, R723
  deleting unselected cases, 51
  exact-size sample, R704
  filter status, 51, R310–R311
  filtering unselected cases, 51, R310–R311
  if condition is satisfied, 51–52, R723–R727
  proportional sample, R704

random sample, 52
  selecting, 49–54, R723–R727, R803–R805
  selection variable, 50
  temporary sample, R704
substrings, R55
subtitles, R767–R768
  apostrophes in, R767
  length, R767
  quotation marks in, R767
  suppressing, R767
  with inline data, R767
sum
  in Descriptives procedure, 81, R239
  in Frequencies procedure, 64, R335
  in Report Summaries in Columns procedure, 348
  in Report Summaries in Rows procedure, 339, R685
sum function, 4
summary reports, 325
summary statistics, 73–76
sums of squares
  in regression, 231
survival tables
  writing to a file, R596–R597
sweep matrix
  in Linear Regression procedure, R628
SYLK files
  read ranges, R376
  read variable names, R375
  reading, R370–R378
  saving, R719
syntax, R11–R19
syntax charts, R11–R12
system variables, R32
system-missing value, R492

t distribution function, R50
t test
  in Independent-Samples T Test procedure, 172–175, R791
  in Paired-Samples T Test procedure, 175–177, R791
  independent samples, 166–169
  one-sample, 151–159
  one-tailed, 168
  paired samples, 170–171
  pooled-variance, 166
  significance level, 167–168
  two-sample, 166–169
  two-tailed, 168
T4253H smoothing, 28, R171
tab-delimited files
  reading, R370–R378
  saving, R718–R719, R720
table lookup files, 39, R458
table percentage, 104
target variables
  computing values, 2, R148
  counting values, R161, R162
  formats, R149–R150
  in COMPUTE command, R52
tau. *See* Goodman and Kruskal's tau
tau-*a*. *See* Kendall's tau-*a*
tau-*b*. *See* Kendall's tau-*b*
tau-*b*. *See* Kendall's tau-*b*
tau-*c*. *See* Kendall's tau-*c*
templates
  in charts, R407
temporary transformations, R770–R772
temporary variables, R770
Tests for Several Independent Samples procedure, 314–316, R522, R525
  grouping variables, 314, R522, R525
  missing values, 316
  statistics, 316
Tests for Several Related Samples procedure, 319–320, R518–R520, R522–R523
  statistics, 320
thousands separator
  specifying, R736
tied pairs, 119
time functions, R62–R75
time intervals, R62–R75
time series analysis
  autocorrelation, 507–510, R76–R82
  cross-correlation, 510–511, R135–R140
  curve estimation, 285
  data file structure, 23
  data transformations, 23–30, R163–R171, R208–R215, R700–R703
  date variables, 24–25, R208–R215
  forecasting, 288, 501

partial autocorrelation, 509–510, R551–R556
predicting cases, 288
preferences, R775–R779
residuals, 502
seasonal trends, 500–501
sequence charts, 499–502, R124–R134, R781–R790
stationary series, 511
time series functions, 26–28, R165–R171
time series variables, 26
   creating, 26–28, R163–R171
titles, R773–R774
   apostrophes in, R773
   displaying, R735
   length, R773
   quotation marks in, R773
   with inline data, R773
   See also subtitles
tolerance, 267
   in Linear Regression procedure, 273, R629, R630, R631
   time series settings, R779
total percentage
   in Crosstabs procedure, 126, R178
transaction files, R796–R802
Transform menu. *See* data transformations
transformations
   data, 1–30
   file, 31–55
   temporary, R770–R772
translating data files. *See* data files
transposing cases and variables, 32–33, R318–R321
treatment effects
   analysis of variance, R111
trimmed mean, 94
   in Explore procedure, 98, R281
truncate function, 3
Tukey's *b*
   in One-Way ANOVA procedure, 190
Tukey's transformation, 21, R602
   in normal probability plots, 497, R533
Two-Independent-Samples Tests procedure, 311–313, R521, R523–R524, R526, R528–R529
   defining groups, 312
   grouping variables, 311, R521, R523–R524, R526, R528

   missing values, 313
   outlier trimming, R526
   statistics, 313
Two-Related-Samples Tests procedure, 316–318, R524, R527–R528, R529
   missing values, 318
   statistics, 318
two-sample *t* test. *See t* test
two-tailed test, 168

u charts, 483–485, 489–491, R758–R760
   data organization, 477, 478, R759
   nonconforming values, 484, 491
   sample size, 490
   sigma, 491, R760
   subgroup identifier, 484, 490, R759
U. *See* Mann-Whitney *U*
uncertainty coefficient
   in Crosstabs procedure, 125, R178
uniform distribution function, R50
update documentation, R425, R427
updating data files, R796–R802
   dropping variables, R801
   flag variables, R801–R802
   input files, R799
   keeping variables, R801
   key variables, R796–R802
   limitations, R798
   master files, R796–R802
   raw data files, R799
   renaming variables, R800–R801
   transaction files, R796–R802
   variable map, R802
upper case
   specifying, R734–R735
user-missing values, R492–R494

V. See Cramér's *V*
valid percentage, 58
value
   syntax, R16–R17
value labels, R90–R92, R806–R808
   adding, R806–R808
   apostrophes in, R806

concatenating strings, R806, R807
length, R806
revising, R90–R92
string data, R91–R92, R806
Van der Waerden's transformation, 21, R602
  in normal probability plots, 497, R533
variability, 69
variable labels, R809–R810
  apostrophes in, R809
  concatenating strings, R809, R810
variables
  controlling default format, R734
  defining, R199–R207, R539–R540, R610–R618, R765–R766
  naming rules, R200
  temporary, R770
variance, 75
  in Descriptives procedure, 81, R239
  in Explore procedure, 98, R281
  in Frequencies procedure, 64, R334
  in Linear Regression procedure, R628, R634
  in Means procedure, 136, R489
  in Report Summaries in Columns procedure, 348
  in Report Summaries in Rows procedure, 339, R685
variance function, 4
variance inflation factor, 267
  in Linear Regression procedure, 273, R628
vectors, R811–R816
  index, R811, R815–R816
  variable list, R811

W. *See* Kendall's *W*
Wald-Wolfowitz test
  in Two-Independent-Samples Tests procedure, 312, R528–R529
warnings
  displaying, R732–R733
  maximum number, R731–R732
Weibull distribution function, R50
weighted least-squares
  in Linear Regression procedure, 271, R632
weighting cases, 54–55, R819–R821
Wilcoxon signed-ranks test, 293
Wilcoxon test
  in Two-Related-Samples Tests procedure, 317, R529
within-groups variability, 183–184
write formats, R827–R829
writing cases, R822–R826

X-bar charts, 478–480, 485–487, R751–R754
  control limits, 491, R761
  data organization, 476, 477, R752
  minimum sample size, 492, R760
  sigma, 491, R760
  subgroup identifier, 479, 486, R753

Yates' correction for continuity, 111
  in Crosstabs procedure, 125, R178

Z scores, 78–79
  in Descriptives procedure, 80, R236–R237
  saving as variables, 80, R236–R237
zero-order correlations, 216
  in Partial Correlations procedure, 221